Blackstone's

Custody Officers' Manual

Blackstone's

Custody Officers' Manual

Huw Smart

Third edition

OXFORD
UNIVERSITY PRESS

OXFORD
UNIVERSITY PRESS

Great Clarendon Street, Oxford OX2 6DP

Oxford University Press is a department of the University of Oxford.
It furthers the University's objective of excellence in research, scholarship,
and education by publishing worldwide in

Oxford New York

Auckland Cape Town Dar es Salaam Hong Kong Karachi
Kuala Lumpur Madrid Melbourne Mexico City Nairobi
New Delhi Shanghai Taipei Toronto

With offices in

Argentina Austria Brazil Chile Czech Republic France Greece
Guatemala Hungary Italy Japan Poland Portugal Singapore
South Korea Switzerland Thailand Turkey Ukraine Vietnam

Oxford is a registered trade mark of Oxford University Press
in the UK and in certain other countries

Published in the United States
by Oxford University Press Inc., New York

© Huw Smart 2008

First published 2004
Third edition published 2008

British Library Cataloguing in Publication Data

Data available

Library of Congress Cataloging in Publication Data
Smart, Huw.
    Blackstone's custody officers' manual / Huw Smart. —3rd ed.
        p. cm.
    Includes bibliographical references and index.
    ISBN 978-0-19-955144-6 (pbk. : alk. paper) 1. Prisoners—Legal status, laws,
etc.—England. 2. Prisoners—Legal status, laws, etc.—Wales. 3. Dock (Criminal
procedure)—England. 4. Dock (Criminal procedure)—Wales. I. Title. II. Title:
Custody officers' manual.
    KD8450.S63 2008
    345.42'052—dc22

                                                                                    2008039141

Typeset by Laserwords Private Limited, Chennai, India
Printed in Great Britain
on acid-free paper by
CPI Antony Rowe, Chippenham, Wiltshire

ISBN 978-0-19-955144-6

10 9 8 7 6 5 4 3 2 1

Preface

The original idea for the first edition of this book came about approximately six years ago. At that time, there appeared to be very little assistance nationally for custody officers in terms of updated legislation or national policy. Even today, most custody officers receive excellent initial training, but how many forces provide regular updates or re-training relating to changes in legislation? This is compounded by the fact that, on average, two to three Acts of Parliament a year are introduced which have an impact on the Police and Criminal Evidence Act 1984 and the *Codes of Practice*.

So why this particular book? There are some excellent publications that deal with PACE, such as Zander's *Police and Criminal Evidence Act 1984*, the Blackstone's Police Manuals and *Blackstone's Criminal Practice*. I have tried to keep this book as practical as possible by using my experience as a serving police officer to assist other serving police officers who may have no-one to turn to for out-of-hours advice on custody-related matters. Readers will notice that my style of writing is not the same as in some classic law textbooks, a matter that has been commented on by some reviewers. I make no apologies for this, because I have tried to simplify the subject and provide plenty of practical operational solutions.

The main purpose of this book is to provide access in one place to all the legislation and procedures that affect custody officers. All custody officers should be provided with a copy of the *Codes of Practice*, but what use is this if they do not have access to the original Act, or the many updates that have been introduced since 1984? Inevitably, someone will read this book and consider that I have missed something out. This could be for two reasons. First, in the research and writing phases, I have tried to limit the book to matters relevant to an operational custody officer. Secondly, it's almost guaranteed that the moment this new edition is published, some new legislation will be introduced which affects custody matters. If I have omitted something important, I am not averse to receiving feedback, so that future editions may be amended.

Finally, what qualifies me to write this particular book? I have been a serving police officer with South Wales Police for the past 26 years. I have experience of writing, being the co-author of the Blackstone's Police Q&A series, published by Oxford University Press. I am also a part-time lecturer at the University of Glamorgan, South Wales. Most importantly, I spent two years performing the duties of a custody officer and six years as an operational inspector, providing full-time cover as a review officer. Currently, as an acting superintendent with operational responsibilities, I deal regularly with custody issues and 24-hour extensions.

I have researched opinions and case law for the legislation and procedure that appears in this book. However, where none exists, I have included my own interpretation. For this reason, I strongly recommend that readers consult with their own force policy on issues that are in doubt. I have attempted to highlight such issues as they arise. Again, any feedback would be welcome for future editions of the book.

For more information on police books from Blackstone's, please visit <http://www. blackstonespolicemanuals.com> or if you have any comments or questions, email police.uk@oup.com.

Huw Smart
July 2008

Acknowledgements

Thanks must go to a knowledgeable and dedicated group of custody officers and custody officer trainers around the country, who have been involved in this book at the beginning; from the first meeting as a focus group at Oxford, to the regular reviews I receive on the book's contents.

Many thanks to: Jacky Smith, Paul Rutter, David Towers, John Halfpenny, Nick Walter, John Atha, Andrew Johnson and Keith Floyd.

I would also like to thank the team at Oxford University Press for their continuing support for this project. I would particularly like to acknowledge Lindsey, Katie and Jodi for continuing to push me to deliver on time for this and other publications. Alistair McQueen, formerly of Blackstone's, also deserves mention, for suggesting this idea a long time ago.

Finally, I must thank my family for the love and support they have given me over the last few years—my parents (Dad, sorry I forgot Father's Day while writing this book!)—the eldest kids, Lawrence and Maddie, who make me so proud—the youngest kids, Hâf and Nia, two beautiful young girls.

Anyone who tries to hold a full-time job and have a family life, whilst trying to write books in their spare time, will acknowledge that you need space, time and a loving, patient partner. I am lucky to receive all these unconditionally from Caroline, without whom this book would not have been written.

Contents

Contents

Contents

APPENDIX 2: Home Office Circulars

Table of Cases

Tables of Legislation

Table of PACE Codes of Practice

Special Features

The book contains several special features that make it more helpful to the reader. These are defined and explained below:

Indexing
The indexing in the book is easy to follow. Chapters are numbered 1–18. Each subject area is then given its own subheading and a unique number.

Legislative provisions
People involved in the custody process, particularly custody officers, will always want to be able to point to a lawful authority to back up their decisions. Therefore, at the beginning of each section, readers will find the legislative provisions that apply to that particular area of law. Readers will also see that where a specific point is made in the following text; this will be cross-referenced with the legislative provisions.

Case law
The book makes extensive use of case law. This assists the reader to understand various legislative points, using a balance of the author's own interpretation, together with decisions made by the courts.

Keynotes
Keynote boxes appear in most chapters. These are used to reinforce a particular legislative point, or to draw the reader's attention to a significant issue.

Tables
The book often uses tables within the text, in order to help provide a focus for key terms.

Case studies
Many chapters contain case studies, which are used to reinforce points of law. These may either be based on the author's own practical experience as a custody officer and reviewing officer, or on decisions made by the court. Either way, the scenarios used are based on real-life experiences, which should assist custody officers in their working environment.

Summing-Up boxes
At the end of each chapter, the summing-up boxes contain a précis of the issues examined. These should provide a quick guide to readers of the key

issues contained in the chapter. However, these boxes should only be used as a quick reference once the chapter has been read thoroughly. The text within the chapters contains extensive detail and interpretation of legislation, whereas the summing-up boxes contain less detail.

Local procedures boxes

At the end of each chapter, there is a local procedures box. Readers will find that occasionally the author recommends consulting local procedures on specific issues. This will usually be where no national guidance exists. Some issues will already be highlighted in the boxes, but readers are welcome to add their own text and contact details.

The Human Rights Act 1998

Most decisions during the custody procedure will be made under the authority of the Police and Criminal Evidence Act 1984 (PACE) and/or the *Codes of Practice*. However, arresting officers, custody officers and reviewing officers will always have to bear in mind the provisions of the Human Rights Act 1998, when making decisions in relation to the arrest, detention and welfare of detainees. Where applicable, reference is made to the provisions of the 1998 Act in the chapter introductions.

Appendices—Flow charts

In the Appendices at the end of the book are a number of flow charts, which provide an easy guide to readers in relation to some specific legislative definitions.

Appendices—Home Office Circulars

The book contains many references to Home Office Circulars which are specific to the custody process. The most important circulars are reproduced in their entirety; however, the Appendices also provide the reference numbers of other, important circulars which can be located on the Home Office website at <http://www.homeoffice.gov.uk>.

The Role of the Custody Officer

1.1 **Introduction**

Can custody officers be truly independent? The provisions of the Police and Criminal Evidence Act 1984 require the custody officer to remain impartial and independent from the investigation of a person in police detention. At the same time, however, s. 36(3) of the Act requires a custody officer to be 'at least the rank of sergeant', in other words a police officer.

Throughout this book, we will be referring to the custody officer as though he/she is a dedicated person, performing that function at all times (which is common in police forces who appoint dedicated custody staff at centralised custody offices). However, the reality is that often custody officers are brought in to work at the last minute, sometimes to cover whole shifts, or sometimes for only a few hours. Whoever does act as a custody officer will have to take full-time responsibility for detainees at the custody office, and may be held liable for actions taken for and against such persons, even by other people.

This chapter examines the role of the custody officer in this context, whether the detainee is taken to a designated station or a non-designated station. We will also be looking at the issue of non-appointed custody officers dealing with detainees and the rare occasions that an investigating officer may also perform the role of a custody officer. It must be emphasised that an officer who does perform this role must at all times comply with the *Codes of Practice*, and protect the human rights of the detainee.

The concept of detention officers was introduced by the Police Reform Act 2002. As a result, non-police officers now act as 'gaolers' in many custody offices throughout England and Wales. Section 120 of the Serious Organised Crime and Police Act 2005 has widened this concept, so that 'staff custody officers' may now be appointed to work in custody offices, in place of police sergeants. The implications of this addition are examined in this chapter.

Lastly, the chapter examines the leadership skills that must be displayed by custody officers. Some of these skills are particularly relevant when the custody officer finds himself/herself in dispute with an officer of a higher rank who makes a decision which is 'at variance' with the one made by him or her.

The Human Rights Act 1998

Article 5 of the Human Rights Act 1998 states that everyone has the right to liberty and security of the person. No one shall be deprived of his liberty save in the following cases and in accordance with a procedure prescribed by law:

(c) the lawful arrest or detention of a person effected for the purpose of bringing him before the competent legal authority on reasonable suspicion of having committed an offence or when it is reasonably considered necessary to prevent his committing an offence or fleeing after having done so.

The custody officer has a duty under this Act to protect the arrested person's human rights. Any arrest and subsequent detention must be lawful, with the ultimate intention of bringing him/her before a 'competent legal authority'.

1.2 **Responsibility and Liability**

1.2.1 **Legislative provisions**

Section 39(1) PACE

Subject to s. 39(2) and 39(4) below, it shall be the duty of the custody officer at a police station to ensure—

(a) that all persons in police detention at a station are treated in accordance with this Act and any code of practice issued under it and relating to the treatment of persons in police detention; and

(b) that all matters relating to such persons which are required by this Act or by such codes of practice to be recorded are recorded in the custody records relating to such persons.

Section 39(2) PACE

If the custody officer, in accordance with any code of practice issued under this Act, transfers or permits the transfer of a person in police detention—

(a) to the custody of a police officer investigating an offence for which that person is in police detention; or

(b) to the custody of an officer who has charge of that person outside the police station

the custody officer shall cease in relation to that person to be subject to the duty imposed on him by s. 39(1)(a) above; and it shall be the duty of the officer to whom the transfer is made to ensure that he is treated in accordance with the provisions of the Act and any such codes of practice as are mentioned in s. 39(1) above.

1.2.2 **Responsibility**

Section 39(1) above makes it clear that the custody officer has overall responsibility for ensuring that detainees are treated in accordance with PACE and the *Codes of Practice*, whilst in police detention. There are two exceptions to this rule.

First, when a detainee is delivered to the investigating officer—usually for interview; or to another officer who takes the detainee outside the custody office—possibly to go to court, to visit the scene of a crime, or for an intimate search at a hospital.

The only other exception, referred to in s. 39(1) above, is where a detainee is transferred to the care of the local authority, under s. 38(6) of the Act (see **Chapter 15—Continued Detention After Charge** for full details of this section).

Where the custody officer does release a detainee to the custody of another officer, the custody record should be endorsed as to the detainee's location. When the officer returns the detainee to the custody officer, he or she must report to the custody officer as to whether PACE and the *Codes of Practice* have been complied with, and the custody record must be updated.

It should be noted that any other time the custody officer releases the detainee to the care of other people in the custody office, he/she still retains responsibility under PACE; for example, when the detainee is being fingerprinted and photographed, undergoing examination by a doctor, or undergoing a station breath test procedure.

1.2.3 **Liability**

We have established that the custody officer is responsible for the treatment and welfare of a person held in police detention, but can the custody officer be held personally liable for everything that happens to the detainee? What if the detainee is assaulted while he/she is being fingerprinted by another officer? Would the custody officer be liable? What if the custody officer informs the detention officer to make visits every fifteen minutes and rouse the detainee and the detention officer doesn't actually go in the cell? Would the custody officer be liable if the detainee died from positional asphyxia?

Obviously, each case will be taken on its own merits, but even though the custody officer is responsible for what happens in the custody office, it will be difficult to see them being held liable for the actions of others who act illegally.

Custody officers often face difficult situations that will require the use of force and whilst this is covered by s. 117 of PACE, custody officers' actions are frequently examined in court. For example, in the case of *Butcher* v *DPP* [2003] EWHC 580 (Admin), the custody officer physically escorted the detainee's appropriate adult from the custody suite as she had entered the custody suite without being invited and had been verbally abusive and aggressive. The court held that the custody sergeant had not detained the appropriate adult, but had merely used reasonable force to remove her in order to maintain the operational effectiveness of the custody suite. The court held that the custody sergeant was entirely entitled to ask her to leave and use reasonable force when she failed to comply with that request.

Such use of force was further examined in *R* v *Jones* (1999) *The Times*, 21 April, where it was held that, although s. 117 of PACE confers a power to use force on a constable, it is not a blanket power to use force. The court said that

s. 117 should not be interpreted as giving a right to police to exercise force whenever the consent of a suspect was not required.

One of the biggest worries for custody officers has been whether or not they should take out insurance for personal liability because of decisions they make in work. As yet, there appears to be no precedent for custody officers themselves being sued regularly for breaches of the *Codes of Practice*, with cases still being brought against chief officers on behalf of forces.

However, it should be remembered that if a custody officer is found to have committed a deliberate act contrary to PACE or the *Codes of Practice*, they may not receive protection from their own chief officer, who may seek to persuade any court that the custody officer was responsible for his/her own actions.

1.2.4 **Leadership**

A Google search for the word 'leadership' brings back a phenomenal 126,000,000 hits. This section concentrates on matters a little closer to home.

The *Practitioner Guide to the Police Leadership Qualities Framework (PLQF)*, developed by Centrex and Skills for Justice®, identifies that:

> The Police Service is almost unique amongst organisations in that everyone from the newest constable to the highest ranks understands that from the moment they choose to serve, they accept the leadership responsibility that goes along with that.

Leadership in the custody office is vital. Visitors, whether they are detainees, solicitors, arresting officers or senior officers, must be left in no doubt that the custody officer is in charge.

The above guide identifies that leadership is not confined to 'taking command' at times of critical need and the research into PLQF showed that that there were behaviours associated with effective leadership that were fundamental to an individual's ability to operate effectively:

Personal Integrity—outstanding leaders possess high levels of integrity and moral courage, which inspires trust and loyalty

Personal Awareness—outstanding leaders have high levels of personal awareness that look beyond themselves and include an understanding of others and how others perceive them

Passion to Achieve—outstanding leaders are driven by an inner desire to achieve objectives and to constantly improve.

The *Practitioner Guide* notes that the existing Integrated Competency Framework (ICF) was not specifically designed to be a leadership competency framework. The *Guide* concludes that the ICF behaviours should be re-aligned into the following four new domains, to complement the PLQF:

Leading People

Communication	Communicates ideas and information effectively, both verbally and in writing. Uses language and a style of communication that is appropriate to the situation and people being addressed. Makes sure that others understand what is going on.
Team Working	Develops strong working relationships inside and outside the team to achieve common goals. Breaks down barriers between groups and involves others in discussions and decisions.
Maximising Potential	Actively encourages and supports the development of people. Motivates others to achieve organisational goals.

Leading the Organisation

Problem Solving	Gathers information from a range of sources. Analyses information to identify problems and issues, and makes effective decisions.
Planning and Organisation	Plans, organises and supervises activities to make sure resources are used efficiently and effectively to achieve organisational goals.
Community and Customer Focus	Focuses on the customer and provides a high-quality service that is tailored to meet their individual needs. Understands the communities that are served and shows an active commitment to policing that reflects their needs and concerns.

Leading the Way

Negotiation and Influencing	Persuades and influences others using logic and reason. Sells the benefits of the position they are proposing, and negotiates to find solutions that everyone will accept.
Strategic Perspective	Looks at issues with a broad view to achieve the organisation's goals. Thinks ahead and prepares for the future.
Respect for Race and Diversity	Considers and shows respect for the opinions, circumstances and feelings of colleagues and members of the public, no matter what their race, religion, position, background, circumstances, status or appearance.

Personal Qualities and Values

Personal Responsibility	*Takes personal responsibility for making things happen and achieving results. Displays motivation, commitment, perseverance and conscientiousness. Acts with a high degree of integrity.*
Resilience	*Shows resilience, even in difficult circumstances. Prepared to make difficult decisions and has the confidence to see them through.*
Openness to Change	*Recognises and responds to the need for change, and uses it to improve organisational performance.*

To conclude this section, the 2004 Home Office report, *Police Leadership: Expectations and Impact* (the catalyst for the PLQF research), showed wide variations in the standards of leadership being experienced by people working in the police service, including examples of 'leaders' who were lazy, unethical, disinterested, or who failed to deal with poor performers.

However, the report found a lot of common ground in terms of the kinds of behaviour which were perceived as 'good leadership'—

- being committed to achieving a high quality service to the community and supporting staff to achieve this;
- displaying high personal and professional standards and challenging poor behaviour;
- enabling, valuing and developing staff;
- having relevant knowledge and skills.

It is difficult not to conclude that custody officers must strive to achieve the highest levels of leadership in all areas, in order to deliver a quality service to internal and external customers.

1.3 **Designated and Non-Designated Police Stations**

1.3.1 **Legislative provisions**

Section 35(1) PACE

The chief officer of police for each police area shall designate the police stations in his area which, subject to s. 30(3) and (5), are to be the stations in that area to be used for the purpose of detaining arrested persons.

Section 30(3) PACE

A constable to whom this subsection applies may take an arrested person to any police station unless it appears to the constable that it may be necessary to keep the arrested person for more than six hours.

Section 30(4) PACE

Subsection (3) above applies—

(a)   to a constable who is working in a locality covered by a police station which is not a designated police station; and

(b)   to a constable belonging to a body of constables maintained by an authority other than a police authority.

Section 30(5) PACE

Any constable may take an arrested person to any police station if—

(a)   either of the following conditions is satisfied—

    (i)   the constable has arrested him without the assistance of any other constable and no other constable is available to assist him;

    (ii)   the constable has taken him into custody from a person other than a constable without the assistance of any other constable and no other constable is available to assist him; and

(b)   it appears to the constable that he will be unable to take the arrested person to a designated police station without the arrested person injuring himself, the constable or some other person.

1.3.2 Designated police stations

Under s. 30(1A) of PACE, when a person is arrested for an offence at any place other than a police station, he or she shall be taken to a police station as soon as practicable after the arrest. However, the Government has driven through several changes in legislation to compel officers to seek alternatives to arresting people at the scene of offences and conveying them directly to the custody office. For example, s. 4 of the Criminal Justice Act 2003 inserted s. 30A to s. 30D into PACE, which provides police officers with the power to grant an arrested person immediate bail at the scene. This power is commonly known as 'street bail' and is covered in depth in **16.8 'Street bail'**.

More recently, Part 3 of the Serious Organised Crime and Police Act 2005 amended s. 24 of PACE and repealed s. 25. The term 'arrestable offence' no longer exists and potentially, a person may be arrested for any offence, whether indictable or summary. However, s. 24(4) of PACE states that the power of arrest is exercisable only if the constable has reasonable grounds for believing that it is *necessary* to arrest the person in question. Once again, police officers are forced to consider alternatives, such as proceeding by way of summons or Penalty Notices for Disorder. Indeed, Code G, para. 1.3 of the *Codes of Practice* states that the use of the power to arrest must be fully justified and officers exercising the power should consider if the necessary objectives can be met by other, less intrusive means. If an offender is dealt with by either of these methods (and they have not been arrested), they will not be subject to s. 30(1A) of PACE.

Under s. 30(2) of the Act, where a person is arrested and taken to a police station, they shall be taken to a 'designated' police station, which is suitable for detaining arrested persons (unless the exceptions in **1.3.3 Non-designated police stations** below apply).

KEYNOTE

Subsection (1) above will not apply, when the presence of that person elsewhere is necessary in order to carry out such investigations as it is reasonable to carry out immediately (see s. 30(10)). The point that the investigation must be immediate was addressed in *R* v *Kerawalla* [1991] Crim LR 451.

A chief officer of police may only designate a police station which appears to 'provide enough accommodation for that purpose' (see s. 35(2)).

Some flexibility is allowed by the Act, as a chief officer may choose to designate a police station which was not previously designated, or may direct that a designation of a police station previously made shall cease to operate (see s. 35(3)).

KEYNOTE

A 'designated police station' means a police station for the time being designated under this section (see s. 35(4)).

1.3.3 **Non-designated police stations**

There are three general exceptions to the rule that all arrested persons must be taken to a designated police station:

1. where the constable works in an area covered by a police station which is not a designated police station (e.g. a rural police station, or a temporary detention area at a football ground); *or*

2. where a constable works for a police force which is not maintained by a police authority (e.g. British Transport Police); *or*

3. where any constable, wherever they work, has arrested a person while they are working alone, and it appears that to take the person to a designated police station would expose that person, the officer, or some other person to injury.

In all of the above cases, the detainee must have been arrested for an offence, for which the constable believes the detainee will not be in police detention for longer than six hours.

Some police areas have set rules which prevent an arrested person being taken to a non-designated police station, whatever the circumstances. This approach would appear to be sensible, if those stations lack the facilities to detain a person safely.

Additionally, if such stations do not have a custody officer available, the integrity of the detention process may be compromised (see **1.6.3 Custody officers at non-designated police stations** below for the situation regarding custody officers at non-designated police stations).

However, if the officer has no choice other than to take a person to a non-designated police station for safety reasons, their actions would be covered by s. 30(5) above. If this situation does occur, it is recommended that this should be viewed as a temporary measure only, and the officer should arrange to transport the arrested person as soon as possible to a designated police station.

In other police areas, arrested persons are taken routinely to non-designated police stations, when the offence is straightforward (e.g. shoplifting), and the detainee is unlikely to be held in police detention for longer than six hours. (See **flow chart 1 in Appendix 1** for an easy guide).

1.4 Appointment of Custody Officers

1.4.1 Legislative provisions

Section 36(1) PACE

One or more custody officers shall be appointed for each designated police station.

Section 36(2) PACE

A custody officer for a designated police station shall be appointed—

(a) by the chief officer of police for the area in which the designated police station is situated, or

(b) by such other police officer as the chief officer of police for that area may direct.

Section 36(3) PACE

No person may be appointed a custody officer unless—

(a) he is a police officer of at least the rank of sergeant; or

(b) he is a staff custody officer.

Section 36(4) PACE

An officer of any rank may perform the functions of a custody officer at a designated police station if a custody officer is not readily available to perform them.

1.4.2 Who should be appointed?

Although the chief officer of police is responsible for appointing custody officers, in practice, this function is generally delegated to the operational commander for the area covering the designated station (under s. 36(2)(b) above).

Section 120 of the Serious Organised Crime and Police Act 2005 amended s. 38 of the Police Reform Act 2002 (police powers for police authority employees), to introduce the concept of 'police staff custody officers'. Section 36(3) of PACE (see above) is amended accordingly, which means that the role of a custody officer may be 'civilianised'.

A police staff custody officer has the powers to perform all the functions of a custody officer under the 1984 Act (except those under s. 45A(4) of that Act, relating to reviews conducted by video links) and under any other enactment which confers functions on such a custody officer. But in relation to a police station designated under s. 35(1) of the 1984 Act, the person must first be appointed a custody officer for that police station under s. 36(2) of that Act.

KEYNOTE

Note that Code C, Note for Guidance 1J states that:

The designation of police staff custody officers applies only in police areas where an order commencing the provisions of the Police Reform Act 2002, section 38 and Schedule 4A for designating police staff custody officers is in effect.

Therefore, although the Serious Organised Crime and Police Act 2005 provides the facility for appointing police staff custody officers, certain police areas will be appointed to pilot the scheme before such people are more widely appointed.

There is nothing preventing a police officer of any other rank performing the role of a custody officer, if one is not readily available (including an officer of a higher rank).

A custody officer should only be appointed once the chief officer is satisfied that he/she is trained, capable and competent.

The situation as regards a custody officer being 'readily available' was examined by the Court of Appeal, in *Vince v Chief Constable of Dorset* [1993] 1 WLR 415. In this case, it was held that there was no requirement for a designated police station to appoint sufficient custody officers, so that one was available at all times (s. 36(1) merely requires one or more to be appointed). Further, the Court of Appeal held that a constable could perform the role, if there was no other sergeant available at the station and one could not be brought there without impacting on the operational capability of the police. This is something of a grey area; for example, what if there is a sergeant working in the police station in a non-operational role? It may be argued that such a person should take on the responsibilities of a custody officer, as this would not affect the operational capability of the police. In the absence of any further guidance, it would be sensible to follow this course of action. If no other sergeants are available, as a last resort a constable may perform these duties.

In most designated police stations, more than one sergeant will be appointed as custody officers, in order to supply 24-hour coverage and to account for leave and sickness.

KEYNOTE

Any references in PACE and the *Codes of Practice* to a custody officer, will also include those performing the functions of a custody officer (when they have not been appointed as one) (see Code C, para. 1.9).

1.5 **Designated Persons**

1.5.1 **Legislative provisions**

Code C, Para. 1.13

In this Code:

(a) 'designated person' means a person other than a police officer, designate under the Police Reform Act 2002, Part 4, who has specified powers and duties of police officers conferred or imposed on them;

(b) reference to a police officer includes a designated person acting in the exercise or performance of the powers and duties conferred on them by their designation.

1.5.2 **The Police Reform Act 2002**

The concept of 'designated persons' was introduced by the Police Reform Act 2002, with a view to 'civilianising' some police functions. Under the Act, chief officers of police may appoint the following:

- Police Community Support Officers (to deal with crime and disorder issues whilst on patrol);
- Investigating Officers (to assist in investigation and interviewing in some specialist areas);
- Detention Officers (to act as gaolers in custody offices);
- Escort Officers (to assist in transporting arrested persons to and from police stations, and to other locations as directed by the custody officer).

This book will concentrate on the powers given to detention officers, as they apply in the custody office.

1.5.3 **Powers given to detention officers**

Prior to the introduction of the 2002 Act, some custody offices utilised 'civilian' detention officers as gaolers. However, those members of staff did not share many of the powers given to police officers, such as taking fingerprints by force. In order to circumvent this, police forces would appoint 'civilian' detention officers as Special Constables.

KEYNOTE

Note that there is nothing preventing police forces from utilising any civilian member of staff who is employed by a police force to perform tasks in the custody office, provided that PACE allows them to do so (see Code C, para. 1.15).

These functions could include:

- administrative duties;
- conducting visits;
- providing meals and refreshments;
- itemising property.

Schedule 4, Part 3 of the 2002 Act provides detention officers with a range of powers which may be utilised in the custody office. The below table outlines the powers available:

Power	PACE Section	Police Reform Act 2002
Require person to attend the police station to have their fingerprints taken	s. 27(1)	Para. 25
Conduct non-intimate searches	s. 54	Para. 26
Conduct searches and examinations to establish identity, or photograph identifying marks	s. 54A	Para. 27
Seize items during non-intimate searches	s. 54	Para. 28
Conduct intimate searches	s. 55	Para. 28
Take fingerprints without consent	s. 61	Para. 29
Give warning before an intimate sample is to be taken (no power to actually take the sample)	s. 62(7)	Para. 30
Take non-intimate sample	s. 63	Para. 31
Require a person who has been charged with or convicted of a recordable offence to attend the station to provide a DNA sample	s. 63A(4)	Para. 32
Photograph a detainee	s. 64A	Para. 33

It should be noted that under Code C, para. 1.14 of the *Codes of Practice*, if any of the above powers allow the reasonable use of force by a constable, a detention officer may also use reasonable force in the exercise of their powers. Paragraph 1.14 provides particular examples of when reasonable force may be used by a designated person, as follows:

(a) when exercising a power conferred on them which allows a police officer exercising that power to use reasonable force, a designated person has the same entitlement to use force; and

(b) at other times when carrying out duties conferred or imposed on them that also entitle them to use reasonable force, for example:

   – when at a police station carrying out the duty to keep detainees for whom they are responsible under control and to assist any other police officer or designated person to keep any detainee under control and to prevent their escape;

   – when securing, or assisting any other police officer or designated person in securing, the detention of a person at a police station;

   – when escorting, or assisting any other police officer or designated person in escorting, a detainee within a police station;

   – for the purpose of saving life or limb or preventing serious damage to property.

KEYNOTE

Detention officers or any other civilian members of staff must have regard to any of the relevant *Codes of Practice* when performing their duties (see Code C, para. 1.16).

1.6 Custody Officers and Impartiality

1.6.1 Legislative provisions

Section 36(5) PACE

Subject to the following provisions of this section and to s. 39(2) below, none of the functions of a custody officer in relation to a person shall be performed by an officer who at the time when the function falls to be performed is involved in the investigation of an offence for which that person is in police detention at that time.

Section 36(7) PACE

Where an arrested person is taken to a police station which is not a designated police station, the functions in relation to him which at a designated police station would be the functions of a custody officer shall be performed—

(a) by an officer who is not involved in the investigation of an offence for which he is in police detention, if such an officer is readily available; and

(b) if no such officer is readily available, by the officer who took him to the station or any other officer.

Section 36(9) PACE

Where by virtue of ss. (7) above an officer of a force maintained by a police authority who took an arrested person to a police station is to perform the functions of a custody officer in relation to him, the officer shall inform an officer who—

(a) is attached to a designated station; and

(b) is of at least the rank of inspector,

that he is to do so.

1.6.2 Impartial investigation

The custody officer must be seen to uphold a detainee's rights and welfare. For that reason, it is clear from PACE and the *Codes of Practice* that the custody officer is expected to remain independent from the investigation.

KEYNOTE

Although custody officers must remain impartial, there is nothing preventing them giving procedural advice and guidance, for example in areas relating to preservation of evidence from the detainee (walking scene of crime).

Consider the following:

Case Study

Sergeant PRING worked at a large station in the centre of a town, as the patrol sergeant. She started work on a day shift one day, to find that the regular custody officer had reported sick. As Sergeant PRING was the only other qualified officer, she had to work in the custody office for that shift.

During the morning, THOMPSON attended the custody office, having answered bail in relation to an offence of assault. Coincidentally, the arresting officer for that offence was Sergeant PRING, the custody officer that day. THOMPSON was due to be charged with the offence, due to evidence obtained from further witnesses.

Would Sergeant PRING be able to act as custody officer in relation to THOMPSON, in these circumstances?

....

We can find the answer to the question in s. 36(5) of PACE (see above). Although there is a general expectation that the custody officer will remain independent from the investigation, the set of circumstances above could easily happen.

Under s. 35(6), the functions of a custody officer should not be performed if at the time when the function falls to be performed, he or she is involved in the investigation of an offence for which that person is in police detention at that time. It could be argued, therefore, that whilst it is not ideal for the arresting officer to later become the custody officer, in the circumstances, the custody officer will not be investigating the offence at this time, but will merely be making a decision as to charging and bailing.

It would be a different matter if it was necessary to re-interview the detainee. In those circumstances, the custody officer should not be involved in the interview, and should either find another custody officer to perform that role, or delegate the investigation to another officer.

KEYNOTE

Under s. 36(6), a custody officer will not be prevented from conducting some functions which by their nature may be seen as being part of the investigative process, for example:

- searching detainees;
- removing property from detainees;
- taking fingerprints or DNA;
- taking photographs or searching the detainee for identification purposes;
- carrying out a station breath test procedure;
- serving forms on a detainee for an identification parade.

1.6.3 **Custody officers at non-designated police stations**

We examined the circumstances in which an arrested person may be taken to a non-designated station in **1.3.3 Non-designated police stations** above. In this section, we will discuss the situation in respect of custody officers when this happens.

Where an arrested person has been taken to a non-designated police station, the custody officer's functions should be performed by an officer who is not involved in the investigation. This is in keeping with the provisions of s. 36(5) above, but what if there is no-one else available to act as a custody officer in the station? This situation is covered by s. 36(7)(b) above, which allows for either the arresting officer to perform these duties, or any other officer. Clearly, if another officer is available, it would be preferable for that person to act as the custody officer, but as a last resort, the arresting officer may do so under this subsection.

If it is necessary for an arresting officer to perform the duties of a custody officer at a non-designated station, the officer must inform an inspector at a designated station, as soon as practicable (see s. 36(9)–(10)). This provision ensures that the arrested person's detention will effectively be reviewed by an inspector at the earliest opportunity, who may decide that it is appropriate to transport the person to a designated police station.

KEYNOTE

Note that the requirement to inform an inspector under s. 36(9) above only applies where the arresting officer intends performing the duties of a custody officer and where the officer is employed by a force maintained by a Police Authority.

1.7 **Explaining the Term 'At Variance'**

1.7.1 **Legislative provisions**

Section 39(6) PACE

Where—

(a) an officer of a higher rank than the custody officer gives directions relating to a person in police detention; and

(b) the directions are at variance—

   (i) with any decision made or action taken by the custody officer in the performance of a duty imposed on him under this Part of this Act; or

    (ii)   with any decision or action which would but for the direction have been made or taken by him in the performance of such a duty,

the custody officer shall refer the matter at once to an officer of the rank of superintendent or above who is responsible for the police station for which the custody officer is acting as custody officer.

1.7.2 **Custody officers' authority**

Throughout this chapter and the rest of the book, it will be obvious that the custody officer has full authority under PACE to deal with detainees in the custody office. Of course, the policing structure expects officers and staff of a lower rank to follow orders from senior officers, so how does this fit in with the custody officer's authority in respect of detainees?

Section 39(6) above ensures that the custody officer cannot be ordered by an officer of a higher rank to make a decision he or she is not comfortable with. This will apply to any decision already made, or one that the custody officer is about to make. However, the above will not apply when a decision is made by an inspector to release a detainee, when the inspector is conducting a review and considers the grounds for detention no longer exist. In these cases, the inspector will have primacy over the decision.

In practice, issues relating to s. 39(6) above usually occur when the investigating officer is in dispute with a custody officer. The investigating officer may consult with his/her own senior officer, who will be of a higher rank than the custody officer. The officer of a higher rank may then try to persuade the custody officer to change their decision. If this happens, the custody officer will have the option to either change their mind or not. If the senior officer orders the custody officer to change their decision, it will be for the custody officer to contact the superintendent responsible for the station. The superintendent should mediate and then make the final decision and the custody record should be endorsed accordingly. It should be noted that similar provisions exist under s. 40(11) of the Act, which protect inspectors who are conducting reviews from directions which are at variance with their decisions. As with s. 39(6) above, a superintendent should be called to mediate.

1.8 **Summing Up**

Responsibility

1.   It is the custody officer's duty to ensure:

    (a)   all detainees are treated in accordance with PACE and the *Codes of Practice*; and

(b)   that all matters relating to such are recorded in the custody records of detainees.

(s. 39(1) PACE)

2.   The custody officer ceases to have the above responsibility if he/she transfers the custody of the detainee to:

- the investigating officer;
- a person who is in charge of the detainee outside the police station;
- the local authority in the case of a juvenile.

(s. 39(2) PACE)

Designated and non-designated police stations

1.   When a person has been arrested, he or she should be taken to a designated police station as soon as practicable after the arrest.

(s. 30(1)–(2) PACE)

2.   An arrested person may be taken to any police station if it appears that the person may only be in police detention for less than six hours, and:

- the constable is working in a locality covered by a police station which is not a designated police station; or
- the constable belongs to a police force which is not maintained by a police authority; or
- where any constable, wherever they work, and while they are working alone, has arrested a person, and it appears that to take the person to a designated police station would expose that person, the officer, or some other person to injury.

(s. 30(3)–(5) PACE)

Appointment of custody officers

1.   No officer may be appointed a custody officer unless he/she is of at least the rank of sergeant, or he/she is a staff custody officer.

(s. 36(3) PACE)

2.   An officer of any rank may perform the functions of a custody officer at a designated police station if a custody officer is not readily available to perform them.

(s. 36(4) PACE)

Designated persons

1. A 'designated person' means a person other than a police officer, designate under the Police Reform Act 2002, Part 4, who has specified powers and duties of police officers conferred or imposed on them.

(Code C, para. 1.13)

2. A designated person has the power to:
    *   require a person to attend a police station to have their fingerprints taken;
    *   carry out non-intimate searches;
    *   carry out searches and examinations to establish identity/photograph identifying marks;
    *   seize items taken during non-intimate searches;
    *   carry out intimate searches;
    *   take fingerprints without consent;
    *   to give warning required before an intimate sample is taken (no power to actually take the sample);
    *   take non-intimate samples;
    *   require a person who has been charged with or convicted of a recordable offence to attend a station to provide a DNA sample; and
    *   photograph a detained suspect.

(Police Reform Act 2002, Sch. 4, Pt 3)

3. Force may be used by a designated person:
    *   when exercising a power which would allow a police officer exercising that power to use reasonable force; and
    *   when carrying out duties conferred or imposed on them that also entitle them to use reasonable force, for example:
        *   when at a police station keeping detainees under control and to assist any police officer or designated person to keep any detainee under control and to prevent their escape;
        *   when securing, or assisting a police officer or designated person in securing, the detention of a person at a police station;
        *   when escorting, or assisting a police officer or designated person in escorting, a detainee within a police station;
        *   to save life or limb or preventing serious damage to property.

(Code C, para. 1.14)

Impartiality

1. None of the functions of a custody officer in relation to a detainee shall be performed by an officer who at the time when the function falls to be performed is involved in the investigation of an offence for which that person is in police detention at that time, unless the arrested person is taken to a non-designated police station, when the functions of a custody officer shall be performed:

    (a) by an officer who is not involved in the investigation of an offence for which the person is in police detention, if such an officer is readily available; and

    (b) if no such officer is readily available, by the officer who took the person to the station or any other officer.

2. Where an officer does perform custody duties as above, he/she shall inform an inspector at a designated police station as soon as practicable.

(ss. 36(7), (9) & (10) PACE)

'At variance'

Where an officer of a higher rank than the custody officer gives directions relating to a person in police detention; and the directions are at variance:

*   with any decision made or action taken by the custody officer; or
*   with any decision or action, which the custody officer is about to make,

the custody officer shall refer the matter at once to a superintendent, who is responsible for the police station.

(s. 39(6) PACE)

1. Does your force have a policy relating to the detention of persons at a non-designated police station?

SPACE FOR NOTES

SPACE FOR NOTES

SPACE FOR NOTES

2

Detainees—Initial Action

2.1 **Introduction**

This chapter will deal with the initial duties of a custody officer to consider whether or not to accept a person into police detention, following their arrest. This section of the custody process is crucial, as the custody officer is required to make instant decisions, which are always open to scrutiny at a later date.

The chapter will offer advice on what must be recorded on the custody record, according to PACE and the *Codes of Practice*, as well as what the custody officer may omit from the record, when it is appropriate.

Part 3 of the Serious Organised Crime and Police Act 2005 added a new dimension to the arrest and detention process. A constable must consider whether he/she has reasonable grounds for believing that the arrest was *necessary*. Custody officers must also apply the same 'necessity test' before authorising detention. This information should also be recorded on the custody record.

Inevitably, there are overlaps in this chapter with many others in this book. For example, this chapter examines the 'booking in procedure', which should include a risk assessment of the detainee to establish whether they require medical treatment, or represent a risk to themselves. Because of the importance of these subjects, they are covered in depth in **Chapter 3—Safer Detention**. Also, the custody officer will need to make decisions about when he or she believes there is sufficient evidence to charge a detainee. The decision-making process is covered in this chapter; however, the practicalities of actually charging a person are covered in depth in **Chapter 14—Charging Suspects**.

Human Rights Act 1998

This chapter concentrates mainly on the provisions of PACE and the *Codes of Practice*; however, custody officers must also consider Article 5 of the Human Rights Act 1998 (right to liberty and security).

The starting point for a potential breach of Article 5 will be when the person is actually arrested. However, when a custody officer accepts an arrested person into police detention, any previous breach of this Article may be compounded if the initial arrest was unlawful. Custody officers must recognise that there is a balance to be struck between the duty of the police to investigate crime and apprehend criminals and the rights of the private citizen (see *R* v *Chief Constable of Kent Constabulary, ex parte Kent Police Federation Joint Branch Board* [2000] 2 Cr App R 196).

2.2 **Accepting Custody of a Detainee**

2.2.1 **Legislative provisions**

Code C, Para. 2.1A

When a person is brought to a police station—

- under arrest;
- is arrested at the police station having attended there voluntarily; or
- attends a police station to answer bail;

they should be brought before the custody officer as soon as practicable after their arrival at the station or, if appropriate, following arrest after attending the police station voluntarily. This applies to designated and non-designated police stations. A person is deemed to be 'at a police station' for these purposes if they are within the boundary of any building or enclosed yard which forms part of that police station.

Section 37(1) PACE

Where—

(a) a person is arrested for an offence—

    (i) without a warrant, or

    (ii) under a warrant not endorsed for bail, *or*

(b) . . .

the custody officer at each police station where he is detained after his arrest shall determine whether he has before him sufficient evidence to charge that person with the offence for which he was arrested and may detain him at the police station for such period as is necessary to enable him to do so.

Section 37(2) PACE

If the custody officer determines that he does not have such evidence before him, the person arrested shall be released either on bail or without bail, unless the custody officer has reasonable grounds for believing that his detention without being charged is necessary to secure or preserve evidence relating to an offence for which he is under arrest or to obtain such evidence by questioning him.

Section 37(3) PACE

If the custody officer has reasonable grounds for so believing, he may authorise the person arrested to be kept in police detention.

Section 37(9) PACE

If the person arrested is not in a fit state to be dealt with under ss. (7) above, he may be kept in police detention until he is.

2.2.2 'At a Police Station'

It should be noted that para. 2.1A determines that a person will be 'at a police station' if he or she is within the boundary of any building or enclosed yard that forms part of that police station.

There will often be a delay in bringing an arrested person before the custody officer, because of circumstances in a custody office at the time, such as a number of persons arriving at the same time, or the custody officer may be engaged in charging or bailing another detainee. Paragraph 2.1A recognises this fact, by requiring an arrested person to be brought before the custody officer 'as soon as practicable' following their arrest.

Note that para. 2.1A applies whether the person is taken to a designated or non-designated police station.

2.2.3 Initial action by custody officer

Very few people who have been arrested and brought before the custody officer at a police station will be dealt with immediately on entering the custody office. There will usually be some delay in the process, even if there is sufficient evidence to charge the person straight away. The custody officer will need to make a decision whether or not to detain that person under s. 37 of PACE (see **flow chart 2 in Appendix 1** for an easy guide). In arriving at this decision, the custody officer will need to consider the following questions:

1. Why is the person here?
2. Was he/she lawfully detained?
3. Was the arrest necessary?
4. Why is further detention necessary?
5. On what authority is detention to be made?

6. What procedures will have to be considered for this person whilst in custody?

7. What special needs does this person have?

In the majority of cases, answering the seven questions listed above should be fairly straightforward and the arrested person will be detained for relatively simple offences. However, this will not always be the case, and it will be necessary for the custody officer to consider these issues separately, as we will do now.

1. Why is the person here?

The arresting officer will need to outline the basic nature of the offence to the custody officer, who should record the facts of the arrest on the custody record. Further guidance as to what should actually be recorded on the custody record is given below in **2.4 What else must be recorded on the custody record?**

2. Was he/she lawfully detained?

The custody officer will also need to decide whether or not the arrest was lawful. The custody officer may assume that an arrest is lawful in the absence of any evidence to the contrary (see *DPP* v *L* [1999] Crim LR 752). In this case, the arrest was later deemed to be unlawful, because the detainee was not informed that she was under arrest. However, the custody officer was entitled to assume that correct procedure had been followed at the point of authorising detention. It would be a different matter if, when the custody officer is given the facts of the arrest by the arresting officer, he or she identifies that the arrest was unlawful. In these circumstances, the custody officer would need to consider whether the detention of the person can be justified.

KEYNOTE

If information given to an arresting officer by a superior was insufficient to supply to the arresting officer reasonable grounds for suspicion of the arrested person, the arresting officer could not claim that he/she thought the superior probably did have other information justifying the arrest that he or she had not been informed of. Simply 'obeying orders' is not a justification for making an arrest in these circumstances (see *O'Hara* v *Chief Constable of the Royal Ulster Constabulary* [1997] AC 286 and *Sonia Raissi & Mohamed Raissi* v *Commissioner of Police of the Metropolis* [2007] EWHC 2842 (QB)).

KEYNOTE

If a custody officer does identify that a person's arrest was unlawful and subsequently releases them from custody, the custody officer should nevertheless open a custody record and note the fact that the person had attended the custody office (see Code C, para. 2.1, which requires a custody record to be opened for every person brought to the station under arrest, or who has been arrested at the station, having gone there voluntarily).

---

3. Was the arrest necessary?

Part 3 of the Serious Organised Crime and Police Act 2005 added a new dimension to the arrest and detention process. Under s. 24(4) of PACE, before making an arrest, a constable must consider whether he/she has reasonable grounds for believing that the arrest was *necessary*. The 'necessity test' laid down in the 2005 Act ensures that every arrest made falls in line with the general provisions of Article 5 of the European Convention on Human Rights, incorporated in the Human Rights Act 1998 (right to liberty and security), which states:

> Everyone has the right to liberty and security of person. No one shall be deprived of his liberty save in the following cases and in accordance with a procedure prescribed by law:

> (c) the lawful arrest or detention of a person effected for the purpose of bringing him before the competent legal authority on reasonable suspicion of having committed an offence or when it is reasonably considered *necessary* to prevent his committing an offence or fleeing after having done so;

It remains to be seen what kind of challenges officers will face in court when asked to explain why an arrest was necessary. However, if a court rules that the officer could have dealt with the offence by one of the alternative methods, such as Street Bail, Penalty Notice or summons, a challenge may be brought under Article 5 above. It follows that custody officers are also under a duty to consider the same 'necessity test' *before* authorising a person's detention. Code G, para. 1.4 specifically states that if the provisions of the Act and this Code are not observed, both the arrest and the conduct of any subsequent investigation may be open to question. Custody officers will need to be intrusive to ensure that the officer has complied with Code G, and a failure to follow this Code may lead to any subsequent detention being seen as unlawful by the court.

KEYNOTE

Note that people who attend police stations voluntarily to assist the police with their investigations are not subject to s. 37 PACE (custody officer determining arrest was necessary).

However, if an officer forms a view that the person should be arrested at the police station for the purpose of interview and informs the custody officer of this view, the custody officer can authorise detention for the interview and is entitled to assume the arrest by the officer is lawful (see *Al Fayed* v *Metropolitan Police Commissioner* [2004] EWCA Civ 1579).

---

4. Why is further detention necessary?

Once the custody officer has decided that the person has been lawfully arrested and that the arrest was necessary, he or she may accept that person into police detention. If the custody officer determines that there are no grounds to detain the person under s. 37(2) that person should be released immediately either on bail or otherwise. If the decision is that the detainee is to be released without bail, there can be no delay (see *Nellins* v *Chief Constable of the Royal Ulster Constabulary* [1998] N.I. 1 (QBD), where the person was detained unlawfully for a medical examination after the decision had been made to release them).

If the custody officer decides to detain the arrested person, he/she will have to consider why it is necessary to hold the person further. In general terms, this may be either because there is sufficient evidence to charge the arrested person, or because there is insufficient evidence to charge him/her (we will deal below with the situation where there is insufficient evidence to charge).

When a person has been arrested for an offence (or is under a warrant issued by the court to arrest for an offence), the custody officer must consider, under s. 37(1) above, whether or not there is sufficient evidence to charge that person. In arriving at this decision, the custody officer will need to consider s. 37(7) of PACE, which requires him or her to determine whether there is sufficient evidence to charge the detainee with the offence for which he or she was arrested and to make one of the following decisions:

(a) release the person without charge and on bail for the purpose of enabling the Director of Public Prosecutions to make a decision under s. 37B below;

(b) release the person without charge and on bail but not for that purpose;

(c) release the person without charge and without bail; *or*

(d) charge the person.

This subsection was altered significantly by the Criminal Justice Act 2003, which requires the police to consult with the Crown Prosecution Service on charging matters and is dealt with in more depth in **Chapter 14—Charging Suspects**. If the custody officer determines that there is sufficient evidence to charge a suspect, he or she may authorise the person to be detained under s. 37(1) at the police station for such period as is necessary to enable him/her to do so.

KEYNOTE

Remember that where the person has answered deferred bail, the period of detention may be restricted by the amount of time remaining on the person's detention clock from their previous time in custody.

Some people arriving before the custody officer may require charging immediately. This will usually occur when there is no requirement to interview the detainee, or gather further evidence while he/she is actually in custody. The most common situations are:

- where the person has previously been in custody and has been released on deferred bail for further enquiries, or pending a decision from the Crown Prosecution Service, and when they return, the custody officer determines that there is sufficient evidence to charge;
- where the person has been arrested for a public order offence and no interview is required, and the detainee is fit to be charged.

5. On what authority is detention to be made?

Many people who have been arrested will not be charged immediately, and the custody officer will have to authorise their further detention. This will have to be done lawfully, and in accordance with s. 37(2) of PACE (see above).

If there is not sufficient evidence to charge the detainee immediately, what should the person be detained for? Section 37(2) above deals with two situations, namely:

- where detention is necessary to secure or preserve evidence relating to an offence for which he/she is under arrest; or
- to obtain such evidence by questioning.

The situation as regards obtaining evidence by questioning is dealt with in more depth in **Chapter 18—Interviewing**.

There can be a number of reasons to authorise detention to secure or preserve evidence, such as:

- making enquiries to arrest a co-accused;
- interviewing a co-accused;
- taking statements from witnesses;

- conducting house-to-house enquiries;
- conducting a search of the detainee's premises under s. 18 of the Act;
- dealing with forensic issues;
- viewing CCTV evidence.

The above list is not exhaustive, and there may be many other reasons to detain a person to secure and preserve evidence. The custody officer must make the decision on the basis that it is necessary to do so in relation to an offence for which the person is under arrest.

As well as detaining a person under s. 37(2) above, a custody officer may also authorise further detention without charge for other reasons, for example, where the person has been arrested:

- on warrant (for production in court);
- for a breach of bail (for production in court);
- for an injunction with a power of arrest;
- for being unlawfully at large;
- to prevent a breach of the peace;
- to provide a sample of breath under s. 7 of the Road Traffic Act 1988;
- to supply fingerprints/DNA samples;
- under the Mental Health Act 1983;
- under the Immigration Act 1971;
- under the Terrorism Act 2000;
- under the Army Act 1955/Navy Act 1955/Air Force Act 1957 (deserters etc.);
- under s. 25 of PACE.

Lastly, a person may be detained, when the custody officer considers there is sufficient evidence to charge, but because of the detainee's condition or behaviour, he or she is unfit to be dealt with. Such a person may be kept in police custody until he/she is fit to be dealt with (see s. 37(9) above).

6. What procedures will have to be considered for this person whilst in custody?

There are several initial and ongoing procedures that must be considered in relation to all detainees. These will include such things as:

- complying with the *Codes of Practice*;
- notifying the detainee of their rights and entitlements;
- conducting a risk assessment of the detainee;
- looking after the detainee's welfare;
- searching;
- reviewing the detainee.

All of the above matters are dealt with elsewhere in this book.

7. What special needs does this person have?

The detainee may be considered to be vulnerable, or in need of an interpreter. These issues are dealt with in depth in **Chapter 7—Vulnerable People and Appropriate Adults**.

The custody officer is also required to conduct a risk assessment of the detainee's mental state, as well as establishing whether they require medical attention or medication. These subjects are covered in **Chapter 3—Safer Detention** and **Chapter 4—Clinical Treatment and Attention** respectively.

KEYNOTE

Note that any decision made by the custody officer under s. 37(1) above must be carried out as soon as practicable after the person arrives at the police station or, in the case of a person arrested at the police station, as soon as practicable after the arrest (see s. 37(10) PACE).

Further to the above, under Code C, para. 1.1, all persons in custody must be dealt with expeditiously, and released as soon as the need for detention no longer applies.

KEYNOTE

The provisions dealt with in this section, should be considered throughout a person's period of detention, and not only when the person is first brought into custody.

This issue is especially important when a custody officer is taking over at the beginning of a new shift. The custody officer must consider the seven questions mentioned above.

2.3 The Custody Record

2.3.1 Legislative provisions

Section 37(4) PACE

Where a custody officer authorises a person who has not been charged to be kept in police detention, he shall, as soon as is practicable, make a written record of the grounds for the detention.

Section 37(5) PACE

Subject to subsection (6) below, the written record shall be made in the presence of the person arrested who shall at that time be informed by the custody officer of the grounds for his detention.

Section 37(6) PACE

Subsection (5) above shall not apply where the person arrested is, at the time when the written record is made—

(a)   incapable of understanding what is said to him;

(b)   asleep;

(c)   violent or likely to become violent; or

(d)   in urgent need of medical attention.

2.3.2 **Opening the custody record**

Once the custody officer has determined that there are sufficient grounds to detain an arrested person, he or she must open a custody record and record the grounds for detention under s. 37(4) above.

The recorded grounds will obviously depend on the offence the person was arrested for and/or the enquiries necessary to gather sufficient evidence to charge the person, as described above in **2.2.3 Initial action by custody officer.**

KEYNOTE

Note that under Code C, para. 2.1, a separate custody record must be opened for each detainee.

The custody officer is also required to link any documentation held in relation to an arrest, with the custody record, when a person is answering street bail (see Code C, para. 3.25).

2.3.3 **Recording the decision in presence of the detainee**

Section 37(5) above requires the custody officer to record their decision in the presence of the detainee. At the same time, the detainee must also be told of the reason for their detention.

Most custody offices have computerised custody records, which prompt the custody officer as to what should be recorded at this point. Whether the custody record is handwritten or computerised, the grounds recorded should follow the examples below:

> I am satisfied that there is sufficient evidence to charge you with an offence. I am authorising your detention as being necessary for that purpose, or

> I am not satisfied that there is sufficient evidence to charge you with an offence. I am authorising your detention as being necessary for the purpose of obtaining evidence by questioning, or

> I am not satisfied that there is sufficient evidence to charge you with an offence. I am authorising your detention as being necessary for the purposes of securing and preserving evidence.

Under s. 37(6) above, when a detainee is incapable of understanding what is said, asleep, violent or likely to become violent, or in urgent need of medical attention, the custody officer need not record the grounds for detention in the detainee's presence.

But what happens later when the detainee becomes capable of understanding what is being said, or is no longer in need of urgent medical attention? Consider the following.

Case Study

FREEMAN was arrested for being found drunk in a public place. On her arrival at the custody office, the custody officer attempted to inform FREEMAN of the grounds for her detention. However, it was clear that she was unfit to understand what was being said. The custody officer ordered her to be placed in a cell and recorded the grounds for her detention while FREEMAN was in the cell. She was also not informed of the grounds due to her condition.

When FREEMAN does become capable of understanding what is being said (or is no longer violent or in need of urgent medical attention) will the custody officer:

(a) be required to re-record the grounds for her arrest in her presence?

(b) be required to inform her of the grounds for her arrest?

....

In relation to question (a) above, s. 37 does not require the custody officer to re-record the grounds for the arrest in the presence of the detainee at this time—this requirement is only necessary 'at the time when the written record is made' (see s. 37(6) above).

In relation to question (b) above, the answer may be found in the *Codes of Practice*, and not under s. 37 of PACE. Under para. 3.4 of the codes, if the custody officer authorises a person's detention, the detainee must be informed of the grounds as soon as practicable and before they are questioned about any offence. The custody officer must, therefore, inform the detainee of the grounds for their detention when they are in a fit state to understand what is being said.

This is reinforced by Code C, para. 1.8, which states that where a person was required to be given certain information which was not given to them because of one of the reasons listed in s. 37(6) above, 'they must be given it as soon as practicable'.

2.4 **What Else Must be Recorded on the Custody Record?**

The introduction by the Serious Organised Crime and Police Act 2005 of the requirement to inform a person of why their arrest was necessary impacted on the role of the custody officer, in respect of what must be recorded on the custody record when the detainee arrives at the police station. This section is divided broadly into the following areas, which we will examine separately:

- Requirement to inform the person of the reason for the arrest
- Recording the circumstances of the arrest
- Recording why the arrest was necessary
- Recording comments made by the arrested person

2.4.1 **Legislative provisions**

Section 28(1) PACE

Subject to s. 28(5) below, when a person is arrested otherwise than by being informed that he is under arrest, the arrest is not lawful unless the person is informed that he is under arrest as soon as practicable after his arrest.

Section 28(3) PACE

Subject to ss. (5) below, no arrest is lawful unless the person arrested is informed of the ground for the arrest at the time of, or as soon as practicable after the arrest.

Code G, Para. 2.1

A lawful arrest requires two elements:

A person's involvement or suspected involvement or attempted involvement in the commission of a criminal offence;

AND

Reasonable grounds for believing that the person's arrest is necessary.

Code G, Para. 2.2

Arresting officers are required to inform the person arrested that they have been arrested, even if this fact is obvious, and of the relevant circumstances of the arrest in relation to both elements and to inform the custody officer of these on arrival at the police station. See Code C, para. 3.4.

Code C, Para. 2.3

The custody officer is responsible for the custody record's accuracy and completeness and for making sure the record or copy of the record accompanies a detainee if they are transferred to another police station.

Code G, Para. 4.3

On arrival at the police station, the custody officer shall open the custody record (see para. 1.1A and s. 2 of Code C). The information given by the arresting officer on the circumstances and reason or reasons for arrest shall be recorded as part of the custody record. Alternatively, a copy of the record made by the officer in accordance with para. 4.1 above shall be attached as part of the custody record.

Code G, Para. 4.4

The custody record will serve as a record of the arrest. Copies of the custody record will be provided in accordance with paras. 2.4 and 2.4A of Code C and access for inspection of the original record in accordance with para. 2.5 of Code C.

Code C, Para. 3.4

The custody officer shall:

- record the offence(s) that the detainee has been arrested for and the reason(s) for the arrest on the custody record (see Code G, s. 2).

- note on the custody record any comment the detainee makes in relation to the arresting officer's account but shall not invite comment. If the arresting officer is not physically present when the detainee is brought to a police station, the arresting officer's account must be made available to the custody officer remotely or by a third party on the arresting officer's behalf.

- note any comment the detainee makes in respect of the decision to detain them but shall not invite comment.

2.4.2 Requirement to inform the person of the reason for the arrest

Under s. 28 of PACE (see above), the arresting officer is required to inform a person that he/she is under arrest (s. 28(1)) and to inform them of the grounds (s. 28(4)) (even if the facts are obvious). This information should be given at the time of the arrest; however, s. 28(5) states that the above information need not be given, if it was not reasonably practicable to do so at the time by reason of the person having escaped before the information could be given. There is an additional requirement, under Code G, para. 2.2, to inform the person of why the arrest was necessary and, further, to inform the custody officer of both the grounds and the necessity for the arrest on arrival at the police station. Code G, Note for Guidance 3 states that *vague or technical language should be avoided* when informing the arrested person.

It is clear that if the information is not given at the time of arrest, it should be given when the person is brought before the custody officer (bearing in mind the requirement to do so as soon as practicable).

Under Article 5 of the European Convention on Human Rights, incorporated in the Human Rights Act 1998 (right to liberty and security):

> everyone who is arrested shall be informed promptly, in a language which he understands, of the reasons for his arrest and of any charge against him.

Consider circumstances in which a person is arrested who does not understand English. They may not understand completely why they have been arrested until they have spoken to an interpreter. Most forces now use Language Line, which enables custody officers to comply with Article 5 above (see **7.13.3 Interpreters** for further discussion on this issue).

> **KEYNOTE**
>
> Note that if s. 28 above is not complied with, the arrest will be unlawful, regard-less of whether the grounds were given later (see *Wilson* v *Chief Constable of Lancashire* [2000] LTL 23 November).

2.4.3 Recording the circumstances of the arrest

The circumstances of the arrest may be given either by the arresting officer, or if he or she is not present, it may be given remotely (e.g. by telephone or radio message, or presumably even by email), or by another officer on behalf of the arresting officer. This addition to the *Codes of Practice* recognises that the arresting officer is often delayed at the scene of arrest and people are brought to the custody office by other police officers.

The Home Office guidance on the changes in the August 2004 edition of the *Codes of Practice* also states that this provision has been inserted to:

> Enable officers to remain on front-line duties without being taken 'off the street' to travel to and from the police station. Enable greater use of desig-nated detention officers under sections 38 & 39 of Police Reform Act 2002. The Code does not require the arresting officer to be present at the point at which the suspect is brought before the custody officer.

Other than s. 28 above, no specific guidance can be found in either PACE or the *Codes of Practice* as to what should be noted down from the arresting officer's account. Generally, the custody officer should note down brief details of the offence and the circumstances surrounding the arrest. The following is an example:

> The detainee has been arrested for theft. The detainee was seen by a store detective in a shop in High Street. She was seen to select two bottles of perfume from the display, total value £30.00, place them in her pocket, and leave the store without paying.

The arresting officer may have given far more information than this, but it is not necessary to note down everything he or she says in relation to the arrest.

The following people may have access to the custody record at some future date:

- Other custody officers taking over a new shift;
- Reviewing officers;
- Superintendents (for authorisations);
- Professional standards department (for complaints and discipline);
- Defence solicitors;
- Appropriate adults;

- The Crown Prosecution Service;
- The courts;
- Independent Custody Visitors;
- The detainee himself/herself;
- The custody officer himself/herself (for court cases or civil claims).

There must, therefore, be sufficient information for anyone else reading the custody record to be able to easily identify why the person was detained.

There may be occasions when the custody officer will legitimately note down even fewer details than above. Let us look at a set of circumstances which occur occasionally:

Case Study

FOLEY was arrested for being in possession of a Class A drug, with intent to supply it, having been under surveillance by the drug squad for two months. On their arrival at the custody office, the arresting officer asked the custody officer if she could speak with him in private. She told the custody officer the full details of the surveillance operation, but asked him not to include these details in the custody record. The custody officer noted the following details:

> Detainee arrested for possession of Class A drugs, with intent to supply to another. Having spoken to the arresting officer, I am satisfied that there are grounds to detain this person.

FOLEY's solicitor attended the custody office and requested a copy of the custody record. Having read it, the solicitor complained to the custody officer that she was unable to advise her client, because of a lack of information on the custody record. Her complaint was that more detail should have been noted in the circumstances of arrest.

Consider the following questions:

(a) Should the circumstances of the arrest have been given in the detainee's presence?

(b) Is the solicitor's complaint valid in these circumstances?

....

Occasionally, custody officers may be asked by the arresting officer not to note all the details of the arrest on the custody record. The detainee in the circumstances above had been under surveillance for some time, and the arresting officer did not wish to reveal full details of their enquiries to the solicitor or the detainee. The custody officer was quite within his/her rights not to reveal these details on this occasion.

Section 28 of PACE (see above) does require the detainee to be informed of the reason and the grounds for his/her arrest. However, it does not state that the detainee must be told every detail surrounding the case against him/her. These details may be provided to the detainee in simple terms and are normally given by the arresting officer at the time of arrest.

There is nothing in PACE that instructs a custody officer to record the reasons for the arrest in the detainee's presence. Section 37(5) above only requires the custody officer to record the grounds for detention in the presence of the detainee.

Therefore, the custody officer may hear the facts of the arrest outside of the detainee's hearing, and then record the grounds for detention afterwards in their presence.

KEYNOTE

It is suggested that the custody officer records the circumstances of the arrest somewhere in circumstances such as those above. This could be done either in the form of a statement or in a pocket book, which will be available in future should the custody officer ever have to defend their decision.

What about the solicitor's complaint that she is unable to advise her client because of a lack of information? Again, there is nothing in either PACE or the *Codes of Practice* stating that the detainee must be given further details at this time. In the circumstances above, the detainee will be aware that he has been arrested for supplying controlled drugs as he should have been told this at the time of his arrest. He or she will also have been told by the custody officer the grounds for his detention (i.e. to obtain evidence by questioning etc.).

It should be remembered that it is the custody officer who must be satisfied that the grounds exist to detain a person—and he or she may be held accountable in the future for decisions made.

As to the solicitor's complaint that she is unable to advise her client, there is no requirement either under PACE, or the Criminal Justice and Public Order Act 1994, for the police to disclose information to the legal representative (other than allowing him/her to see the custody record (*Codes of Practice*, para. 2.4)). The officer in the case does face the risk of the detainee making no comment, and later claiming that since there had not been full disclosure prior to the interview, the court should not draw any inference from this silence. However, see *R v Argent* [1997] Crim LR 346, where the court dismissed this submission (this issue is also dealt with in **13.5—Initial disclosure to solicitors**).

The investigating officer will need to strike a balance between providing enough information to the solicitor to allow him/her to properly represent the client, and providing the detainee with a ready-made defence prior to the interview.

KEYNOTE

In *R* v *Imran* [1997] Crim LR 754 it was held that the police need not present the suspect with their whole case prior to interview.

There may be other occasions when the custody officer feels it necessary to withhold information from the circumstances of the arrest. The request will normally come from the arresting officer, and could be for any of the following reasons:

- To protect a covert human intelligence source;
- To protect a vulnerable or intimidated witness;
- To delay informing the detainee of forensic evidence linking him/her with the offence;
- To delay informing the detainee of issues under the Proceeds of Crime Act 2002;
- Where other people are to be arrested for the offence.

2.4.4 Recording why the arrest was necessary

In addition to recording the circumstances of the arrest when opening the custody record, Code G, para. 4.3 above, also requires the custody officer to record the reason or reasons for the arrest. Alternatively, a copy of the record made by the arresting officer may be attached as part of the custody record. Under Code G, para. 4.1, the arresting officer is required to record the following information in his/her pocket book or by other methods used for recording information:

- the nature and circumstances of the offence leading to the arrest;
- the reason or reasons why arrest was necessary;
- the giving of the caution;
- anything said by the person at the time of arrest.

Additionally, according to Code G, para. 4.4 above, the custody record will serve as a record of the arrest. It follows that the custody officer should also record on the custody record *why the arrest was necessary*. In order for the record to withstand scrutiny, it should at least contain the same information as the arresting officer's notes.

2.4.5 **Recording comments made by the arrested person**

We have examined the requirement to record the grounds for a person's detention on the custody record above in **2.3.2 Opening the custody record**. Also, it can be seen from Code C, para. 3.4 above that the custody officer must note any comment made by the detainee in respect of the decision to detain them, as well as recording any comment the detainee makes in relation to the arresting officer's account.

KEYNOTE

Note that if the custody officer does put specific questions to the detainee regarding their involvement in any offence, or in respect of any comments they may make in response to the arresting officer's account, or the decision to place them in detention, such an exchange is likely to constitute an interview as in the *Codes of Practice*, para. 11.1A. This subject is covered in more depth in Chapter 18—Interviewing.

2.5 **Signing the Custody Record**

2.5.1 **Legislative provisions**

Code C, Para. 3.5

The custody officer shall:

(a)   ask the detainee, whether at this time, they:

    (i)   would like legal advice,

    (ii)   want someone informed of their detention;

(b)   ask the detainee to sign the custody record to confirm their decisions in respect of (a);

Code C, Para. 2.6

Subject to para. 2.6A, all entries in custody records must be timed and signed by the maker. Records entered on computer shall be timed and contain the operator's identification.

Code C, Para. 2.7

The fact and time of any detainee's refusal to sign a custody record, when asked in accordance with this code, must be recorded.

2.5.2 **Signatures**

The issue of notifying the detainee of their rights (referred to in Code C, para. 3.5 above) is dealt with in depth in **Chapter 6—The Detainee's Entitlements**. It is important to ensure that the detainee signs the custody record as to whether they would like legal advice, or someone informed of their detention. This will offer protection from any claims in future by the detainee that their fundamental human rights have been infringed.

Paragraph 2.6 above is aimed at both the custody officer and any other person who makes an entry on the custody record. Where a computerised custody record is in use, the person making the entry will usually be identified by their operator number. This security measure is important to ensure that people making decisions on a person's detention are entitled to do so because of their rank (i.e. constables are not conducting inspector's reviews).

Paragraph 2.6A of the *Codes of Practice* (referred to above), allows for the identities of custody staff and investigating officers to be protected in cases linked to the investigation of terrorism, or where they are likely to be placed in danger.

2.6 **Delay in Updating the Custody Record**

2.6.1 **Legislative provisions**

Code C, Para. 2.1

All information recorded under this code must be recorded as soon as practicable in the custody record unless otherwise specified.

Code C, Para. 1.1A

A custody officer must perform the functions in this Code as soon as practicable. A custody officer will not be in breach of this Code if delay is justifiable and reasonable steps are taken to prevent unnecessary delay. The custody record shall show when a delay has occurred and the reason.

Code C, Note for Guidance 1H

Paragraph 1.1A is intended to cover delays which may occur in processing detainees e.g. if:

- a large number of suspects are brought into the station simultaneously to be placed in custody;
- interview rooms are all being used;
- there are difficulties contacting an appropriate adult, solicitor or interpreter.

2.6.2 **Reasonable delay**

The provisions referred to above will apply as much when detention is first authorised and the custody record is being opened, as any other entries made during the detention period. Experienced custody staff will know that delays occur frequently, especially in busy custody offices.

The requirement under Code C, para. 1.1A to update the custody record when a delay has occurred and show the reason for that delay is important to note. Because custody records relate to a single detainee, anyone reading them in the future will be unable to appreciate how busy the custody office was at the time of the delayed entry.

What if the custody officer is challenged in court as to a delay in contacting a solicitor? If the reason for a delay is not recorded on the custody record, the custody officer may find it difficult to remember *why* the information was not added when it should have been, leaving him or her open to challenges by the defence solicitor. Provided the delay is reasonable and justified, and the custody record is updated as to the reason, Code C, para. 1.1A will have been complied with.

2.7 **Transferring Detainees**

2.7.1 **Legislative provisions**

Code C, Para. 2.3

The custody officer is responsible for the custody record's accuracy and completeness and for making sure the record accompanies a detainee if they are transferred to another police station. The record shall show the:

- time and reason for transfer;
- time a person is released from detention.

Section 56(8) PACE

The rights conferred by this section on a person detained at a police station or other premises are exercisable whenever he is transferred from one place to another; and this section applies to each subsequent occasion on which they are exercisable as it applies to the first such occasion.

Section 58(1) PACE

A person arrested and held in custody at a police station or other premises shall be entitled, if he so requests, to consult a solicitor privately at any time.

2.7.2 **Transferring to another station**

Code C, para. 2.3 above makes it clear that the custody officer is responsible for ensuring that the original custody record is taken with the detainee, when he or she is transferred to another police station for continued detention. The detainee may either be transferred to another station in the same force area, or to a station in a different force area. Paragraph 2.3 will apply whichever is the case. Where a written document exists, this should also be taken with the detainee as it is part of the custody record.

2.7.3 **Accepting a detainee from another police station**

When a person arrives at a custody office, having been transferred from another police station, the custody officer will have to decide whether or not to accept that person's detention. In doing so, the custody officer must consider the requirements of s. 37 above. In other words, he or she must base the decision on the following questions:

- Why is the person here?
- Was he/she lawfully detained?
- Was the arrest necessary?
- Why is further detention necessary?
- On what authority is detention to be made?
- What procedures will have to be considered for this person whilst in custody?
- What special needs does this person have?

These questions and the answers to them are discussed in depth above, in **2.2.3 Initial action by custody officer**. If the custody officer cannot justify authorising detention having considered the above, he/she must release the detainee immediately, regardless of any decisions made by previous custody officers.

In addition to considering the above questions, the custody officer must also inform the detainee of the grounds for his/her detention, remind the detainee of his/her right to have someone informed of their arrest (see s. 56(8) above), and the right to consult with a solicitor (see s. 58(1) above).

The custody officer should also seek to establish whether the detainee requires medical attention, or has injuries.

Consider the following:

Case Study

EVANS was arrested and taken to a non-designated police station for an offence contrary to the Public Order Act 1986. On his arrival, a custody record was opened and it was intended that he would be charged with the offence. However, it was discovered that he was also wanted for an offence of burglary.

He was arrested for burglary and the decision was made to transfer him to a designated police station nearby, as he was likely to be in custody for some time. On his way to the designated police station EVANS became extremely violent and when he arrived, he was taken straight to a cell because of his continued violent behaviour.

EVANS' solicitor had been contacted while EVANS was at the non-designated station, and was informed that EVANS was at the new station. On his arrival, he was allowed to consult with EVANS; however, after a few minutes, he emerged and informed the custody officer that his client had an injury to his head, and was claiming that he had been assaulted by the officers who transferred him.

What do you think were the implications of the custody officer failing to ensure that the detainee had no injuries when he arrived at the designated station?

···

The detainee in this scenario subsequently made a complaint that he was assaulted by the officers who transferred him to the designated station. From the custody record commenced in the non-designated station, it was clear that EVANS had no injuries when he arrived there. This meant that the injuries could have occurred either while he was being transported, or in the cells complex in the designated station. The continuation of the custody record at the designated station did not indicate whether or not EVANS had injuries, because he had been placed straight in a cell. Eventually, the police officers who transferred EVANS were saved by the CCTV coverage at the designated station, which clearly showed that the detainee did not have an injury when he arrived there. The person later admitted that he had made up the complaint, and that he had caused the injury to himself by banging his head on a wall in the designated station.

The custody officer at the designated station in this scenario had to consider whether he had acted correctly at the time. Although he acted within the guidelines of PACE and the *Codes of Practice* by not speaking to EVANS when he first arrived, he did not identify that he had an injury, which left him and the other officers exposed to the complaint.

2.7.4 Transferring a detainee to court

When a detainee is transferred to court, from a custody office, the custody record remains at the last police station he/she was at prior to the transfer. The custody officer must note the time that the detainee leaves police detention, under Code C, para. 2.3 above.

KEYNOTE

Note that when a detainee is transferred either to another custody office, or to court or prison, whether he/she is considered to be 'at risk' or not, the custody officer must complete a Prisoner Escort Record (PER) Form, which should accompany the detainee. (See **Chapter 3—Safer Detention** for a full discussion on risk assessments.)

2.8 **Summing Up**

Where a person is arrested for an offence, without a warrant, or under a warrant not endorsed for bail, the custody officer shall determine whether or not there is sufficient evidence to charge that person and may detain him at the police station for such period as is necessary to enable him/her to do so.

(s. 37(1) PACE)

If the custody officer determines that there is insufficient evidence to charge, the person shall be released either on bail or without bail, unless there are reasonable grounds for believing that detention without charge is necessary to secure or preserve evidence relating to an offence for which the person is under arrest or to obtain such evidence by questioning.

(s. 37(2) PACE)

If the custody officer has reasonable grounds for so believing, he/she may authorise the person to be kept in police detention.

(s. 37(3) PACE)

The 'seven questions'

In arriving at the decision as to whether a person should be detained, the custody officer will need to consider the following questions:

1.   Why is the person here?
2.   Was he/she lawfully detained?
3.   Was the arrest necessary?
4.   Why is further detention necessary?
5.   On what authority is detention to be made?
6.   What procedures will have to be considered for this person whilst in custody?
7.   What special needs does this person have?

Written record in presence of detainee

Where a custody officer authorises a person who has not been charged to be kept in police detention, he/she shall, as soon as is practicable, make a written record of the grounds for the detention, in the presence of the person arrested who shall at that time be informed by the custody officer of the grounds for his/her detention. Unless, he or she is:

(a)   incapable of understanding what is said to him/her;
(b)   violent or likely to become violent; or

(c)   in urgent need of medical attention.

(s. 37(4), (5) & (6) PACE)

Recording comments in the custody record

The custody officer shall:

• note on the custody record any comment the detainee makes in relation to the arresting officer's account but shall not invite comment. If the arresting officer is not physically present when the detainee is brought to a police station, the arresting officer's account must be made available to the custody officer remotely or by a third party on the arresting officer's behalf.

• note any comment the detainee makes in respect of the decision to detain them but shall not invite comment;

(Code C, para. 3.4)

Delay in recording entries in the custody record

All information recorded under this code must be recorded as soon as practicable in the custody record unless otherwise specified.

(Code C, para. 2.1)

A custody officer must perform the functions in this Code as soon as practicable. A custody officer will not be in breach of this Code if delay is justifiable and reasonable steps are taken to prevent unnecessary delay.
The custody record shall show when a delay has occurred and the reason.

(Code C, para. 2.1)

Transfer of detainee to another police station

The custody officer is responsible for the custody record's accuracy and completeness and for making sure the record accompanies a detainee if they are transferred to another police station. The record shall show the:

• time and reason for transfer;

• time a person is released from detention.

(Code C, para. 2.3)

The right to have a person informed of their arrest for a person detained at a police station or other premises is exercisable whenever he/she is transferred from one place to another; and on each subsequent occasion.

(s 56(8) PACE)

LOCAL PROCEDURES

1. If your force has a computerised custody handling system, are original custody records transferred with the detainee, when he/she moves to a different police station?

SPACE FOR NOTES

SPACE FOR NOTES

SPACE FOR NOTES

3

Safer Detention

3.1 **Introduction**

In the first draft of the first edition of this book, consideration was given to 'tagging on' the subject of risk assessments to the previous chapter on 'booking in' detainees. However, it became abundantly clear that this subject was important enough to merit a complete chapter of its own. Ask most experienced custody officers what the most worrying aspect of their job is and they will invariably point to the risk of a person dying, or committing suicide, while in their detention. Indeed, the *Guidance on the Safer Detention and Handling of Persons in Police Custody 2006* (produced by the National Centre for Policing Excellence (NCPE), on behalf of the Association of Chief Police Officers (ACPO) and the Home Office) is absolutely clear that responsibility for managing the first action following an adverse incident lies with the custody officer.

The above *Guidance* was still in draft form when the previous edition of this book was published; however, it is now the main focus for advice and guidance to custody officers on how to manage the risk posed by certain detainees. Further guidance can be found in Home Office Circulars 13/2002, 28/2002 and 32/2000 (see **Appendix 2** of this book).

Code C of the PACE *Codes of Practice* also contains advice relating to the care and treatment of detainees, to ensure custody officers take responsibility for risk assessing people in police detention who may be 'at risk'.

'At risk' detainees fall into two broad categories:

1.   those at risk from suicide and self-harm;

2.   those at risk from illnesses or injuries;

This chapter concentrates mainly on the first category of people and is divided into two general areas:

•   minimising the physical risk by identifying vulnerable areas in the custody office that may assist a person determined to self-harm; and

•   identifying individuals who may have a tendency towards self-harm and assessing and managing the risk.

Chapter 4—Clinical Treatment and Attention concentrates on dealing with detainees who may be at risk from illness or injuries, although there will inevitably be some overlap between these two chapters (as well as with **Chapter 2—Detainees—Initial Action** and **Chapter 5—Conditions of Detention**).

The Human Rights Act 1998

Article 2 of the Human Rights Act 1998 provides that 'everyone's right to life shall be protected by law' and Article 2(1) imposes a positive obligation on the State to ensure these rights are upheld. The police have a duty of care to ensure reasonable steps are taken to identify individuals who have a tendency to self-harm, and prevent them from doing so, and this chapter contains several references to the Human Rights Act 1998, specifically in **3.5.1 Recognising 'at risk' detainees**.

3.2 **Deaths In or Following Police Custody**

3.2.1 **Categorising 'deaths in or following police custody'**

All police forces in England and Wales have a statutory obligation to refer to the Independent Police Complaints Commission (IPCC) any incident involving a death or serious injury which has arisen from police contact. The IPCC considers the circumstances of all cases referred to it and will determine the mode of investigation for the death (see **3.2.3 Referral to the IPCC** below for details relating to investigations).

The IPCC must produce an annual report containing the number of deaths during or following police contact for England and Wales and an overview of the nature and circumstances of the deaths which occurred (see **3.2.4 Facts and figures** below for further details). The report is divided into the four categories listed in Home Office Circular 13/2002, as follows:

- *Category 1—Fatal road traffic incidents involving the police*—e.g. during a police pursuit;
- *Category 2—Fatal shooting incidents involving the police*—e.g. where an officer fires a fatal shot;
- *Category 3—Deaths in or following police custody*—e.g. where a person is arrested or otherwise detained by the police, where a person is in police detention and where a person has left police detention;
- *Category 4—Deaths during or following other types of contact with the police*—e.g. where the person is actively attempting to evade arrest and the death occurs otherwise than as the result of a road traffic incident or where a person is present at a demonstration and is struck by a police baton and subsequently dies.

For the purposes of this chapter, we will concentrate on deaths in *Category 3* above. The death may have taken place on police, private, or medical premises, in a public place or in a police or other vehicle.

This would include the following:

- deaths which occur during or following police custody where injuries which contributed to the death were sustained during the period of detention;
- deaths which occur in or on the way to hospital (or other medical premises) following or during transfer from police custody;

- deaths which occur as a result of injuries or other medical problems which are identified or develop while in custody;
- deaths which occur while the person is in police custody having been detained under s. 136 of the Mental Health Act 1983 or other legislation.

This would not include the following:

- deaths (including suicides) which occur following release from police custody, except those which meet the criteria outlined above;
- deaths of individuals who have been transferred to the care of another agency and subsequently die whilst in their care;
- deaths of those attending police stations as innocent visitors or witnesses who are not suspects.

KEYNOTE

It is important to note that a person may be considered to be in 'police custody' for these purposes before, during or after their time in 'police detention', as authorised by the custody officer.

KEYNOTE

- The term 'police' includes police civilians as well as police officers.
- Deaths involving off-duty police personnel are not included.

3.2.2 Initial action by custody officers

The *Guidance on the Safer Detention and Handling of Persons in Police Custody 2006* contains comprehensive checklists on the initial actions custody officers should take following an adverse incident when a person dies or is seriously injured while in police detention. The following is a general list for guidance only—custody officers should familiarize themselves with the entire chapter in the above publication.

Initial actions that should be taken:

- render first aid and consider an ambulance if required;
- identify all potential scenes and secure as appropriate;
- close the custody record for that detainee and ensure that all future actions are recorded in a scene log;
- on paper custody records underline the last entry in red (timed and signed) or secure the IT record and a make suitable entry on it;

- inform the duty inspector;
- photograph the whiteboard;
- complete a self-harm report.

The *Guidance* lists further actions for the custody officer; however, in reality, many of these are likely to be conducted by the on-duty inspector:

- consider relief of custody staff for remaining shift and their next shift;
- inform the Professional Standards Department (PSD)—they will consider compliance with the statutory reporting to the Independent Police Complaints Commission (IPCC);
- identify witnesses, the last person to see the detainee alive and the person who first saw the deceased detainee—they need to be available as required;
- inform the relevant Police Federation representative, who can advise the officers involved and secure legal representation if required;
- consider moving those detainees who may be witnesses;
- consider closing the custody suite and transferring all the detainees;
- arrange a critical incident debrief for staff involved. This should be carried out only after the officers involved have provided their initial account and the needs of the investigation have been met. It may be that such a debrief only takes place following conclusion of the investigation. These considerations do not, however, preclude speaking to relevant staff on issues of welfare and the next stages of any PSD and IPCC actions.

Importantly, the welfare of staff, other detainees and the relatives of the deceased must be considered in addition to the needs of the ongoing investigation.

3.2.3 **Referral to the IPCC**

Once an incident involving a fatality has been referred to the IPCC, it will consider the circumstances of the case and decide how the death will be investigated, in accordance with its own manual of guidance—IPCC (2005), *Making the New Police Complaints System Work Better: Statutory Guidance*. In making the decision, the IPCC will have regard for the seriousness of the case and the public interest.

The *Statutory Guidance* refers to four categories of investigation, which are outlined below:

Independent Investigation An investigation conducted solely by IPCC staff into incidents that cause the greatest level of public concern, have the greatest potential to impact on communities or have serious implications for the reputation of the police service.

In independent investigations, IPCC investigators have the powers of a police constable, and are able to enter police premises and seize and retain documentation or other evidence where necessary.

The complainant has no right of appeal in an independent investigation.

Managed Investigation An investigation conducted by the police under the direction and control of the IPCC, when an incident, or a complaint or allegation of misconduct, is of such significance and probable public concern that the investigation of it needs to be under the direction and control of the IPCC but does not need an independent investigation.

The IPCC is responsible for setting the Terms of Reference for the investigation in consultation with the force. An IPCC Commissioner agrees the Terms of Reference and approves the choice of Investigating Officer (IO) who is nominated by the force. The IPCC Regional Director or Investigator manages the investigation and receives regular progress reports.

Responsibility for maintaining the record of decisions and for conducting a timely investigation rests with the IPCC.

The complainant has no right of appeal in a managed investigation.

Supervised Investigation An investigation conducted by the police when the IPCC decides that an incident or a complaint or allegation of misconduct is of less significance and probable public concern than for an independent or managed investigation but oversight by the Commission is appropriate.

An IPCC Commissioner approves the choice of IO, and agrees the Terms of Reference and investigation plan; both are drafted by the force. An IPCC process for regular review including risk assessment, may be agreed at the outset depending on the nature and scale of the investigation and included in the Terms of Reference. In these cases any changes should be recorded.

Responsibility for maintaining the record of decisions and for conducting a timely investigation rests with the force.

The complainant has the right of appeal to the IPCC at the end of the investigation.

Local Investigation A local investigation is appropriate where the IPCC concludes that none of the factors identified in terms of the seriousness of the case or public interest exists and that the police have the necessary resources and experience to carry out an investigation without external assistance. The case is then referred back to the force to be dealt with by way of a local investigation.

The complainant has the right of appeal to the IPCC at the end of the investigation.

Of the deaths in or following police custody during the period 2006/07, 30 per cent were actually returned to forces for *Local Investigation*. Thirty-seven per cent were *Independently Investigated* by the IPCC, 30 per cent were *Managed* and 3 per cent were *Supervised*.

However, during the period 2005/06, the IPCC was involved in 92 per cent of investigations (compared to 70 per cent above), with only 8 per cent being returned to forces. Clearly, the IPCC will continue to have greater involvement in incidents that cause the greatest level of public concern, have the greatest potential to impact on communities or have serious implications for the reputation of the police service, but there appears to be increasing trust in police forces' ability to independently investigate their own staff.

3.2.4 **Facts and figures**

Statistics relating to deaths in police custody were first collated in 1981, when the recorded figure was 49. The IPCC has a statutory duty to collate and publish figures of people who die during or following police contact. The first IPCC report was published in November 2005, reporting on the 2004/05 figures. Previous figures were collated and published by the Police Leadership and Powers Unit (PLPU). The table below shows some of the statistics gathered by the PLPU between 1997 and 2002 for deaths in police custody.

Year	Overall Number of Deaths	Number of Deaths in Police Stations	Percentage of Deaths in Police Stations
1997/98	69	11	16%
1998/99	67	16	24%
1999/00	70	7	10%
2000/01	52	5	10%
2001/02	70	3	4%

In 2002, Home Office Circular 13/2002 was published and the counting rules were changed to widen the definition of people who died in custody, or following police contact (as identified in the four categories in **3.2.1 Categorising 'deaths in or following police custody'** above).

The table below shows the statistics gathered between 2002 and 2007, under *Category 3*, according to the new counting rules.

Year	Overall Number of Deaths	Number of Deaths in or Following Police Custody	Number of Deaths in Police Stations	Percentage Of Deaths in Police Stations
2002/03	104	40	8	8%
2003/04	100	38	7	7%
2004/05	106	36	7	6%
2005/06	118	28	3	2.5%
2006/07	82	27	4	5%

It can be seen that although the numbers of deaths in custody remained steady over a 10-year period, the number of deaths in police stations fell. It has to be noted that early figures gathered were quite basic and do not identify whether the 'deaths in police stations' actually occurred in custody offices, but it would be safe to assume that most of them did.

The figures produced are more meaningful each year, which will assist in further reducing the number of casualties as well as informing the police of specific trends. For example, the statistics show that the majority of people who die in police stations are white males, in their forties. Alcohol and drugs are significant factors in deaths in and following police custody and this issue is dealt with in depth later in this chapter.

Statistics are also used to identify the number of people from minority ethnic backgrounds who have died in or following police custody. An example of this occurred during 2002/03, where the figures showed there was a significant increase in the number of people from minority ethnic groups who died during or following police contact. There were 22 such deaths in 2002/03 (21 per cent), compared to just 7 recorded for 2001/02 (10 per cent).

The steep rise on the previous year raised concern that there might be some underlying reason linked to ethnicity. An independent research was commissioned, which was published in July 2004 and suggested that while there are grounds for concern relating to some aspects of the general treatment of all detainees, there is little evidence to suggest that this concern can be directly linked to racial stereotyping, perceptions or different treatment of people from minority ethnic groups.

During 2003/04, there was a significant decrease in the number of people from minority ethnic groups who died during or following contact with the police (10 such deaths, representing 10 per cent of the overall figure). This figure has remained fairly low since initial concerns.

This section represents only a snapshot of the comprehensive figures produced. A visit to the IPCC website, http://www.ipcc.gov.uk, is recommended for a more in-depth look at the statistics.

3.2.5 **Learning Lessons**

In the *Guidance on the Safer Detention and Handling of Persons in Police Custody 2006*, lessons learned are divided into two categories:

- Fast-Time Learning—learning points which emerge immediately after an incident is reported, and
- Slow-Time Learning—learning points which were not obvious immediately following the incident may emerge over time as a result of the ongoing investigation or enquiry.

The IPCC recommends that forces must have established procedures for investigations into deaths and adverse incidents. Forces must also have procedures for learning lessons from such incidents and Professional Standards Departments and the IPCC will produce recommendations following an investigation. These recommendations could include instructions to liaise with other stakeholder and practitioner groups to cross-share information.

The IPPC itself is part of The Learning the Lessons Committee, which is a multi-agency committee that has been established to disseminate and promote learning across the police service. Its members are:

- Association of Chief Police Officers;
- Association of Police Authorities;
- Home Office;
- Independent Police Complaints Commission;
- Her Majesty's Inspectorate of Constabulary;
- National Policing Improvement Agency.

The Committee aims to produce regular bulletins relating to IPPC investigations, which will include deaths or serious injuries which have arisen from police contact and adverse incidents.

Further, a review conducted by Robert Fulton was commissioned to look at the role and functions of the Forum for Preventing Deaths in Custody and to recommend how these might be strengthened. The review was published in April 2008 and recommended, amongst other things, that a Ministerial Board on Deaths in Custody should be formed, with senior representation from all the organisations which hold people in custody or which are otherwise concerned with the issue.

It is clear that there is a national drive across all agencies to impact on reducing the number and rate of deaths in custody.

3.3 **The 'Cell Environment'**

3.3.1 **Reducing opportunities for self harm**

Much of this chapter will focus on what the custody officer can do to minimise the risk of detainees attempting to self-harm or commit suicide, by observing the detainee's behaviour. However, there are also environmental precautions that can be taken to further minimise the risk. Advice is contained in Home Office Circular 28/2002:

- Cell doors should wherever possible be outwards-opening and have 'piano' hinges;
- Cell hatches should always be kept locked shut. (Older-style 'flap-down', or 'pin-lock', hatches are often ill-fitting and defective. Where combined with door handles other than the standard-issue Home Office handle—the 'T-bar'-door handle—they can be extremely dangerous.)
- As far as possible all cells should be free of:
  - pipework or conduits of any form (even at ground level);
  - sharp angles;
  - gratings;
  - holes;
  - abrasive surfaces;
  - broken or cracked surfaces; or
  - any open joint between fittings and the cell structure.
- No fittings should provide any means of forming a ligature. The stainless steel box units designed to be 'vandal-proof' which are still used in some police stations often have ligature points and should wherever possible be removed. All fittings should be bedded in resin-based, solid-setting, non-corrosive compounds, which will neither peel nor pick, and which are not poisonous. (The height of the openings of 'slot'-style hand wash units should not exceed 125 mm, as people have wedged their heads in larger ones and then broken their necks.)
- Air-vents offer one of the main means of committing suicide by ligature. They should wherever possible be purpose-built, stainless steel plated and with holes no greater than 2 mm in diameter.
- Only light fittings of designs specifically recommended by Home Office staff should be used, and they must be out of reach. (It should be noted that light fittings used by the Prison Service often have ligature points and are therefore normally unsuitable for police cells.)

- Closed-circuit television (CCTV) cameras should where possible be installed in all cells designated for vulnerable people. All people in police cells should be monitored closely.

- In shower areas showerheads must be as robust as possible, and with no ligature points. Shower curtains, rails etc. are inappropriate in a police custody context.

- In exercise yards there should as far as possible be no exposed pipework, conduits etc. except at roof level. CCTV cameras and mountings must be out of reach.

- All maintenance of police cells and custody areas should be carried out by people fully trained in issues around ligature points.

As well as ensuring that the environment is safe, custody officers should consider the clothing and other materials the detainee has in the cell, such as blankets or pillows. As identified in the *Guidance on the Safer Detention and Handling of Persons in Police Custody 2006*, to commit suicide by ligature a person requires both the means of forming the ligature and the means of attachment, normally to the structure. Removing one or preferably both opportunities minimises the risk of suicide or self-harm.

Custody offices should also be equipped with first-aid kits that conform to the minimum standards set out by the ACPO Working Group in First Aid Skills in the *ACPO/CENTREX Police First Aid Training Programme*. The above *Guidance* recommends issuing suicide intervention packs to custody staff, consisting of ligature knives or emergency cut-down tools, which should be carried at all times when in the custody suite.

KEYNOTE

It may be that custody officers have no direct influence on the condition of the cells they are in charge of, but the above advice offers an opportunity for issues to be highlighted to senior management. In any case, generic risk assessments of cells complexes should be undertaken as part of Health and Safety precautions (please refer to your own force policy to see whether this takes place).

65

3.4 **Risk Assessments**

3.4.1 **Legislative provisions**

Code C, Para. 3.6

The custody officer is responsible for initiating an assessment to consider whether the detainee is likely to present specific risks to custody staff or themselves. Such assessments should always include a check on the Police National Computer (PNC), to be carried out as soon as practicable, to identify any risks highlighted in relation to the detainee.

Although such assessments are primarily custody officers' responsibility, it may be necessary for them to consult and involve others, e.g. the arresting officer or an appropriate healthcare professional (see para. 9.13). Reasons for delaying the initiation or completion of the assessment must be recorded.

Code C, Para. 3.7

Chief Officers should ensure that arrangements for proper and effective risk assessments required by para. 3.6 above are implemented in respect of all detainees at police stations in their area.

Code C, Para. 3.8

Risk assessments must follow a structured process which clearly defines the categories of risk to be considered and the results must be incorporated in the detainee's custody record. The custody officer is responsible for making sure those responsible for the detainee's custody are appropriately briefed about the risks. If no specific risks are identified by the assessment that should be noted in the custody record. See Note 3E and para. 9.14.

Code C, Para. 3.9

The custody officer is responsible for implementing the response to any specific risk assessment, for example:

• reducing opportunities for self-harm;

- calling a healthcare professional;
- increasing levels of monitoring or observation.

Code C, Note for Guidance 3E

Home Office Circular 32/2000 provides more detailed guidance on risk assessments and identifies key risk areas which should always be considered.

3.4.2 **Initial assessment**

As well as dealing with the physical risks posed by the cell environment, custody officers have a duty to identify the potential risk posed by detainees themselves and their capacity for self-harm.

The *Guidance on the Safer Detention and Handling of Persons in Police Custody 2006* and para. 3 of the *Codes of Practice* emphasise the importance of conducting risk assessments on detainees and place the custody officer right in the centre of this process, with responsibility for:

- conducting an initial assessment and considering whether or not the person should be detained (balanced against the risk posed);
- visually assessing the detainee's general health and any injuries and recording these matters on the custody record;
- interpreting behaviour in the context of health and risk issues;
- liaising with a healthcare professional;
- determining levels of monitoring or observation and increasing them if necessary;
- reducing opportunities for self-harm.

The custody officer also has responsibility for making sure the arresting officer (and anyone else who has had contact with the detainee) has passed on any relevant information about the detainee to the custody staff. Equally as important, as outlined in the above Guidance, custody officers must conduct effective briefing and debriefing when handing over responsibility for detainees, particularly at shift change-over.

The case of *R (on the application of JL)* v *Secretary of State for the Home Department* [2007] EWCA Civ 767 (CA) provided a useful insight into circumstances where the risk assessment process broke down. *L* was remanded to custody in prison, where a risk assessment stated that he was at risk of self-harm, due to anxiety over an argument with his girlfriend. He was found in a distressed state, having made a noose out of his bed sheets. A later review concluded that *L* was no longer at risk of self-harm and the relevant risk form was filed.

A week later, *L* was found suspended from the bars in his cell, with a sheet around his neck. He was resuscitated, but suffered a permanent brain injury.

Custody officers must also check the PNC and local intelligence systems, recording relevant warning markers on the custody record before the detainee is placed in a cell, as identified in Code C, para. 3.6. Custody officers also have a duty to check and record whether approved restraint techniques and equipment have been used. The use of restraints is covered in more depth in **Chapter 5—Conditions of Detention**.

At this initial stage, the custody officer will have to determine the levels of monitoring or observation, based on the risk assessment. The *Guidance on the Safer Detention and Handling of Persons in Police Custody 2006* has produced extensive guidance on observation and engagement. Monitoring levels and frequency of visits are also dealt with in more depth in **Chapter 5—Conditions of Detention**.

All decisions relating to risk assessments must be recorded in the custody record, in accordance with Code C, para. 3.8 above. This was reinforced in the European Court of Human Rights in the case of *Velikova* v *Bulgaria*, application no. 41488/98 (27 April 2000), where it was held that under Article 2 of the European Convention on Human Rights, the State is under a duty to provide a plausible explanation of events that lead to a death in police custody where the person had originally been detained in good health.

KEYNOTE

It is important to note that custody officers must have regard for any risk to themselves and their staff, as well as to the detainee.

3.4.3 **Guidance on risk assessment**

Home Office Circular 32/2000 provides guidance on the key risk factors which should be considered in every assessment. Although risk assessments are primarily the responsibility of the custody officer, he or she will also have to rely on advice and guidance from healthcare professionals. The results of risk assessments and any advice offered by healthcare professionals should be entered in the custody record, whether or not the person is considered to be at risk.

The circular identifies those detainees who fall under the categories below, and who must always be considered to be 'at risk' to some degree or other:

- Medical/Mental Condition
- Medication Issued
- Special Needs

- First Aid Given
- Violence
- Conceals Weapons
- Escape Risk
- Hostage Taker
- Stalker/Harasser
- Racial Motivation
- Sex Offence
- Drug/Alcohol Issues
- Suicide/Self Harm
- Injuries
- Vulnerable
- Force/Restraint Used
- CS Spray Used

The level of risk that the detainee poses will be another matter for the custody officer to take into consideration. For example, a detainee may be known to conceal weapons and is subject to a strip search. If nothing is found, the custody officer may decide to reassess the risk relative to this individual. It is the custody officer's responsibility to determine the response to any specific risk assessment. For example, deciding whether or not to call a healthcare professional, or instigating extra levels of monitoring or observation.

KEYNOTE

Risk assessment is an ongoing process and assessments must always be subject to review if circumstances change (see Code C, para. 3.10).

The Prisoner Escort Record (PER) Form

The main purpose of the PER is to ensure that whenever a detainee is moved between locations, those escorting and receiving the detainee are provided with all necessary information about them, particularly in relation to any risks or vulnerabilities they may present. It also enables a record of the detainee's movements and of any relevant incidents occurring during transit to be maintained.

The PER is not intended to serve as the primary record of detainee risk assessment. All persons entering police custody should be subject to a structured process of risk assessment as referred to above, which should be documented on the custody record. The details of any risk identified will obviously be recorded on the PER, if the detainee is moved from the custody office.

69

A PER should be completed whenever a detainee—irrespective of age or reason for detention—is to be escorted from a police station to another location, whether to court, to another police station or another agency, e.g. Health Authorities, Social Services, HM Customs & Excise, Immigration Authorities, etc.

KEYNOTE

It will not be necessary to complete a PER form for every detainee held in custody at a police station.

3.5 Suicide and Self-Harm

3.5.1 Recognising 'at risk' detainees

In 2003, the Police Complaints Commission presented evidence to the Joint Committee on Human Rights Inquiry into Deaths in Custody. In the chapter *Focusing only on deaths in custody*, the Commission described how 50 per cent of all those people who died in or following police custody had a prior indication of mental health problems. Looking after a person with suicidal tendencies places a significant extra burden on the custody officer—especially when he or she has other important duties to perform in a crowded custody office. The House of Lords examined this issue in *Commissioner of Police for the Metropolis* v *Reeves* (A.P.), 15 July 1999. In this case, *Reeves* was the administrator for the estate of *L*, who had committed suicide whilst in police detention. She sued the police for neglect after *L* had been arrested and been allowed to hang himself in his cell using his shirt. The police left the hatch door to the cell open and *L* managed to loop the shirt around a spyhole, which had no glass, and through the open hatch. The court found that the police had a positive duty of care towards *L* and that they were negligent. The court held that the police knew he posed a suicide risk and failed to prevent him from killing himself, and that they could have reasonably foreseen the consequences of leaving the hatch open.

KEYNOTE

In the case of *Orange* v *West Yorkshire Police* [2001] EWCA Civ 611, the police assessed the detainee as not being at risk of committing suicide. He was allowed to keep his belt and was put in a cell which had a gate with bars and not a solid cell door. The detainee hung himself using the bars in the gate.

In this case, it was held that although the police had a duty to assess every prisoner regarding their risk of self-harm, the *Reeves* case referred to above did not mean that the police had an automatic duty to prevent suicide by those who appeared not to be at risk. The police were held not to be negligent.

So, how does a custody officer recognise when a detainee is 'at risk' from suicide or self-harm? It was identified in **3.4.2 Initial assessment** above that custody officers are responsible for conducting an initial risk assessment and visually assessing the detainee's general health and any injuries. But custody officers do not generally receive extensive medical training to assist them in recognising the signs and symptoms and they often have to rely on the detainee's own assessment of their suicidal tendencies.

In 1996, Lancashire Constabulary, working with HM Prison Service, conducted research on this subject: a project entitled 'Self-harm and Suicides by Detained Persons', which received approval from the Police Research Group. As a result of the research, a 'Suicide Awareness Booklet' was produced offering some excellent advice on recognition of the signs displayed by detainees at risk from suicide and self-harm.

The following are just some of the findings:

Some detainees may contemplate self-harm or suicide because of custody-induced stressors, such as:

- fear;
- guilt;
- helplessness or hopelessness;
- loneliness and feelings of isolation;
- uncertainty as to the future—i.e. accused of committing serious offences/ first-time offenders;
- lack of activity/boredom;
- breakdown of relationships;
- lack of contact with family.

Other triggers may be more situational, such as:

- unexpected remand in custody;
- further charges;
- bad news;
- impending trial;
- sleeplessness;
- unexpected conviction or sentence;

71

- suicide attempt by others in custody;
- the detainee has been transferred from prison where there may be fewer opportunities for self-harm.

KEYNOTE

Statistics show that the first five hours of a person's detention time is a high-risk period (Lancashire Constabulary, 'Self-harm and Suicides by Detained Persons'). Also, people in detention for child abuse may be particularly vulnerable to self-harm, especially where the victim may be a member of the suspect's household or family. The same could be said about those who have been detained for domestic abuse.

Home Office Circular 32/2000 instructs that the following questions must be asked of every person entering police custody:

1. Do you have any illness or injury?
2. Have you seen a doctor or been to a hospital for this illness/injury?
3. Are you taking or supposed to be taking any tablets/medication?
4. What are they? What are they for?
5. Are you suffering from any mental health problems or depression?
6. Have you ever tried to harm yourself?

We will be concentrating on the answers to questions 5 and 6 in this section; medical health matters will be dealt with in **Chapter 4—Clinical Treatment and Attention**.

The *Guidance on the Safer Detention and Handling of Persons in Police Custody 2006* builds on the above six questions, outlining that if the detainee answers yes to any of the above, then they should be asked further questions as appropriate:

- How often?
- How long ago?
- How did you harm yourself?
- Have you sought help?
- How are you feeling in yourself now?
- Would you like to speak to the doctor or nurse?
- Is there anything that I can do to help?

The responses to these questions should be entered in the custody record. Statistically, many people who commit suicide have attempted to do so previously. Therefore, any information the custody officers glean from the questionnaire is crucial to how they will treat the detainee when detention is authorised. Also, according to the Lancashire project, previous self-harmers are 12 times more likely to make a determined attempt to commit suicide.

KEYNOTE

Custody officers are under a duty to consider information relating to a risk to detainees from any source (see *R v HM Coroner for Coventry, ex parte Chief Constable of Staffordshire Police* (2000) 164 JP 665).

While the above guidance is of course useful, decision-making can often be hampered by matters beyond the custody officer's control, for example:

- the detainee may be in detention for a short period of time, making it difficult to correctly assess their mental state;
- the detainee may not have been in police detention previously, therefore no records exist of suicidal tendencies (i.e. on the PNC);
- the effects of drugs or alcohol could mask the detainee's behaviour and influence the custody officer's judgement.

If there is any doubt about a detainee's mental state, advice must be sought from a healthcare professional.

Consider the following:

Case Study

HARTSON was arrested and taken to a custody office. He had a criminal record and had previously been imprisoned. He was also a known heroin addict, and had told the officers who arrested him that he had taken heroin that morning. While in custody, HARTSON was seen by a police surgeon, who concluded that he was commencing drug withdrawal, and gave him some medication. She completed her notes and gave them to the custody officer, who copied them incorrectly into the custody record.

Later in the evening HARTSON complained to a different custody officer that the medication had not worked and that he was in pain. This officer then spoke to a different doctor and described the symptoms and complaint. He repeated the incorrect details of the medication given from the custody record. The second doctor said that he would not prescribe any further medication and advised the officers to 'keep an eye' on the detainee and call again if he got any worse.

HARTSON was later allowed to come out of his cell to make a telephone call. However, when he was returned to his cell, the officer forgot to remove HARTSON's trainers, which had long laces. He was then not checked for nearly three-quarters of an hour. When he was checked he was found dead in his cell, hanging by the neck from the toilet plunger on the sink, which had provided a ligature point for his shoelaces.

The above set of circumstances are used as a test case in Home Office Circular 28/2002—*Learning the Lessons from Adverse Incidents*. It should be noted that the second doctor has stated that, had he been given correct information about the medication given, he would have made a different decision.

The circular identified four lessons from the incident:

1. Ligature points

When the cells were inspected it was found that all of them contained stainless steel toilet-and-sink units with hot and cold taps and plungers. Since this case the units have been boxed in with wood panelling, pending a final decision as to whether they should be removed from these cells altogether.

However, there may still be cells in other police stations which have similar designs. All police stations should be checked to see if there are any cells containing taps, plungers or other easily accessible ligature points. If there are any, they should be removed.

2. The Human Rights Act 1998

Although it seems that not removing the young man's trainers in this case was an oversight, one of the investigating officers did suggest that laces were not always removed due to the requirement for proportionality under the Human Rights Act. It is true that people have a range of rights under the European Convention on Human Rights (ECHR), which the police must have due regard to in their dealings with members of the public and others. However, under Article 2 of the ECHR, 'Everyone's right to life shall be protected by law' and the police must have the highest regard for this. But how do the police make sure that everything that people might use to harm themselves is removed? Items such as shoelaces and belts that can most easily be used in this way should always be removed, especially where there are grounds for believing that someone may be a suicide risk.

The circular found that members of the police service can be assured that there is no legal obstacle under the Human Rights Act to doing this.

3. Non-medically qualified persons 'copying' doctors' notes into custody records

The consequences in the above case of notes not being copied accurately speak for themselves. Doctors must therefore be invited to make the relevant entry directly into the custody record themselves, attaching their original notes.

4. Liaison between the Prison Service and the police service

The young man in this case had previously been in prison, and was known by the Prison Service to be a suicide risk. However, there was nothing to this effect on the Police National Computer (PNC).

This issue is being examined and a Prison Service/ACPO Prison Intelligence Working Group initiative is taking place in the Leicestershire Police Area to ensure that warning markers are placed on PNC regardless of the agency at the source of the information. Much of the advice offered in this chapter should address the issues arising out of the above case.

Some police forces are using advanced technology to assist custody officers, for example, testing has begun on a life signs monitoring system which uses low power microwave transceivers to detect movement within custody cells. Progressive warnings are sounded if an occupant's breathing becomes very low or ceases altogether. The system is currently being assessed. Early indications are favourable and a further letter will be sent to police forces shortly.

One force is researching the possibility of installing electronic information screens in new cells. The screen will relay messages to the detainee in various languages and it is possible that it may be developed to show video/DVD/television pictures, adverts such as Crimestoppers and about drug/alcohol referral services, Alcoholics Anonymous, Samaritans etc. The screens will be touch sensitive and will be able to withstand attack. They may be able to display such messages as 'solicitor contacted and on way to station' and could be linked to a hands-free telephone system to allow calls from solicitors to be taken in cells.

KEYNOTE

Note if the detainee is unable to understand, violent or in need of urgent medical attention, asking questions may be delayed until it is safe and appropriate to do so.

However, if the custody officer is in any doubt, the advice of an appropriate health-care professional should be sought (see below).

If video cameras are installed in the custody area, notices shall be prominently displayed showing cameras are in use. Any request to have video cameras switched off shall be refused (see Code C, para. 3.11).

3.6 **Health and Safety in the Custody Office**

Under Code C, para. 3.7 of the *Codes of Practice* (see **3.4.1 Legislative provisions** above), Chief Officers are required to ensure that arrangements for proper and effective risk assessments are implemented in respect of all detainees at police stations in their area. Although this relates mainly to the dynamic risk assessment of detainees in police detention, custody officers are under a general duty to consider health and safety risks in the custody office and abide by a regular inspection regime. The table below outlines the advice contained in the *Custody Policy Document* (PD), *(February 2004) New Build Only, Home Office* on such inspections:

Frequency of Routine	Actions to be Taken	By Whom
DAILY	• Test cell call system (should be checked when detainee is placed in a cell); • Inspect for damage in custody suite (risk assess for continued use); • Inspect cells each time they are vacated; • Clean suites daily, although some areas may need to be cleaned more frequently; • Check contents of first-aid kits and any suicide intervention kits, replacing any used or missing articles; • Ensure recording equipment is tested before use if it does not have autotest facility.	All custody staff
WEEKLY	• Test the fire alarm; • Test the emergency call alarm system; • Check the cleaning of all surfaces; • Inspect exercise yard/van dock for damage/potential problems.	Custody Inspector or Custody Manager equivalent
MONTHLY	• Assess the need for any specialist cleaning regime; • Check the cleaning and topping up of floor gullies, including exercise yard. **Note:** Some internal gullies may require more regular topping up due to evaporation; • Ensure a testing regime for power failure is completed to maintain uninterrupted power supply (UPS) and generator working capability.	Custody Inspector or Custody Manager equivalent
QUARTERLY	• Quarterly inspection of all areas with the building surveyor with the Custody Officer or Custody Manager; • Checks of operating efficiency of heating, cooling and ventilation plan including filter replacement; • Health and Safety Risk Assessment 'walk through'—this must be carried out after, for example, each change in layout and change in equipment use.	Custody Inspector or Custody Manager equivalent and a Health and Safety representative

(continued)

Frequency of Routine	Actions to be Taken	By Whom
ANNUALLY	• Annual checks undertaken by specialist suppliers/manufacturers; • Decoration check (bi-annually and redecorate as required); • Annual search of the custody suite (this could be an opportunity for the search team to carry out training); • Calibration check of building management control systems; • Undertake the testing regime for a power failure to ensure UPS and generator working capability; • Water testing, disinfecting and certification; • Deep cleaning of suite by professional cleaning company; • Practice evacuation drills.	Custody Inspector or Custody Manager equivalent and a Health and Safety representative

It should be noted that the above is only advice and not subject to legislative requirements. However, demonstration of a strict health and safety inspection programme could potentially assist in any claims against forces.

At the least, custody offices must have an evacuation policy in the event of an emergency, such as a fire, and should have been issued with a fire certificate. Custody staff should be familiar with the emergency procedures and drills should be carried out regularly.

3.7 Summing Up

Deaths in police custody

Home Office Circular 13/2002 lists the categories which will be declared a death in or following police custody:

1. fatal road traffic incidents involving the police;

2. fatal shooting incidents involving the police;

3. deaths in or following custody;

4. deaths during or following other types of contact with the police.

Risk assessments

* The custody officer is responsible for initiating an assessment as to whether the detainee is likely to present specific risks to custody staff or themselves;
* Assessments should include a check on the PNC;
* Chief Officers should ensure that arrangements for risk assessments are implemented in respect of all detainees at police stations in their area;
* The results of risk assessments must be incorporated in the detainee's custody record.

(Code C, para. 3.6–3.9)

Risk assessment is an ongoing process and assessments must always be subject to review if circumstances change.

(Code C, para. 3.10)

Recognising 'at risk' detainees

Some detainees may contemplate self-harm or suicide because of custody induced stressors, such as:

* fear;
* guilt;
* helplessness or hopelessness;
* loneliness and feelings of isolation;
* uncertainty as to future—i.e. accused of committing serious offences/first-time offenders;
* lack of activity/boredom;
* breakdown of relationships;
* lack of contact with family.

Other triggers may be more situational, such as:

* unexpected remand in custody;
* further charges;
* bad news;
* impending trial;
* sleeplessness;
* unexpected conviction or sentence;
* suicide attempt by others in custody.

Statistics show that the first five hours of a person's detention time is a high-risk period.

Health and Safety

Health and safety risks in the custody office should be identified through a regular inspection regime.

LOCAL PROCEDURES

1.   Does your force have a questionnaire aimed at identifying 'at risk' detainees when they are first brought into police detention?

2.   Does your force have a medical history questionnaire aimed at identifying medical issues that custody officers should be aware of?

3.   Does your force implement a regular Health and Safety inspection regime?

SPACE FOR NOTES

SPACE FOR NOTES

SPACE FOR NOTES

4

Clinical Treatment and Attention

4.1 **Introduction**

In the previous chapter, it was identified that 'at risk' detainees fall into two broad categories:

1. those at risk from suicide and self-harm, and

2. those at risk from illnesses or injuries.

This chapter concentrates on dealing with detainees who may be at risk from illness or injuries, although there will of course be some overlap between these two chapters (as well as with **Chapter 2—Detainees—Initial Action** and **Chapter 5—Conditions of Detention**). The risk posed to a person in detention from illness or injury is just as great as the risk of a person self-harming. Any adverse incident would have to be referred to the IPCC; therefore, custody staff must be equally as vigilant when dealing with this category of detainee.

Code C of the *Codes of Practice* features heavily in this chapter—the legislative provisions contained in PACE govern when medical attention should be sought for a detainee, as well as determining who can administer medication.

Research shows that detainees who are under the influence of drugs or alcohol pose the greatest risk to themselves, and to custody staff. Therefore, the chapter includes advice from the Association of Police Surgeons on recognising the dangers to detainees in these categories.

Further information and advice has been taken from the *Guidance on the Safer Detention and Handling of Persons in Police Custody 2006* to assist with writing this chapter.

The Human Rights Act 1998

Article 2 of the Human Rights Act 1998 provides that 'everyone's right to life shall be protected by law' and Article 2(1) imposes a positive obligation on the State to ensure these rights are upheld. The police have a duty of care to ensure reasonable steps are taken to identify individuals who are at risk because of a medical condition while in police detention and to ensure that such people receive the required care and attention.

4.2 **Identifying Medical Issues**

Research shows that more detainees will be 'at risk' from an adverse incident or death in custody for medical reasons, than those who are 'at risk' from self-harm.

In **Chapter 3—Safer Detention**, we examined the recommendation in Home Office Circular 32/2000 to produce a questionnaire that custody officers should use to identify detainees 'at risk' from self-harm or suicide. The recommendations in the circular were also identified as good practice in the ACPO report, 'Police First Aid Training', July 1999. This report stated that custody staff faced difficulties in identifying persons who are suffering from physical or mental illness, or injury. As a result, most forces should have produced medical questionnaires to assist custody officers.

We will revisit the questions that should be asked of all detainees:

1. Do you have any illness or injury?

2. Have you seen a doctor or been to hospital for this illness/injury?

3. Are you taking or supposed to be taking any tablets/medication?

4. What are they for?

5. Are you suffering from any mental health problems or depression?

6. Have you ever tried to harm yourself?

The last two questions are dealt with in **3.5.1 Recognising 'at risk' detainees** above.

It can be seen that the questions are of a private nature, and some detainees may decide not to answer, which they are entitled to do, as they have a right to privacy under the Human Rights Act 1998. However, the questions are proportionate and necessary because they assist the custody officer to determine whether a person is at risk from self-harming. Also, any answers to questions will only be disclosed to medical practitioners, and would not be used in evidence.

The custody record should be updated either if the detainee refuses to answer the questions, or if he/she provides details of illnesses, injuries or medication.

4.3 **Clinical Treatment**

When the custody officer, possibly through the medical questions above, identifies that a detainee may either be at risk from self-harm, or may have a medical condition or injury, he/she may need to consult with an appropriate healthcare professional.

This area may be divided into two sections:

1. where the custody officer identifies that a detainee may require medical attention; and

2. where the detainee requests medical attention.

In this section we will deal with these issues separately (see **flow chart 3 in Appendix 1** for an easy guide).

4.3.1 **Legislative provisions**

Code C, Para. 3.5

The custody officer shall:

(a)   determine whether the detainee:

    (i)   is, or might be, in need of medical treatment or attention;

    (ii)   requires:

- an appropriate adult,
- help to check documentation,
- an interpreter;

(b)   record the decision in respect of (a).

Code C, Para. 9.5

The custody officer has a duty to make sure a detainee receives clinical attention as soon as reasonably practicable if the person:

- appears to be suffering from physical illness, or
- is injured, or
- appears to be suffering from a mental disorder, or
- appears to need clinical attention.

This applies even if the detainee makes no request for medical attention and whether or not they have already received clinical attention elsewhere. If the need for clinical attention is urgent, the nearest available health care professional or an ambulance must be called immediately.

Code C, Note for Guidance 9C

Paragraph 9.5 does not apply to minor ailments or injuries which do not need attention.

However, all such ailments and injuries must be recorded on the custody record and any doubts must be resolved in favour of calling the appropriate health care professional.

Code C, Para. 9.8

If the detainee requests a clinical examination, an appropriate health care professional must be called as soon as practicable to assess the detainee's needs. If a safe and appropriate care plan cannot be provided, the police surgeon's advice must be sought. The detainee may also be examined by a medical practitioner of their choice at their expense.

Code C, Para. 9.13

Whenever an appropriate health care professional is called in accordance with this section to examine or treat a detainee, the custody officer shall ask for their opinion about:

- any risks or problems which the police need to take into account when making decisions about a detainee's continued detention;
- when to carry out an interview if applicable; and
- the needs for safeguards.

4.3.2 When the custody officer recognises medical attention is required

Code C, para. 3.5 above is divided into two parts; the requirement for the custody officer to establish whether or not the detainee requires:

(i) medical attention, and

(ii) an appropriate adult or interpreter.

We will be concentrating in this section on the requirement to provide medical attention, as the subjects of appropriate adults and interpreters are dealt with in depth in **Chapter 7—Vulnerable People and Appropriate Adults.**

The custody officer is required to adopt a proactive approach to identifying medical issues, hence the reason for the medical questions that should be asked of detainees when they are accepted into custody. Particular attention should be paid to a detainee who appears drunk or behaves abnormally, as they may also be suffering from illness, the effects of drugs or may have sustained injury, particularly a head injury, which is not apparent.

A detainee who needs, or is dependent on, certain drugs, including alcohol, may experience harmful effects within a short time of being deprived of their supply. In these circumstances, when there is any doubt, police should always act urgently to call an appropriate healthcare professional or an ambulance (see Code C, para. 9.5B and Note for Guidance 9C).

If the custody officer has determined that they are supervising an 'at risk' detainee, either because they may cause harm to themselves, or because they are ill, he or she must then make a judgement as to whether the detainee requires medical attention. If a decision is made that the detainee does require medical attention, the custody officer will have to decide:

1. can the matter be dealt with routinely by the custody officer? *or*

2. should the custody officer contact a healthcare professional for advice? *or*

3. is the matter urgent enough to call an ambulance?

We will deal with the above points separately:

Point 1

If the custody officer identifies that a detainee poses a risk to themself, but judges that he or she can manage that risk, there will be no need to call an appropriate healthcare professional. We have examined several tactical ways of ensuring that the detainee is prevented from self-harming in **3.5.1 Recognising 'at risk' detainees** above. The custody officer will need to identify the most suitable method of protecting the detainee while he or she is in custody.

KEYNOTE

Note if the custody officer identifies a risk to the detainee, and decides to deal with the matter without contacting an appropriate healthcare professional, the following procedure must take place:

- note on the custody record the particular risk the detainee poses;
- note on the custody record the action taken to minimise the risk;
- ensure all staff working in the custody office are aware of the risk and the action plan to address it;
- ensure that new custody staff coming on duty are made aware of the risk.

What if the detainee has a minor aliment or injury? Code C, Note for Guidance 9C above is clear that not all injuries need to be treated medically.

KEYNOTE

The custody officer should also note, on the custody record, any visible injuries that the detainee has, even if the injuries are of a minor nature. This will protect the custody officer and their staff from any allegations made by a detainee that they have been assaulted whilst in custody, as there will be a record that the injury occurred prior to detention being authorised.

Point 2

The custody officer's main reason for contacting an appropriate healthcare professional will be for an expert opinion as to whether a person is fit to be detained in police custody. This may be either because the detainee is exhibiting signs that he or she may self-harm, or that he or she may be injured or suffering from illness.

Consider the following:

Case Study

MICHAELS was arrested for causing criminal damage to the front door of his ex-girlfriend's house. When the police arrived, he was causing a disturbance trying to get her to open the door and talk to him.

He was taken to the police station and during the 'booking in' procedure, it emerged that he had recently been in prison, and that whilst he was there, he made several attempts at committing suicide. The custody officer was concerned about MICHAELS' mental condition and contacted the on-call police surgeon. Following an examination, the doctor concluded that MICHAELS posed a significant risk to himself and that it was extremely likely that he would attempt to commit suicide again. The doctor recommended that MICHAELS should be released immediately, as he was not fit to be detained.

What action should the custody officer now take?

....

There is nothing in either PACE or the *Codes of Practice* stating that the custody officer must actually follow advice from the appropriate healthcare professional. In fact, para. 13 above makes it clear that the custody officer is seeking an opinion from the healthcare professional, which may be taken into account when making decisions about a detainee's continued detention.

This means that the custody officer has the ultimate decision-making powers with regard to detention issues, following advice from the healthcare professional.

This is all very well, but what if the custody officer fails to take heed of the advice given, and the detainee does commit suicide while in custody? The answer is not straightforward. Obviously the officer in the case and the victim would prefer that the person is kept in police detention, so that the crime may be investigated properly. However, the custody officer will be concerned with ensuring that the detainee leaves the custody office safe and well.

The custody officer could consider placing the detainee under constant observation, but this can be resource-intensive and would depend on how many other detainees are in custody at the same time, or whether any resources are available operationally.

The use of CCTV could also be considered, if available. However, custody officers will be aware that relying on a television monitor is not the perfect solution. Often, the custody officer's attention is taken away because of other duties, such as dealing with other detainees. The *Guidance on the Safer Detention and Handling of*

Persons in Police Custody 2006 identifies that monitoring vulnerable detainees can be improved by using technology, but physical checks and visits must also be made irrespective of the use of technology. Again, using CCTV can be resource-intensive.

Lastly, the custody officer could consider following the doctor's advice and bail the detainee for another day.

The custody officer will need to make a balanced judgement, based on the risk that the individual poses to himself/herself, the ability to supervise him/her while in custody and the seriousness of the allegation against him or her.

KEYNOTE

Remember that the custody officer's actions need to be both proportionate and necessary in order to comply with Human Rights legislation.

Point 3

The issue of whether a custody officer should send a detainee to the hospital is not straightforward. Guidance can be found on this issue from the Association of Police Surgeons, whose advice is fairly simple:

If in doubt trust your instincts and call an ambulance.

There are some occasions when hospitalisation will almost certainly have to occur, for example, where:

- the detainee is suffering chest pains;
- the detainee is having difficulty breathing;
- there is concern for the detainee's level of consciousness;
- the detainee is suffering from severe injuries (i.e. head injuries, deformed limbs, wounds that require suturing).

If there is any doubt as to the urgency of the care needed, custody officers must err on the side of caution and send the person to hospital.

KEYNOTE

There is no need to delay sending a person to hospital simply to consult with an appropriate healthcare professional (although this may be done if there is time). If the injury or illness is serious enough to warrant hospital treatment, the person should be taken straight away, by ambulance if necessary.

4.3.3 **When the detainee requests medical attention**

Code C, para. 9.8 above clearly requires the custody officer to act on instruc-tions given by the detainee. Many 'regular' detainees will be aware of this fact and will insist on receiving medical treatment as soon as they enter the cus-tody office. How many times have we heard these words:

I want my solicitor and I want to see a doctor now

Although the custody officer is obliged to call a doctor, in practice, police surgeons do not attend the custody office on every occasion. Advice is often given by telephone.

KEYNOTE

Note that the custody officer also has an obligation, under para. 9.4, to bring to the attention of the health care professional any:

'relevant information which might assist in the treatment of the detainee'.

If the detainee makes a request to be examined by a medical practitioner of their choice at their expense, it is recommended practice that the examina-tion be conducted in the presence of the police surgeon. If the police surgeon is not available, it may be conducted in the presence of the custody officer or an officer of the same gender as the detainee.

4.4 **Medication**

4.4.1 **Legislative provisions**

Code C, Para. 9.9

If a detainee is required to take or apply any medication, prescribed before their deten-tion, the custody officer must consult the appropriate health care professional before the use of the medication. Subject to the restrictions of para. 9.10 , the custody officer is responsible for the safekeeping of any medication and for making sure the detainee is given the opportunity to take or apply prescribed or approved medication. Any such consultation and its outcome shall be recorded on the custody record.

Code C, Para. 9.10

No police officer may administer or supervise the self-administration of medically pre-scribed controlled drugs of the types and forms listed in the Misuse of Drugs Regu-lations 2001, Schs. 2 or 3. A detainee may only self-administer such drugs under the personal supervision of the registered medical practitioner authorising their use.

Drugs listed in Schs. 4 or 5 may be distributed by the custody officer for self adminis-tration if they have consulted the registered medical practitioner authorising their use, this may be done by telephone, and both parties are satisfied self-administration will not expose the detainee, police officers or anyone else to the risk of harm or injury.

Code C, Para. 9.11

When appropriate health care professionals administer drugs or supervise their self-administration, it must be within current medicines legislation and the scope of prac-tice determined by their relevant professional body.

4.4.2 **Administering medication**

Paragraph 9.9 above envisages situations where a detainee has arrived at the custody office with their medication in their possession. However, custody officers will know that things are not always so straightforward. Very often, the detainee will require medication which is at their home and the onus is usually on the custody officer to arrange for it to be obtained. Although there is nothing in the *Codes of Practice* stating that custody officers must do this, the alternative is to call out the police surgeon to issue a prescription, which will obviously incur a cost.

There are literally hundreds of drugs listed in Schs. 2–5 of the Misuse of Drugs Regulations 2001 (referred to in para. 9.10 above).

Note that where drugs fall within Schs. 2–3 of the Regulations, police officers may not supervise the detainee's self-administration. Paragraph 9.10 above refers to *medically prescribed* controlled drugs. In other words, the detainee must not be allowed to self-administer drugs which would be unlaw-fully in their possession. A detainee may only self-administer such drugs under the personal supervision of the registered medical practitioner (i.e. doc-tor), authorising their use.

Schedules 2–3 include such drugs as:

- Cannabis and cannabis resin
- Raw opium

- Cocaine
- Benzethidine
- Morphine
- Methadone
- Amphetamine
- Codeine
- Temazepam

In contrast to the above, drugs listed in Schs. 4 or 5 of the Regulations may be distributed by the custody officer (or an appropriate healthcare professional) for self-administration by the detainee after the custody officer has consulted the registered medical practitioner authorising their use, and both parties are satisfied that the detainee, police officers or anyone else will not be exposed to risk of harm or injury (note that consultation may take place by telephone).

Schedule 4 and 5 include such drugs as:

- Diazepam
- Tetrazepam
- Nandrolone
- Testosterone
- Methandriol

KEYNOTE

When administering medication, the following advice should be noted (although custody officers should check their own force procedures on this issue):

- Another officer as a witness should accompany the police or civilian detention officer issuing the medication;
- The detainee should be observed taking the medication (to prevent hoarding);
- Following the issue, an entry must be made in the detainee's custody record, including the date, time and quantity of medication given;
- Refusal to take medication should be recorded in the custody record, and the police surgeon informed;
- Disposal of unused medication must be undertaken following instructions given by the police surgeon.

> **KEYNOTE**
>
> Some police forces have adopted the following procedure:
>
> Where a custody officer undertakes a medical risk assessment and the only risk factor apparent is alleged drug withdrawal, the detainee should be notified that a police surgeon will not normally prescribe medication for drug withdrawal until at least six hours after arrest have elapsed. (Again, custody officers should check their own force procedures for clarification.)

4.4.3 **Documentation**

Again, the *Codes of Practice*, paras. 9.15–9.17 cover this issue extensively. Below is a summary of the relevant provisions:

The custody record must show:

- the arrangements made for examination by the healthcare professional and any complaint made by the detainee;
- any request made by the detainee for clinical examination;
- any injury, aliment, condition or other reason making it necessary to arrange a clinical examination;
- any clinical directions given by the healthcare professional and any treatment given;
- where decisions have been recorded, if the healthcare professional does not update the custody record;
- all medication a detainee has in their possession on arrival at the police station;
- a note of any medication a detainee claims to need, but does not have with them.

4.4.4 **Other matters**

Finally, the issues below should be noted from the *Codes of Practice*:

- Where it appears to the custody officer that a detainee has an infectious or contagious disease or condition, he or she must take reasonable steps to safeguard the health of the detainee and others at the station. Medical advice should be sought and the custody officer has the discretion to isolate the person and their property until clinical directions have been sought (Code C, para. 9.7);
- A detainee's right to privacy must be respected and details of their health must be kept confidential and only disclosed with their consent or in

accordance with clinical advice when it is necessary to protect the detainee's health or others that come into contact with him/her (see Code C, Note for Guidance 9E).

4.5 **Drugs and Alcohol**

In this section, we will be examining the significance of people who have been detained while suffering from the effects of drugs and/or alcohol. We will deal with these subjects separately.

4.5.1 **Detainees under the influence of drugs**

The unpredictability of detainees who are under the influence of drugs can cause many problems for custody officers and their staff. There are risks relating to self-harm or suicide, as well as personal risks to custody staff, who face being assaulted.

The Association of Police Surgeons has produced some guidance to assist custody officers in the recognition of drug-related problems. General guidance includes making sure that custody staff are aware of drug trends in their area, and that substance misuse and mental illness may co-exist. Further matters that custody officers should be aware of relate to the symptoms of people who may be under the influence of certain drugs, such as:

Opiates—Heroin/Methadone

- Intoxication (drowsy, decreasing level of consciousness, pinpoint pupils, respiration level falls, snoring);
- Combination with other drugs can be potentially lethal;
- Withdrawal less of a problem—may be treated in custody.

Benzodiazepines

- Intoxication similar to alcohol;
- Fits may occur with withdrawal.

Stimulants—Cocaine/Amphetamine

- Death may occur from cardiac problems, stroke, cocaine-agitated delirium;
- Withdrawal—risk of self-harm.

The lists above are obviously general guides, and custody officers are advised to seek medical advice if there are any doubts about a detainee's symptoms.

The report *Drug-related deaths in police custody* was published in June 2003 by the Police Complaints Authority (PCA) research department. The document quoted a British Crime Survey report outlining that drug use was gradually increasing but there had been a disproportionate increase in their use by young adults (16–19 year olds) and in the use of Class A drugs, particularly heroin and cocaine.

Research was conducted into 43 drug-related deaths in police care or custody between 1998 and 2002 and some of the following issues were identified:

- 90 per cent of the sample were male and 86 per cent were white with an average age of 32;
- the most commonly used drug was cocaine, which had been consumed by more than half, and the most common method of consumption was swallowing;
- 39 of the 43 deaths involved the use of more than one substance (one person had consumed alcohol and six different drugs);
- mental health problems were much more prevalent among drinkers and drug users:
  - 18 individuals, or 40 per cent of those who died, had histories of mental health problems;
  - 5 individuals had psychotic symptoms;
  - 5 individuals had histories of self-harm;
  - 8 individuals had indications of clinical depression or anxiety;
- on average individuals were perceived to have fallen ill about 5 hours after the initial contact with police.

Some elements of the above research will come as no surprise to custody officers, who have to deal with the effects of drugs and alcohol on a daily basis. What the report highlights is that the behaviour of detainees who are under the influence of drugs can be unpredictable and they need to be monitored constantly.

KEYNOTE

If a detainee admits to having taken drugs immediately prior to being brought into custody, the advice of a police surgeon must be sought. Often, a detainee who has taken drugs may deteriorate rapidly, and in these cases, consideration should be given to transferring them to hospital immediately.

The Home Office Drugs Intervention Programme views the police service as a key player in the treatment and rehabilitation of drug users, and in assisting with interventions in the crime/drugs cycle. Code C, para. 17 of the *Codes of Practice* provides the police with the power to test detainees for Class A drugs in certain circumstances, a power which will be useful in monitoring drug misuse in an area. The information will also be of use to the courts when deciding whether or not to grant bail to a detainee. Also, because emphasis should be placed on rehabilitation, the information should also be of use to drug referral agencies. Paragraph 17.1 applies only in selected police stations in police areas, where the provisions for drug testing under s. 63B of PACE (as amended by s. 5 of the Criminal Justice Act 2003 and s. 7 of the Drugs Act 2005) are in force (see **12.10 Testing for presence of Class A drugs** for a full discussion of these powers).

4.5.2 Detainees under the influence of alcohol

The report by Dr David Best and Amakai Kefas—*The Role of Alcohol in Police-Related Deaths (Analysis of Deaths in Custody (Category 3) between 2000 and 2001)*—highlights the issue of alcohol as a contributory factor in deaths in custody. Analysis showed that 86 per cent of deaths in police custody were linked to recent alcohol consumption or chronic alcohol abuse. In 81 per cent of *head injury* deaths in police custody, the deceased was suspected of intoxication and in many of these cases the link may not have been apparent to officers at the time of arrest.

Further, alcohol-related death was cited as the second most prominent cause of death in police custody following death by hanging, and 42 per cent of those who died as a result of hanging were thought to be intoxicated with alcohol or drugs. Only 3 of 11 detainees arrested for being drunk and incapable were assessed by a police doctor prior to death.

This report is too lengthy to include in this book, but is essential reading for custody officers and custody trainers and can now be found on the Home Office website, at http://www.homeoffice.gov.uk.

The statistics bulletin by the Police Leadership and Powers Unit (PLPU) referred to above in **3.2.4 Facts and figures** further outlines issues of good practice when dealing with detainees who are drunk. The document recognises that drunkenness remains a significant factor in some deaths in custody and it imposes a burden on the police, who have to deal with severely intoxicated people who might be better cared for elsewhere. The bulletin goes on to state that there has been recognition for many years that people who are incapable through drink would usually be better and more safely cared for in dedicated facilities rather than at a police station.

In July 2003, the Home Office published the findings of a research study (Home Office Research Findings 171, 2003) that investigated the extent to which detainees in custody had been arrested for alcohol-specific offences or had been drinking at the time of arrest, and the problems for the police when such detainees are held in custody.

1,575 custody records relating to three metropolitan police stations were examined. The key findings include:

- Almost a third of the custody records sampled indicated that alcohol was a factor in the arrest;

- 15 per cent of detainees had been arrested for an alcohol-specific offences (e.g., drunkenness or drink driving). 16 per cent were alcohol-related in that the detainee was drunk or had been drinking prior to arrest;

- Alcohol-related detainees spent significantly longer in custody than other detainees (average of 8.7 hours and 6.9 hours respectively) mainly because detainees needed to sober up before interviewing and processing;

- Many detainees arrested for alcohol-specific offences were held to allow them to sober up in a supervised environment and were released without any charges being brought;

- 53 per cent of those arrested for alcohol-related offences and 36 per cent of those arrested for alcohol-specific offences required the attention of a police surgeon (or Forensic Medical Examiner (FME)) (this was compared to 24 per cent of other arrestees who required attention from the FME);

- The FME recommended that custody staff closely observe about a quarter of these detainees while they were being held;

- Detainees arrested for alcohol-related or alcohol-specific offences were more likely to be noisy, disruptive, agitated, abusive, aggressive, and violent while in custody.

Once again, custody officers will be familiar with the problems highlighted in the above report. With approximately a third of all detainees being under the influence of alcohol, custody staff will need to take extra care in order to protect them from harm.

KEYNOTE

Note that detainees who are under the influence of drink or drugs must be visited and roused every half hour (this is discussed in depth in **Chapter 5—Conditions of Detention**).

4.6 **Other Medical Issues**

4.6.1 **Legislative Provisions**

Code C, Para. 9.12

If a detainee is in possession, or claims to need, medication in relation to a heart condition, diabetes, epilepsy or a condition of comparable potential seriousness then, even though para. 9.5 may not apply, the advice of the appropriate health care professional must be sought.

4.6.2 **Diabetes and other serious medical conditions**

Code C, para. 9.12 above leaves the custody officer with no choice; if the detained person has, or claims to need, medication relating to a heart condition, diabetes, epilepsy, or a condition of comparable potential seriousness then, the advice of the Police Surgeon must be obtained. Diabetes is a particularly important medical condition for custody officers to be aware of. Some people receive treatment for their diabetes with insulin and may carry syringes with them. Consequently, they may be mistaken for drug addicts. Also, people with diabetes may suffer incidents of 'hypoglycemia' (or low blood sugar). The symptoms associated with hypoglycemia can be similar to drunkenness, leading sometimes to arrests for the wrong reasons.

Other medical issues to note are:

• Asthmatic detainees and those suffering from angina can be adversely affected by having their inhalers withheld (however, it is possible to overdose by inhaling too frequently—such detainees should not be allowed to retain their inhalers for use as required but should be seen by a Police Surgeon);

• Inhalers should be examined to ensure they have not been tampered with or used to conceal other substances;

• A person believed to be receiving steroid therapy, or found in possession of an identification card showing that they are receiving steroid therapy, may be endangered if medical advice is not sought as soon as possible. A Police Surgeon must be called immediately to examine them;

• Persons thought to be suffering from schizophrenia must be seen by the Police Surgeon at the earliest opportunity.

4.6.3 **Positional asphyxia**

Positional asphyxia can occur when the person has been involved in a violent confrontation, and they are suffering from exertion. The *Guidance on the Safer Detention and Handling of Persons in Police Custody 2006* contains a checklist of factors, which can contribute towards a death during restraint. These include situations where:

- the body position of a person results in partial or complete obstruction of the airway and the subject is unable to escape from that position;
- pressure is applied to the back of the neck, torso or abdomen of a person held in the prone position;
- pressure is applied restricting the shoulder girdle or accessory muscles of respiration while the person is lying down in any position;
- the person is intoxicated through drink or drugs;
- the person is left in the prone position;
- the person is obese (particularly those with large stomachs and abdomens);
- the person has heightened levels of stress;
- the person may be suffering respiratory muscle failure related to earlier violent muscular activity (such as after a struggle).

The person may be in danger if left in one of the following positions, which may affect their ability to breathe:

- lying face down;
- sitting against a wall, with their head forward restricting the windpipe;
- slumped forward, where the chest or abdomen is compressed.

The prone position should be avoided if at all possible, or the period for which it is used minimised. Bodyweight should not be used on the upper body to hold down the detainee and if possible, staff should avoid restraining a person on the floor face down, with pressure being applied on their back (particularly with the knee).

Custody staff should receive personal safety training, which should include proper restraint techniques.

KEYNOTE

A person who is unconscious should be placed in the recovery position on a mattress on the floor to ensure an open airway and prevent the inhalation of vomit. An ambulance must be called immediately.

4.6.4 **Excited Delirium**

The condition is also known as Acute Exhaustive Mania. Custody officers may have come across this condition in detainees, which can occur when a person is behaving in a particularly violent manner. People who suffer from this condition are often found to be under the influence of drugs (usually cocaine) and/or alcohol. They may also be suffering from a psychiatric illness. A person suffering from this condition may show extraordinary strength and will struggle violently, with no apparent regard for pain or CS incapacitant sprays. The main danger from this condition is the person suffering from a heart attack or similar condition.

4.6.5 **CS spray and other incapacitants**

Detainees who are brought into custody offices, having been affected by CS incapacitant should be examined by a police surgeon as soon as possible, because the spray may have an effect on the person's breathing (especially if they suffer from asthma or a similar condition). Consideration should be given to removing the detainee's clothes; otherwise if he/she is placed in a cell, the effects of the spray will not disperse. The detainee should be segregated from other detainees and should be made the subject of more frequent cell visits. To treat the effects of CS spray, the detainee should have dry air blown into their faces (most custody offices have fans for this purpose). The skin (but not the eyes) may be washed with soapy water.

4.7 **Protecting Custody Staff from Risk**

This chapter has focused mainly on what custody officers should do to ensure the safety of detainees. However, it should also be remembered that custody staff need to be protected from injury, illness and disease. Experienced custody staff will know that even though previously violent detainees may have calmed down once they have been placed in a cell, they still represent a risk to custody staff.

The case of *David Glyn Lloyd* v *Ministry of Justice* [2007] EWHC 2475 (QB) examined the duty of the employer to protect staff from injury. *L* was a prison officer who entered the cell of a prisoner who was on remand for robbery, when he was subjected to an unprovoked attack, sustaining a serious eye injury which ended his career. It later transpired that the prisoner had previously been responsible for 20 violent incidents, 14 of which involved assaults or attempted assaults on prison officers.

L claimed he was unaware of the prisoner's history of violence and that had he known, he would have taken further precautions. *L's* employers argued that he would have known of the prisoner's violent tendencies from an incident the previous day, where the prisoner was extracted from his cell, having barricaded himself in, and that in any event it was *L's* responsibility to brief himself on a person's history.

The court heard that the prisoner's history sheet could and should have included the simple warning that he had a history of assaulting prison officers and further it was never brought to the segregation unit where *L* worked. In addition, the internal computer system did not hold all the relevant information or hold it in an understandable form.

It was held that *L's* employers had a duty to keep him reasonably safe and that the senior officer in charge had a duty to obtain all relevant information and disseminate it to staff. The court found that *L's* employers were negligent.

There is a distinct connection between this case and the duty of police organisations and custody officers to inform staff of specific risks involving prisoners in detention so that appropriate safety precautions can be put in place.

Custody staff must be fully trained to the standards required by the *ACPO/ NCPE Custody Officer Training Programme*, specifically in respect of:

- personal safety training;
- control and restraint techniques;
- searching detainees in cells;
- risk assessment;
- first aid;
- PNC.

Custody staff should be aware that, regardless of their training, complacency is their worst enemy in the cells complex. Consider the following:

- try to avoid being isolated in the cells—i.e. at least two custody staff on duty at all times;
- make sure you are aware of any emergency buzzers in the cells and where they are located;
- before opening the cell door, use the spy hole or hatch to check where the prisoner is;
- never walk in front of a detainee, to avoid being attacked from behind;
- be firm, and clear the custody office regularly of any people who should not be there;
- regularly check your environment for articles left or new damage.

These are just a few things that staff can do to protect themselves, but mainly they should always be on their guard from attack and be aware of their surroundings.

Staff working in custody offices should also consider immunisation against Hepatitis B as a minimum requirement.

4.8 **Summing Up**

Identifying medical issues

Custody officers should ask the following questions of all detainees:

1. Do you have any illness or injury?

2. Have you seen a doctor or been to hospital for this illness/injury?

3. Are you taking or supposed to be taking any tablets/medication?

4. What are they for?

5. Are you suffering from any mental health problems or depression?

6. Have you ever tried to harm yourself?

Clinical treatment

1. The custody officer must ensure a detainee receives clinical attention as soon as reasonably practicable if the person:

    *   appears to be suffering from physical illness; *or*

    *   is injured; *or*

    *   appears to be suffering from a mental disorder; *or*

    *   appears to need clinical attention.

2. If the detainee requests a clinical examination, an appropriate healthcare professional must be called as soon as practicable.

(Code C, para. 9.5–9.8)

Medication

*   If a detainee is required to take or apply any medication, the custody officer must consult the appropriate healthcare professional before the use of the medication.

*   No police officer may administer or supervise the self-administration of a controlled drug listed in the Misuse of Drugs Regs 2001, Schedule 1, 2 or 3. A detainee may only self-administer such drugs under the personal supervision of the registered medical practitioner authorising their use.

*   Drugs listed in Schedule 4 or 5 may be distributed by the custody officer for self administration if they have consulted the registered medical practitioner authorising their use.

- If a detainee is in possession of, or claims to need, medication in relation to a heart condition, diabetes, epilepsy or a condition of comparable potential seriousness, then the advice of the appropriate health care professional must be sought.

(Code C, para. 9.10–9.12)

Custody staff must be fully trained to the standards required by the *ACPO/NCPE Custody Officer Training Programme*, specifically in respect of:

- personal safety training;
- control and restraint techniques;
- searching detainees in cells;
- risk assessment;
- first aid;
- PNC.

LOCAL PROCEDURES

1. Does your force adopt the 'six-hour rule', where a detainee requests medication for a drug dependency?
2. Are you and your staff fully trained to the standards required by the *ACPO/NCPE Custody Officer Training Programme*?

SPACE FOR NOTES

103

SPACE FOR NOTES

SPACE FOR NOTES

5

Conditions of Detention

5.1 **Introduction**

The issues surrounding a detained person's conditions of detention can mainly be found in Code C of the *Codes of Practice*. The majority of this chapter examines the custody officer's duty to maintain a high standard of care in relation to a detainee's treatment and welfare while they are in police detention.

Clearly the main focus of a detained person's time in custody will be on evidence gathering; however, even if such evidence is obtained fairly, the whole case may be placed at risk by a custody officer who ignores the seemingly less important issues contained within the *Codes of Practice*. At the very least, a custody officer may be called to court to account for his or her decision-making during the time the detained person was in his or her care.

This chapter deals with the provisions of paras. 8 and 12 of the *Codes of Practice*:

- cells and detention rooms and cell sharing;
- heating and lighting;
- washing facilities;
- additional restraints and cell relocation;
- clothing, bedding and blankets;
- meals and refreshments;
- exercise;
- juveniles and cells;
- visits (observation and monitoring);
- rest periods.

The *Codes of Practice* provide specific guidelines as to the accommodation provided in a custody office and the comfort of detained persons, and the guidance should be viewed as a minimum requirement in relation to the detainee's welfare.

Lastly, this chapter will examine the role of the independent custody visitor, in the protection of the welfare of detainees at the custody office.

Human Rights Act 1998

It should also be noted that by failing to comply with these particular *Codes of Practice*, custody officers (and their employers) run the risk of a claim being brought by the detained person that their human rights have been breached under Article 3 of the Convention Rights (inhuman or degrading treatment). While this might seem harsh, Article 3 specifically deals with treatment giving rise to fear and anguish in the victim, causing feelings of inferiority and humiliation (see *Ireland* v *United Kingdom* (1978) 2 EHRR 25, where the UK was found to have breached the human rights of certain detainees in Northern Ireland prisons). This area is largely untested as yet in relation to the *Codes of Practice*. However, a failure to provide food, washing facilities or adequate comfort to a detainee could certainly attract such claims in the future. In general, provided the Codes are complied with, the custody officer's actions should withstand scrutiny under the Human Rights Act 1998.

5.2 Cells and Detention Rooms

5.2.1 Conditions of detention

In **Chapter 3—Safer Detention**, we examined the issue of safely designed custody offices to minimise opportunities for detainees to self-harm. There are other requirements, contained in the *Codes of Practice*, to ensure that the welfare and comfort of detained persons is provided for, such as the condition of cells and facilities and the capacity of the custody office.

Perhaps taking this concept a step too far, the courts have had to consider whether a police cell is a 'dwelling' for the purposes of the Public Order Act 1986. In *R v CF* [2006] EWCA Crim 3323 (CA), the defendant had been charged with an offence under s. 4A of the Act (causing racially aggravated harassment, alarm or distress), having allegedly made a racially obscene remark to a police officer while being detained in a police cell.

The defendant was acquitted in Crown Court, having successfully argued that the police cell constituted a dwelling (within the meaning of s. 8 of Act) while she 'resided' there and therefore the offence could not be made out.

The Crown appealed against this decision and the Court of Appeal held that the judge was wrong to conclude that a police cell was a dwelling within the meaning of s. 8; the appeal was upheld.

Moving to more conventional matters, the *Guidance on the Safer Detention and Handling of Persons in Police Custody 2006* identifies that the safe operating capacity of a custody office depends on a number of factors:

- the number and type of detainees currently being held;
- identified risks;
- the number of trained and competent staff available on duty;
- operational commitments of the area;
- the actual number of cells in operation.

Custody officers will be well aware that the day-to-day capacity for a cell complex will depend on how well they can monitor the safety and welfare of detainees, as well as their own staff. It will be a decision for the custody officer as to whether he or she can accept further detainees, or whether they need to be taken elsewhere. Such decisions are not always popular with operational staff; however, the custody officer has ultimate responsibility for what happens in the custody office and must take a firm stance on these matters.

5.2.2 **Cell sharing**

Code C, para. 8.1 states:

So far as is practicable, not more than one person shall be detained in each cell.

The *Guidance on the Safer Detention and Handling of Persons in Police Custody 2006* identifies that cell sharing is only appropriate in exceptional circumstances. Custody officers should consider the detainee's privacy (especially relating to toilet and showering facilities) and whether they may be in breach of Article 8 of the European Convention on Human Rights (the right to respect for private and family life).

Cell sharing must *not* take place where:

- the detainee requires special provisions for any reason, e.g., disability;
- there are any diversity issues that would make cell sharing inappropriate, e.g., religious beliefs and the inability to meet religious obligations;
- the detainees are not of the same gender;
- the detainee is a juvenile.

Where a custody officer makes the decision to allow cell sharing, a risk assessment must be endorsed on *all* custody records of the people affected. The custody should also seek the views of the detainees themselves before making the decision and record those views. The risk assessment must cover the following points:

- any medical condition the detainee has;
- whether the detainee has to take medication while in detention (to avoid medication being passed to the other detainee);
- demeanour on arrival (e.g. violent, use of substances or alcohol);
- known or suspected tendencies to self-harm;
- known or suspected tendencies to conceal articles in custody (e.g. drugs or weapons);
- current demeanour;
- known or suspected racist or homophobic attitudes;
- other discriminatory attitudes;
- any warning markers that the detainees may have (particularly relating to any of the above issues);

- whether both persons have been thoroughly searched;
- whether there is a risk of losing evidence connected to a case (custody officers should liaise with the investigating officer);
- whether the detainees are likely to be in custody for a long time (e.g. sufficient beds or bedding);
- whether one of the detainees is likely to receive visits from a legal representative (e.g. if the cell is used for consultation, privacy will be affected).

The list is not exhaustive, but a detainee should not be allowed to share a cell with someone who may pose one of the above risks. This is particularly important in relation to potentially violent detainees, because any death in custody in such circumstances would almost certainly amount to a breach of Article 2 of the European Convention on Human Rights (the right to life).

Where all risks have been discounted and a custody officer does make the decision to cell share, the custody record should also be endorsed as to the frequency of visits (it is suggested that visits should be increased in these circumstances) and consideration should be given to using a cell equipped with CCTV.

KEYNOTE

Note that issues relating to juveniles and cells are dealt with in **5.5 Juveniles and Cells** below.

5.2.3 **Heating and lighting**

Under Code C, para. 8.2, cells in use must be adequately heated, cleaned and ventilated. They must be adequately lit, subject to such dimming as is compatible with safety and security to allow people detained overnight to sleep. This is linked directly with Code C, para. 12.2, which deals with a detainee's period of uninterrupted rest. If the cell's lighting is so bright that it impedes the detainee's ability to sleep, then it follows that there may be a breach of both Codes.

Contrast the above requirement with the situation of a vulnerable detainee, who may be placed in a cell with CCTV monitoring facilities. In this case, it is vital that there is sufficient lighting to monitor that person, notwithstanding their need to sleep. Cells may be fitted with dimmer switches to strike the balance between the need to monitor a person safely and allow them adequate rest.

In **3.6 Health and safety in the custody office**, we discussed the requirement for custody officers to consider health and safety risks in the custody office and abide by a regular inspection regime. If such inspections take place regularly, para. 8.2 above should be complied with.

110

5.2.4 **Toilets and washing facilities**

Paragraph 8.4 of Code C simply states that 'access to toilet and washing facilities must be provided'. Once again, this paragraph is self-explanatory, but some degree of caution is required, as always.

KEYNOTE

Allowing detainees of either gender to use toilet and in particular washing facilities has potential danger in relation to exposing the person to implements which may be used to self-harm.

For example, disposable razors, toothbrushes, containers. If there is any doubt as to whether a detainee is in possession of such articles, custody officers should utilise their powers to search, under s. 54 of PACE (see **Chapter 8—Dealing with Property and Searching**), before and after a detained person uses toilet and washing facilities.

5.3 **Restraint and Conflict Management**

5.3.1 **Legislative provisions**

Code C, Para. 8.2

No additional restraints shall be used within a locked cell unless absolutely necessary and then only restraint equipment, approved for use in that force by the Chief Officer, which is reasonable and necessary in the circumstances having regard to the detainee's demeanour and with a view to ensuring their safety and the safety of others.

If a detainee is deaf, mentally disordered or otherwise mentally vulnerable, particular care must be taken when deciding whether to use any form of approved restraints.

Code C, Para. 8.11

The use of any restraints on a detainee whilst in a cell, the reasons for it and, if appropriate, the arrangements for enhanced supervision of the detainee whilst so restrained, shall be recorded.

5.3.2 **Additional restraints**

Considerable care should be taken when deciding whether or not to use restraints on a person in a locked cell, particularly when dealing with vulnerable people. The decision must not be taken lightly and can have an impact on public confidence if an adverse incident occurs due to their use.

Firstly, a custody officer must believe that it is absolutely necessary to allow a person to be restrained once they are placed in a cell—that is, *all other alternatives* have been considered and dismissed before the decision is taken to do so. There will always be alternatives, such as being in the cell with the detainee and restraining them physically, or monitoring from outside the cell, either with the door open or through CCTV. The tactical options used will depend on the level of risk posed by the detainee to himself/herself or others.

Clearly, it would be appropriate to use additional restraints when intervention is required to prevent detainees from harming themselves, especially if they are likely to cause serious damage by punching, kicking and head butting the cell walls. Under these conditions, detainees may need to be restrained whilst awaiting the arrival of a medical practitioner and other suitably trained professionals and custody staff may have no alternative but to use restraints rather than put themselves in danger.

If the decision is taken to use additional restraints on a person in a locked cell, only restraint equipment 'approved for use in that force by the Chief Officer' should be used. Paragraph 8.2 above offers no further guidance as to which restraints may be 'approved'; however, rigid handcuffs (or 'quick cuffs') often have a tendency to exaggerate a person's injuries, if not properly applied. Therefore, rigid handcuffs should only be used in accordance with the training given and should be double locked. Alternatively, 'bracelet' type handcuffs may be used. Leg restraints also offer an alternative option. Custody officers should research their own force policy.

Restraints should be removed as soon as it is considered safe to do so and care must be taken to prevent positional asphyxia.

KEYNOTE

The *Guidance on the Safer Detention and Handling of Persons in Police Custody 2006* recommends that if additional restraints are required, the detainee should be placed either under constant observation (Level 3) or in close proximity (Level 4) so that all vital signs can be monitored and appropriate intervention made if a medical emergency arises.

Note the requirement under para. 8.11 to record the reasons for the use of additional restraints and the arrangements for enhanced supervision of the detainee whilst so restrained.

5.3.3 **Cell relocation**

The *Guidance on the Safer Detention and Handling of Persons in Police Custody 2006* also offers advice on cell relocation of violent detainees from one location in the custody office to another. Below is a summary of the guidance:

- the custody officer should maintain supervision and not be physically involved;
- the custody officer should ensure sufficient staff are available (unless the need to move the person is urgent);
- the custody officer is accountable for the way the incident is managed, but all staff involved have a responsibility to be aware of signs of distress and trauma.

The simple message from the *Guidance* is that moving a person who is violent or likely to become violent is accompanied by a high risk of injury to the detainee and staff—if you don't need to, don't do it!

5.4 **Welfare Issues**

5.4.1 **Legislative provisions**

Code C, Para. 8.3

Blankets, mattresses, pillows and other bedding supplied shall be of a reasonable standard and in a clean and sanitary condition.

Code C, Para. 8.5

If it is necessary to remove a person's clothes for the purposes of investigation, for hygiene or health reasons or for cleaning, replacement clothing of a reasonable standard of comfort and cleanliness shall be provided. A person may not be interviewed unless adequate clothing has been offered to him.

Code C, Para. 8.6

At least two light meals and one main meal shall be offered in any period of 24 hours. [see Note 8B] Drinks should be provided at meal times and upon reasonable request between meal times. Whenever necessary, advice shall be sought from the health care professional on medical or dietary matters. As far as practicable, meals provided shall offer a varied diet and meet any special dietary needs or religious beliefs that the person may have; he may also have meals supplied by family or friends at his own expense.

Code C, Note for Guidance 8A

In deciding whether to allow meals to be supplied by family or friends, the custody officer is entitled to take account of the risk of items being concealed in any food or package and the officer's duties and responsibilities under food handling legislation.

Meals should so far as practicable be offered at recognised meal times.

5.4.2 **Blankets and bedding**

Paragraph 8.3 of Code C, deals with a detained person's comfort while in custody and does not require extensive de-briefing. Note for Guidance 8A states that:

> the provisions in para. 8.3 regarding bedding and a varied diet are of particular importance in the case of a person detained under the Terrorism Act 2000, immigration detainees and others who are likely to be detained for an extended period.

Care should be taken when giving blankets to particularly vulnerable detainees as they may be used as a ligature point. People have been known to set fire to them using lighters smuggled into the custody office!

5.4.3 **Clothing**

There may be occasions where it is necessary to remove a detained person's clothing while they are in custody. Paragraph 8.5 of Code C above gives specific advice about replacement clothing.

A person's clothing is often important in the course of an investigation as a 'crime scene'. The authority to seize a person's clothing is derived from s. 54 of PACE. A full discussion on this and other aspects of searching is contained in **Chapter 8—Dealing with Property and Searching**.

It may also be necessary to provide alternative clothing for sanitary reasons, if the detainee's has become soiled, or if the person is suffering from the affects of CS spray.

It is common practice when a detained person is likely to be in custody for some time to allow family to bring clothing to the custody office. All such clothing must be searched for weapons, drugs or other articles which may assist a person to escape (see **Chapter 8—Dealing with Property and Searching**).

Custody offices should have a store of purpose-made 'rip suits' to issue to detainees who have had their clothing removed. Giving the detainee a blanket would probably not comply with the requirement to provide 'clothing'.

KEYNOTE

Note that a person must not be interviewed unless adequate clothing has been offered to him or her. Paragraph 8.5 appears slightly vague as to what would happen if a detained person refuses the offer of replacement clothing. However, interviewing a semi-naked person would appear to be a clear breach of Article 3 of the Convention Rights (Inhuman or Degrading Treatment). At the very least, the interview may be deemed oppressive and any evidence obtained may be considered inadmissible.

KEYNOTE

Under Code C, para. 8.11, a record must be kept of any replacement clothing offered to the detained person, and why their own clothes were taken.

5.4.4 **Meals and refreshments**

Among the varied duties given to a custody officer by the *Codes of Practice* are the provision of meals, refreshments and drinks to detainees.

Consider the following:

Case Study

PICARD has been in police detention for four hours, having been arrested for an offence of robbery. The officer in the case is conducting enquiries and is likely to return soon to interview PICARD. It is 6.00pm and the custody officer is wondering whether or not PICARD should be provided with a meal.

What should the custody officer consider in these circumstances?

- How long has the person been in custody?
- How long is the person likely to be in custody?
- The time of day?

The length of time a person has been in custody may be considered when deciding whether or not to provide a meal. But a person need not have been in custody for 24 hours before they are entitled to one. It may be appropriate at any time during the 24-hour period.

The amount of time a person is likely to be in custody may be taken into account. If the person is likely to be in custody only a short period and they are there during a recognised meal time, they would not automatically qualify for a meal under para. 8.6 above.

The *Codes of Practice* allow for the flexibility of providing meals outside recognised meal times, depending on the circumstances of each case. It may be necessary for some detainees, for example during Ramadan.

If the detained person has already been in custody for six hours, it is likely that they have not eaten since the night before (bearing in mind the time of day). It would seem appropriate to provide a meal in these circumstances.

Note the requirement in para. 8.6 to consider varied diets for the following reasons:

- religious beliefs;
- medical grounds (e.g. diabetes, Coeliac disease or any other, such as those who suffer from the inability of the body to absorb fatty food);
- vegetarians and vegans.

KEYNOTE

The custody officer should attempt to establish from the officer in the case how long the interview is likely to last and their thoughts on what is likely to happen afterwards.

Obviously no firm decisions can be made in relation to the person's further detention until the conclusion of interviews, but the custody officer will be able to make an informed decision from such a conversation.

Lastly, and most obviously, the prisoner should be consulted to see if they are hungry.

KEYNOTE

Note also that custody officers should monitor detainees who have declined meals that have been offered. Consideration should be given to calling a police surgeon if a detainee declines two meals.

5.4.5 **Exercise**

Code C, para. 8.7 deals with exercise and is self-explanatory. Simply, 'Brief outdoor exercise shall be offered daily if practicable'. This will be a decision for the custody officer, taking into consideration such things as availability of exercise facilities, the weather, ability to supervise detainees and simply how busy the custody office is at the time.

A record must be kept of the fact that a person was granted a period of exercise.

5.5 **Juveniles and Cells**

5.5.1 **Legislative provisions**

Code C, Para. 8.8

A juvenile shall not be placed in a police cell unless no other secure accommodation is available and the custody officer considers that it is not practicable to supervise them if they are not placed in a cell or the custody officer considers that a cell provides more comfortable accommodation than other secure accommodation in the police station. A juvenile may not be placed in a cell with a detained adult.

5.5.2 **Juveniles and cell sharing**

The *Codes of Practice* offer specific guidelines under para. 8.8 in relation to the detention of juveniles in custody offices. This paragraph should be read in conjunction with **5.2.2 Cell sharing**, above.

Under para. 8.8 above, there are only two reasons for placing a juvenile in a cell:

- if there is no other secure accommodation available and the custody officer considers it is not practicable to supervise the juvenile if he/she is not placed in a cell;
- a juvenile detainee may be placed in a cell if it would offer more comfortable accommodation than other secure accommodation in the police station.

Neither para. 8.1 nor para. 8.8 above appears to prohibit placing two juveniles in the same detention room (or indeed the same cell). However, refer to the discussion in **5.5.2 Cell sharing**, above, relating to the dangers of cell sharing.

KEYNOTE

- No juvenile may ever be placed in the same cell as an adult detainee.
- If a juvenile is placed in a cell, the reason must be recorded in accordance with para. 8.10 of the *Codes of Practice*.

Placing a juvenile in a cell should be viewed as a temporary measure and as soon as a detention room becomes available, the juvenile should be moved. This is often overlooked by custody officers.

Consider the following:

Case Study

What if two juveniles, X and Y, have been arrested for a robbery. The custody office has one juvenile detention room and two female cells in one corridor and eight male cells in a second corridor. Both female cells are occupied and there is a male adult in one of the male cells. Juvenile X has been in custody numerous times in the past, while juvenile Y has never been arrested before and appears to be disturbed by the experience of being in custody.

What issues must be considered?

1. Can they be detained without being placed in a cell?
2. The availability of detention rooms and cells?
3. The vulnerability of the detainee?

....

It would be useful to consider each of the points in the exercise separately:

1. Occasionally, it may be appropriate to process a juvenile detainee without placing him/her in a detention room or a cell. For example, when he or she has been arrested for a simple offence by appointment, when attending the station with a parent.

It would depend on whether the custody office has convenient locations available, such as medical rooms, interview rooms or solicitor's consultation areas. It would also depend on whether such rooms may be used without the juvenile detainee coming into contact with other detainees in the custody office.

The serious nature of the offence may also influence the custody officer's decision. Investigating officers would certainly wish detainees involved in a joint case to be segregated, to prevent them discussing the offence and possibly for forensic reasons.

2. Clearly only one of the juveniles can be detained in the detention room, while the other needs to be located elsewhere. Had they been unoccupied, the female cells would seem the logical place to locate the juvenile, as they are situated away from the male cells, which would separate the juvenile from other adult detainees.

However, since this is not an option, one juvenile must be placed in a male cell. Consideration should be given to placing the juvenile as far away from the other adult detainee as possible.

3. It would seem logical at first to place juvenile *X* in the adult cell, because of this person's previous history.

However, there is potential for juvenile *Y* to self-harm and this must be a consideration. Had the juvenile detention room been fitted with CCTV, the decision would present no difficulty.

The serious nature of the offence and the time they are likely to spend in custody may also affect the state of mind of detainee *Y*.

Considering all of the above points, at least one of the juveniles will have to be placed in a male cell, as there is no other place to detain him. As there may be doubts as to his state of mind, it would seem sensible to place juvenile *Y* in the cell, if the custody officer considers it is safer to place him there than the detention room.

KEYNOTE

There is a requirement under s. 31 of the Children and Young Persons Act 1933 that detained females under the age of 17 must be under the care of a woman. This may be either a police officer or a member of police staff, who need not physically be with the detainee at all times.

5.6 Observing and Monitoring Detainees

5.6.1 Legislative provisions

Code C, Para. 9.3

Detainees should be visited at least every hour. If no reasonably foreseeable risk was identified in the risk assessment, there is no need to wake a sleeping detainee. Those suspected of being intoxicated through drink or drugs or having swallowed drugs, see Note 9CA, or whose level of consciousness causes concern must, subject to any clinical directions given by the appropriate healthcare professional:

- be visited and roused at least every half hour;
- have their condition assessed as in Annex H;
- and clinical treatment arranged if appropriate.

Code C, Note for Guidance 9F

Custody officers should always seek to clarify directions that the detainee requires constant observation or supervision and should ask the appropriate healthcare professional to explain precisely what action needs to be taken to implement such directions.

Code C, Para. 1.1A

A custody officer is required to perform the functions specified in this code as soon as is practicable. A custody officer shall not be in breach of this code in the event of delay provided that the delay is justifiable and that every reasonable step is taken to prevent unnecessary delay. The custody record shall indicate where a delay has occurred and the reason why. [See Note 1H]

Code C, Note for Guidance 1H

Paragraph 1.1A is intended to cover the kinds of delays which may occur in the processing of detained persons because, for example, a large number of suspects are brought into the police station simultaneously to be placed in custody, or interview rooms are all being used, or where there are difficulties in contacting an appropriate adult, solicitor or interpreter.

5.6.2 **Observation**

The *Guidance on the Safer Detention and Handling of Persons in Police Custody 2006* outlines the four levels of observation. This is an excellent guide which has become standard practice for custody officers, and should always be used. As outlined in Code C, para. 9.3, custody officers should conduct a risk assessment on each detainee when detention is first authorised; however, the risk should be assessed continuously in case there are changes in circumstances.

Level 1—General Observation

This is the least intrusive observation level and the minimum acceptable standard outlined in para. 9.3, where detainees are checked **every hour**. If no reasonably foreseeable risk has been identified, there is no need to wake the detainee, but if the detainee is awake, custody staff should engage him/her in conversation as part of the ongoing risk assessment.

120

Level 2—Intermittent Observation

This level of observation is again referred to in para. 9.3 and relates to those detainees who are suspected of being intoxicated through drink or drugs or having swallowed drugs, or whose level of consciousness causes concern. Subject to any clinical directions given by the healthcare professional, the detainee is visited and roused at least every **30 minutes**.

The visit must be conducted in accordance with the Detained Persons Observation List, outlined in Annex H of Code C (see **5.6.3 Rousability** below). This type of visit will require custody staff to actively engage with the detainee on every visit, which will include physical checks and conversations.

Custody officers may wish to review the risk assessment with the healthcare professional; however, Annex H states that if a detainee fails to respond to questions or commands outlined in the Observation List, an appropriate healthcare professional or an ambulance must be called.

Where a person is in police custody by order of a magistrates' court under the Criminal Justice Act 1988, s. 152 (as amended by the Drugs Act 2005, s. 8) to facilitate the recovery of evidence after being charged with drug possession or drug trafficking and suspected of having swallowed drugs, there is no requirement for the detainee to be roused, unless there are any clinical directions to do so (see Note for Guidance 9CA).

Again, all visits and observations must be recorded, including changes in the detainee's condition or behaviour, and the custody officer informed immediately of any changes.

Level 3—Constant Observation

This observation level relates to a detainee, whose risk assessment indicates the likelihood of self-harm. The risk assessment in this case must be reviewed by the healthcare professional. The detainee will be monitored **at all times** while in police detention unless the risk assessment changes. Custody staff must actively engage with the detainee at regular intervals, including physical checks and conversations. This will require custody staff to look out for any possible ligatures in the cell or anything else the detainee may use to self-harm.

Level 4—Close Proximity

The detainee will have been identified as at high risk of self-harm. The detainee will be physically supervised **in close proximity**. This will require a member of staff either sitting in a cell with the detainee, or outside with the door open. The detainee must not be left alone and staff must be constantly vigilant for ligatures or anything else the detainee may use to self-harm.

Again, custody staff must actively engage with the detainee at regular intervals, including physical checks and conversations and the risk assessment must be reviewed by the healthcare professional.

121

KEYNOTE

In all cases, visits and observations must be recorded in the custody record, including changes in the detainee's condition or behaviour. The custody officer must be informed immediately if there are any changes.

KEYNOTE

CCTV and other technologies can be used in addition to personal visits, even where the detainee needs to be constantly monitored or supervised in close proximity. However, visits must still take place according to the risk assessment and the technology must be used to enhance the process, not replace it.

5.6.3 **Rousability**

Where a detainee is suspected of being intoxicated through drink or drugs or having swallowed drugs, or whose level of consciousness causes concern, the custody officer is likely to determine that the person be subject to Level 2 observations (see **5.6.2 Observation** above). The visit must be conducted in accordance with the Detained Persons Observation List, outlined in Annex H of Code C.

If a detainee fails to respond to questions or commands outlined below, an appropriate healthcare professional or an ambulance must be called. Annex H states:

When assessing the level of rousability, consider:

Rousability—can they be woken?

- go into the cell
- call their name
- shake gently

Response to questions—can they give appropriate answers to questions such as:

- What's your name?
- Where do you live?
- Where do you think you are?

Response to commands—can they respond appropriately to commands such as:

- Open your eyes!
- Lift one arm, now the other arm!

122

Remember to take into account the possibility or presence of other illnesses, injury or mental condition. A person who is drowsy and smells of alcohol may also have the following:

- diabetes
- epilepsy
- head injury
- drug intoxication or overdose
- stroke

When a person has been roused, a note should be made of their response to questioning. The purpose of attempting to rouse such persons using the procedure in Annex H is to enable any change in the individual's consciousness level to be noted and clinical treatment arranged if appropriate.

KEYNOTE

Note that the custody officer may not be aware of the condition or illness. Assistance may be provided to recognise these symptoms by:

- early risk assessment, and correct completion of medical questionnaires (as recommended by the Police Complaints Authority);
- early PNC checks (these should be done before a person is placed in a cell);
- drug recognition tests (there is a standard course on this subject).

Failing to comply with the *Codes of Practice* or to follow the *Guidance on the Safer Detention and Handling of Persons in Police Custody 2006* places the detainee at risk, as well as exposing the custody officer to potential litigation.

The above *Guidance* states that the custody officer should record the following in the custody record:

- the level of observation required for a detainee;
- the reasons for the decision;
- clear directions that specify the name and title of the persons carrying out the observations;
- the name of the person responsible for carrying out the review of the required observation level.

In my experience, mistakes are often made by staff who do not wish to wake up a prisoner who has only just gone to sleep after banging the cell door for three hours. The key is in the direction given by the custody officer to custody staff, who must be instructed to record exactly what they did and how the detainee responded. Custody record entries such as 'visit correct' or 'checked in order' are insufficient.

Remember that the real danger time for at-risk detainees is when the cell is quiet. The intoxicated prisoner who is banging on a cell door or singing and shouting can more often than not be assumed to be healthy. However, when the detainee stops banging and falls asleep, they become vulnerable to positional asphyxia, or even choking on their own vomit (for further information relating to positional asphyxia, see **Chapter 4—Clinical Treatment and Attention**). The sound of a detainee snoring may be music to a custody officer's ears, especially if that person has been making a racket while they were awake. However, a person could also be snoring because their air supply is constricted.

KEYNOTE

The following are practical tips for custody officers in relation to vulnerable detainees:

- when a detainee is considered vulnerable, it is good practice to vary the times of visits. If a person is contemplating suicide and they are being visited exactly every half an hour, they will know they have 30 minutes in which to act, before the next visit;

- when a detainee is not vulnerable, try to round up visits to every hour or half hour rather than having different times for visiting each prisoner—it avoids the possibility of missing a visit;

- stations may be fitted with alarms outside cells, forcing custody staff to make timely visits—alternatively, use an alarm clock or stopwatch;

- protect an at-risk person by ensuring that they are sleeping in the recovery position. Also, use low bunks to protect people who fall out of bed;

- another way of keeping a close eye on such a person is to try to place them in the cell nearest to the custody reception area. This way, anyone going into the cells complex area will have to pass the detainee and can look in on them.

Code C, Note for Guidance 9F above offers additional guidance to custody staff in relation to medical directions. Directions may have been given to the custody officer by a healthcare professional in relation to the detainee's medical care (which could include the frequency of visits). It is important that the custody officer understands what is expected of him/her.

So far as possible, the above requirements in relation to visiting detained people must be adhered to. However, in reality, busy custody staff find it difficult to keep strictly to the *Codes of Practice*. Paragraph 9.3 above specifies that people detained 'shall' be visited every hour, and an intoxicated detainee 'shall' be visited every half hour, which leaves little room for interpretation.

Note for Guidance 9B above is slightly less prescriptive, stating that 'wherever possible' juveniles and persons at risk should be visited more frequently. This shows that where the delay is justifiable and every reasonable step was taken to prevent the delay, visits may even be made less frequently. This is reflected in Code C, para. 1.1A above.

> **KEYNOTE**
>
> Note—the custody record must be endorsed as to the reason why a delay was necessary.

5.6.4 **Rest periods**

Code C, para. 12 deals with interviewing detained persons in police stations. This section also provides information about rest periods for detained persons (see para. 12.2). Although this issue obviously relates to a detainee's welfare, for continuity the matter is dealt with fully in **Chapter 18—Interviewing**.

5.7 **Independent Custody Visitors**

Independent custody visiting, formerly known as 'lay visiting', is a system whereby volunteers attend to make random inspections in custody offices, to check on the treatment of detainees and the conditions in which they are held. The original impetus for the introduction of lay visiting came from Lord Scarman's inquiry into the Brixton disorders in 1981 and was intended to open up police activity to scrutiny and enhance public confidence in their work. Pilot visiting schemes were successfully established in 1983 and subsequent Home Office guidance encouraged their wider application. Section 51 of the Police Reform Act 2002 placed independent custody visiting on a statutory basis and a Code of Practice was produced, which commenced on 1 April 2003. It contains full guidance on the respective roles of custody officers and independent custody visitors. This section is meant as a guide to custody officers on their role within the scheme.

5.7.1 **The purpose of independent custody visiting**

Independent custody visiting has a number of connected purposes:

- it offers an extra level of protection to detainees by providing independent scrutiny of their treatment and the conditions in which they are held;

- by giving approved members of the local community an opportunity to observe, comment and report on these matters, it can reassure that community, improve citizens' understanding of procedures at police stations and strengthen their confidence that these are properly applied;
- from a police perspective, it is a clear demonstration of their commitment to transparency and openness in relation to this critical aspect of their duties;
- it can improve police management of their own performance by pointing out areas where problems have occurred and which may have implications for policy, training, communications or the daily work of officers responsible for custody at police stations;
- for police authorities, independent custody visiting can be an extremely important aid in fulfilling their responsibility to ensure that policing in their areas is carried out fairly, in accordance with statutory and other rules and with respect for the human rights of all those coming into contact with the police.

5.7.2 Selection as an independent custody visitor (ICV)

The Home Office provides central guidance on how independent custody visiting should be organised and carried out. Responsibility for delivery lies with police authorities in consultation with forces.

Visitors should be over 18 and police authorities must seek to ensure that the overall set of ICVs is representative of the local community and provides a suitable balance in terms of age, gender, ethnicity and disability. Appointments are for three years, with a six-month probationary period.

Serving police officers and other serving members of police staff may not become ICVs. The same will apply to special constables, justices of the peace and members of the police authority.

Basic training should be provided in such things as the relevant aspects of Code C covering detention, treatment and questioning, communication skills, equal opportunities and race awareness, health and safety, data protection, the Police Complaints System.

KEYNOTE

Visits must be undertaken by pairs of ICVs working together.

ICVs may act as appropriate adults in certain circumstances. However, they must not switch between the role of independent custody visitor and appropriate adult during the course of a visit to the same police station.

5.7.3 **The custody officer's duties**

ICVs should normally be admitted immediately to the custody area. Any delay in allowing visitors into the custody office may be viewed as affecting the independence of the scheme.

ICVs should never be denied entry into the custody officer altogether—access may only ever be delayed if the visitors may be placed in immediate danger, for example if there is a disturbance in progress in the custody area.

The Independent Custody Visiting Association has its own targets, with key performance indicators being frequency of visits and speed of access to the custody area. Ninety-five per cent of urban police stations should be visited once per week and 95 per cent of rural police stations should be visited twice per month. According to targets, 85 per cent of visitors should be allowed immediate access to the custody area and this is broken down into:

- the percentage of visits allowed immediate access;
- the percentage of visits delayed by less than five minutes;
- the percentage of visits delayed by less than 15 minutes;
- the percentage of visits delayed by more than 15 minutes;
- the percentage of visits denied access or aborted;

Custody officers should not delay access simply because they are too busy to allow the visitor into the custody area. If the custody officer is busy, he or she should invite the visitors in and ask them to wait until someone is available to show them around. The custody officer should then offer an explanation as to why access was delayed, which may be included in the visitors' report.

ICVs should be accompanied on their visit by a member of police staff. The escorting officer should normally remain in sight, but out of hearing, during discussions between visitors and detainees.

Visitors should be allowed access to all parts of the custody area, including:

- cells and detention rooms (whether occupied or not);
- charging areas;
- interview rooms (but not when an interview is in progress);
- washing facilities;
- kitchen or food preparation areas;
- medical rooms (but not the drugs cabinet);
- relevant storage areas.

Visitors will wish to satisfy themselves that these areas are clean, tidy and in a reasonable state of repair and decoration, and that bedding in cells is clean and adequate.

KEYNOTE

Visitors may not visit CID rooms or other operational parts of the station.

5.7.4 **Access to detainees**

ICVs should normally have access to any person detained at a police station. In exceptional circumstances the police may judge that it is necessary for a detained person not to be seen by a visitor in order to avoid any possible risk of prejudicing an important investigation. Any denial of a visitor in these circumstances must be authorised by an inspector, and the custody record should be updated. However, even in these circumstances, it may be possible to arrange a visit, so that the detainee is out of sight from the visitor, but within their hearing, so that a conversation may take place relating to welfare issues.

Otherwise, the following procedures must be adopted:

- the detainee should be asked by the escorting officer, in the presence of the visitor, whether he or she consents to a visit;
- if the detainee declines to see a visitor, the escorting officer should attempt to obtain permission from him or her to allow their custody record to be viewed by the visitor;
- if a detainee is suffering from the effects of drink or drugs, or a mental illness, the escorting officer should still allow access unless it is considered that the visitors' safety would be at risk (visitors may wish to speak to the detainee through the cell hatch);
- detainees can be woken at the discretion of the escorting officer to seek consent to a visit (unless this would involve interrupting the continuous period of eight hours rest—the person may be observed through the cell hatch in these circumstances);
- juveniles may be visited without the presence of an appropriate adult.

KEYNOTE

The purpose of an independent visit is to check whether or not detainees have been offered their rights and entitlements under PACE. Visitors should not involve themselves in any way in the process of investigation.

Conversations should focus on confirming whether the conditions of detention are adequate.

5.7.5 **Custody records**

If the detainee consents, visitors may view their custody record to check its contents against what they have been told by the detainee. Visitors will seek to establish:

- if entitlements under PACE have been given and signed for;
- that medication, injuries, medical examinations, meals/diet are recorded;
- that procedures to assess special risks/vulnerabilities presented by the detainee have been properly recorded;
- the timing and frequency of cell inspections of inebriated or otherwise vulnerable detainees;
- the timing of reviews of the continuing need for detention.

KEYNOTE

If a detainee is incapable of giving permission to their custody record being viewed, the custody officer should consider allowing visitors to examine the record regardless.

KEYNOTE

It should be noted that the Home Office view is that visitors should carry out their functions in person and not by viewing either live CCTV pictures or recorded footage.

This does not mean that visitors should not be allowed to view CCTV, but they should only do so when specific incidents are brought to their attention by a detainee, and permission has been given by both the detainee and the custody officer.

5.7.6 **Reporting procedure**

At the end of each visit, and while they are still at the police station ICVs should complete a report with their findings. Custody officers should not be present while visitors discuss and complete their reports. The visitor may, however, discuss issues with the custody officer that require immediate attention. A copy of the report will normally be placed in a sealed envelope for the attention of the officer in charge.

Other copies of the report will be passed to the local police authority and to the co-ordinator of the local independent custody visiting group. Police authorities should regularly review reports in order to address recurring issues in their area.

5.8 **Summing Up**

Cells and detention rooms

So far as is practicable, no more than one person shall be detained in each cell.

(Code C, para. 8.1)

Cell sharing must *not* take place where:

- the detainee requires special provisions for any reason, e.g., disability;
- there are any diversity issues that would make cell sharing inappropriate, e.g., religious beliefs and the inability to meet religious obligations;
- the detainees are not of the same gender;
- the detainee is a juvenile;

Additional restraints

Should not be used in a locked cell unless absolutely necessary, and then only approved equipment. Care should be used in the case of a deaf, mentally disordered or mentally vulnerable person.

(Code C, para. 8.2)

Clothing

If it is necessary to remove a person's clothes, replacement clothing of a reasonable standard of comfort and cleanliness shall be provided. A person may not be interviewed unless adequate clothing has been offered to him.

(Code C, para. 8.5)

Meals and refreshments

- At least two light meals and one main meal shall be offered in any period of 24 hours;
- Drinks should be provided at meal times and upon reasonable request between meal times;

- As far as practicable meals provided shall offer a varied diet and meet any special dietary needs or religious beliefs that a person may have.

(Code C, para. 8.6)

Juveniles and cells

- A juvenile shall not be placed in a police cell unless no other secure accommodation is available and the custody officer considers that it is not practicable to supervise him if he is not placed in a cell; or
- The custody officer considers that a cell provides more comfortable accommodation than other secure accommodation in the police station;
- A juvenile may not be placed in a cell with a detained adult.

(Code C, para. 8.8)

Observation

Level 1—General Observation

The least intrusive observation level and the minimal acceptable standard outlined in para. 9.3, where detainees are checked **every hour**.

Level 2—Intermittent Observation

Relates to detainees suspected of being intoxicated through drink or drugs or having swallowed drugs, or whose level of consciousness causes concern. Detainee should be visited and roused at least every **30 minutes**. The visit must be conducted in accordance with the Detained Persons Observation List, outlined in Annex H.

Level 3—Constant Observation

Relates to a detainee whose risk assessment indicates the likelihood of self-harm. The risk assessment must be reviewed by the healthcare professional. The detainee will be monitored **at all times** unless the risk assessment changes. Custody staff must actively engage with the detainee at regular intervals, including physical checks and conversations.

Level 4—Close Proximity

The detainee has been identified as at high risk of self-harm and will be physically supervised **in close proximity**. A member of staff will either sit in a cell with the detainee, or outside with the door open. The detainee must not be left alone and staff must be constantly vigilant for ligatures or anything else the detainee may use to self-harm.

Rousability

When assessing the level of rousability, consider:

Rousability—can they be woken?

Response to questions—can they give appropriate answers to questions?

Response to commands—can they respond appropriately to commands?

When a person has been roused, a note should be made of their response to questioning. The purpose of attempting to rouse such persons using the procedure in Annex H is to enable any change in the individual's consciousness level to be noted and clinical treatment arranged if appropriate.

Independent custody visitors

Independent custody visitors should normally be admitted immediately to the custody area.

Custody officers should not delay access simply because they are too busy to allow the visitor into the custody area. If the custody officer is busy, he or she should invite the visitors in and ask them to wait until someone is available to show them around.

Access may be delayed if an inspector reasonably believes the visitors may be placed in immediate danger.

LOCAL PROCEDURES

1. Does your force have a policy in relation to allowing more than one detainee in a police cell?

2. Does your force provide custody officers with non-rigid handcuffs for use in cells?

3. Do your staff comply with the four levels of observation as outlined in the *Guidance on the Safer Detention and Handling of Persons in Police Custody 2006*?

4. Does your force comply with policies relating to independent custody visitors?

SPACE FOR NOTES

SPACE FOR NOTES

6

The Detainee's Entitlements

6.1 **Introduction**

This chapter deals with a detainee's right both to have a person informed of their arrest and to consult with a solicitor. Detainees must be informed of their rights, and then given the opportunity to exercise those rights. In certain circumstances the detainee's rights may be delayed by applying ss. 56 and 58 of PACE.

Juveniles and vulnerable people enjoy extended rights under the Act, and the *Codes of Practice*. These additional rights are dealt with in **Chapter 7—Vulnerable People and Appropriate Adults**.

This chapter also deals with the authority to interview a detainee without a solicitor being present, when legal advice has been requested. **Chapter 18—Interviewing** actually deals with the legislation concerning interviews themselves and there is an obvious overlap with this chapter.

There are further powers to exclude legal representatives from interviews, because of their conduct. This power is dealt with in **Chapter 13—Dealing with Legal Representatives**.

Remember that a detainee has a fundamental human right to have a person informed of their arrest, and to be legally represented. Any delays to these rights may only be authorised under the Police and Criminal Evidence Act 1984, or the *Codes of Practice*.

It should be noted that the rights referred to in this chapter will only ever be delayed until the reason has passed. For example, when a drunken person has sobered up, they must be informed of their rights, or when the risk of serious injury has been averted and authorisation has been given under s. 56 of the Act.

Human Rights Act 1998

Once again, the main Articles which the custody officer will need to consider in respect of this chapter are Article 5 (right to liberty and security) and Article 6 (right to a fair trial). The detainee's human rights may be affected if the *Codes of Practice* are not complied with in respect of allowing access to a solicitor, and notifications of arrest.

6.2 **What the Detainee Must be Told**

6.2.1 **Legislative provisions**

Code C, Para. 3.1

When a detainee is brought to a police station under arrest or arrested at the station having gone there voluntarily, the custody officer must make sure the person is told

136

about the following continuing rights which may be exercised at any stage during the period in custody:

(i)   the right to have someone informed of their arrest;

(ii) the right to consult privately with a solicitor and that free independent advice is available;

(iii) the right to consult these *Codes of Practice*.

Code C, Para. 1.8

If this Code requires a person to be given certain information, they do not have to be given it if at the time they are incapable of understanding what is said, are violent or may become violent or in need of urgent medical attention; but they must be given it as soon as practicable.

6.2.2 **Detainee to be made aware of rights**

Sections 56 and 58 of the Act are discussed in depth below; however, both sections refer to a detainee requesting someone to be informed of their arrest, or access to legal advice. Before a person can make such requests, they must be made aware that they are entitled to them. This is outlined in para. 3.1 above. Paragraph 3.1 is clear that the rights are continuing, as long as the detainee is in detention.

Under para. 3.2, a written notice must be given to the detainee outlining the rights referred to in para. 3.1 above. The notice must also set out the arrangements for obtaining legal advice, the right to a copy of the custody record and outline the terms of the caution. The detainee shall be asked to sign the custody record to acknowledge receipt of these notices. Any refusal must be recorded on the custody record.

Note for Guidance 3A states that an additional written notice must be given to the detainee, which briefly sets out their entitlements while in custody. This notice should:

• list the entitlements in this Code, including:

  – visits and contact with outside parties, including special provisions for Commonwealth citizens and foreign nationals;

  – reasonable standards of physical comfort;

  – adequate food and drink;

  – access to toilets and washing facilities, clothing, medical attention, and exercise when practicable.

- mention the:

  - provisions relating to the conduct of interviews;

  - circumstances in which an appropriate adult should be available to assist the detainee and their statutory rights to make representation whenever the period of their detention is reviewed.

KEYNOTE

In addition to notices in English, translations should be available in Welsh, the main minority ethnic languages and the principal European languages, whenever they are likely to be helpful. Audio versions of the notice should also be made available (see Note for Guidance 3B).

Not everyone who comes into police detention will need to be informed of their rights straight away, as Code C, para. 1.8 shows (see above). However, if the information is not given at the time, it must be given as soon as practicable (i.e. when they are capable of understanding, no longer violent, or have been treated medically).

KEYNOTE

Custody officers should remember that detainees will suffer different levels of sobriety. This means that even though a person may be unfit to be interviewed for an offence, they may actually be able to understand their right to legal advice.

This will be a subjective test, and the custody officer will have to provide a rationalised decision, depending on the circumstances.

6.3 Right to have Someone Notified when Arrested

6.3.1 Legislative provisions

Section 56(1) PACE

Where a person has been arrested and is being held in custody in a police station or other premises, he shall be entitled, if he so requests, to have one friend or relative or other person who is known to him or who is likely to take an interest in his welfare told, as soon as is practicable except to the extent that delay is permitted by this section, that he has been arrested and is being detained there.

6.3.2 **Informing the detainee**

Code C, para. 5 describes this as a 'Right not to be held Incommunicado'. In other words, the detainee has a right not to be held in police custody without some other person knowing that he or she is being so held.

KEYNOTE

The person nominated must be someone who would be likely to take an interest in the detainee's welfare.

In addition to s. 56(1), under para. 5.1, if the person nominated by the detainee cannot be contacted, he or she may 'choose up to two alternatives'. If the alternative people cannot be contacted, the person in charge of detention or the investigation 'may allow further attempts until the information has been conveyed'. Note that the right conferred in s. 56(1) above may be exercised each time a detainee is moved to another police station. This means that a detainee may have the same, or another, person told that they have been moved (see Code C, para. 5.3).

KEYNOTE

If the detainee does not know anyone to contact for advice and support, custody officers may wish to contact local voluntary bodies and organisations who may offer help (see Code C, Note for Guidance 5C).

Consider the following:

Case Study

BLOOM was in custody for burglary and did not exercise his right to have someone informed of his arrest. He had been there for three hours when the custody officer received a telephone call from BLOOM'S girlfriend, asking about his welfare.

What action should the custody officer take in these circumstances?

....

The situation in the exercise above occurs quite frequently, as friends and family may be told about a person's detention. Paragraph 5.5 of the *Codes of Practice* allows for information on the suspect to be passed on, 'if the suspect agrees'. The detainee should be consulted before any information is given out, to ensure their right to privacy is protected.

However, where authorisation has been given for the detainee's rights to be delayed, information must not be given. Paragraph 5.5 specifically allows the custody officer to refuse to provide details in these circumstances. (See below for full details of delaying a detainee's rights.)

6.4 Delay in Notification of Arrest (Incommunicado)

6.4.1 Legislative provisions

Code C, Annex B, Para. 1

The exercise of the rights in s. 5 or s. 6, or both, may be delayed if the person is in police detention, as in PACE, s. 118(2), in connection with an indictable offence, has not yet been charged with an offence, and an officer of superintendent rank or above, or inspector rank or above only for the rights in s. 5, has reasonable grounds for believing their exercise will:

(i) lead to:

  • interference with, or harm to, evidence connected with an indictable offence; or

  • interference with, or physical harm to, other people; or

(ii) lead to alerting other people suspected of having committed an indictable offence but not yet arrested for it; or

(iii) hinder the recovery of property obtained in consequence of the commission of such an offence.

6.4.2 Authorisation for delay of right to notification of arrest

The authority to delay a detainee's right to have a person notified of his/her arrest derives from s. 56(2) of PACE. An officer of the rank of inspector may authorise a detained person's rights to be delayed, if he or she is in police detention for an indictable offence, which he or she has not yet been charged with. (This power was previously given to an officer of the rank of superintendent only.) (See **flow chart 4 in Appendix 1** for an easy guide.)

In order to authorise a delay to a person's rights under this section, the inspector must have reasonable grounds to believe that one of the consequences in Annex B, para. 1 above will occur, if the detainee is allowed to have someone informed of his/her detention. This section will not apply if one of the situations referred to above has already happened and it is not anticipated there will be a re-occurrence—for example where a person is seriously injured during an assault, the inspector must have reasonable grounds to believe that someone else will be seriously injured if the detainee is allowed to exercise his or her right under this section.

KEYNOTE

Note that a detainee's right to have a person notified of his/her arrest may also be delayed if the authorising officer has reasonable grounds to believe that:

- the person detained for an indictable offence has benefited from their criminal conduct (decided in accordance with Part 2 of the Proceeds of Crime Act 2002); and
- the recovery of the value of the property constituting that benefit will be hindered by the exercise of either right.

(see Code C, Annex B, para. 2)

If a delay is authorised under Annex B, the detained person must be told the reason for it, and the reason must be noted on his/her custody record as soon as practicable.

KEYNOTE

It should be noted that with the introduction of the Serious Organised Crime and Police Act 2005, and the removal of the term 'serious arrestable offence' from PACE, there is potential for an inspector to authorise a delay in notification of arrest for any indictable offence, which would include minor offences such as theft or criminal damage.

However, the *Codes of Practice* have been amended to protect the detainee's basic human rights and ensure that a delay under this section is only authorised for more serious offences. Code C, para. 5.7A states:

any delay or denial of the rights in this section should be proportionate and should last no longer than necessary.

6.4.3 Authorisation in writing as soon as practicable

An officer may give an authorisation to delay a person's rights under s. 56(2) orally or in writing but, if he/she gives it orally, the officer shall confirm it in writing as soon as is practicable (see s. 56(4)).

> **KEYNOTE**
>
> Where a detained person's rights have been delayed under this section, he or she must be permitted to exercise the right within 36 hours from the relevant time (see s. 56(3)).
>
> There may be no further delay in permitting the exercise of the right, once the reason for authorising delay ceases to exist (see s. 56(9)).

6.5 Other Entitlements

In addition to the right to have someone informed of their arrest, a detainee may also have access to writing materials, make a telephone call and receive visits. These are dealt with separately below.

6.5.1 Legislative provisions

Code C, Para. 5.6

The detainee shall be given writing materials, on request, and allowed to telephone one person for a reasonable time. Either or both of these privileges may be denied or delayed if an officer of inspector rank or above considers sending a letter or making a telephone call may result in the consequences in:

(a) Annex B, paras. 1 and 2 and the person is detained in connection with 'an indictable offence'.

(b) Annex B, paras. 8 and 9 and the person is detained under the Terrorism Act 2000.

Nothing in this paragraph permits the restriction or denial of the rights in paras. 5.1 and 6.1.

6.5.2 Telephone calls and writing materials

This issue is covered by Code C, para. 5.6 above. Custody officers often confuse this right with the one listed in s. 56(1) of PACE above (i.e. the right not to be held incommunicado). Note for Guidance 5E and para. 5.6 clarify this position, stating that the entitlement to a telephone call is an additional entitlement to the one in s. 56(1).

Writing materials or a telephone call must be given on request. However, unlike s. 56 above, there is nothing in the *Codes of Practice* which requires the detainee to be informed of this entitlement (see para. 3.1 above).

The detainee is only entitled to one telephone call under para. 5.6 above. However, custody officers often use their discretion and allow more than one call, especially when a person is in detention for a long time.

KEYNOTE

Before any letter is sent or telephone call made, the detainee must be warned that what they say may be read or listened to and may be given in evidence. A telephone call may be terminated if it is being abused.

However, this does not apply to communication with a solicitor (see Code C, para. 5.7).

6.5.3 Delaying or denying access to telephone calls and writing materials

The privileges in para. 5.6 may either be denied or delayed and there appears to be no limit as to how long they may be delayed (unlike s. 56 above, which states that a person must not be held incommunicado for longer than 36 hours from the relevant time). Effectively, this means that the right to have someone informed of the arrest may be delayed, whereas the entitlement to a telephone call or writing materials may be denied altogether. The entitlement may be denied or delayed by an inspector where the person is suspected of committing an indictable offence (this section does not include non-indictable offences, such as drink driving and some public order offences). The inspector authorising the delay under this section may only do so if he or she considers that sending a letter or making a telephone call may result in the consequences set out in Annex B of the *Codes of Practice*. These are identical to those listed in s. 56(5) of PACE (delaying notification of arrest).

KEYNOTE

Note that Code C, para. 5.7A applies to delaying or denying access to telephone calls and writing material as well as delaying notification of arrest.

Code C, para. 5.7A states:

any delay or denial of the rights in this section should be proportionate and should last no longer than necessary.

6.5.4 Visits

Under Code C, para. 5.4, the detainee may receive visits at the custody officer's discretion.

The custody officer has discretion to deny visits if:

143

- there are insufficient personnel available to supervise the visit; or
- the visit is likely to prove a possible hindrance to the investigation.

KEYNOTE

Note that consideration must be given to searching the detainee before and after a visit, even when it is supervised.

6.6 Citizens who are Foreign Nationals

6.6.1 Legislative provisions

Code C, Para. 7.1

Any citizen of an independent Commonwealth country, or national of a foreign country, including the Republic of Ireland, may communicate at any time with the appropriate High Commission, Embassy or Consulate.

The detainee must be told as soon as possible of:

- this right;
- their right, upon request, to have their High Commission, Embassy or Consulate told of their whereabouts and the grounds for their detention. The request should be acted upon as soon as practicable.

6.6.2 Custody procedure

Most force areas these days deal with an increasing number of political refugees and asylum seekers entering the country. In most cases, asylum seekers and refugees will be dealt with as 'illegal immigrants', and the Immigration Department of the Customs and Excise service will be involved in the investigation. Initially, such people will be dealt with as 'PACE prisoners', enjoying all the rights and entitlements of any other detainee.

Custody officers may have to deal with other 'illegal immigrants' who are not refugees or asylum seekers, and have merely entered the country illegally. There are specific powers of arrest under the Immigration Act 1971 to deal with all such detainees. It is likely that the Immigration Department will want to interview detainees falling in these categories to establish how they entered the country, and to establish their status (whether political or otherwise). Following this, the detainee may be served with an immigration or deportation notice, to leave the country at the next available opportunity.

144

Alternatively, political refugees may be taken to a holding centre, depending on an appeal to remain in the country.

Once a deportation order has been served on a detainee, they cease to enjoy the rights and entitlements of a PACE detainee; however,

> the provisions on conditions of detention and standards in sections 8 and 9 must be considered as the minimum standards of treatment for such detainees.
>
> (See Code C, para. 1.12)

The rights of persons from outside the United Kingdom are quite straightforward. The requirement to inform the detainee of his or her rights as soon as possible, under Code C, para. 7.1 (see **6.6.1 Legislative provisions** above), will depend on the availability of interpreters. Most forces should be familiar with the Language Line facility to assist in these matters.

Note that consular officers may visit one of their nationals in police detention and talk to them and, if required, arrange legal advice. Such visits will take place outside the hearing of a police officer (Code C, para. 7.3).

KEYNOTE

If a detainee is a citizen of a country with which a bilateral consular convention or agreement is in force requiring notification of arrest, the appropriate High Commission, Embassy or Consulate shall be informed as soon as practicable (see Code C, para. 7.2).

The requirement above is mandatory, whatever the detainee's wishes, unless the detainee is a political refugee, or is seeking asylum (in which case, consular officers should not be informed unless the detainee expressly requests it) (see Code C, para. 7.4).

The countries to which para. 7.2 apply are listed in Code C, Annex F.

6.7 Access to Legal Representation

Under Article 6 of the European Convention on Human Rights, every person has a right to a fair trial. An essential part of this right will be for the detainee to receive legal advice while in police detention and a breach of Code C is fundamental in affecting the fairness of the evidence (see *R* v *Aspinall* [1999] 2 Cr App R 115).

6.7.1 **Legislative provisions**

Code C, Para. 6.1

Unless Annex B applies, all detainees must be informed that they may at any time consult and communicate privately with a solicitor, whether in person, in writing or by telephone, and that free independent legal advice is available (see Notes 6B, 6B1, 6B2 and Note 6J).

Code C, Para. 6.4

No police officer should, at any time, do or say anything with the intention of dissuading a detainee from obtaining legal advice.

6.7.2 **Detainees to be informed of the right to consult with a solicitor**

A detainee may communicate privately with a solicitor at any time while they are in police detention (unless Annex B applies—see **6.8 Delay in access to legal advice** below). The custody officer must act without delay to secure the provision of legal advice, when it has been requested by a detainee (Code C, para. 6.5).

Once a person has requested a solicitor, this must be provided without delay; what will be considered to be without delay will be a question of fact in each case (*Whitley* v *DPP* [2003] EWHC 2512 (QB)). In *Kirkup* v *DPP* [2003] EWHC 2354 (QB), the Court considered whether a breach of Code C had occurred due to a seven-minute delay between the request and subsequent phone call to the solicitor. It was held that the delay only just gave rise to a breach of Code C, but that it was so short a period that it did not lead to the exclusion of any evidence obtained. (Note that where the delay is justified, Code C, para 1.1A may apply.)

Code C, Note for Guidance 6B contains advice for custody staff as to how solicitors should be contacted; however, with effect from 21 April 2008, the contents of Notes for Guidance 6B were superseded by Note for Guidance 6B2 in all forces in England and Wales. Legal Aid reforms have resulted in the commencement of a publicly funded telephone call centre authorised by the Legal Services Commission (LSC) to deal with calls from the police station, known as the Defence Solicitor Call Centre (DSCC).

A detainee who asks for legal advice to be paid for by himself/herself should now be given an opportunity to consult a specific solicitor or another solicitor from that solicitor's firm (as opposed to an on-call solicitor who is unknown to the detainee). If the solicitor is unavailable by these means, the detainee may choose up to two alternatives. If these attempts are unsuccessful, the custody officer has discretion to allow further attempts until a solicitor has been contacted and agrees to provide legal advice.

If the detainee does not wish to, or is unable to pay for, legal advice, then publicly funded legal advice must be accessed by telephoning the DSCC, who will determine whether legal advice should be limited to telephone advice or whether a solicitor should attend the police station. Legal advice may be given by telephone if a detainee has been:

- detained for a non-imprisonable offence;
- arrested on a bench warrant for failing to appear and being held for production before the court (except where the solicitor has clear documentary evidence available that would result in the client being released from custody);
- arrested on suspicion of driving with excess alcohol (failure to provide a specimen, driving whilst unfit/drunk in charge of a motor vehicle); or
- detained in relation to breach of police or court bail conditions.

In determining whether telephone advice is appropriate, the DSCC will consider whether:

- the police are going to carry out an interview or an identification parade;
- the detainee is eligible for assistance from an appropriate adult;
- the detainee is unable to communicate over the telephone;
- the detainee alleges serious maltreatment by the police.

It is probable that the custody officer will be involved in providing this information, however, Note for Guidance 6B is explicit in that apart from carrying out these duties, an officer must not advise the suspect about any particular firm of solicitors. Para. 6.4 above builds on this theme that police officers should do nothing to dissuade a detainee from obtaining legal advice. In *R* v *Alladice* (1988) 87 Cr App R 380, the Court of Appeal held that no matter how strongly and however justifiably the police may feel that their investigation and detection of crime are being hindered by the presence of a solicitor, they are nevertheless confined to the narrow limits imposed by Code C.

However, detainees often ask custody staff their opinion as to whether or not they should seek legal advice, or which particular firm of solicitors they should speak to. While custody officers have an active role to play in arranging legal advice for a detainee, they should avoid giving advice on such issues.

KEYNOTE

A detainee is not obliged to give reasons for declining legal advice and should not be pressed to do so.
Code C, Note for Guidance 6K

6.7.3 **Consultation to be in private**

Under Code C, Note for Guidance 6J, the detainee has a 'fundamental' right to consult with their solicitor in private and if the detainee is not allowed to consult in private, and his or her conversation is listened to, without his or her consent, the right will effectively have been denied.

If consultation is to take place by telephone, this should still be the case, provided the layout of the custody office allows this. However, Note for Guidance 6J continues that there is an expectation that such facilities will be available at all stations.

The Divisional Court found that there had not been a breach of this right in *R (on the application of La Rose)* v *Commissioner of Police of the Metropolis* [2002] Crim LR 215. The officer had been at the custody desk when the individual was consulting with a solicitor by telephone, but the court took the view that there was no evidence that the officer had listened to the conversation, which meant that there was no evidence that the applicant's rights had been interfered with.

On the other hand, the European Court of Human Rights found that there had been a breach of Article 6(3)(c), in *Brennan* v *United Kingdom* [2001] 34 EHRR 507, para. 58 Crim LR 216. In this case, an officer was present at the detainee's consultation with a solicitor (see **17.4.2 Private access to a solicitor** for the effect of this decision in relation to cases under the Terrorism Act 2000). (See also *S* v *Switzerland* [1992] 14 EHRR 670 for a similar judgment.)

It remains to be seen whether this issue will be challenged further and it would appear that the majority of custody offices do not have the facilities to allow a detainee to consult with a solicitor by telephone in private.

6.8 **Delay in Access to Legal Advice**

6.8.1 **Legislative provisions**

Code C, Annex B, Para. 1

The exercise of the rights in s. 5 or s. 6, or both, may be delayed if the person is in police detention, as in PACE, s. 118(2), in connection with an indictable offence, has not yet been charged with an offence and an officer of superintendent rank or above, or inspector rank or above only for the rights in s. 5, has reasonable grounds for believing their exercise will:

(i) lead to:

- interference with, or harm to, evidence connected with an indictable offence; or
- interference with, or physical harm to, other people; or

(ii) lead to alerting other people suspected of having committed an indictable offence but not yet arrested for it; or

(iii) hinder the recovery of property obtained in consequence of the commission of such an offence.

Code C, Annex B, Para. 5

The fact that the the grounds for delaying notification of arrest may be satisfied does not automatically mean the grounds for delaying access to legal advice will also be satisfied.

6.8.2 Authorisation for delay in access to legal advice

The authority to delay access to legal advice derives from s. 58(6) of PACE; however, unlike the authority to delay notification of arrest (see **6.4.2 Authorisation for delay of right to notification of arrest** above), only a superintendent may authorise a delay under this section. Perhaps because of the serious implications of making such a decision, this power was not given to inspectors by the most recent changes to the *Codes of Practice*. (See **flow chart 4 in Appendix 1** for an easy guide.)

It should be made clear that a decision to delay access to a solicitor will be a very rare occurrence, and only when the provisions of Annex B, para. 1 above apply. However, in certain, very restricted circumstances, it may be done. Guidance is contained in Code C, Annex B, Note B3, which states that such a delay may only occur:

> when it can be shown the suspect is capable of misleading that particular solicitor and there is more than a substantial risk that the suspect will succeed in causing information to be conveyed which will lead to one or more of the specified consequences (in Annex B).

Further guidance is contained in Annex B, para. 3, which goes on to say that the authorising officer must have reasonable grounds to believe that the solicitor the detainee wants to consult with will, 'inadvertently or otherwise', pass on a message from the detainee or act in some other way which will have any of the consequences set out in Annex B. In these circumstances, the detainee must be allowed to choose another solicitor.

The above extracts from the *Codes of Practice* more or less confirm the decision in the case of *R* v *Samuel* [1988] QB 615, where the Court of Appeal held that denying access to legal advice on the grounds that the solicitor may alert other suspects is not sufficient. The police would have to have a strongly held belief that the solicitor would unlawfully alert other suspects, or would do so inadvertently or otherwise. The court held that it would be rare for a police officer to form an opinion in either case about a solicitor.

KEYNOTE

When authorising a delay in access to legal advice, consideration must be given to the admissibility of any interview that takes place without a solicitor being present. In *R* v *Sanusi* [1992] Crim LR 43, a person from another country was denied access to a solicitor. The court excluded the defendant's confession on the grounds that his right to advice was particularly affected by his unfamiliarity with legislative procedures in this country.

The detainee will be entitled to some form of legal advice, either from the solicitor he or she has chosen, or from an alternative one. The *Codes of Practice* do not envisage that a detainee will remain entirely unrepresented while in custody (if they have requested a solicitor). Code C, Annex B, para. 5 (see **6.8.1 Legislative provisions** above), makes it clear that the decision to delay access to legal advice must be considered separately from any decision to delay notification of arrest. This would also be the case where grounds exist to deny access to writing material or telephone calls.

KEYNOTE

Note that a detainee's right to have a person notified of his/her arrest may also be delayed if the authorising officer has reasonable grounds to believe that:

- the person detained for an indictable offence has benefited from their criminal conduct (decided in accordance with Part 2 of the Proceeds of Crime Act 2002); and
- the recovery of the value of the property constituting that benefit will be hindered by the exercise of either right.

(see Code C, Annex B, para. 2)

> **KEYNOTE**
>
> The introduction of the Serious Organised Crime and Police Act 2005, and the removal of the term 'serious arrestable offence' from PACE, caused a change to the *Codes of Practice* in para. 5 (relating to delaying notification of arrest and delaying or denying access to telephone calls and writing material).
>
> Code C, para. 5.7A states:
>
> any delay or denial of the rights in this section should be proportionate and should last no longer than necessary.
>
> Curiously, no such instruction appears in para. 6 (relating to legal advice). However, since a superintendent may now delay access to legal advice for any *indictable* offence (as opposed to a serious arrestable offence), the principles set out in para. 5.7A above in respect of proportionality and necessity should be applied to avoid a breach of a person's human rights.

6.8.3 **Detainee's rights**

Some issues connected with s. 58 (delaying access to legal advice) are similar to those in s. 56 above (delaying notification of arrest):

- If delay is authorised, the detained person shall be told the reason for it, and the reason shall be noted on his custody record, as soon as is practicable;
- Where a person's access to legal advice has been delayed, he or she must be permitted to consult a solicitor within 36 hours from the relevant time (s. 58(5)).

Also, there may be no further delay in permitting the exercise of the right conferred by ss. (1) above once the reason for authorising delay ceases to subsist (s. 58(11)).

> **KEYNOTE**
>
> Some other points to note:
>
> - if a detainee wishes to see a solicitor, access may not be delayed on the grounds that they might advise the detainee not to answer questions;
> - access may not be delayed on the grounds that the solicitor was asked to attend the station by another person (unless of course s. 58(8) above applies);
> - if a solicitor has attended the station, as a result of being asked by someone else, the detainee must be told and asked to sign the custody record to signify whether they want to see the solicitor; however, this will only apply where the

solicitor has attended the custody office—it will not apply if a solicitor merely telephones the custody office (see Code C, para. 6.15).

6.9 **Interviews Without a Solicitor being Present**

Generally, when a detained person has requested legal advice, that person may not be interviewed until he or she has received advice. However, there will be occasions where it is necessary to conduct an interview before such legal advice is received.

These occasions are divided into two broad areas:

1. where, for reasons outlined below, authorisation is given to interview the detainee before he/she receives legal advice;

2. where the detainee chooses to be interviewed before he/she receives legal advice.

Interviews described in 1 above may only be authorised by a superintendent, whereas interviews described in 2 above may be authorised by an inspector. These situations will be examined separately below.

6.9.1 **Legislative provisions**

Code C, Para. 6.6

A detainee who wants legal advice may not be interviewed or continue to be interviewed until they have received such advice unless:

(a) Annex B applies;

OR

(b) An officer of superintendent or above has reasonable grounds for believing that:

(i) the consequent delay might:

- lead to interference with, or harm to, evidence connected with an offence;

- lead to interference with or physical harm to other persons;

- lead to serious loss of, or damage to, property;

- lead to alerting other people suspected of having committed an offence but not yet arrested for it;

- hinder the recovery of any property obtained in the commission of an offence.

> (ii) when a solicitor, including a duty solicitor, has been contacted and has agreed to attend, awaiting their arrival would cause an unreasonable delay to the process of the investigation.
>
> OR
>
> (c) the solicitor the detainee has nominated or selected from a list:
>
> (i) cannot be contacted; *or*
>
> (ii) has previously indicated they do not wish to be contacted; *or*
>
> (iii) having been contacted has declined to attend, and
>
> the detainee has been advised of the Duty Solicitor Scheme but has declined to ask for the duty solicitor. In these circumstances the interview may be started or continued without further delay provided an inspector has agreed to the interview proceeding.
>
> OR
>
> (d) the detainee changes their mind about wanting legal advice.
>
> In these circumstances the interview may be started or continued without delay provided that:
>
> (i) the detainee agrees to do so, in writing or on the interview record made in accordance with Code E or F; and
>
> (ii) an officer of inspector or above has inquired about the reasons for the detainee's change of mind and gives authority for the interview to proceed.

Code C, Note for Guidance 6A

In considering if para. 6.6(b) applies, the officer should, if practicable, ask the solicitor for an estimate of how long it will take to come to the station and relate this to the time detention is permitted, the time of day (i.e. whether a period of rest is imminent), and the requirements of the investigation.

If the solicitor is on their way or is about to set off immediately, it will not normally be appropriate to begin the interview before they arrive.

If it appears necessary to begin an interview before the solicitor's arrival, they should be given an indication of how long the police would be able to wait before para. 6.6(b) applies, so there is an opportunity to make arrangements for someone else to provide legal advice.

Code C, Note for Guidance 6G

Subject to the constraints of Annex B, a solicitor may advise more than one client in an investigation if they wish. Any question of a conflict of interest is for the solicitor under their professional code of conduct. If, however, waiting for a solicitor to give advice to one client may lead to unreasonable delay in interviewing another, para. 6.6(b) may apply.

6.9.2 **Superintendent's authority (urgent interviews)**

Code C, para. 6.6(a)–(b) deals with this situation (see **6.9.1 Legislative provisions** above). In keeping with s. 58 above, only a superintendent may authorise an interview in these circumstances.

Paragraph 6.6(a)–(b) is divided into three different areas:

• where Annex B applies (see s. 58 above);

• where a superintendent reasonably believes that one of the consequences in Code C, para. 6.6(b)(i) above may occur;

• where a solicitor has been contacted and there is an unreasonable delay in his/her attendance.

The requirements in Annex B are similar to those in para. 6.6(b)(i) above; however, there are two differences:

1. this paragraph extends the circumstances in which an interview may take place, without a solicitor, to when a person has been arrested for an offence; and

2. authorisation may be given where a delay is likely to lead to 'serious loss of, or damage to, property'.

In relation to para. 6.6(b)(ii) above, a superintendent may authorise the interview to proceed when a solicitor has actually been contacted, but awaiting their arrival may cause an 'unreasonable delay to the process of the investigation'. However, Code C, Note for Guidance 6A (see **6.9.1 Legislative provisions** above) reinforces that the superintendent must consider carefully any alternatives, before authorising an interview under para. 6.6(b). The power granted by para. 6.6(b) above is broad and requires a subjective test by the superintendent authorising it. They must consider carefully what would constitute 'serious loss of, or damage to, property', or 'an unreasonable delay'.

It must be remembered that the right to consult with a solicitor prior to being questioned is fundamental, and there must be a very good reason for withholding or delaying that right.

> **KEYNOTE**
>
> A detainee who has been permitted to consult a solicitor shall be entitled on re-
> quest to have the solicitor present when they are interviewed unless one of the
> exceptions in para. 6.6 applies (see Code C, para. 6.8).

> **KEYNOTE**
>
> Note also, that Article 5 of the Human Rights Act 1998 (right to liberty and secur-
> ity) may apply in these circumstances, and the authorisation must be found to be
> lawful, aimed at a legitimate objective and proportionate.

6.9.3 **Conflict of interest**

Where a solicitor intends representing more than one detained person at the
same time, the provisions of Code C, Note for Guidance 6G will apply (see
6.9.1 Legislative provisions above). It is for the solicitor to decide whether
or not a conflict of interests exists.

> **KEYNOTE**
>
> Note, however, that if the investigation is likely to suffer as a result of a solici-
> tor representing two or more clients simultaneously, para. 6.6(b) may apply, and
> a superintendent may authorise an interview to take place without the solicitor
> being present. In such circumstances, however, if would be advisable to establish
> with the solicitor whether or not another solicitor can be contacted to assist.

6.9.4 **Inspector's authority**

There are two specific occasions when an inspector may authorise an interview to take place without a solicitor being present, when the detainee has
previously requested legal advice:

- when a solicitor has been contacted and is not available;
- where the detainee has requested legal advice, and has subsequently
  changed his/her mind.

When a solicitor has been contacted and is not available

In the circumstances outlined in Code C, para. 6.6(c) (see **6.9.1 Legislative
provisions** above), the presumption is that the detainee has asked for a specific solicitor, who either cannot be contacted, or has previously stated they

do not wish to attend the station, or has declined to attend on this occasion. If any of the above circumstances apply, the detainee must be given the opportunity to speak to a duty solicitor. If the detainee is not informed of the Duty Solicitor Scheme, there is a substantial risk that any subsequent interview may be held inadmissible (see *R v Vernon* [1988] Crim LR 445 and *R v Sanusi* above).

If the detainee does elect to be represented by the duty solicitor, the interview must be delayed until they have received advice from that person (unless either Code C, para. 6.6(a) or (b) apply). On the other hand, if the detainee declines to be represented by the duty solicitor in these circumstances, the interview may take place without a solicitor being present, with the authorisation of an inspector.

The significant aspect of para. 6.6(c), and where the detainee changes their mind (see para. 6.6(d) below), is that the detainee has chosen to be interviewed without a solicitor being present. This is in contrast to para. 6.6(a) and (b) above, where the interview has been authorised by a superintendent. Where the detainee makes their own choice to be interviewed without a solicitor being present, authorisation for the interview to take place is needed from an inspector, not a superintendent.

Change of mind

Paragraph 6.6(d) is quite straightforward; the detainee may either indicate their wishes in writing, or on the interview record (whether it is conducted audibly or visually), before the interview commences. The name of the authorising inspector should be recorded either on the audible or visual record, or a written interview record.

KEYNOTE

Where a person changes their mind about wanting a solicitor, the inspector authorising the interview may do so over the telephone, provided he/she is satisfied about the detainee's reasons for changing his/her mind, and that it is proper for the interview to continue (see Code C, Note for Guidance 6I).

6.10 **Inferences from Silence**

Where authorisation has been granted under para. 6.6(a) or (b), and an interview takes place without a solicitor, adverse inferences from any silence may not be drawn, as the detainee has not had the opportunity to consult with a solicitor. This is significant, as the detainee may refuse to answer questions in such an interview, and if evidence is subsequently found by other means, the court cannot ask themselves, 'Why didn't the detainee mention this when he/she was interviewed?' Of course, if the detainee does answer questions put to him/her in these circumstances, anything said may be used in evidence (provided para. 6.6 has been applied correctly).

On the other hand, if an interview takes place, having been authorised by an inspector under para. 6.6(c) or (d), the detainee will have had the opportunity to consult with a solicitor, and adverse inferences may be drawn from any silences.

Consider the following:

Case Study

An armed robbery occurred in a building society, where £20,000 was stolen by two men. A car registered to KENT was seen driving away from the scene.

About 30 minutes after the robbery, KENT was stopped while driving his car. He was unaccompanied at the time and the car was searched—no weapon or money was found.

When he arrived at the station, KENT requested a solicitor; however, the superintendent in charge of the station authorised an interview to take place under para. 6.6 of the *Codes of Practice*, to allow the investigating officers to speak to him without delay, about the whereabouts of the stolen cash and firearm. KENT refused to come out of his cell to answer any questions.

What action could the investigating officer take in these circumstances?

....

The authority given by the superintendent, under para. 6.6(a) or (b), would allow the interview to take place in these circumstances. However, whether or not the detainee will answer questions put to him or her is another matter.

The answer to the question in the scenario may be found in Code E, para. 3.4, which states:

> If a person refuses to go into or remain in a suitable interview room and the custody officer considers, on reasonable grounds, that the interview should not be delayed the interview may, at the custody officer's discretion, be conducted in a cell using portable recording equipment or, if none is available, in writing. The reason for this shall be recorded.

Of course, the detainee may still refuse to answer questions, but the interview would, at least, be considered lawful. Note that, as discussed above, no inferences may be drawn from any silences, but if the detainee does provide information, this may be used in evidence.

6.11 **Summing Up**

What the detainee must be told

Detainees must be told they have continuing rights which may be exercised at any stage during the period in custody:

- the right to have someone informed of their arrest;
- the right to consult privately with a solicitor and that free independent advice is available;
- the right to consult these *Codes of Practice*.

(Code C, para. 3.1)

Right to have someone informed when arrested

The detainee shall be entitled, if he/she so requests, to have one friend or relative or other person who is known to him/her or who is likely to take an interest in his/her welfare told, as soon as is practicable except to the extent that delay is permitted by this section, that he/she has been arrested and is being detained there.

(s. 56(1) PACE)

Delay in notification of arrest (incommunicado)

An inspector may authorise a delay, when a person is in custody for an indictable offence where he/she has reasonable grounds for believing that telling the named person of the arrest:

(a) will lead to interference with or harm to evidence connected with an indictable offence or interference with or physical injury to other persons; *or*

(b) will lead to the alerting of other persons suspected of having committed such an offence but not yet arrested for it; *or*

(c) will hinder the recovery of any property obtained as a result of such an offence.

(Code C, Annex B)

Any delay or denial of the rights in this section should be proportionate and should last no longer than necessary.

(Code C, para. 5.7A)

Other entitlements

The detainee shall be given writing materials and allowed to telephone one person for a reasonable time. Either or both of these privileges may be denied or delayed by an inspector if he/she considers sending a letter or making a telephone call may result in the consequences in Annex B, and the person is detained in connection with an indictable offence.

(Code C, para. 5.6)

Any delay or denial of the rights in this section should be proportionate and should last no longer than necessary.

(Code C, para. 5.7A)

The detainee may receive visits at the custody officer's discretion.

(Code C, para. 5.4)

Citizens who are foreign nationals

Any citizen of an independent Commonwealth country, or national of a foreign country, including the Republic of Ireland, may communicate at any time with the appropriate High Commission, Embassy or Consulate.

(Code C, para. 7.1)

If a detainee is a citizen of a country with which a bilateral consular convention or agreement is in force requiring notification of arrest, the appropriate High Commission, Embassy or Consulate shall be informed as soon as practicable.

(Code C, para. 7.2)

Access to legal representation

A person arrested and held in custody in a police station or other premises shall be entitled, if he/she so requests, to consult a solicitor privately at any time.

Delay in access to legal advice

Delay in compliance with a request for legal advice is only permitted:

(a)   where a person is in detention for an indictable offence; and

(b)   if an officer of at least the rank of superintendent authorises it.

(s. 58(6) PACE)

An officer may only authorise delay where he/she has reasonable grounds for believing that the exercise of the right will:

(a)   lead to interference with or harm to evidence connected with an indictable offence or interference with or physical injury to other persons; *or*

(b)   lead to the alerting of other persons suspected of having committed such an offence but not yet arrested for it, *or*

(c)   hinder the recovery of any property obtained as a result of such an offence.

(s. 58(8) PACE)

Urgent interviews

A detainee who wants legal advice may not be interviewed or continue to be interviewed until they have received such advice unless:

(a)   Annex B applies, or

(b)   An officer of superintendent or above has reasonable grounds for believing that:

    (i)   the consequent delay might:

- lead to interference with, or harm to, evidence connected with an offence;
- lead to interference with or physical harm to other persons;
- lead to serious loss of, or damage to, property;
- lead to alerting other people suspected of having committed an offence but not yet arrested for it;
- hinder the recovery of any property obtained in the commission of an offence.

    (ii)   when a solicitor, including a duty solicitor, has been contacted and has agreed to attend, awaiting their arrival would cause an unreasonable delay to the process of the investigation.

(Code C, para. 6.6(a)–(b))

When a solicitor has been contacted and is not available

An inspector may authorise a detainee's interview to take place without a solicitor being present, and when the detainee has requested legal advice if:

(a)   the solicitor the detainee has nominated or selected from a list:

    (i)   cannot be contacted; *or*

    (ii)   has previously indicated they do not wish to be contacted; *or*

(iii)   having been contacted has declined to attend.

AND

The detainee has been advised of the Duty Solicitor Scheme but has declined to ask for the duty solicitor.

(Code C, para. 6.6(c))

Change of mind about legal advice

A detainee who has requested legal advice may only be interviewed without their legal representative being present if:

(i)   the detainee agrees to do so, in writing or as part of an audible or visual interview record; *and*

(ii)   an inspector has inquired about the reasons for the detainee's change of mind and gives authority for the interview to proceed.

(Code C, para. 6.6(d))

Inferences from silence

1.   Where authorisation has been granted under para. 6.6(a) or (b) above, and an interview takes place without a solicitor, adverse inferences from any silence may not be drawn, as the detainee has not had the opportunity to consult with a solicitor.

2.   If an interview takes place, having been authorised under para. 6.6(c) or (d), the detainee will have had the opportunity to consult with a solicitor, and adverse inferences may be drawn from any silences.

LOCAL PROCEDURES

1.   Does your custody office have the facility to allow a detainee to consult with their solicitor on the telephone in private?

SPACE FOR NOTES

SPACE FOR NOTES

7

Vulnerable People
and Appropriate Adults

7.1 **Introduction**

Juveniles and other 'mentally disordered or otherwise mentally vulnerable people' (referred to in this chapter as 'vulnerable detainees') have the same right to have someone informed of their arrest and to consult with a solicitor as any other person in police detention. However, both PACE and the *Codes of Practice* create additional protection for those classes of people, who may have difficulty in understanding the procedures relating to their arrest and detention. This chapter deals with the procedure laid down for custody officers under the Act and the *Codes of Practice*.

Additionally, the chapter deals with other aspects of vulnerability, for example, people who have been detained under s. 136 of the Mental Health Act 1983, and the procedure for arranging their transfer to hospitals.

This chapter also examines the specific issues relating to people who may be deaf, blind, seriously visually impaired, unable to read, or where there is doubt about their ability to speak English. Such people will require interpreters and there are measures in the *Codes of Practice* designed to protect them.

Inevitably, there are areas within this chapter that overlap with others in this book. Juveniles and vulnerable adults are dealt with in the original Act and several different paragraphs in the *Codes of Practice*. All aspects of vulnerable detainees are dealt with in one chapter. Where necessary, those subjects are cross-referred with the main chapters, including **Chapter 14—Charging Suspects, Chapter 16—Bail** and **Chapter 18—Interviewing**.

The overriding message that should be taken from this chapter is that the rights of vulnerable detainees must be protected while they are in police detention. However, by failing to comply with the Act or *Codes of Practice*, officers risk jeopardising their case, if the defence can show that the vulnerable detainee did not understand decisions made in relation to their detention, or questions being put to them in interview.

7.2 **Detained Persons—Special Groups**

Code C, para. 3(b) deals specifically with 'special groups' of detainees. According to this paragraph, special groups will fall into three broad categories:

1. where there is doubt about the detainee's ability to hear, speak, or understand English;

2. where the detainee is a juvenile;

3. where the detainee is mentally disordered or otherwise mentally vulnerable.

This chapter will deal with people in categories 2 and 3 first, and category 1 last.

7.3 **Appropriate Adults—General Issues**

The *Codes of Practice* are divided into specific issues, which affect only juvenile detainees or adult detainees requiring appropriate adults, and some general issues, which affect both classes of people. We will examine the general issues first.

7.3.1 **Legislative provisions**

Code C, Note for Guidance 1B

A person, including a parent or guardian, should not be an appropriate adult, either if they are:

- suspected of involvement in the offence;
- the victim;
- a witness;
- involved in the investigation;

  or

if they have received admissions prior to attending to act as the appropriate adult.

7.3.2 **Who may act as appropriate adult?**

Code C, para. 1.7(a) lists the people who should act as an appropriate adult for a juvenile detainee. They are as follows:

- the parent or guardian; or
- where the juvenile is in local authority or voluntary organisation care, or is otherwise being looked after under the Children Act 1989, a person representing that organisation; or
- a social worker of a local authority; or
- failing these, some other responsible adult aged 18 or over who is not a police officer or employed by the police.

The above list, and the order it appears in, has been taken from the *Codes of Practice*. Custody officers should ensure that it is followed. Care should be taken when a parent, guardian or official from the local authority is unavailable, and a decision is made to call some other responsible adult. For example, an elder sibling or relative who has a criminal record may not be suitable to act as appropriate adult. The custody officer should make sure that the person is acting in the best interests of the detainee.

KEYNOTE

The *Codes of Practice* are prescriptive in terms of who should act as an appropriate adult. It follows, therefore, that if someone has already been appointed, and it is subsequently discovered that they are involved in the case, or are not acting in the best interests of the juvenile, the person should be excluded and another appropriate adult called.

The situation in respect of adult detainees is discussed in **7.11.3 Appropriate adults for adult detainees** below.

KEYNOTE

It may be argued that the police have a duty of care towards the appropriate adult. This issue was discussed in *Leach* v *Chief Constable of Gloucestershire Constabulary* [1999] 1 All ER 215. Leach was called out to act as an appropriate adult for a murder suspect who turned out to be Fred West, and claimed that after a number of weeks of acting as appropriate adult in the case, she suffered from post-traumatic stress, psychological injury and a stroke. Because of the gruesome details of the case, a number of people involved were offered counselling (even the defence team was offered some assistance). Such help was not made available to Leach. The court held that it was foreseeable that some kind of psychological harm might arise and it would have been appropriate to have offered some counselling or trained help.

7.3.3 Who may not act as appropriate adult?

The position as to who should not act as an appropriate adult is less straightforward. Code C, Note for Guidance 1B (see **7.3.1 Legislative provisions** above), gives specific instructions in relation to this issue. It can be seen from this guidance that the *Codes of Practice* intend that the appropriate adult should remain completely independent from the investigation.

Consider the following:

Case Study

WILLIAMS works for the local youth offending team. She has contacted the police to say that she overheard a conversation between NORRIS and LARTER, who were attending a recent session at her office. WILLIAMS stated that the two juveniles were discussing a burglary they had committed the previous evening, where property had been stolen.

NORRIS and LARTER have been arrested by the police for the burglary and are in custody, awaiting the arrival of an appropriate adult for the interviews.

Would WILLIAMS be able to act as appropriate adult in these circumstances?

....

Code C, Note for Guidance 1B above would not cover the set of circumstances in the exercise, as neither of the juveniles has actually admitted the offence to the member of the youth offending team.

However, this issue is covered by Code C, Note for Guidance 1C, which states that,

> if a juvenile admits an offence to, or in the presence of a social worker or member of a youth offending team other than during the time that the person is acting as the juvenile's appropriate adult, another appropriate adult should be appointed in the interests of fairness.

Clearly the member of the youth offending team should not act as an appropriate adult in the circumstances outlined above, because, even though she has not received admissions from the juveniles (as covered by Note for Guidance 1B), the offence was discussed in her presence (as covered by Note for Guidance 1C).

KEYNOTE

Note for Guidance 1C only appears to apply to juveniles who require appropriate adults.

KEYNOTE

A solicitor acting for a detainee may not act as appropriate adult (see *R* v *Lewis* [1996] Crim LR 260). This is also confirmed in Code C, Note for Guidance 1F, which extends the provision to independent Custody Visitors (see **5.7 Independent Custody Visitors** for further information).

7.4 **Contacting the Appropriate Adult**

7.4.1 **Legislative provisions**

Code C, Para. 3.15

If the detainee is a juvenile, mentally disordered or otherwise mentally vulnerable, the custody officer must, as soon as practicable:

1. inform the appropriate adult, who in the case of a juvenile may or may not be a person responsible for their welfare, of:

    - the grounds for their detention;

    - their whereabouts;

    and

2. ask the adult to come to the police station to see the detainee.

7.4.2 **The appropriate adult's role**

In addition to contacting the appropriate adult as soon as practicable, Code C, para. 3.18 provides that the custody officer must advise the detainee that:

- the duties of the appropriate adult include giving advice and assistance;
- they can consult privately with the appropriate adult at any time.

The appropriate adult may be expected to advise the detainee on matters relating to the case. They may also be expected to advise the detainee as to their right to have someone informed of their arrest, or to consult with a solicitor.

If the appropriate adult is already at the police station, the above rights must be given in the appropriate adult's presence. However, if the appropriate adult is not at the station when the detainee is given his/her rights and entitlements, the custody officer must notify the detainee of his/her rights in the presence of the appropriate adult when he/she arrives.

See **7.6 Legal Advice** below for a full discussion on legal advice in respect of vulnerable detainees.

KEYNOTE

The custody officer must advise the appropriate adult and the detainee about the right to legal advice and record any reasons for waiving it (see Code C, Note for Guidance 1I).

7.5 **Vulnerable Detainees Held Incommunicado**

7.5.1 **Legislative provisions**

Section 57(9) PACE

The rights conferred on a child or young person to have a person responsible for their welfare informed that they are in police detention are in addition to his rights under s. 56 of the Act (right not to be held incommunicado).

7.5.2 **Juveniles held incommunicado**

The effect of s. 57(9) of PACE is that when a juvenile has been arrested and a decision has been made under s. 56 of the Act to hold him/her incommunicado, the juvenile is still entitled to be advised by an appropriate adult.

KEYNOTE

This above point is reinforced by Code C, Annex B, Note for Guidance B1, which also extends the provision to adult detainees who are mentally disordered or otherwise mentally vulnerable.

Consider the following:

Case Study

STILLMAN, aged 19, has been arrested for raping his 12-year-old sister. The custody officer considers that he is mentally vulnerable and requires an appropriate adult.

STILLMAN has asked for his parents to be informed of his arrest; however, a decision has been made to withhold his right to have someone informed of his arrest, as the investigating officer believes that some members of his family were involved in abusing the girl.

What arrangements should the custody officer make in order to ensure STILLMAN is able to consult with an appropriate adult while in custody?

....

Clearly, it would be wrong for either of STILLMAN's parents to represent him as an appropriate adult, as they may be implicated in the offence. However, the custody officer has identified that STILLMAN is mentally vulnerable, and requires an appropriate adult and he/she must comply with Code C, para.3.15, which requires an appropriate adult to be called as soon as practicable.

The Court of Appeal emphasised the importance of appropriate adults in the case of *R* v *Aspinall* [1999] 2 Cr App R 115. There it was held that an appropriate adult played a significant role in respect of a vulnerable person whose condition rendered him/her liable to provide information which was unreliable, misleading or self-incriminating. This is reinforced by Code C, Annex B, Note for Guidance B1, which is clear that even though a decision may have been made to withhold a person's rights to have someone informed of their arrest, an appropriate adult will still be required if the detainee is a juvenile or vulnerable adult.

Therefore, the custody officer should call a different appropriate adult to represent STILLMAN's interests. This may be a friend or relative, if they are not believed to be involved in the case. Some local authorities provide an appropriate adult service for adult detainees. If this facility is available, it would provide the most logical answer to the scenario above, as the appropriate adult would be completely independent from the investigation.

Custody officers should check local procedures as to whether an appropriate adult service is available for adult detainees.

7.6 **Legal Advice**

7.6.1 **Legislative provisions**

Code C, Para. 3.19

If the detainee, or appropriate adult on the detainee's behalf, asks for a solicitor to be called to give legal advice, the provisions of s. 6 apply.

Code C, Para. 6.5A

In the case of a juvenile, an appropriate adult should consider whether legal advice from a solicitor is required. If the juvenile indicates that they do not want legal advice, the appropriate adult has the right to ask for a solicitor to attend if this would be in the best interests of the person. However, the detained person cannot be forced to see the solicitor if he or she is adamant that he/she does not wish to do so.

Code C, Annex E, Note for Guidance E1

The purpose of the provision at Code C, para. 3.19 is to protect the rights of a mentally disordered or otherwise mentally vulnerable detained person who does not understand the significance of what is said to him/her. If the detained person wants to exercise the right to legal advice, the appropriate action should be taken and not delayed until the appropriate adult arrives.

7.6.2 **Decision to contact a solicitor**

Juveniles and other vulnerable people have the same right to legal advice, under s. 58 of PACE, as any other person in police detention, but are afforded additional protection by the *Codes of Practice*. In *Aspinall* (see **7.5.2 Juveniles held incommunicado** above), the court stated that the right to access to legal advice was a fundamental right under Article 6 of the European Convention on Human Rights and even greater importance had to be attached to advice for a vulnerable person.

Code C, para. 3.19 above makes it clear that either the detainee, or the appropriate adult, may request legal advice on the detainee's behalf, and that the provisions of Code C, para. 6 (right to legal advice, which is dealt with in more depth in **Chapter 6—The Detainee's Entitlements**), will apply whoever makes the request. Paragraph 3.19 applies to both juveniles and adult detainees.

Conflict often occurs where a juvenile detainee is in custody and a member of the local youth offending team is acting as appropriate adult. Most local authorities insist on legal representation even if the juvenile detainee disagrees. Paragraph 6.5A of the *Codes of Practice* clears up any ambiguity in this area. According to this paragraph, an appropriate adult acting on behalf of a juvenile detainee still has the right to ask for a solicitor to attend to represent that person; however, the detainee cannot be forced to see a solicitor if he or she does not wish to do so. In practice, most juvenile detainees will accept the advice of their appropriate adult in these circumstances. It should be noted that para. 6.5A above only applies to juvenile detainees.

KEYNOTE

Under Code C, Note for Guidance 1E, the detainee should always be given an opportunity, when an appropriate adult is called to the police station, to consult privately with a solicitor in the appropriate adult's absence if they wish.

However, it should be noted that an appropriate adult is not subject to legal privilege and there is nothing to prevent a person acting as an appropriate adult from being asked by the police to provide a statement or to be required by a court to give evidence of contact with the detainee.

Note for Guidance 1K expands on this theme, by outlining that, in principle, all citizens have a duty to help police officers to prevent crime and discover offenders. This is a civic rather than a legal duty; but when a police officer is trying to discover whether, or by whom, an offence has been committed he or she is entitled to question any person from whom he/she thinks useful information can be obtained. The entitlement to ask such questions is not altered by the fact that the person may be unwilling to assist the police.

7.7 **Interviews**

Once again, there is an overlap between this chapter and another chapter in the book. **Chapter 18—Interviewing**, deals specifically with matters affecting custody officers when it comes to interviews. However, there are certain aspects within the *Codes of Practice* relating to juveniles and other vulnerable adults.

7.7.1 **Legislative provisions**

Code C, Para. 11.1

A juvenile or mentally disordered or otherwise mentally vulnerable person must not be interviewed in the absence of the appropriate adult unless the consequent delay would be likely to:

(a) lead to:

- interference with, or harm to, evidence connected with an offence;
- interference with, or physical harm to, other people;
- serious loss of, or damage to, property;

(b) lead to alerting other people suspected of committing an offence but not yet arrested for it;

(c) hinder the recovery of property obtained in the consequence of the commission of an offence.

Code C, Para. 11.17

If an appropriate adult is present at an interview, they shall be informed that they are not expected to act simply as an observer; and the purpose of their presence is to:

- advise the person being interviewed;
- observe whether the interview is being conducted properly and fairly;
- facilitate communication with the person being interviewed.

7.7.2 Urgent interviews

Generally, juveniles or vulnerable adults may not be interviewed in the absence of an appropriate adult (Code C, para. 11.15). However, in certain circumstances, an interview may take place provided a superintendent authorises it. These interviews are known as 'urgent interviews', and should only take place in 'exceptional cases' (Code C, Annex E, Note for Guidance E3), hence the requirement for a superintendent's authorisation (and not an inspector's).

The superintendent granting the authorisation must consider that a delay to the interview may lead to one of the consequences in Code C, para. 11.1(a)–(c) above, and:

> that the interview would not significantly harm the person's physical or mental state.

The advice below is taken from Code C, Annex E, Note for Guidance E2:

> Although people who are mentally disordered or otherwise mentally vulnerable are often capable of providing reliable evidence, they may, without knowing or wanting to do so, be particularly prone in certain circumstances to provide information that may be unreliable, misleading or self-incriminating.

Code C, Annex E, Note for Guidance E2 goes on to say:

> Special care should always be taken when questioning such a person, and the appropriate adult should be involved if there is any doubt about a person's mental state or capacity. Because of the risk of unreliable evidence, it is important to obtain corroboration of any facts admitted whenever possible.

KEYNOTE

Questioning suspects may not continue in the absence of the appropriate adult once sufficient information to avert the risk has been obtained. A record shall be made of the grounds for the decision to begin the interview (see Code C, Annex E.8).

KEYNOTE

Note that there are other matters contained in the *Codes of Practice* relating to interviewing, such as Annex G—Fitness to be interviewed. This subject is dealt with in depth in **Chapter 18—Interviewing**.

7.8 **Charging the Detainee**

The issue of charging detainees is dealt with in depth in **Chapter 14—Charging Suspects**; however, there are some issues that are worth mentioning in this chapter, as there are specific provisions that apply to detainees who require appropriate adults.

7.8.1 **Legislative provisions**

Code C, Para. 16.6

The provisions of paras. 16.2–16.5 (charging suspects) must be complied with in the appropriate adult's presence if they are already at the police station. If they are not at the police station then these provisions must be complied with again in their presence when they arrive, unless the detainee has been released.

Code C, Note for Guidance 16C

There is no power under PACE to detain a person and delay paras. 16.2–16.5 to await the arrival of an appropriate adult.

7.8.2 **Presence of an appropriate adult**

When a decision has been made to charge a juvenile or vulnerable adult, the procedure for charging and cautioning must be conducted in the same way as for any detainee, except that the procedure must be completed in the presence of an appropriate adult (Code C, para. 16.1), and the appropriate adult must be given the notice of charge (Code C, para. 16.3).

You will notice from Code C, para. 16.6 above that the appropriate adult must be present when a vulnerable person is charged, 'unless the detainee has been released'.

Consider the following:

Case Study

HUDSON, aged 15, has been arrested at 0100 hrs for an offence contrary to s. 5 of the Public Order Act 1986. The custody officer has authorised her detention for charging purposes, and it is not intended to interview her. Officers have attended her home address, but there is no appropriate adult available. The local youth offending team will not attend during the night.

What action should the custody officer take, in order to charge HUDSON with the offence?

....

There may be occasions, such as in the middle of the night, when the custody officer is unable to contact an appropriate adult. The situation in the scenario above is quite common. In the past, the custody officer might have delayed charging a juvenile, or other vulnerable person until an appropriate adult was available.

The situation changed when Code C, Note for Guidance 16C was introduced into the *Codes of Practice* (see above). This paragraph shows that if there is evidence to charge a detainee, he or she should be charged without delay, even if the appropriate adult has not yet arrived.

The situation would be different if the person needed to be interviewed. This is not mentioned in Note for Guidance 16C; however, Code C, para. 11.15 deals with the subject, and such a person should not be interviewed without an appropriate adult being present unless Code C, paras. 11.1, 11.18 to 11.20 apply (see **7.7.2 Urgent interviews** above). Therefore, if the juvenile in the scenario was to be interviewed, it should be delayed until the appropriate adult arrives.

Normally, if the appropriate adult is present for an interview, and there are indications that the detainee is likely to be charged, the appropriate adult will remain available until that time.

The next consideration for the custody officer is whether or not to bail the detainee. Once again, if the person has been charged without an appropriate adult being present, should the custody officer do likewise when it comes to bail? This matter is discussed in **7.9.2 Presence of an appropriate adult** below.

KEYNOTE

Note that Code C, Note for Guidance 16C above applies to all detainees who require an appropriate adult, not just juveniles.

7.9 **Bail**

The issue of bailing suspects is dealt with in depth in **Chapter 16—Bail**; however, once again, there are specific matters relating to juveniles and vulnerable adults that should be discussed here. For example, we have discussed above that the charging of a suspect should not be delayed to await the arrival of an appropriate adult. What happens after a suspect requiring an appropriate adult is charged in accordance with Code C, Note for Guidance 16C (see **7.8.1 Legislative provisions** above)? **Chapter 16—Bail** also covers in depth the situation regarding detention of a juvenile suspect after charge.

7.9.1 **Legislative provisions**

Code C, Note for Guidance 16C

After charge, bail cannot be refused or delayed simply because an appropriate adult has not arrived, unless the absence of the appropriate adult provides the custody officer with the necessary grounds to authorise detention after charge under PACE s. 38.

Section 38(1)(b)(ii)

. . . the custody officer shall order his release from police detention, either on bail or without bail, unless—

(b) if the person is an arrested juvenile—

   (i) any of the requirements of paragraph (a) above is satisfied; *or*

   (ii) the custody officer has reasonable grounds for believing that he ought to be detained in his own interests.

7.9.2 **Presence of an appropriate adult**

It can be seen from Code C, Note for Guidance 16C above that once a juvenile or vulnerable adult has been charged, the custody officer must not delay bailing the detainee simply because there is no appropriate adult available. Note for Guidance 16C will obviously pose practical questions for custody officers. For example, returning to the scenario above, involving a 15-year-old juvenile: Would a custody officer release such a person from the custody office in the early hours of the morning to find his/her own way home? Obviously not, as the custody officer would have some duty of care for the welfare of the juvenile. So what options are available to the custody officer in these circumstances?

Note for Guidance 16C above does provide a practical solution to custody officers, depending on the circumstances. In the situation above, the custody officer may believe that there are grounds to detain the juvenile after charge, under s. 38(1)(b)(ii) of PACE (see above). Section 38(1)(b)(ii) shows that the juvenile in our scenario may be detained 'in his own interests'.

However, what if the detainee is a vulnerable adult, who has been charged and there is no appropriate adult available? Section 38(1)(a)(ii) covers this situation, where bail may be denied to a detainee when the custody officer:

> has reasonable grounds for believing that the detention of a person arrested is necessary for his/her own protection. . . .

This means that the juvenile (or vulnerable adult) could be detained at the police station for his/her own protection, but could be released on bail if an appropriate adult becomes available later.

Other options available to custody officers include taking the suspect home and bailing them in the presence of an appropriate adult, or bailing them, taking them home and handing the bail sheet to an appropriate adult.

As usual with PACE, the custody officer will have to use common sense and each case will have to be considered on its own merits. Whether or not a custody officer decides to bail a juvenile or vulnerable adult without an appropriate adult present will depend on the circumstances. He or she would have to take into account such things as the time of day (i.e. middle of the night), and the age of the suspect and their ability to understand what is being said to them (i.e. they may fail to answer their bail).

Of course, there may be grounds to keep the detainee in custody under s. 38(1)(a) of PACE, which relates to denying bail for other reasons, such as when a name and address cannot be ascertained or the detainee may fail to answer bail. These subjects are dealt with in more depth in **Chapter 16—Bail**. (Of course, if detention were necessary under that subsection, the custody officer would not need to worry about Note for Guidance 16C.)

7.10 **Specific Matters Affecting Juvenile Detainees**

7.10.1 **Legislative provisions**

Code C, Para. 1.5

If a person appears to be under 17, they shall be treated as a juvenile for the purposes of this Code in the absence of any clear evidence that they are older.

Section 57(2)

Where a child or young person is in police detention, such steps as are practical shall be taken to ascertain the person responsible for his welfare.

Section 57(5)

The person responsible for a child or young person's welfare will be:

'his parent or guardian, or any other person who has, for the time being, assumed responsibility for his welfare'.

7.10.2 **Appropriate adults for juvenile detainees**

Additional guidance as to who should act as appropriate adult for a juvenile detainee can be found in Code C, Note for Guidance 3C, which provides that if a juvenile is in local authority or voluntary organisation care but living with their parents or other adults responsible for their welfare, although there is no legal obligation to inform them, they should normally be contacted, as well as the authority or organisation, unless they are suspected of involvement with the offence concerned.

Even if the juvenile is not living with their parents, consideration should be given to informing them.

Under Code C, paras. 3.13 and 3.14, the following groups of people may be notified of a child or young person's detention:

- the parent or guardian;
- if the juvenile is in local authority or voluntary care, a person appointed by that authority or organisation;

- any other person who has, for the time being assumed responsibility for the juvenile's welfare;
- if the detainee is the subject of a court order, the person responsible for supervising or monitoring him/her (this person will normally be a member of the local authority youth offending team);
- where the juvenile is the subject of a curfew order which involves electronic tagging, the contractor responsible for the monitoring should be informed.

KEYNOTE

If a juvenile's parent is estranged from the juvenile, they should not be asked to act as the appropriate adult if the juvenile expressly and specifically objects to their presence (see Code C, Note for Guidance 1B).

Also, a parent who is unable to understand the seriousness of the detainee's position, because they are mentally vulnerable, should not act as an appropriate adult (see *R v Morse* [1991] Crim LR 195).

KEYNOTE

Note that if the parent or guardian who has attended as an appropriate adult appears to be deaf, or there is doubt about their hearing or speaking ability, an interpreter should be called, unless the detainee agrees in writing to the interview proceeding without one (see Code C, para. 13.6).

7.11 Specific Matters Affecting Vulnerable Adults

7.11.1 Legislative provisions

Code C, Note for Guidance 1G

'Mentally vulnerable' applies to any detainee who, because of their mental state or capacity, may not understand the significance of what is said, of questions or of their replies. 'Mental disorder' is defined in the Mental Health Act 1983, s. 1(2) as 'mental illness, arrested or incomplete development of mind, psychopathic disorder and any other disorder or disability of mind'.

Code C, Para. 1.4

If an officer has any suspicion, or is told in good faith, that a person of any age may be mentally disordered or otherwise mentally vulnerable, in the absence of clear evidence to dispel that suspicion, the person shall be treated as such for the purposes of this Code.

Code C, Annex E.2

In the case of a person who is mentally disordered or otherwise mentally vulnerable, 'the appropriate adult' means:

1. a relative, guardian or other person responsible for their care or custody;
2. someone experienced in dealing with mentally disordered or mentally vulnerable people but who is not a police officer or employed by the police;
3. failing these, some other responsible adult aged 18 or over who is not a police officer or employed by the police.

Code C, Note for Guidance 1D

In the case of people who are mentally disordered or otherwise mentally vulnerable, it may be more satisfactory if the appropriate adult is someone experienced or trained in their care rather than a relative lacking such qualifications. But if the detainee prefers a relative to a better qualified stranger or objects to a particular person, their wishes should, if practicable, be respected.

7.11.2 **When an appropriate adult should be called**

In most cases, police officers will not be experts on 'mental illness', or personality disorders. If there is any doubt as to a detainee's state of mind, custody officers should seek expert advice. The integrity of any interview or custody process may be called into question if the defence can show that the detainee was unable to fully understand what was being said to him or her.

The wording in Code C, para. 1.4 above should be noted. The term 'any suspicion' does not appear to leave much room for interpretation. If the custody officer or investigating officer has the slightest belief that a person is mentally disordered or otherwise mentally vulnerable, they should be treated as such.

Also, the officer may be told in good faith of a person's vulnerability. This information may come from any source, such as the detainee, a member of his/her family, or a legal representative. Wherever the information comes from, it should be acted on, and an appropriate adult called.

7.11.3 **Appropriate adults for adult detainees**

As in the case of juvenile detainees, the appropriate adult for an adult detainee should be a person who has the interests of the detainee in mind. If a member of the detainee's family cannot be contacted, most local authorities offer an appropriate adult service for vulnerable adults.

KEYNOTE

Note that the person attending as appropriate adult must not be employed by the police.

The guidance contained in Annex E.2 above, and Code C, Note for Guidance 1D, seem to suggest an order of preference, as follows:

1. a relative or guardian with previous experience or training in caring for the detainee;

2. some other person with experience or training in caring for mentally disordered or otherwise mentally vulnerable people;

3. some other responsible adult aged 18 or over, who is not employed by the police.

Ultimately, if practicable, the detainee should be consulted as to who they would prefer to act as appropriate adult on their behalf. The custody officer and interviewing officer must aim for the correct balance to ensure:

- that the detainee's rights are complied with;
- that any evidence gained is not compromised by failing to follow the *Codes of Practice.*

7.12 **Mental Health Act 1983**

7.12.1 **Legislative provisions**

Section 136 (1) & (2) Mental Health Act 1983

---

(1) If a constable finds in a place to which the public have access a person who appears to him to be suffering from mental disorder and to be in immediate need of care or control, the constable may, if he thinks it necessary to do so in the interests of that person or for the protection of other persons, remove that person to a place of safety within the meaning of section 135 above.

(2) A person removed to a place of safety under this section may be detained there for a period not exceeding 72 hours for the purpose of enabling him to be examined by a registered medical practitioner and to be interviewed by an approved social worker and of making any necessary arrangements for his treatment or care.

Code C, Para. 3.16

It is imperative that a mentally disordered or otherwise mentally vulnerable person, detained under the Mental Health Act 1983, section 136, be assessed as soon as possible. If that assessment is to take place at the police station, an approved social worker and a registered medical practitioner shall be called to the station as soon as possible in order to interview and examine the detainee. Once the detainee has been interviewed, examined and suitable arrangements made for their treatment or care, they can no longer be detained under section 136. A detainee must be immediately discharged from detention under section 136 if a registered medical practitioner, having examined them, concludes they are not mentally disordered within the meaning of the Act.

7.12.2 **Place of safety**

The power created by s. 136(1) is listed among the powers preserved by s. 26(2) of PACE; however, strictly speaking it is not a power of arrest, but a power of removal from a public place to a place of safety. Further, a person brought to the station utilising this power is not classed as being in police detention under PACE.

A place of safety is defined in s. 135(6) of the Act as:

- residential accommodation provided by a Local Social Services Authority (LSSA);

183

- a hospital (including an independent hospital);
- a police station;
- a care home for mentally disordered people; or
- any other suitable place where the occupier is willing temporarily to receive the patient.

A person removed to a place of safety under s. 136(1) above may be detained there for a period not exceeding 72 hours for the purpose of enabling him or her to be examined by an approved mental health professional and of making any necessary arrangements for his/her treatment or care (s. 136(2)).

Although police stations are listed as places of safety under s. 135(6) above, they are not always the most suitable places to detain a person suffering from a mental disorder. Home Office Circular 007/2008 (The Use of Police Stations as Places of Safety under s. 136 of the Mental Health Act 1983) states:

> It is widely recognised that a police station is not a suitable place of safety for detaining persons under section 136 of the Mental Health Act 1983, save for exceptional circumstances involving the risk or threat of serious harm posed by the person to themselves or those tasked with looking after their healthcare needs.

The Mental Health Act 1983 was updated on the 30 April 2008 by the Mental Health Act 2007 to offer a solution to the problem. A new s. 136(3) has been created, which states:

> A constable, an approved mental health professional or a person authorised by either of them for the purposes of this subsection may, before the end of the period of 72 hours mentioned in subsection (2) above, take a person detained in a place of safety under that subsection to one or more other places of safety.

The aim of this provision is to deal with the problem that, under the 1983 Act, once a person was admitted to a police cell as a place of safety, there was no power to move them to a more suitable clinical location, even for purposes of assessing their mental health treatment needs. This change should give the police, the NHS and social services greater flexibility when making arrangements for the detention of a person at a place of safety and to transfer them to a more suitable location within the 72-hour period.

Curiously, the 2008 PACE *Codes of Practice* make no mention of this new provision and Code C, Note for Guidance 9D still states:

> Wherever practicable, arrangements should be made for persons detained for assessment under s. 136 of the Mental Health Act to be taken to hospital. There is no power under that Act to transfer them from one place of safety to another place of safety for assessment.

Clearly the provisions contained in the Mental Health Act 2007 supersede Note for Guidance 9D, which is likely to be updated in the next version of the *Codes of Practice*.

Where a person has been taken from one place of a safety to another, under sub-section (3) above, they may be detained there for assessment for a period ending no later than 72 hours (s. 136(4)).

The police have further powers to detain people under s. 135 of the 1983 Act. Under this section, a constable may enter any premises, under a warrant issued by magistrates, to detain a person suspected to be suffering from a 'mental disorder' and take them to a place of safety, and to recover a person who has absconded from a place where they are being treated while an order is in place for their treatment under the Act.

Section 135 has also been amended by the Mental Health Act 2007, to allow a constable, an approved mental health professional, or a person authorised by either of them, to move a person who has been detained under this section to different place of safety under the same circumstances as in s. 136 above.

The Mental Health Act 2007 has defined 'mental disorder' as any disorder or dis-ability of the mind. Previous terms, such as 'severe mental impairment', 'mental impairment' and 'psychopathic disorder', have been removed from the 1983 Act.

7.12.3 Assessing the detainee

Code C, para. 3.16 above is clear that a person detained under s. 136 should be assessed as soon as possible and that once the detainee has been interviewed, examined and suitable arrangements made for their treatment or care, they can no longer be detained under s. 136 and should be released. A detainee should also be immediately released if a registered medical practitioner, having examined them, concludes they are not mentally disordered within the meaning of the Act. However, as usual with custody and detention, matters are not always straightforward.

Consider the following:

Case Study

SANCHEZ was arrested for assault at his home, after officers were called there. He had been in a domestic argument with his wife, and had used violence towards her. He was taken to the custody office and his detention was authorised.

While he was at the custody office, he began to exhibit bizarre behaviour by taking his clothes off and trying to harm himself. It was discovered that he had a history of psychiatric problems and the custody officer had serious concerns for his well-being.

In the meantime, SANCHEZ's wife withdrew her complaint.

Would the custody officer be able to detain SANCHEZ under the Mental Health Act 1983 in these circumstances?

The situation in the exercise occurs frequently. Assuming that there is insufficient evidence to charge SANCHEZ for an offence, what powers would the custody officer have to further detain him for assessment under the Mental Health Act 1983?

Technically, there is nothing under that Act allowing a person's detention to be converted in this way. Section 136(1) of the Act simply allows a person to be taken from a public place to a place of safety. Since he was arrested in his home, this has clearly not happened in the circumstances outlined above. There would be no power to actually arrest him under the Mental Health Act 1983 in these circumstances.

However, would it be correct for the custody officer simply to release SANCHEZ, knowing that he has psychiatric problems? The custody officer would feel some sort of duty of care to ensure that the person did not harm either himself or his wife.

The Mental Capacity Act 2005 (Commencement No. 2) Order 2007 (2007/1897) brought into force certain provisions in the Mental Capacity Act 2005 on 1 October 2007. Certain provisions of this Act have an impact on policing vulnerable people.

Section 5 of the Act provides a power to make decisions on behalf of people who lack the mental capacity to do so themselves, in connection with their care and treatment. Section 5 also provides protection from legal liability if such decisions are made in the person's best interests.

Section 6 of the Act permits restraint where the person using it believes that it is necessary to prevent harm to the person they are restraining and the restraint is a proportionate response to the likelihood and seriousness of the harm (harm is not confined to physical harm).

While restraint is allowed under this s. 6, this should not be taken as a power of arrest; therefore, officers would have to look to other legislation to deprive a person of their liberty in these circumstances, which links back to the scenario above. Baroness Hale dealt with a related matter in the case of *Seal* v *Chief Constable of South Wales Police* [2007] UKHL 31. Seal had been arrested inside his mother's home by the police for a breach of the peace—once taken outside, he was then detained under s.136(1) of the 1983 Act.

Baroness Hale commented:

If a constable finds in a place to which the public have access a person who appears to him to be suffering from mental disorder and to be in immediate need of care or control, the constable may, if he thinks it necessary to do so in the interests of that person or for the protection of other persons, remove that person to a place of safety . . .

Baroness Hale further stated:

The police may well have an answer to Mr. Seal's claim. But their case is not without difficulty. If he was 'removed' under section 136 of the Mental Health Act from his mother's home, he cannot have been 'found in a place to which the public have access'. If he was arrested in her home for a breach of the peace, and then 'removed' under Section 136 after they had taken him outside, can it be said that they 'found' him there? (To say otherwise would deprive Section 136 of much of its usefulness when an arrested person is later discovered to have a mental disorder).

The situation in the custody office is similar and essentially, the custody officer faces a choice between considering SANCHEZ's right not to be detained unlawfully, and protecting him from harming himself or others. One possible option could be to further detain the person for a common law breach of the peace, or to attempt to get the detainee examined as soon as possible. However, the answer to the situation is far from clear and if the custody officer did detain SANCHEZ, he or she might face a claim similar to the one above even if they were acting reasonably and in the detainee's interests.

While the powers created in both the Mental Health Act 1983 and the Mental Capacity Act 2005 are useful, they do not always provide answers to the practical problems that occur daily in custody offices. As a custody officer and a reviewing officer, I have authorised further detention to have the person examined in circumstances similar to the SANCHEZ scenario, making a full entry in the custody record, outlining my decision-making rationale. I would do so again in the same circumstances if it was necessary to protect individuals and the public.

7.12.4 Local procedures

Home Office Circular 007/2008 outlines that a clear and robust local policy is required for the effective and efficient multi-agency handling of persons who need to be detained at a place of safety. Without such a policy, agencies are unlikely to be able to deliver place of safety services to an acceptable good practice standard.

Good practice advice is set out in detail in Home Office Circular 17/2004 and should include:

• the local social services authority, hospitals, NHS commissioners, police forces and ambulance services ensuring that they have a clear and jointly agreed policy for use of the powers under s. 135 and s. 136, as well as the operation of agreed places of safety within their localities; and

• all professionals involved in its implementation understanding the power and its purpose, the roles and responsibilities of other people involved, and following the local policy; and

• those professionals receiving the necessary training to do so;

• providing prompt assessment and, where appropriate, admission to hospital for further assessment and/or treatment.

According to the above circular:

• the process for identification of the most appropriate place of safety to which a particular patient is removed should be clearly outlined in the local policy;

• every effort should be made to ensure that a police station is used only on an exceptional basis in cases, for example, where the person's behaviour would pose an unmanageably high risk to other patients, staff or users of a healthcare setting. It is preferable for a person thought to be suffering from mental disorder to be detained in a hospital, or other healthcare setting, where mental health services are provided (subject, of course, to any urgent physical healthcare needs they may have);

• a police station should not be assumed to be the automatic second choice if the first choice place of safety is not immediately available. Other available options, e.g. a residential care home or the home of a relative or friend of the person who is willing to accept them temporarily, should also be considered. If a police station must be used, health and social care agencies should work with the police in supporting the care and welfare of the person while in police custody and assist in arranging, where appropriate, the transfer of the patient to a more suitable place of safety;

• in identifying the most appropriate place of safety for an individual, consideration should be given to the impact that the proposed place of safety (and the journey to it) may have on the person held and the examination and interview. It should always be borne in mind that the use of a police station can give the impression that the person detained is viewed as a criminal. This will cause distress and anxiety to the person concerned and is likely to affect their co-operation with, and therefore the effectiveness of, the assessment process;

- where the police remove an individual to a place of safety it is recommended that:
  - where the place of safety will be a hospital, immediate contact is made with both the hospital and the Local Social Services Authority (LSSA) (or the people arranging Approved Mental Health Professional (AMHP) services on its behalf) by the police, and this should take place prior to arrival at the place of safety. This will allow arrangements to be made for the patient to be interviewed and examined as soon as possible. Where a warrant has been issued under s. 135, these arrangements should, wherever possible, have been made in advance.
  - where a police station is to be used as the place of safety, contact should be quickly made with the LSSA (or its AMHP service) and an appropriate doctor. This will enable the examination and interview to be commenced as quickly as possible to ensure that the person spends no longer than necessary in police custody before being released or taken to hospital. Early assessment will also allow consideration to be given to the possibility of a transfer to an alternative place of safety as soon as this is considered to be safe and appropriate in all of the circumstances.

The Department of Health has produced a revised Mental Health Code of Practice, which is in draft form at the time of writing and is due for implementation in autumn 2008. The Code of Practice will include the above guidelines. In addition, the Home Office, in co-operation with the National Custody Forum and the Chairs of the Regional Custody Network, intends providing half-yearly progress reports on implementation of these arrangements.

7.13 **Other Vulnerable Detainees**

There are certain aspects of the *Codes of Practice* that overlap once again. Code 13 deals with issues relating to people who are deaf, blind, seriously visually impaired or unable to read. Those people should be classed as 'vulnerable detainees' and are dealt with in this chapter.

7.13.1 **Legislative provisions**

Code C, Para. 3.20

If the detainee is blind, seriously visually impaired or unable to read, the custody officer shall make sure their solicitor, relative, appropriate adult or some other person likely to take an interest in them and not involved in the investigation is available to help check any documentation.

Code C, Para. 3.12

If the detainee appears deaf or there is doubt about their hearing or speaking ability or ability to understand English, and the custody officer cannot establish effective communication, the custody officer must, as soon as practicable, call an interpreter for assistance in the action under paras. 3.1–3.5.

Code C, Para. 13.4

In the case of a person making a statement to a police officer or other police staff other than in English:

(a)   the interpreter shall record the statement in the language it is made;

(b)   the person shall be invited to sign it;

an official English translation shall be made in due course.

Code C, Para. 13.9

The interpreter may not be a police officer or a support staff member when interpretation is needed for the purposes of obtaining legal advice.

In all other cases a police officer or a support staff member may only interpret if the detainee and the appropriate adult, if applicable, give their agreement in writing or if the interview is audibly recorded or visually recorded as in Code E or F.

7.13.2 **Appropriate adults**

Code C, para. 3.20 ensures that people who may have difficulties in communicating are protected by the presence of an appropriate adult. This paragraph ensures that detainees are given assistance to understand the documentary issues that arise during the custody administrative procedures. This paragraph also allows for the appropriate adult to sign for any documentation, if the detainee prefers.

7.13.3 **Interpreters**

Chief Officers are responsible for making sure appropriate arrangements are in place for provision of suitably qualified interpreters (Code C, para. 13.1). The custody officer or interviewing officer has a duty to make sure that the detained person and the interpreter are able to communicate effectively and understand each other. It may be necessary to have more than one interpreter to allow the detained person to understand and be understood (see *R* v *West London Youth Court, ex parte J* [2000] 1 All ER 823).

Under Code C, para. 13.2, unless paras. 11.1, 11.18 to 11.20 apply (provisions relating to urgent interviews), a person must not be interviewed in the absence of a person capable of interpreting if:

1. they have difficulty understanding English;
2. the interviewer cannot speak the person's own language;
3. the person wants an interpreter present.

The above provisions also apply if a person appears to be deaf or there is doubt about their hearing or speaking ability (Code C, para. 13.5).

> **KEYNOTE**
>
> All reasonable attempts should be made to make the detainee understand that interpreters will be provided at public expense (Code C, para. 13.8).

Initially, the interpreter's duty will be to assist with informing a person of their rights. Later, the interpreter may be expected to assist the detainee in consulting with a legal representative and interview within the custody office and may later be required for court hearings. However, this may cause problems in relation to the interpreter's independence, an issue that was examined in the case of *Bozkurt* v *Thames Magistrates' Court* [2001] EWHC 400 (Admin).

In this case, an interpreter was called out to interpret for a station breath test procedure in a drink-drive case. The police arranged for the interpreter to attend court and the interpreter translated for the defendant while he took advice from his solicitor. The interpreter failed to inform the solicitor that he had translated for the drink-drive procedure at the police station. The court held that in these circumstances it would have been preferable for a different interpreter to be used and that the interpreter is there for the benefit of the detained person and should not be considered to be part of the prosecution team.

7.13.4 Interview procedures

The procedures relating to interpreters apply when an officer is either interviewing a suspect or taking a statement. When taking a witness statement, Code C, para. 13.4 above applies.

When an officer is interviewing a suspect, he or she must follow the procedures laid out in Code C, para. 13.3. These are outlined below:

- the interviewer shall make sure the interpreter makes a note of the interview time in the person's language;
- the interviewer should allow sufficient time for the interpreter to note each question and answer after each is put, given, and interpreted;
- the person should be allowed to read the record or have it read and sign it as correct or indicate the respects in which they consider it inaccurate;
- if the interview is audibly recorded or visually recorded, the arrangements in Code E or F apply (Codes of Practice for recording interviews either audibly or visually).

KEYNOTE

Note that when the custody officer cannot establish effective communication with a person charged with an offence, who appears deaf or there is doubt about their ability to hear, speak or to understand English, arrangements must be made as soon as practicable for an interpreter to explain the offence and any other information given by the custody officer (see Code C, para. 13.10).

7.13.5 **Who may act as an interpreter?**

Paragraph 13.1 of the *Codes of Practice* requires that, whenever possible, interpreters are drawn from the National Register of Public Service Interpreters (NRPSI) or the Council for the Advancement of Communication with Deaf People (CACDP) Directory of British Sign Language/English Interpreters. Home Office Circular 17/2006 (Use of Interpreters within the Criminal Justice System) advised that care should be taken when using interpreters not registered with the above bodies, in case the person fails to meet the required standards in terms of academic qualifications and proven experience of interpreting within the criminal justice system and professional accountability.

The Circular recommends that an interpreter's identity should be checked on arrival, both to ensure that the person arriving for the assignment is the person who has been contracted for that assignment, and therefore has the skills and experience to carry out the task, and also to assist in confirming that relevant checks have been conducted on that person. NRPSI- and CACDP-registered interpreters are issued with photo-identity cards and should be in possession of them. Registered interpreters should have a standard or enhanced Criminal Records Bureau (CRB) disclosure certificate; and agencies are strongly recommended to ask any interpreters they employ whether they have a CRB disclosure certificate, and if they do, to ask to see it.

In cases where interpreters are not registered, consideration should be given to the security clearance issue—especially in cases where high standards of security clearance are required. In these circumstances, agencies are advised to undertake their own additional checks.

NRPSI interpreters have their own Disciplinary Framework and Code of Conduct, which can be found at <http://www.nrpsi.co.uk/publications>. The site also contains guidelines and good practice for public service officers working with interpreters before, during and after interviews.

Home Office Circular 17/2006 also issued guidance on the use of telephone interpreting, which is summarised below:

- telephone interpreting is suitable only for brief and straightforward communications, for example, arranging appointments or handling front-desk enquiries (which could include booking in at the custody office) at police stations. It is not appropriate for use in evidential procedures;
- it may be used in cases (e.g. for procedures under the Road Traffic Act 1988) where it is not possible to secure the attendance of a face-to-face interpreter within a reasonable amount of time, and the matter is time-critical (i.e. there is a risk that evidence will degrade). If telephone interpreting is used, the interpreter should be UK based and drawn from the NRPSI;
- in cases where there is no alternative to using a non-UK-based telephone interpreter, care should be taken to ensure that they are suitably qualified and subject to codes of conduct and good practice;
- in all cases where telephone interpreting is used, audio-recordings of both ends of the conversation should be made via, for example, a speakerphone.

Unlike the rules relating to appropriate adults, dealt with earlier in this chapter, police personnel may, in some circumstances, act as an interpreter. Code C, para. 13.9 above permits this use only when the interview is audibly recorded or visually recorded or the detainee (and appropriate adult if applicable) agree in writing (however, see above in relation to appropriate qualifications).

If the interview is not recorded electronically, police personnel may still act as an interpreter if the detainee agrees in writing. However, care should be taken, as the defence may challenge the accuracy of the interpretation.

KEYNOTE

If the detainee cannot communicate with the solicitor because of language, hearing or speech difficulties, an interpreter must be called (see Code C, para. 13.9).

The reason for this is obvious: if a police officer were to act as an interpreter when the detainee was receiving legal advice, the consultation could not be deemed to be in private.

7.14 **Summing Up**

Who may not act as appropriate adult?

A person, including a parent or guardian, should not be an appropriate adult, either if they are:

- suspected of involvement in the offence;
- the victim;
- a witness;
- involved in the investigation;

or

if they have received admissions prior to attending to act as the appropriate adult.

(Code C, Note for Guidance 1B)

Contacting the appropriate adult

The custody officer must, as soon as practicable, inform the appropriate adult of the grounds for the person's detention, their whereabouts and ask the adult to come to the police station to see the detainee.

(Code C, para. 3.15)

Vulnerable detainees held incommunicado

A child or young person has the right to have a person responsible for their welfare informed that they are in police detention in addition to his/her rights under section 56 of the Act (right not to be held incommunicado).

(s. 57(9), PACE)

Legal Advice

Legal advice should be arranged if either the detainee makes the request, or the appropriate adult does so, on the detainee's behalf.

(Code C, para. 3.19)

However, a juvenile detainee cannot be forced to see a solicitor if he or she does not wish to do so.

(Code C, para. 6.5A)

Interviews

A juvenile or mentally disordered or otherwise mentally vulnerable person must not be interviewed in the absence of the appropriate adult unless the provisions of Annex B apply.

(Code C, para. 11.1)

Charging the detainee

The detainee must be charged in the appropriate adult's presence if they are already at the police station. If they are not at the police station then these provisions must be complied with again in their presence when they arrive unless the detainee has been released.

(Code C, para. 16.6)

There is no power under PACE to detain a person and delay charging them, to await the arrival of an appropriate adult.

(Code C, Note for Guidance 16C)

Bail

After charge, bail cannot be refused or delayed, simply because an appropriate adult has not arrived, unless the absence of the appropriate adult provides the custody officer with the necessary grounds to authorise detention after charge under PACE section 38.

(Code C, Note for Guidance 16C)

Appropriate adults for juvenile detainees

The person responsible for a child or young person's welfare will be:

'his/her parent or guardian, or any other person who has, for the time being, assumed responsibility for his/her welfare'.

(s. 57(5) PACE).

Specific matters affecting vulnerable adults

If an officer has any suspicion, or is told in good faith, that a person of any age may be mentally disordered or otherwise mentally vulnerable, in the absence of clear evidence to dispel that suspicion, the person shall be treated as such.

(Code C, para. 1.4)

In the case of a person who is mentally disordered or otherwise mentally vulnerable, 'the appropriate adult' means:

1.   a relative, guardian or other person responsible for their care or custody;

2.   someone experienced in dealing with mentally disordered or mentally vulnerable people but who is not a police officer or employed by the police;

3.   failing these, some other responsible adult aged 18 or over who is not a police officer or employed by the police.

(Code C, Annex E.2)

The Mental Health Act 1983

A person removed to a place of safety under the Act may be detained there for a period not exceeding 72 hours.

(s. 136(2) Mental Health Act 1983)

A mentally disordered or otherwise mentally vulnerable person, detained under the Mental Health Act 1983, s. 136, must be assessed as soon as possible.

(Code C, para. 3.16)

A constable, an approved mental health professional or a person authorised by either of them for the purposes of this subsection may, before the end of the period of 72 hours mentioned in subsection (2) above, take a person detained in a place of safety under that subsection to one or more other places of safety.

(s. 136(3) Mental Health Act 1983)

Where a person has been taken from one place of safety to another, under subsection (3) above, they may be detained there for assessment for a period ending no later than 72 hours.

(s. 136(4) Mental Health Act 1983)

Once the detainee has been interviewed, examined and suitable arrangements made for their treatment or care, they can no longer be detained under s. 136.

(Code C, para. 3.16)

A detainee must be immediately discharged from detention under s. 136 if a registered medical practitioner, having examined them, concludes they are not mentally disordered.

(Code C, para. 3.16)

Wherever practicable, arrangements should be made for persons detained for assessment under s. 136 of the Mental Health Act to be taken to hospital (in preference to the police station).

(Code C, Note for Guidance 9D)

Interpreters

- If the detainee appears deaf or there is doubt about their hearing or speaking ability or ability to understand English, and the custody officer cannot establish effective communication, the custody officer must, as soon as practicable, call an interpreter.

(Code C, para. 3.12)

- Police officers or civilian support staff may only interpret if the detainee and the appropriate adult, if applicable, give their agreement in writing or if the interview is audibly recorded or visually recorded.

(Code C, para. 3.19)

- Police officers or civilian support staff may not interpret when the detainee is consulting with their legal representative.

(Code C, para. 3.12)

LOCAL PROCEDURES

1. Does your force have a call-out procedure for vulnerable adults, who require an appropriate adult?
2. Does the local authority in your area insist on a juvenile detainee being represented by a solicitor?
3. Does your force have a local arrangement with a secure hospital, allowing mentally vulnerable people to be taken straight there?
4. Does your force make use of the 'Language Line' facility, or do you have some other method of contacting an interpreter?
5. Does your force have a dedicated call-out list for interpreters?
6. Does your force have a clear and robust local policy, required by Home Office Circular 007/2008, for the effective and efficient multi-agency handling of persons who need to be detained at a place of safety?

SPACE FOR NOTES

SPACE FOR NOTES

Dealing with Property and Searching

8.1 **Introduction**

This chapter concentrates mainly on ss. 54 and 55 of the Police and Criminal Evidence Act 1984, and Code C, para. 4 of the *Codes of Practice*. This part of the Act deals with three areas:

1. Recording detainees' property
2. Seizing detainees' property
3. Searching detainees

It will be necessary in this chapter to refer to both the Act and the *Codes of Practice*, in order to clarify this piece of legislation. The intention of this chapter is to simplify the duties given to custody officers in relation to detained persons' property and searching.

The first part of s. 54 of PACE deals with the requirement to ascertain and record a detainee's property. The Criminal Justice Act 2003, Part 1, amended s. 54, allowing the custody officer to choose what he/she records in relation to a detainee's property.

The second part of s. 54 provides custody officers with powers to seize property, including clothes and personal effects from detainees in certain circumstances (s. 54(3)). Further guidance will be given on the extent to which officers may search, in order to seize property. The chapter will cover both strip searches, and intimate searches, under s. 55 of the Act.

From the 1 January 2006, s. 5 of the Drugs Act 2005 inserted s. 55A into the Police and Criminal Evidence Act 1984, which enables a police officer to authorise an x-ray or ultrasound scan of a person who is arrested for an offence and who is suspected of swallowing a Class A drug, which he or she had in his/her possession with intent to supply or to export unlawfully.

Further, s. 8 of the Drugs Act 2005 inserted s. 152(1A) into the Criminal Justice Act 1988, enabling the police to apply to the magistrates' court to commit a person charged with either possession of a controlled drug or a drug trafficking offence to custody for a period of up to 192 hours (8 days). Home Office Circular 55/2005 outlines the procedures that will apply to such a remand in custody—these are described in this chapter.

It should be noted that under the Police Reform Act 2002, detention officers have the same powers to conduct searches under PACE as a constable. See **Chapter 1—The Role of the Custody Officer** for a full breakdown of the powers given to detention officers.

The Anti-Terrorism, Crime and Security Act 2001 inserted s. 54A and s. 64A into PACE, allowing detainees to be searched and photographed, to establish their identities. These matters are dealt with in depth in **Chapter 12—Identification and Samples**.

Other powers exist to search persons in places to which the public has access, under s. 1 of the Police and Criminal Evidence Act 1984 (stop and search), but these powers are not dealt with in this book.

Human Rights Act 1998

Readers are reminded of the need to comply with the Human Rights Act 1998. However, in relation to searching persons in custody, custody officers may be presented with a double-edged sword:

- Article 1 of the 1st Protocol states: 'Every natural or legal person is entitled to the peaceful enjoyment of his possessions'. Custody officers will require a 'lawful' reason for seizing and retaining a detained person's possessions.

- Article 2 of the Convention states: 'Everyone's right to life shall be protected by law'. Under this article, the State has a positive duty to protect life. This duty may well include the removal of articles from detainees, which they could use in order to kill themselves or others whilst in custody.

- Article 3 of the Convention states that, 'No-one shall be subjected to torture or to inhuman or degrading treatment or punishment.' This Article may have effect in relation to both intimate searches and the removal of clothing from detainees (the issue of providing alternative clothing is dealt with in more depth in **Chapter 5—Conditions of Detention**).

The police have a duty to rationalise their actions and show that it was necessary, proportional and legal to conduct an intimate search, or remove a detained person's item of property, or indeed allow them to retain their property. It is important to realise that even if property is correctly seized under PACE, but is subsequently retained unnecessarily, this would be unlawful and could lead to a claim for damages (*Martin* v *Chief Constable of Nottingham*, 29 October 1999, unreported (CA)).

8.2 **Recording Property**

8.2.1 **Legislative provisions**

Code C, Para. 4.1

The custody officer is responsible for:

(a)   ascertaining what property a detainee:

    (i)   has with them when they come to the police station, whether on:

- arrest or re-detention on answering to bail;
- commitment to prison custody on the order or sentence of a court;
- lodgement at the police station with a view to their production in court from prison custody;
- transfer from detention at another station or hospital;

- detention under the Mental Health Act 1983, s. 135 or 136;
- remand into police custody on the authority of a court;

(ii) might have acquired for an unlawful or harmful purpose while in custody;

(b) the safekeeping of any property taken from a detainee which remains at the police station.

Code C, Para. 4.4

It is a matter for the custody officer to determine whether a record should be made of the property a detained person has with him or had taken from him on arrest. Any record made is not required to be kept as part of the custody record but the custody record should be noted as to where such a record exists. Whenever a record is made, the detainee shall be allowed to check and sign the record of property as correct. Any refusal to sign shall be recorded.

Code C, Note for Guidance 4A

Section 54(1) of PACE and para. 4.1 require a detained person to be searched where it is clear that the custody officer will have continuing duties in relation to that person or where that detainee's behaviour or offence makes an inventory appropriate.

They do not require every detained person to be searched; e.g. if it is clear a person will only be detained for a short period and is not to be placed in a cell, the custody officer may decide not to search them. In such a case the custody record will be endorsed 'not searched', para. 4 will not apply, and the detainee will be invited to sign the entry. If the detainee refuses, the custody officer will be obliged to ascertain what property they have in accordance with para. 4.1.

8.2.2 Ascertaining and recording property

Code C, para. 4.1 above makes the custody officer responsible for ascertaining what property a detainee has with him/her, and for its safekeeping. The paragraph appears to cover all occasions where a person has been arrested and brought before the custody officer or is detained there as a result of an order from the court.

Previously, under s. 54 of PACE, the custody officer was required to ascertain and record or cause to be recorded everything which a detained person had with him/her. However, the Criminal Justice Act 2003, Part 1, amended this section, so that the custody officer has been given a choice. He or she still has an obligation to ascertain the property the detainee has, but now has the option not to record all of the property. If a record is made of any property the detainee has with him/her, the custody officer also has a choice as to where such a record is made. By virtue of s. 8 of the Criminal Justice Act 2003, the *Codes of Practice* were amended to reflect this change.

Unfortunately, PACE gives no specific guidance as to what should not be recorded in relation to property; however, if, for example, an arrested person has a suitcase full of clothes, the custody officer could record 'suitcase and clothes' on the custody record. Similarly, a person may have a 'handbag and contents' with them.

Custody officers will be keen to protect themselves against allegations of theft, which are sometimes made by detainees. As such, they may still be advised to record valuable items the detainee has with them as part of the custody record. Fortunately, many custody offices are equipped with CCTV cameras, which should have reduced such complaints.

KEYNOTE

What if the custody officer makes the decision not to record property, but the detainee asks for some record to be made? This situation is not covered specifically in the Act, but common sense would suggest that the custody officer should record property in these circumstances, to avoid any allegations by the detainee.

It can be seen from Note for Guidance 4A above that if the custody officer determines that he/she will not have continuing duties in relation to the detainee, their property need not be recorded. An example could be a person who has answered bail only to be charged, who will not be taken to a cell. In such a case, the custody record will be endorsed 'not searched'.

This point is reinforced by the case of *Brazil* v *Chief Constable of Surrey* [1983] 3 ALL ER 537 (QB). In this case, it was decided that even though force standing orders stated that all detained persons should be searched, this did not provide the custody officer with the automatic right to do so.

The detained person should be invited to sign the custody record when they have not been searched. However, if a person refuses to sign, the custody officer will be obliged to ascertain what property he or she has with him or her, in accordance with para. 4.1 (and s. 54(1)).

8.3 **Seizing Property**

8.3.1 **Legislative provisions**

Section 54(4)

Clothes and personal effects may only be seized if the custody officer—

(a) believes that the person from whom they are seized may use them—

    (i) to cause physical injury to himself or any other person;

    (ii) to damage property;

    (iii) to interfere with evidence; or

    (iv) to assist him to escape;

    or

(b) has reasonable grounds for believing that they may be evidence relating to an offence.

Code C, Para. 4.3

Personal effects are those items which a person may lawfully need or use or refer to while in detention but do not include cash and other items of value.

8.3.2 **What may be seized?**

At the same time as ascertaining and recording property, the custody officer will need to decide which items of property may be retained by the detainee and which should be seized, under s. 54(4) above.

Under s. 54(3), a custody officer may seize and retain any item of property a person has with them, when they have been arrested and detained. However, s. 54(4) makes an exception in the case of a detained person's clothes and personal effects. Section 54(4) only allows this category of property to be seized in certain circumstances. As with s. 54(1), we have to look at both PACE and the *Codes of Practice* to try to make sense of s. 54(4). We should examine the main elements of s. 54(4) separately:

• most of the time, it will be obvious to the custody officer when a person has an item with them which may harm another person, cause damage or assist with their escape (s. 54(4)(a)(i), (ii) & (iv));

- allowing a detainee to keep a mobile phone in the cell may assist them with interfering with evidence. Therefore, it will be easy to justify seizing personal effects in these circumstances (s. 54(4)(a)(iii));
- however, a person could cause physical injury to themselves with almost any item of clothing or personal effect (s. 54(4)(a)(i)).

The custody officer should conduct a risk assessment in respect of every detained person, to assess their vulnerability to self-harm (risk assessments are covered in more depth in **Chapter 3—Safer Detention**).

The most common reason for removing clothing is when the custody officer believes the detainee may use the item to cause harm to themselves (such as belts, shoe laces or even trousers and shirts). This is permissible under s. 54(4)(a)(i) above.

KEYNOTE

If it is necessary to remove a person's clothes, replacement clothing of a reasonable standard of comfort and cleanliness shall be provided. (Most custody offices are equipped with 'paper suits' or 'rip suits', which tear if a detainee tries to use them as a ligature.)

A person may not be interviewed unless adequate clothing has been offered to him/her (Code C, para. 8.5, see **Chapter 5—Conditions of Detention**).

There is no requirement to routinely record items of clothing worn by the detained person, unless withheld by the custody officer for any of the above reasons (see Code C, Note for Guidance 4C).

The custody officer will often be guided by the arresting officer as to whether a detainee is in possession of property which is believed to be evidence relating to an offence. However, the confiscation of property is not restricted to the offence for which the detainee has been arrested (e.g. a person may be in possession of a stolen credit card, or drugs).

Clothing may also be removed for evidential purposes, normally to be retained for forensic reasons (such as blood stains, fibres and shoe casts). This is also permissible under s. 54(4)(b) above.

KEYNOTE

If property has been seized from a third party in the course of the investigation, the property can only be retained for so long as it is necessary in accordance with s. 22(1) PACE (constable's power to seize anything which is on the premises if he has reasonable grounds to believe that it has been obtained in consequence

---

of the commission of an offence, or that it is evidence in relation to an offence); even if it might be needed for another matter, it should be returned to the third party unless there was an additional power to seize the item (see *Settelen* v *Metropolitan Police Commissioner* [2004] EWHC 2171 (Ch)).

8.3.3 **Personal effects**

It will be obvious to the custody officer what an item of clothing is; however, personal effects are given their own definition under Code C, para. 4.3 above. Unfortunately, this definition does not provide instant clarification of 'personal effects'. However, they could include items such as diaries, books, newspapers, letters etc.

When it comes to seizing cash and items of value, matters are not quite so clear. Code C, para. 4.3 above states specifically that cash and items of value do not amount to personal effects, and are therefore not covered by s. 54(4) above. If this is the case, what right does a custody officer have to seize such items? Neither PACE, nor the *Codes of Practice*, actually states that cash and other items of value may be seized by the custody officer. On the other hand, they do not state that such items may not be seized. The assumption, therefore, is that cash and other items of value may be seized by the custody officer.

Since this area is unclear in PACE and the *Codes of Practice*, custody officers will have to rationalise why such items are seized. Usually, valuable items are taken for 'safekeeping', which offers protection to custody staff from allegations by detainees of theft of their property. Many custody offices have CCTV installed in the reception area, offering additional protection. If necessary, cash and jewellery may also be seized if the custody officer considers that the detainee may use them to self-harm (i.e. swallowing coins or necklaces). The custody officer should be able to justify the decision to seize property, whatever it is, and should consult their force policy if unsure.

KEYNOTE

There is no requirement to record on the custody record property in possession of the person on arrest if, by virtue of its nature, quantity or size, it is not practicable to remove it to the police station (see Code C, Note for Guidance 4B). (This could include a vehicle, where the detained person has been arrested for a positive breath test.)

8.3.4 **Standard of belief**

Under s. 54(4)(a), a custody officer must believe that a person may use their clothing or personal effects to do one of the four things listed above. Whereas under s. 54(4)(b), a custody officer must have reasonable grounds for believing that the property may be evidence relating to an offence. The standard for the custody officer's belief would appear to be less demanding under s. 54(4)(a) than it is under s. 54(4)(b).

Custody officers may be accused of 'oppressive' confiscation of property, if they do not apply the above standards of belief on every occasion that clothing or personal effects are seized. This matter was referred to in the Introduction to this chapter, but is worth repeating here. Protocol 1, Article 1 to the Convention states: 'Every natural or legal person is entitled to the peaceful enjoyment of his possessions.' Custody officers will require a 'lawful' reason for seizing and retaining a detained person's possessions.

> **KEYNOTE**
>
> Under s. 54(5), the detainee must be told why an item of property was seized, unless he/she is:
>
> (a) violent or likely to become violent; or
>
> (b) incapable of understanding what is said to him/her.

8.4 **Searching Detainees**

8.4.1 **Legislative provisions**

Section 54(6)

Subject to s. 54(7) below, a person may be searched if the custody officer considers it necessary to enable him to carry out his duty under s. 54(1) above and to the extent that the custody officer considers it necessary for that purpose.

8.4.2 **Power to search**

Section 54(6) of the Act deals with the power to authorise the search of a detainee. This power enables a custody officer to carry out his/her duty under s. 54(1), to ascertain and record detained persons' property. Subsection (7) provides the power to conduct an intimate search and is dealt with in more detail below (see **8.8 Intimate Search**).

8.4.3 Reasonable force

Searching officers may use reasonable force, if necessary, to exercise the above power (see s. 117, PACE).

KEYNOTE

Note that the power to search under s. 54 above is extended to a detention officer, who has been designated under para. 26 of the Police Reform Act 2002. A detention officer may also use reasonable force, if necessary, to conduct a search.

8.4.4 Continuing responsibility to search

Custody officers will have a continuing responsibility to monitor a detained person's property while they are in custody. This will include the safekeeping of any property which is taken from him/her and which remains at the police station, and any property he or she might have acquired for an unlawful or harmful purpose while in custody (see Code C, para. 4.1).

The custody officer may also allow the detainee to receive visits while they are in custody. It is essential for the safety of the detainee and custody staff that the detainee is searched following a visit. Many items, such as weapons, drugs and cigarette lighters may be smuggled in during visits and passed on to detainees.

Other ways of avoiding problems are to ensure that all visits are supervised and by searching cells and detention rooms at regular intervals. Some custody offices have secure rooms with partitions so that items cannot be passed to detainees.

Remember that if there is any doubt, the custody officer has the discretion to deny visits if they cannot be supervised properly, or the visit may hinder the investigation (see Code C, Note for Guidance 5B).

KEYNOTE

Detainees often receive food parcels from friends and members of their family, or fresh clothes are brought in for those likely to be in custody for some time. First, the custody officer has the duty to record such property on the custody record.

Secondly, anything brought into the custody office in this manner must be searched in order to avoid the detained person from coming into possession of unlawful or harmful items. This is specifically catered for in Code C, Note for Guidance 8A (see **Chapter 5—Conditions of Detention**).

8.5 **The Extent of the Search**

The extent of the search will be determined by the custody officer on the basis of what he/she honestly believes is necessary in order to comply with his/her duties under s. 54(1). It may be important to consider cultural issues that might affect the detained person, for instance would it be necessary and justifiable to search a Sikh's turban (see *Brazil* v *Chief Constable of Surrey* [1983] 3 ALL ER 537 (QB))? Once again, the custody officer will need to conduct a risk assessment on each detainee before making their decision. Custody officers will be assisted in their decision by such things as:

- previous knowledge of the detainee;
- warning signals on PNC or custody computers;
- advice from the arresting officer;
- the offence for which the detainee has been arrested;
- medical questionnaires;
- metal detectors, which are often used to identify sharp objects.

Once the custody officer has considered the above issues, and he or she has determined that a search is necessary, one of the following types of search may take place:

1. routine search;
2. strip search;
3. intimate search.

8.6 **'Routine' Search**

The majority of people held in police detention will be subjected to some kind of search before being placed in a cell. In most of these cases, the detainees will require nothing more than an ordinary 'pat down' search. They will ordinarily be asked to turn out their pockets and the search will not involve removing more than outer clothing, or examining orifices.

This type of search may be authorised by the custody officer.

8.7 **'Strip Search'**

8.7.1 **Legislative provisions**

Code C, Annex A, Para. 9

A strip search is a search involving the removal of more than outer clothing. In this code, outer clothing includes shoes and socks.

Code C, Annex A, Para. 10

A strip search may take place only if it is considered necessary to remove an article which a person would not be allowed to keep and an officer reasonably considers that the person might have concealed such an article.

8.7.2 **What is a 'strip search'?**

Strip searches are not actually defined in the Police and Criminal Evidence Act 1984. However, the definition can be found in Code C, Annex A, para. 9 of the *Codes of Practice* above.

8.7.3 **Authorisation to conduct a strip search**

A custody officer may authorise a strip search, and the power to do so comes from two sources:

(a)   s. 54(6) of the Act allows a search to be conducted to the extent that the custody officer considers necessary for that purpose (provided he or she is satisfied that s. 54(1) and (4) apply).

(b)   Code C, Annex A, para. 10 above provides further guidance.

Paragraph 10 does not identify the types of articles which a person would not be allowed to keep; however, since s. 54(3) of the Act allows a custody officer to seize any article a person has with him/her (subject to s. 54(4)), this paragraph will apply to any item of property.

The belief that a person has concealed an article must be reasonably held. This belief may be as a result of:

• information from the arresting officer;
• information from the detained person;

- prior information that the custody officer has (i.e. PNC or custody computer checks);
- the offence for which the person has been arrested.

The custody officer must consider carefully all of the above information before justifying the authorisation of a strip search. He or she must also consider whether or not the article he or she is seeking may be recovered by other means (such as asking the detainee).

KEYNOTE

It must be remembered that strip searches must not be routinely carried out where there is no reason to consider that articles have been concealed (see Code C, Annex A, para. 10).

8.7.4 Conduct of strip searches

Further guidance as to the conduct of strip searches may be found in the *Codes of Practice*, Code C, Annex A, paras. 9–12. The following is a summary:

- a police officer carrying out a strip search must be of the same sex as the person searched;
- the search shall take place in an area where the person being searched cannot be seen by anyone who does not need to be present, nor by a member of the opposite sex (except an appropriate adult who has been specifically requested by the person being searched—see below);
- except in cases of urgency, where there is a risk of serious harm to the person detained or to others, whenever a strip search involves exposure of intimate parts of the body, there must be at least two people present other than the person searched;
- except in cases of urgency, where there is a risk of serious harm to the person detained or to others, if the search is of a juvenile or a mentally disordered or mentally handicapped person, one of the people present must be the appropriate adult;
- other than in urgent cases as above, a search of a juvenile will normally take place in the presence of an appropriate adult, unless the juvenile signifies in the presence of the appropriate adult that he/she prefers the search to be done in his/her absence and the appropriate adult agrees (a record shall be made of the juvenile's decision and signed by the appropriate adult);
- the search shall be conducted with proper regard to the sensitivity and vulnerability of the person in these circumstances and every reasonable

effort shall be made to secure the person's co-operation and minimise embarrassment;

- people who are searched should not normally be required to have all their clothes removed at the same time (e.g. a man shall be allowed to put on his shirt before removing his trousers, and a woman shall be allowed to put on her blouse and upper garments before further clothing is removed);
- to assist the search, the person may be required to hold his/her arms in the air or to stand with his/her legs apart and to bend forward so that a visual examination may be made of the genital and anal areas provided that no physical contact is made with any body orifice;
- if, during a search, articles are found, the person shall be asked to hand them over. If articles are found within any body orifice other than the mouth, and the person refuses to hand them over, their removal would constitute an intimate search, which must be carried out in accordance with the provisions of part Λ of Annex A;
- a strip search shall be conducted as quickly as possible, and the person searched allowed to dress as soon as the procedure is complete.

8.7.5 **Custody record**

The custody record must be endorsed with the fact that a strip search was authorised and the reason it was considered necessary to undertake it. Those people present must be identified and the result of the search recorded (Code C, Annex A, para. 12).

Remember that some time in the future, the custody officer, or authorising officer, may be asked to justify their decision; therefore it is essential that the decision is rationalised in the record, using the above guidance.

8.8 **Intimate Search**

Intimate searches are covered in s. 55 of the Act, and Code C, Annex A of the *Codes of Practice*.

8.8.1 **Legislative provisions**

Code C, Annex A, Para. 2

Body orifices other than the mouth may be searched only:

(a) if authorised by an officer of inspector rank or above who has reasonable grounds for believing that the person may have concealed on themselves:

(i)   anything which they could and might use to cause physical injury to themselves or others at the station; or

(ii)   a Class A drug which they intended to supply to another or to export;

and the officer has reasonable grounds for believing that an intimate search is the only means of removing those items; and

(b)   if the search is under para. 2(a)(ii) (a drug offence search), the detainee's appropriate consent has been given in writing.

8.8.2 What is an 'intimate search'?

An 'intimate search' is a search which consists of the physical examination of a person's body orifices 'other than the mouth' (Code C, Annex A, para. 2). Careful consideration must be given to the intrusive nature of this type of search. Annex A, para. 1 specifically states that 'the actual and potential risks associated with intimate searches must never be underestimated'.

8.8.3 Authorisation to conduct an intimate search

An intimate search may be authorised by an inspector, under Annex A (previously this was the responsibility of a superintendent). (See **flow chart 5** in **Appendix 1** for an easy guide.) There are only two distinct reasons for authorising an intimate search under Annex A, para. 2:

1.   that the person has concealed either an article that s/he could use to cause injury while in custody, or

2.   that the person has concealed a Class A drug which they intend to supply to another or export (referred to in the Act as the 'appropriate criminal intent').

Consider the following:

Case Studies

Would an intimate search be appropriate in any of these circumstances?

1.   the person concealed a stolen credit card in her vagina;
2.   the person concealed cannabis resin in their anus, which they intended supplying to their friend;
3.   the person concealed a small quantity of heroin in their anus, which was intended for their own personal use;
4.   the person concealed a bag of heroin in their mouth, which they intended supplying to their partner;
5.   the person concealed a small bag of heroin in her vagina, which she intended supplying to her boyfriend.

Here are the answers:

1. The detainee has only concealed stolen property, and although the police would obviously wish to recover it, only a strip search may be authorised in these circumstances.

2. The detainee is in possession of cannabis, which is not a Class A drug. Despite the fact that he/she intended supplying it to another, a search could not be authorised under s. 55(1) of the Act.

3. Here, the detainee is in possession of a Class A drug; however, not with the 'appropriate criminal intent', therefore a search may not be authorised under s. 55(1).

4. The detainee is in possession of a Class A drug, with the 'appropriate criminal intent'; however, the mouth is not considered to be an orifice for the purposes of s. 55(1). The property may be recovered as a result of a 'routine' search in these circumstances.

5. The detainee is in possession of a Class A drug, with the 'appropriate criminal intent'; a search may be authorised under s. 55(1), despite the quantity of drugs involved.

Now that we have examined what cannot be authorised, you may be asking yourself, 'What can be done to recover property in these circumstances?'

With the exception of the final scenario, the answer cannot be found in either the Act or the *Codes of Practice*. It has to be remembered that an intimate search will be seen as an invasion of an individual's privacy. Therefore, legislators would have envisaged police officers conducting such searches only in extreme circumstances; hence the limited powers given in s. 55(1) of the Act. There are some practical solutions to the above scenarios; however, they will not provide all the answers. For example, it could be argued that where a person places something in their anus or vagina, they are exposing themselves to the risk of injury.

However, the authorising officer must have reasonable cause to believe that the person will use the item to cause physical injury to himself/herself or another. This has a slightly different meaning from, 'there is reasonable cause to believe that the item will cause physical injury to the detainee or some other person'. The wording of s. 55(1)(a) suggests that it is intended that the power will only be used when the detainee has concealed some type of weapon.

In respect of the first four scenarios, custody staff could monitor the detainee until the item passes through them (some forces now have clear toilets to assist), but this could take some time and will mean allocating a resource to watch the detainee constantly. Dealing with the property in the custody office in this way will also mean that the detainee's detention clock is still running.

Whatever decision is made, the custody officer should seek medical advice to establish whether the detainee requires hospital treatment.

In respect of the fifth scenario, s. 5 of the Drugs Act 2005 inserted s. 55A into PACE, which enables a police officer to authorise an x-ray or ultrasound scan of a person arrested for an offence and who is suspected of swallowing a Class A drug, which he or she had in his/her possession with intent to supply or to export unlawfully (see **8.10.2 Background to Drugs Act 2005** below for a full discussion of this power).

Because of the potential for causing injury during an intimate search, Annex A, Note for Guidance A1 states that before authorising any intimate search, the authorising officer must make every reasonable effort to persuade the detainee to hand the article over without a search. If the detainee agrees to hand over the article, a registered medical practitioner or registered nurse should whenever possible be asked to assess the risks involved and, if necessary, attend to assist the detainee.

8.8.4 **Use of force to conduct an intimate search**

The Drugs Act 2005 inserted subsection (3A) into s. 55 of PACE, which reflects Annex A, para. 2(b) above. A drug offence search may *not* be carried out unless the detainee has given the appropriate consent in writing. In other words, an intimate search under this section may not be conducted using force. Home Office Circular 55/2005 provides an insight into why the power to conduct an intimate search by force has been altered:

> Some drug dealers conceal drugs in their body cavities to avoid detection. Prior to the Drugs Act 2005, the Police and Criminal Evidence Act 1984 (PACE) allowed for an intimate search of a suspect to be carried out on the satisfaction of certain conditions. Consent was not required under PACE.

> However, unless it was impracticable to do so, intimate searches were carried out by a registered medical practitioner or registered nurse and, in practice, such searches would not normally be undertaken without the suspect's consent. Consequently some suspects would not consent in order to avoid detection. Section 3 of the Drugs Act 2005 is intended to encourage suspects not to withhold consent without good cause by enabling courts to draw such inferences as appear to them to be proper where consent is withheld without good cause.

As no such restriction applies in para. 2(a)(i) above, if the authorising officer has reasonable grounds for believing that the person may have concealed an article which they could and might use to cause physical injury to themselves or others at the station, force may be used to recover such an item. However, if the detainee does not agree to hand the article over without a search, Note for Guidance A2 states that the authorising officer must carefully review all the relevant factors before authorising an intimate search against the person's will. In particular, the officer must consider whether the grounds for believing an article may be concealed are reasonable.

Even though force may be used to recover articles under para. 2(a)(i) above, a registered medical practitioner or registered nurse must be consulted whenever possible. Such people are likely to advise against using force on a detainee to recover articles from body orifices unless the situation is life threatening. Note for Guidance A3 states that if authority is given for a search under para. 2(a)(i), the presumption should be that the search will be conducted by the registered medical practitioner or registered nurse (however, see **8.8.6 Conduct of intimate searches** below for occasions when a police officer may carry out the search). The authorising officer must make every reasonable effort to persuade the detainee to allow the medical practitioner or nurse to conduct the search. This will be the case whether the search is to be conducted with the detainee's consent or not.

8.8.5 **Information to be given to detainee**

Under Annex A, para. 2A, before the search begins, a police officer, designated detention officer or staff custody officer must tell the detainee:

(a)   that the authority to carry out the search has been given;

(b)   the grounds for giving the authorisation and for believing that the article cannot be removed without an intimate search.

Before a detainee is asked to give appropriate consent to a search under para. 2(a)(ii) (a drug offence search), they must be warned that if they refuse without good cause their refusal may harm their case if it comes to trial (see Note for Guidance A6 below). This warning may be given by a police officer or member of police staff. A detainee who is not legally represented must be reminded of their entitlement to have free legal advice and the reminder noted in the custody record (see Annex A, para. 2B).

Note for Guidance A6 states that when warning a detainee who is asked to consent to an intimate drug offence search, the following form of words may be used:

You do not have to allow yourself to be searched, but I must warn you that if you refuse without good cause, your refusal may harm your case if it comes to trial.

KEYNOTE

Where anything is seized under this section, the detainee must be told why it was seized, unless he/she is violent or likely to become violent, or incapable of understanding what is said (s. 55(13) PACE).

8.8.6 **Conduct of intimate searches**

Under Annex A, para. 3, an intimate search may only be carried out by a registered medical practitioner or registered nurse, unless an officer of at least inspector rank considers this is not practicable, in which case a police officer may carry out the search. However, a police officer may only be authorised to conduct an intimate search under para. 2(a)(i) above (articles which may be used to cause physical injury). Any search authorised under para. 2(a)(ii) (a drug offence search) *must* be conducted by a registered medical practitioner or registered nurse.

Paragraph 3A makes matters clear in respect of police officers conducting intimate searches—such a search must only be considered as a last resort and when the authorising officer is satisfied the risks associated with allowing the item to remain with the detainee outweigh the risks associated with removing it. Note for Guidance A4 expands on this theme, stating that a constable should only be authorised to carry out a search as a last resort, when all other approaches have failed.

In these circumstances, the authorising officer must be satisfied the detainee might use the article for one or more of the purposes in para. 2(a)(i) and the physical injury likely to be caused is sufficiently severe to justify authorising a constable to carry out the search. The authorising officer must be able to justify, in writing, such a search taking place (see **8.8.7 Documentation in respect of intimate searches** below).

KEYNOTE

If the authorising officer has any doubts whether to authorise an intimate search by a constable, the officer should seek advice from an officer of superintendent rank or above (Annex A, Note for Guidance A5).

If the authorising officer believes that all other methods of removing an article have failed and considers it necessary for an intimate search under para. 2(a)(i) to be carried out by a police officer, the officer must be of the same sex as the detainee. A minimum of two people, other than the detainee, must be present during the search.

Subject to para. 5 (intimate searches of juveniles or mentally disordered people—see **8.9 Intimate searches of vulnerable people** below), no person of the opposite sex who is not a medical practitioner or nurse shall be present, nor shall anyone whose presence is unnecessary. The search shall be conducted with proper regard to the sensitivity and vulnerability of the detainee (see para. 6).

Annex A, para. 4 gives specific guidance as to where an intimate search may take place. An intimate search under:

- para. 2(a)(i) may take place only at a hospital, surgery, other medical premises or police station;
- para. 2(a)(ii) may take place only at a hospital, surgery or other medical premises and must be carried out by a registered medical practitioner or a registered nurse.

The below table offers a simple guide:

Type of Search	Who may Conduct the Search	Where the Search may be Conducted
Item used to cause injury	Registered medical practitioner or a registered nurse, or if an inspector (previously superintendent) authorises that it is not practicable, a police officer	At a hospital, surgery, or other medical premises or police station
Class A drug	Registered medical practitioner or a registered nurse only	At a hospital, surgery, or other medical premises only

8.8.7 Documentation in respect of intimate searches

Annex A, para. 7 states:

In the case of an intimate search, the following shall be recorded as soon as practicable, in the detainee's custody record:

(a) for searches under para. 2(a)(i) and (ii):

- the authorisation to carry out the search;
- the grounds for giving the authorisation;
- the grounds for believing the article could not be removed without an intimate search;
- which parts of the detainee's body were searched;
- who carried out the search;
- who was present;
- the result;

(b) for searches under para. 2(a)(ii):

- the giving of the warning required by para. 2B;
- the fact that the appropriate consent was given or (as the case may be) refused, and if refused, the reason given for the refusal (if any).

If an intimate search is carried out by a police officer, the reason why it was impracticable for a registered medical practitioner or registered nurse to conduct it must be recorded (see Annex A, para. 8).

KEYNOTE

An inspector may authorise an intimate search orally or in writing, but if orally it must be confirmed in writing as soon as possible (s. 55(3) PACE).

KEYNOTE

Note that where a constable has the power to conduct a search under this section, the same authority is given to a detention officer (para. 26 of the Police Reform Act 2002). A detention officer may also seize items discovered as a result of an intimate search.

8.9 Intimate Searches of Vulnerable People

Because of their potential vulnerability, juveniles and persons who are mentally disordered, or otherwise mentally vulnerable are provided with extra protection by Code C, Annex A, para. 5. A summary of the provisions are contained below:

- an intimate search at a police station of juveniles and persons who are mentally disordered or otherwise mentally vulnerable may take place only in the presence of an appropriate adult of the same sex;

- however, there is an exception to this rule, if the person specifically requests the presence of a particular adult of the opposite sex, who is readily available;

- in the case of a juvenile, the search may take place in the absence of the appropriate adult only if the juvenile signifies in the presence of the appropriate adult that he/she prefers the search to be done in his/her absence and the appropriate adult agrees. A record shall be made of the juvenile's decision and signed by the appropriate adult.

Police forces have a duty to produce annual reports in relation to intimate searches that have been conducted in their areas. The reports must contain information such as the number of searches, who they were carried out by and the results of those searches (s. 51(14), (15) and (16)).

8.10 **X-rays and Ultrasound Scans**

8.10.1 **Legislative provisions**

Code C, Annex K, Para. 1

PACE, s. 55A allows a person who has been arrested and is in police detention to have an x-ray taken of them or an ultrasound scan to be carried out on them (or both) if:

(a) authorised by an officer of inspector rank or above who has reasonable grounds for believing that the detainee:

   (i) may have swallowed a Class A drug; and

   (ii) was in possession of that Class A drug with the intention of supplying it to another or to export; and

(b) the detainee's appropriate consent has been given in writing.

8.10.2 **Background to Drugs Act 2005**

From the 1 January 2006, s. 5 of the Drugs Act 2005 inserted s. 55A into the Police and Criminal Evidence Act 1984 (reflected in Code C, Annex K, para. 1 above). The power enables a police officer to authorise an x-ray or ultrasound scan of a person who is arrested for an offence and who is suspected of swallowing a Class A drug, which he or she had in his/her possession with intent to supply or to export unlawfully. (See **flow chart 6 in Appendix 1** for an easy guide.)

The intention of this section is to target drug dealers, not drug users—therefore, if a person has been arrested for an offence and simply swallows drugs, which were meant for personal use, the power under this section would not apply. Home Office Circular 55/2005 provides further information:

Drug dealers may swallow (wrapped) drugs when arrested in order to conceal the evidence. This provision allows for a senior police officer (inspector and above) to authorise an x-ray and/or ultrasound of a person who is suspected of swallowing a Class A drug which he or she had in their possession with intent to supply or to export unlawfully. The intention is to give police an indication whether a person should be detained to allow the drugs to pass through their body.

This is an area which has caused particular problems to drugs teams in the past. Many custody offices have had 'drugs toilets' installed, which have clear bowls enabling staff to identify when a drug has passed through a detainee who has swallowed a package, but this method is only useful if the detainee passes the package during their detention time. On other occasions, detainees have been taken to hospital to wait for the drugs to pass. However, this method can prove resource-intensive and often officers have to guard a detainee for a number of days.

The Home Office Consultation Paper, *Policing: Modernising Police Powers to Meet Community Needs*, addressed this issue, referring to the Home Office/Cabinet Office Review of PACE and the fact that HM Customs and Excise already had the power to apply to the court to remand a person who had swallowed a parcel into Customs detention to allow the package to pass (an average time of 12 days). The paper recommended providing the police with similar powers of detention, as well as separate powers to x-ray detainees. One of the other recommendations was to allow the courts to draw adverse inferences from a refusal to be x-rayed or submit to an intimate search. Many of these recommendations are now included as a result of the 2005 Act.

8.10.3 Information to be given to detainee

Code C, Annex K, para. 2 states that:

Before an x-ray is taken or an ultrasound scan carried out, a police officer, designated detention officer or staff custody officer must tell the detainee:

(a) that the authority has been given; and

(b) the grounds for giving the authorisation.

Paragraph 3 goes on to state:

Before a detainee is asked to give appropriate consent (which must be given in writing) to an x-ray or an ultrasound scan, they must be warned that if they refuse without good cause their refusal may harm their case if it comes to trial. This warning may be given by a police officer or member of police staff. A detainee who is not legally represented must be reminded of their entitlement to have free legal advice and the reminder noted in the custody record.

Annex K, Note for Guidance K2 states that in warning a detainee who is asked to consent to an x-ray being taken or an ultrasound scan being carried out (or both), as in para. 3 above, the following form of words may be used:

You do not have to allow an x-ray of you to be taken or an ultrasound scan to be carried out on you, but I must warn you that if you refuse without good cause, your refusal may harm your case if it comes to trial.

KEYNOTE

It should be noted that because of Code C, Annex K, para. 1(b) above, an x-ray may only be taken or an ultrasound scan carried out with the person's consent. However, Home Office Circular 55/2005 states that *there is no basis to refuse consent for cultural or religious reasons*.

8.10.4 Conduct of x-rays and ultrasound scans

Specific instructions are contained in the *Codes of Practice* and Home Office Circular 55/2005, as to how an x-ray may be taken, or an ultrasound scan may be carried out, which are dealt with below.

Once the decision has been made and the suspect agrees to an x-ray being taken, or an ultrasound scan being carried out, a registered medical practitioner (a medical practitioner retained by the police and registered with the General Medical Council) must be called to determine the appropriateness of the request to carry out an ultrasound scan or x-ray, or both, with a view to obtaining relevant evidence and will ensure that the detainee is notified of that authorisation and the reason for it. The registered medical practitioner will refer the detainee to the appropriate medical facility and make clear whether the referral is for evidential, medical or for dual purpose.

Forces should consider circulating internal guidance on procedures that should be followed. The registered medical practitioner will refer the detainee to the place where the x-ray or ultrasound will take place. The procedure must be carried out in a suitable place and by a suitably qualified person. An x-ray may be taken, or an ultrasound scan may be carried out, only by a registered medical practitioner or registered nurse, and only at a hospital, surgery or other medical premises (see Annex K, para. 4).

The registered medical practitioner may have to be called in at an earlier stage in the procedure (possibly before an x-ray or ultrasound has been authorised in this way) if there is any reason to be concerned as to the health of the detainee. Current advice from the Association of Forensic Physicians is that persons suspected to have swallowed drugs should be removed to a hospital in the first instance. In cases of 'imminent risk', officers should consider the appropriateness of using an ambulance to transport the detainee to hospital.

If authority is given for an x-ray to be taken or an ultrasound scan to be carried out (or both), consideration should be given to asking a registered medical practitioner or registered nurse to explain to the detainee what is involved and to allay any concerns the detainee might have about the effect which taking an x-ray or carrying out an ultrasound scan might have on them. If appropriate consent is not given, evidence of the explanation may, if the case comes to trial, be relevant to determining whether the detainee had a good cause for refusing (see Annex K, Note for Guidance K1).

Where the detainee gives consent for an x-ray or ultrasound to be taken, the period in detention at a hospital (or other appropriate medical facility) will count towards the total period of detention allowed under PACE, because the detainee will be there for gathering evidence. The detainee will be returned to the police station after the x-ray or ultrasound unless there are medical reasons for remaining at the hospital. In such a case, unless the person is being questioned for the purpose of obtaining evidence relating to an offence (s. 41(6) of PACE), the further period of detention at hospital will *not* count towards the total period of detention under PACE.

Where it is thought that the detainee is at imminent risk, for example, because of swallowing drugs, the registered medical practitioner may also refer the detainee to the appropriate medical facility on health grounds alone for an x-ray or ultrasound scan. In this case, the scan or x-ray (if it has also been properly authorised and consented to as above) would have a dual purpose.

If the detainee consents, the hospital (or other appropriate medical facility) will keep a record for medical purposes and provide police with a record for evidential purposes. However, if consent to the evidential x-ray or ultrasound scan is refused, any x-ray or ultrasound scan obtained with consent for *medical* purposes will be excluded material for the purposes of s. 11 (excluded material) and s. 12 (personal records) of PACE and the hospital will not be required to provide a copy for police to use as evidence.

8.10.5 Documentation required in respect of x-rays and ultrasound scans

Code C, Annex K, para. 5 states that the following shall be recorded as soon as practicable in the detainee's custody record:

(a) the authorisation to take the x-ray or carry out the ultrasound scan (or both);

(b) the grounds for giving the authorisation;

(c) the giving of the warning required by para. 3; and

(d) the fact that the appropriate consent was given or (as the case may be) refused, and if refused, the reason given for the refusal (if any); and

(e) if an x-ray is taken or an ultrasound scan carried out:
- where it was taken or carried out;
- who took it or carried it out;
- who was present;

- the result.

If the detainee is a juvenile or other mentally vulnerable person, paras. 1.4–1.7 of Code C apply, and an appropriate adult should be present when consent is sought to any procedure under Annex K.

8.11 **Extended Detention of Suspected Drug Offenders**

8.11.1 **Background to Drugs Act 2005**

Section 8 of the Drugs Act 2005 inserted s. 152(1A) into the Criminal Justice Act 1988. These new powers have been introduced because, under PACE, a suspect may be detained only for a maximum of 96 hours without charge. This is often not a sufficient length of time to allow swallowed drugs to pass through the body.

Under the Criminal Justice Act 1988 provisions were originally made for a magistrates' court to commit a person charged with either possession of a controlled drug or a drug trafficking offence into the custody of a customs officer for a period of up to 192 hours. Section 8 of the 2005 Act allows a court to similarly remand a person charged with an offence to the custody of a constable for up to 192 hours (eight days), measured from the date and time the court makes the order for the remand. Home Office Circular 55/2005 outlines the procedures that will apply to such a remand in custody—these are described below.

8.11.2 **Application to the magistrates' court**

The extension allows a magistrates' court to commit a person aged 17 or over, who has been charged with an offence under s. 5(2) of the Misuse of Drugs Act 1971 (possession of a controlled drug) *or* a 'drug trafficking offence', into police custody for up to 192 hours to increase the likelihood that swallowed evidence can be recovered. For the purposes of s. 152, drug trafficking offence is defined by s. 151(5) of the Criminal Justice Act 1988 and includes the following offences:

(a) any of the following offences under the Misuse of Drugs Act 1971:

- s. 4(2) or (3) (unlawful production or supply);
- s. 5(3) (possession with intent to supply);
- s. 8 (permitting certain activities);
- s. 20 (assisting in or inducing the commission outside the UK of an offence punishable under a corresponding law);

(b) attempting, conspiring or inciting, or aiding, abetting, counselling or procuring, the commission of any offence specified in (a) above.

8.11.3 Decisions to charge and refuse bail

Decisions to charge a suspect with an offence for which a remand may be sought (see above) and to authorise detention after charge will continue to be made and recorded in accordance with the Director of Public Prosecution's Guidance issued under s. 37A PACE and s. 38 PACE (duties of custody officer after charge). As this will be a remand into police custody, crown prosecutors will apply the threshold test when making their charging decisions.

If the suspect has been charged and bail after charge refused, a remand into police custody under s. 152 will usually be appropriate if the officer in charge of the investigation and CPS have reasonable grounds to believe that:

- the suspect has swallowed or otherwise concealed drugs internally;
- some or all of these drugs are expected to be produced, excreted or to otherwise become available to be recovered after the suspect has been taken to court; and
- a remand into police custody is necessary to enable police to recover the drugs.

The results of any x-rays and/or ultrasound scans taken under s. 55A PACE, supporting admissions, drug test results or other circumstantial evidence such as a refusal to eat or defecate would be relevant to the above decisions and considerations, particularly if no drugs have been produced at the police station.

The officer in charge of the investigation and CPS should assess and agree the remand period to be requested and the reasons to be given in open court when the application is made.

8.11.4 Making the application to the magistrates' court

An application under s. 152 will require sufficient evidence to satisfy the court that a remand to the custody of police is appropriate in the circumstances. Although what is 'appropriate' is not defined, it will usually apply when the main reason for seeking the remand is to enable police to recover swallowed drugs for evidence. It is not necessary to exhaust the PACE provisions regarding the length of detention in police custody before charging a suspect and making an application under s. 152.

Applications under s. 152 should normally be made in open court unless to do so would compromise a source or intelligence-gathering technique. The CPS prosecutor will present the applications.

The granting and length of the remand is entirely at the discretion of the magistrates' court according to the reasons presented. The maximum period that can be granted on any one occasion is 192 hours. If the period granted is insufficient to enable police to recover the drugs, or as the case may be, complete an operation to arrest accomplices, a further application may be made when the person is brought back to court.

8.11.5 When the application has been granted—custody matters

If the court grants the application, they will issue a warrant of commitment to police custody. It will direct police to keep the person in custody and specify the date and time at which the person must re-appear before the court. Commitment warrants must be returned to the court with the person when the hearing resumes and for this reason they should be kept with the custody record.

A person remanded under s. 152 is not in police detention and not subject to the detention provisions and time limits in ss. 37 to 44 PACE. However, although detention under s. 152 is not subject to review under s. 40 PACE, the need for the person to remain in police custody should be periodically reviewed.

The person may be detained at any suitable police station and the station need not be the one where the person was charged and from which they were taken to court. The recovery of evidence from persons suspected of swallowing drugs will require single occupancy cell toilet facilities to allow the drugs to be safely recovered and at the same time, provide evidential continuity. Not all police stations are equipped with such facilities. It will be necessary for police forces to ensure, from existing resources, that a suitably equipped police station will be available before applying for a remand under s. 152 and to inform the court of that police station when making the application.

The commitment warrant is the authority to keep the person in police custody and a new custody record should be opened when the person arrives from court. The reasons for the remand presented in court represent the grounds for detention and should be noted accordingly on the record.

If the reasons for the remand cease to apply in sufficient time to make it practicable to return the person to court before the date specified in the warrant, the court and CPS should be informed so that the necessary arrangements can be made. These will include notifying any solicitor representing the person. This situation may arise if before the specified return date, police are satisfied that all the swallowed drugs have been recovered or that no drugs were swallowed or that an operation to arrest accomplices is completed or abandoned, or that the charge should be withdrawn and proceedings should be discontinued.

KEYNOTE

The police will need to make suitable arrangements to ensure evidential continuity in recovering further drugs, preventing escape and minimising health risks during any period that the charged person is:

- being taken to court for any application or further application;
- at court; and

if the application is granted

- being taken to a police station.

The above matters may require police to carry out all the escort duties rather than the appointed prisoner escort service contractor and to agree the arrangements with the court concerned.

8.11.6 Continuing health risks

Any drugs swallowed may leak from the packages containing them. The risks to health arising from internal concealment of drugs must be managed in accordance with the continuing risk assessment process required by Code C, paras. 3.6 to 3.10 (Risk Assessments) and Code C, section 9 (Care and Treatment of Detained Persons). Code C, para. 9.3 and Note 9CA emphasise the need to pay special attention to these cases. This will apply throughout the person's period in police custody before and after charge and whilst remanded under s. 152.

All police officers and police staff who might have any direct contact with the person in the custody suite or when involved in escorting the person to and from court should be suitably trained and must be made aware of:

- the medical and evidential significance of internal drug concealment; and
- the need to report and record full details of any such relevant occurrences.

Police forces are reminded of their responsibility under relevant legislation to ensure the health and safety of police officers and police staff engaged in the recovery of excreted drugs. They will wish to undertake an appropriate assessment of the risks and put in place control measures to address them, including the provision and use of protective equipment and the introduction and maintenance of an immunisation programme.

8.12 **Summing Up**

Much has been made in this chapter regarding the ongoing 'risk assessments' in relation to all detainees. The risk assessment in relation to detainees' property will be integral to the custody officer's initial 'booking in' process. This subject is dealt with in more depth in **Chapter 3—Safer Detention**. However, in order to justify decisions made in relation to detainees' property, custody officers must consider the following questions on each occasion:

1. Does the detainee need to be searched?
2. To what extent does the detainee need to be searched?
3. Does property need to be seized, or can it be retained by the detainee?

These questions must be considered carefully on each occasion, in conjunction with s. 54 and s. 55 of the Act and the Codes of Practice. Provided this is done, the detainee and custody staff will be protected from risk of harm, and the custody officer will be protected from complaints or litigation.

Recording property

Custody officers are responsible for ascertaining what property a detainee has with him/her when he/she has been:

- arrested or re-detained on answering to bail;
- committed to prison custody by an order or sentence of a court;
- lodged at the police station with a view to their production in court from prison custody;
- transferred from detention at another police station or from hospital;
- detained under ss. 135 or 136 of the Mental Health Act 1983;
- remanded into police custody on the authority of a court.

Custody officers are also responsible for ascertaining any property that a person might have acquired for unlawful or harmful purpose while in custody, and for safekeeping any property taken from a detainee. However, the custody officer is no longer required to record all of the detainee's property as part of the custody record.

(Code C, paras. 4.1 and 4.4)

Not all detainees will require searching; the custody officer may decide not to search detainees who are only in custody for a short period of time. The custody record will be endorsed 'not searched'.

(Code C, Note for Guidance 4A)

What may be seized?

Unless the exception below applies, anything may be seized from a person in police detention, s. 54(3), who falls into the categories above.

Exceptions to the above:

- Clothing or personal effects which the custody officer believes the detainee may use to:

  1. harm themselves or another;

  2. cause damage;

  3. interfere with evidence;

  4. assist with their escape.

(s. 54(4)(a) PACE)

- Clothing or personal effects when the custody officer has reasonable grounds for believing that they may be evidence relating to an offence.

(s. 54(4)(b) PACE)

Power to search persons in custody to the extent that the custody officer considers necessary for that purpose. Force may be used if necessary.

(s. 54(6)).

Extent of search

1. 'Routine' Search:
   - no removal of more than outer garments;
   - no examining bodily orifices;
   - authorised by custody officer.

2. Strip Search:
   - a search involving the removal of more than outer clothing;
   - authorised by custody officer;
   - may only take place if necessary to remove an article which a person would not be allowed to keep and an officer reasonably considers that the person might have concealed such an article;
   - must not be routinely carried out where there is no reason to consider that articles have been concealed.

   Extensive guidance is provided in the *Codes of Practice*, Code C, Annex A, paras. 9–12, as to the conduct of strip searches. A summary is contained in this chapter.

3. Intimate Search

   Body orifices other than the mouth may be searched only:

   (a) if authorised by an inspector who has reasonable grounds for believing that the person may have concealed on themselves:

      (i) anything which they could and might use to cause physical injury to themselves or others at the station; or

      (ii) a Class A drug which they intended to supply to another or to export;

      and the officer has reasonable grounds for believing that an intimate search is the only means of removing those items; and

   (b) if the search is under para. 2(a)(ii) (a drug offence search), the detainee's appropriate consent has been given in writing.

(Code C, Annex A, para. 2)

An intimate search under:

- para. 2(a)(i) may take place only at a hospital, surgery, other medical premises or police station;
- para. 2(a)(ii) may take place only at a hospital, surgery or other medical premises and must be carried out by a registered medical practitioner or a registered nurse.

(Code C, Annex A, para. 4)

4. X-rays and ultrasound scans

   A person who has been arrested and is in police detention may have an x-ray taken of them or an ultrasound scan carried out on them (or both) if:

   (a) authorised by an officer of inspector rank or above who has reasonable grounds for believing that the detainee:

      (i) may have swallowed a Class A drug; and

      (ii) was in possession of that Class A drug with the intention of supplying it to another or to export; and

   (b) the detainee's appropriate consent has been given in writing.

(s. 55A PACE)

An x-ray may be taken, or an ultrasound scan may be carried out, only by a registered medical practitioner or registered nurse, and only at a hospital, surgery or other medical premises.

(Code C, Annex K, para. 4)

5. Extended detention of suspected drug offenders
   A magistrates' court may commit a person aged 17 or over, who has been charged with an offence under s. 5(2) of the Misuse of Drugs Act 1971 (possession of a controlled drug) *or* a 'drug trafficking offence', into police custody for up to 192 hours (eight days) to increase the likelihood that swallowed evidence can be recovered.

(s. 152(1A) Criminal Justice Act 1988)

LOCAL PROCEDURES

1. What does your force policy dictate in relation to seizing cash and other items of value from a detainee?

2. Does your force or custody office have single occupancy cell toilet facilities to allow the recovery of evidence from persons suspected of swallowing drugs?

SPACE FOR NOTES

SPACE FOR NOTES

SPACE FOR NOTES

9

Warrants

9.1 **Introduction**

Unlike the rest of this book, this chapter relies more on established practice and force policy than PACE and the *Codes of Practice* and covers the complications of dealing with detainees who have been arrested on a warrant for failing to appear in court, and are subsequently found to be wanted for other offences, as well as other detainees who have been arrested for a criminal offence and then found to be wanted on warrant. In both of these cases, we examine the requirement to take the detainee to court 'immediately'. We will also study warrants issued by courts to detain people in police custody (known as 'three day lie downs') and the requirement to conduct periodic reviews in respect of such people.

The Human Rights Act 1998

Under Article 5 of the Human Rights Act 1998 (the right to liberty and security), there is a requirement to bring a person before a 'competent legal authority' promptly. Custody officers should bear this in mind when considering the attendance at court of a person who has been arrested for a warrant, or the return to court of a person detained as a result of a 'three day lie down'.

9.2 **Warrants for Failing to Appear**

This section deals with detainees who have been arrested for a fail to appear warrant which is not backed for bail. Generally, when a person has been arrested in such circumstances, the warrant will instruct the police to take the person 'immediately' to the next available court. However, there are two situations, which occur quite frequently, that can cause problems for custody officers and the courts:

1. where the detainee has been arrested for a warrant, and after detention has been authorised, it is discovered that he/she is wanted for another offence;

2. where the detainee has been arrested for an offence and it is discovered that he/she is wanted for a warrant.

There is no specific guidance to be found in either PACE or the *Codes of Practice* on how to deal with these situations and this section offers general guidance; however, you should consult local procedures for your own force policies. We will deal with these issues separately.

KEYNOTE

In its review *Re-balancing the Criminal Justice System in favour of the law-abiding majority*, published in July 2006, the Home Office considered how to restrict the use of 'warrants backed for bail', in order to help speed the return to court of bailed defendants who fail to appear. It considered removing entirely the court's power to issue a warrant backed for bail.

However, following consultation, the Government proposed to restrict the use of these warrants through the identification, dissemination and implementation of good practice guidance through criminal justice partners, rather than by taking a legislative approach.

9.2.1 Arrested on warrant and then found to be wanted for other offences

This situation generally occurs when a person has been arrested for failing to appear in court, and the warrant has been executed. The arresting officer may check the PNC, or the local crime information system, and discover that the person is also wanted for a criminal offence. The warrant will usually instruct the police to bring the detainee before the next available court, and there should be no problem if the next court is sitting the following day. But what if the detainee is arrested during the daytime and the court is sitting at that time? In these circumstances, the magistrates' court will generally prefer the police to deal with the criminal allegation while he/she is in custody. The detainee can then be taken before the next available court, when the police have completed their enquiries. This means that when the detainee arrives in court, there are no outstanding issues, and the magistrates' court can deal with all the facts before them when considering whether or not bail should be granted.

The alternative method of dealing with a person arrested in these circumstances is to allow the detainee to attend court and then arrest him/her after the hearing. However, dealing with the situation in this way suits nobody's purpose; the detainee would have to go through a second period of detention; the courts would have to deal with the detainee twice in 24 hours for separate offences (and consider the issue of bail a second time); the police have to wait to deal with their crime. Common sense would dictate that the detainee should remain in police detention until all matters are dealt with.

KEYNOTE

Whatever decision the custody officer makes in these circumstances, it is recommended that the clerk of the court be informed, as well as the Crown Prosecution Service representative in court.

9.2.2 Arrested for an offence and then found to be wanted on warrant

This situation is slightly different from the one above, in that the detainee will already be under investigation for a criminal offence, when it is discovered that he/she is also wanted for failing to appear in court and a warrant had been issued, which was not backed for bail. The timing of the execution of the warrant is crucial in these circumstances, bearing in mind that a no-bail warrant requires a person to be taken to the next available court.

Consider the following:

Case Study

MADDOX was arrested for an offence of assault, and taken to the police station on a Friday evening. The enquiry was protracted because of the number of witnesses and MADDOX was finally charged with the offence at lunch time on the Saturday.

He was bailed to appear in court; however, before being released he was arrested for an outstanding warrant for failing to appear in the magistrates' court, which the officers had known about shortly after his arrival on the Friday evening. MADDOX was detained to appear before the next available court under the terms of the warrant. Because there was no court on the Saturday afternoon, MADDOX was kept in custody until the following Monday.

MADDOX subsequently sued the police for unlawful detention, arguing that he should have been taken to court on the Saturday morning, as the police had been aware of the existence of the warrant.

Has the custody officer acted lawfully in these circumstances?

....

The above facts are similar to those in the case of *Henderson* v *Chief Constable of Cleveland Constabulary* [2001] The Times, 16 March. Henderson had been detained in similar circumstances, for an offence of deception. He later instituted civil proceedings against Cleveland Police at Middlesbrough County Court, claiming unlawful detention for the time he spent in custody after being arrested for the warrant.

Henderson asked the court to rule on the following issues:

(a) Did the police have the authority to exercise discretion as to when the warrant should be executed? If the police did have such discretion, was it reasonable to delay the execution of the warrant until the investigation into the criminal offence, for which he had been arrested, had been concluded?

(b) Was the delay in executing the warrant a breach of Article 5.1(b) and (c) of the European Convention on Human Rights (the right to liberty and security)?

Henderson argued that the police were required to bring him before the court 'immediately' under the terms of the warrant, and that they had not done so. It was held that the word 'immediately' in the warrant governed procedures after execution of the warrant and that he had been taken to court 'immediately' after the police had executed it. The judge found that there had been no breach of Article 5 and that the police did have discretion as to when a warrant should be executed (however, for a further discussion on this matter, see **15.5.2 Requirement to take the detainee to court**).

Henderson appealed against the decision, and eventually appeared in the Court of Appeal, where he argued that if the police did have discretion as to when a warrant should be executed, that discretion should be exercised reasonably. He submitted that due to the magistrates' court being closed, his detention time from the Saturday to the Monday was unreasonable, and that the police should have taken this into consideration when exercising their discretion.

Lord Chief Justice, Lord Woolf asserted that the word 'immediately' related solely to the taking of the prisoner before a court and had no relevance as to the timing of the arrest. His Lordship concluded that while the use of warrants was an important part of the criminal justice system, the execution of them was at the lower end of the scale compared to investigating more serious criminal allegations.

He concluded that there was no duty imposed on the police to halt a criminal investigation simply because they were in possession of a warrant and that:

(i)   the police had discretion when to execute the warrant;

(ii) the officer must comply with the terms of the warrant; but if he/she exercised discretion, then he/she had complied with the terms of the warrant.

In section **9.2.1 Arrested on warrant and then found to be wanted for other offences**, above, we concluded that there was no direct guidance on the situation when a person had been arrested for a warrant before it was discovered that they were wanted for a criminal offence. However, if we apply the principles laid out in the *Henderson* case above, it would seem logical that the criminal investigation should take precedence, whatever the circumstances.

9.2.3 Warrants for failing to appear in Crown Court ('bench warrants')

In contrast to the two scenarios above, custody officers may find that the situation is different when a detainee has been arrested for a Crown Court, or 'bench', warrant. In theory, the decision in the case of Henderson referred to above should apply as much in the Crown Court as it does in the magistrates' court. In practice, failing to appear in the Crown Court is seen as a more serious offence than failing to appear in any other court, particularly amongst judges. In these cases, Crown Courts will often insist on the detainee being brought before them at the earliest opportunity. This can cause problems with an investigation, especially when the PACE clock is ticking away; however, custody officers have very little choice when Crown Court judges order a detainee to appear before them.

As with matters relating to the magistrates' court, the custody officer should liaise with the Crown Court to negotiate a time when the detainee may be taken there. Custody officers should also check their own force procedures in relation to this matter.

9.3 Warrants to Detain in Police Custody ('Three Day Lie Down')

9.3.1 Legislative provisions

Magistrates' Courts Act 1980, s. 128(7) & (8)

A suspect may be remanded in detention at a police station for a period not exceeding three clear days.

Where a person is committed to detention at a police station—

(a) he shall not be kept in such detention unless there is a need for him to be so detained for the purpose of inquiring into other offences;

(b) if kept in such detention, he shall be brought back before the magistrates' court which committed him, as soon as the need ceases;

(c) his detention shall be subject to periodic reviews at the times set out in s. 40 of PACE (review of police detention).

9.3.2 Period of detention

Generally, when a person is remanded in custody by the magistrates' court, he or she will be taken to prison (or detention centre in the case of a juvenile), while awaiting the next court hearing. However, when a person has been charged with an offence, and the police wish to interview him/her about offences other than the one for which he/she appears in court, the magistrates may order that he/she is returned to police detention for a period not exceeding three clear days. This procedure is also known as a 'three day lie down'.

KEYNOTE

Where the magistrates order the further detention of a person under 17 years of age, the period may not exceed 24 hours (see Magistrates' Courts Act 1980, s. 128(7)).

Section 128(8) of the Magistrates' Courts Act 1980 makes it clear that a person detained under this power must be returned to the court when the police have completed their inquiries. The three day lie down should be viewed as a maximum period of detention. For example, if the police complete their inquiries within 24 hours, the detainee should be returned to the court which remanded him/her before the three day period has expired.

KEYNOTE

Before making an application under this section, the investigating officer should liaise with the Crown Prosecution Service, who will represent their case in court.

9.3.3 **Reviewing detention**

People held at a police station under s. 128(8) must have their detention periodically reviewed. The reason for this, according to Code C, Note for Guidance 15B, is to make sure the detainee is taken back to court no later than the end of the period authorised by the court or when the need for their detention by police ceases, whichever is the sooner.

Neither s. 128(8)(c) nor Note for Guidance 15B is clear on whether the review should be conducted by a sergeant or an inspector. It could be argued that because the detainee has already been charged with an offence, a custody officer should conduct the review. On the other hand, the detainee has been returned to the station for investigation into offences for which he/she has not yet been charged; therefore an inspector could conduct the review.

Elsewhere, Note for Guidance 15B specifically mentions that where people have been arrested for matters not covered by s. 40 or 40A reviews (e.g. fail to appear warrant), their detention should be reviewed by sergeants as a matter of good practice. However, the list does not mention people detained under s. 128(8). Custody officers should check their own force procedures in relation to this issue, but in the absence of any further guidance, I suggest that reviews are conducted by inspectors.

Whoever conducts the review, he/she should take into account:

- the original grounds on which the application was made (i.e. what persuaded the magistrates to remand the detainee in the first place?); and
- that detention is still necessary as per the original application to the court.

9.4 Detainees Produced from Prison ('Production Orders')

Occasionally, detainees are brought to the police station, having been produced from prison (known as 'production orders'). People in prison are often visited by the police to 'clear up' crimes they may have committed prior to being sentenced or remanded in custody. However, where the offence is more serious or the inquiry is of a protracted nature, the police may apply to the Chief Executive (or Governor) of the prison to have the detainee produced to police cells. This may be done for interview and charging procedures, or sometimes to arrange an identification parade.

Detainees produced under this process should be reviewed periodically. Once again, the matter of who conducts the review is debatable. A person produced for these purposes will not be detained under PACE or the *Codes of Practice*; however, in accordance with Code C, Note for Guidance 15B, detainees who are not covered by the Act should still have their detention reviewed periodically as a matter of good practice.

Opinion is divided on who should actually conduct the review. It could be argued that either a custody officer or an inspector could do so, because the detainee is not subject to the provisions of s. 40 of PACE. As with the situation described above in **9.3 Warrants to detain in police custody ('three day lie down')**, custody officers should check their own force policy, but it is difficult to imagine criticism being levelled at a force if an inspector reviews detention in these circumstances.

9.5 Summing Up

Arrested on warrant and found to be wanted for other offences

Police should deal with the criminal offence as a priority and then take the detainee to court. However, custody officers should consult their own force procedures in respect of this issue.

Arrested for an offence and found to be wanted on warrant

The timing of the execution of the warrant is crucial in these circumstances. The case of *Henderson v Chief Constable of Cleveland Constabulary* shows that the police may deal with criminal offences before executing a warrant, even if the warrant was known about at the beginning of the investigation.

Warrants to detain in police custody ('three day lie down')

A suspect may be remanded in detention at a police station (by the magistrates' court) for a period not exceeding three clear days (24 hours in the case of a juvenile), provided:

(a) there is a need to inquire into other offences;

(b) he/she is brought back before the magistrates' court which committed him/her, as soon as the need ceases;

(c) his/her detention is subject to periodic reviews under s. 40 PACE (review of police detention).

LOCAL PROCEDURES

1. Does your force have a policy in relation to people who have been detained for a fail to appear warrant, who are later found to be wanted for another offence?

2. What arrangements does your force have with the Crown Court, when detainees have been arrested for a criminal offence and a bench warrant?

3. When a person has been remanded on a three day lie down, what does your force policy say about who should conduct the review?

4. When a person has been produced from prison (production order), what does your force policy say about who should conduct the review?

SPACE FOR NOTES

SPACE FOR NOTES

SPACE FOR NOTES

10

Reviews and Relevant Time

10.1 **Introduction**

Unsurprisingly, a person may not be held in police detention indefinitely. There are strict guidelines contained within the Police and Criminal Evidence Act 1984 as to how long a person may be kept in police detention, and, just as importantly, how their period of detention is monitored. There is a distinct difference between a person's 'Review Time' and their 'Relevant Time'. Both terms are examined in depth in this chapter, as well as the responsibilities given to custody officers and inspectors in the process. It is important to note that custody officers must have equal understanding of the review duties of an inspector as they do of their own duties.

The review procedure adds integrity to the process, by ensuring that a person's detention is monitored both at regular intervals by an inspector or above and as a continual process by a custody officer. Remember that a person's detention must be lawful and failing to follow the review process correctly may impact on the investigation. To deviate from this may render that detention unlawful, which may mean that any interviews conducted, or evidence secured, during that period are deemed inadmissible by the court. Inevitably, a failure to carry out a timely review of a person's detention in custody before charge may render previously lawful detention unlawful, and may amount to false imprisonment (*Roberts* v *Chief Constable of the Cheshire Constabulary* [1999] 1 WLR 662). It is crucial to record decisions as soon as possible and, where they vary from the Police and Criminal Evidence Act 1984 or the *Codes of Practice*, the reasons they do so.

Guidance as to the timing and conduct of reviews can be found in both the Police and Criminal Evidence Act 1984 and the *Codes of Practice*, but it will come as no surprise that many of the practical issues faced every day are not covered. This chapter will offer guidance and practical advice and, wherever possible, the definitive answer.

The Human Rights Act 1998

Once again, the Human Rights Act 1998 adds an extra dimension to the Police and Criminal Evidence Act 1984. Article 5 of the 1998 Act will be of particular significance to review officers who are monitoring the detainee's lawful arrest and detention.

10.2 **The Detention Clocks**

It should be noted that while a person is in police detention, there will always be two 'clocks' running side by side.

10.2.1 **Detention clock**

The first clock to commence, when a person is in police detention, will be the 'detention clock'. This clock starts when the person first arrives at the police station whilst under arrest. The time at which the 'detention clock' starts is known as the 'Relevant Time'. In most circumstances, the police have 24 hours in which to investigate the offence, unless the person is in custody for an indictable offence, and detention has been extended under s. 42 of PACE by a superintendent, or he/she is in custody for a similar offence, and detention has been extended under s. 43 or s. 44, by a magistrate. Relevant times are discussed in greater depth later in this chapter and extensions to this time (under s. 42, s. 43 and s. 44) are dealt with in **Chapter 11—Extending Detention.**

10.2.2 **Review clock**

The second clock, the 'review clock', commences at the point where a person's detention is first authorised by a custody officer. Reviews are discussed in detail below.

10.3 **Reviews**

10.3.1 **Legislative provisions**

Code C, Note for Guidance 15A

Review officer for the purposes of:

- PACE, ss. 40 and 40A, means, in the case of a person arrested but not charged, an officer of at least inspector rank not directly involved in the investigation and, if a person has been arrested and charged, the custody officer;

- the Terrorism Act 2000, means an officer not directly involved in the investigation connected with the detention and of at least inspector rank, for reviews within 24 hours of the detainee's arrest or superintendent for all other reviews.

10.3.2 **Review officers**

The two review officers identified under s. 40 and s. 40A (telephone reviews of detention) have the same responsibility; to determine whether the grounds for detention are still necessary. Reviews under the Terrorism Act 2000 are dealt with in **Chapter 17—Terrorism Act 2000 Detainees.**

Review officers under PACE may be distinguished as follows:

- Before Charge:
  The review officer for a detained person who has not been charged will be an officer of at least the rank of inspector.
- After Charge:
  The review officer for a detained person who has been charged will be a custody officer.

The issue of reviewing a detainee after charge is dealt with in **Chapter 15— Continued Detention After Charge**. There are occasions where an officer of a lower rank can perform the functions required by a higher rank (see s. 107 of PACE).

10.4 **What is a Review?**

10.4.1 **Legislative provisions**

Section 40(8) PACE

Subject to s. 40(9) below, where a person whose detention is under review, s. 37(1) to (6) above shall have effect in relation to him, but with the substitution:

(a)   of references to the person whose detention is under review for references to the person arrested; and

(b)   of references to the review officer for references to the custody officer.

10.4.2 **Periodic reviews**

The Oxford English Dictionary describes a review as:

> a formal assessment of something with the intention of instituting change if necessary.

PACE deals with the subject of reviews in far more detail. There are two sections within the Act which determine the duties and obligations of reviewing officers, namely s. 34 and s. 40. We will examine the requirements of these sections separately, beginning with s. 40.

10.4.3 **Section 40**

In plain English, s. 40(8) means that whenever a review is conducted, the review officer must also consider s. 37 of the Act. Section 37 is dealt with in depth in **Chapter 2—Detainees—Initial Action** and relates to what the custody officer must consider when first accepting the detainee into custody (e.g. sufficient evidence to charge the detainee, detention is necessary to obtain evidence by questioning or secure and preserve evidence).

Under s. 40, periodic reviews at set intervals are required by a 'review officer' (either the custody officer or the inspector). The review officer has an overseeing role and acts as a 'safety net' for the detention process. When review is due, the review officer must also ask themselves, 'Does this person still need to be in police detention?'

10.4.4 **Section 34**

Under s. 34, a custody officer has a continuing responsibility to ensure that the grounds for a person's detention still apply, from the moment a person's detention is first authorised, until the point that they leave the station (either with or without bail, or to appear in court). Simply, the custody officer must ask themselves, 'Does this person still need to be in police detention?' Although this will not be classed as an official review under s. 40, by doing this, the custody officer will effectively be 'reviewing' the person's detention.

This information may have come about because the custody officer has used intrusive management skills, or because the officer in the case has volunteered it. Either way, action should be taken to make sure the person's detention does not become unlawful.

KEYNOTE

The circumstances of a person's detention can change. For example:

- Has information come to light that it is a case of mistaken identity?
- Has the officer in the case satisfied himself/herself that the detainee is not involved in the offence?
- Has the complaint been withdrawn, or a vital witness refused to make a statement?
- If the detainee has been detained after charge, have the grounds ceased to apply (i.e. an address suitable for bail has been found)?

10.5 **Review Officer's Checklist**

Review officers should follow this practical checklist at every review stage:

- enquire into the reasons for detention;
- determine if there is sufficient evidence to charge;

- determine if detention is still necessary;
- remind the detainee of entitlement to free legal advice;
- allow representations to be made;
- note any comment made;
- record the decision in the presence of the detainee.

Each stage of the review process should be examined separately.

10.5.1 Enquire into the reasons for detention

The review officer should enquire into the progress of the case. If it is before charge, the review officer could obtain this information from the custody officer, or the officer in the case. The review officer before charge should also ensure that the case is being investigated thoroughly, but note that s. 40 of the Act does not mention the words 'diligently' or 'expeditiously'. These terms are only mentioned in s. 42 of the Act (superintendent's authorisation). However, even though there is no requirement to establish diligence and expeditiousness, this would not be an unreasonable test to apply at this stage of the review.

10.5.2 Determine if there is sufficient evidence to charge

The review officer, in this case an inspector, must consider whether there is sufficient evidence to charge the detained person.

In arriving at this decision, the review officer will need to consult with the custody officer and often the officer in the case to establish the status of any investigation. The officer will also need to consider s. 37(7) of PACE, which requires the custody officer to determine whether there is sufficient evidence to charge the detainee with the offence for which he or she was arrested and to make one of the following decisions:

(a) release the person without charge and on bail for the purpose of enabling the Director of Public Prosecutions to make a decision under s. 37B below;

(b) release the person without charge and on bail but not for that purpose;

(c) release the person without charge and without bail; or

(d) charge the person.

This subsection was altered significantly by the Criminal Justice Act 2003, which requires the police to consult with the Crown Prosecution Service on charging matters and is dealt with in more depth in **Chapter 14—Charging Suspects**.

If there is insufficient evidence to charge a detainee, the review officer must decide whether detention continues to be necessary.

10.5.3 **Determine whether detention is still necessary**

Detention may be necessary for several reasons, some of which could be:

- to obtain evidence by questioning;
- to secure and preserve evidence;
- because the person is unfit (see **10.8 Reviewing detainees who are unfit to be dealt with** below);
- to place the detainee before the next available court in accordance with the terms of a warrant.

Consideration should be given to releasing the person, either with or without bail, if detention is no longer necessary.

10.5.4 **Remind the detainee of entitlement to free legal advice**

Before conducting a review, the review officer should ensure that the detained person is reminded of his/her entitlement to free legal advice. It is the responsibility of the review officer to ensure that all such reminders are noted in the custody record (Code C, para. 15.4). The reminder of entitlement to free legal advice must be given before conducting the review. This would allow the detained person the opportunity to consult with a legal representative before making representations on their own behalf.

10.5.5 **Allow representations to be made**

In reaching a decision as to whether a person's detention is still necessary, the review officer must provide an opportunity to the detainee or any legal representative, who is available at the time of the review, to make representations (Code C, para. 15.3).

However, this will not be necessary if:

- the person is asleep (para. 15.3(a)); or
- the detainee is considered by the review officer to be unfit to make representations because of his or her condition or behaviour (para. 15.3B).

The detained person, or his/her representative, may make written representations in relation to their continued detention. Any written representations shall be retained.

KEYNOTE

- There is no need for the review officer to actually contact the detained person's legal representative, unless the detainee specifically asks for them to be contacted. However, if that person is present at the time the review is due, they should be allowed to make representations on behalf of the detainee.
- If the review is conducted while the person is asleep, they must be informed of the decision and the reason as soon as practicable after waking (para. 15.7).

Under Code C, Note 15C, if a detainee's review was due when they were likely to be asleep, the review officer is still under an obligation to bring it forward to allow representations from him/her, provided the 'legal obligations and time constraints permit'.

A detainee *not* asleep during the review must be present when the grounds for their continued detention are recorded and must at the same time be informed of those grounds unless the review officer considers the person is incapable of understanding what is said, violent or likely to become violent or in urgent need of medical attention.

10.5.6 Note any comment made

After hearing representations, the review officer should make their decision and inform the detained person of the result. The review officer must note any comment made by the detained person if the decision is to keep that person in detention (Code C, para. 15.5).

The review officer must not put specific questions to the detained person regarding his or her involvement in an offence (Code C, para. 15.6), as this would constitute an interview under para. 11 of the *Codes of Practice*. The review process does not require the detained person to be cautioned at this time; the detainee could therefore incriminate themselves.

There may be occasions when detainees make unsolicited comments to the review officer. These comments should not be ignored, as they may be of evidential value. As the review process is outside the context of an interview, comments should be recorded and the person should be given the opportunity to sign the record (Code C, para. 11.13).

10.5.7 Record the decision

Review officers should record, as soon as practicable, the outcome of each review, in the presence of the detained person (s. 37(5) PACE and Code C, Note 15E).

However, the decision need not be recorded in the detainee's presence if:

- they are violent or likely to become violent, incapable of understanding, asleep or in urgent need of medical attention (s. 37(6)); or
- the review is conducted in accordance with Code C, para. 15.9 (Telephone Reviews of Detention).

10.5.8 Telephone reviews and video conferencing

The Criminal Justice Act 2003 amended PACE and clarified the position in respect of telephone reviews (s. 40A). In addition, the *Codes of Practice* were amended to include guidance as to how and when such reviews should take place and extensive guidance may be found in Code C, paras. 15.9–15.14.

The Criminal Justice Act 2003 also added s. 45A to PACE, allowing the use of video conferencing to conduct reviews. The use of video conferencing facilities for decisions about detention is subject to the introduction of regulations by the Secretary of State. However, there are currently no regulations in place to conduct such reviews.

Review officer's decision

Under s. 40A of PACE, the officer responsible for reviewing the detention of a person who has not been charged need not attend the police station holding the detainee and may carry out the review by telephone.

The decision as to whether or not the review takes place in person or by telephone is a matter for the review officer, who must take into account the needs of the person held in custody. Each case should be considered on its own merits, but consideration should be given to conducting the review in person if the person is:

- a juvenile (and the age of the juvenile); or
- mentally vulnerable; or
- has been subject to medical attention for other than routine minor ailments; or
- there are presentational or community issues around the person's detention.

Also, under para. 15.9C the review officer may terminate a telephone review and conduct it in person if he or she thinks it is necessary. The reasons for doing so should be noted in the custody record.

Documentation

When a telephone review is carried out, the review officer may require another officer at the station where the detainee is being held to carry out some of the functions required under s. 40 of PACE and para. 15.10, namely:

- making any record connected with the review in the detainee's custody record;
- if applicable, making a record in the presence of the detainee; and
- giving the detainee information about the review.

It must be remembered that the review officer will still be expected to hear representations from a detainee or their representative. Paragraph 15.11 states that this may be done by fax or email, but if these facilities are not available, the review officer must hear representations orally by telephone.

A record must be made of the reason the review officer did not attend the station holding the detainee and where he or she was at the time the review was conducted, as well as the method of any representations made to the custody officer.

The provisions of PACE, s. 40A allowing telephone reviews do not apply to:

- reviews of detention after charge by the custody officer;
- reviews under the Terrorism Act 2000, Sch. 8, Part II in terrorism cases;
- the procedure under s. 42—extending detention.

10.6 **Who Should be Reviewed?**

Only certain persons are subject to reviews, under s. 40 of the Police and Criminal Evidence Act 1984: those who are both:

(a) in police detention, and

(b) subject to the investigation of an offence.

We will examine both of these issues separately.

10.6.1 **Legislative provisions**

Section 118(2) PACE

A person is in police detention if he:

(a) has been taken to a police station after being arrested for an offence; or

(b) is arrested at a police station after attending voluntarily at the station or accompanying a constable to it;

and

is detained there or is detained elsewhere in the charge of a constable.

Code C, Note for Guidance 15B

The detention of persons in police custody not subject to the statutory review requirement in para. 15.1 should still be reviewed periodically as a matter of good practice. Such reviews can be carried out by an officer of the rank of sergeant or above. The purpose of such reviews is to check the particular power under which a detainee is held continues to apply, any associated conditions are complied with and to make sure appropriate action is taken to deal with any changes. This includes the detainee's prompt release when the power no longer applies, or their transfer if the power requires the detainee be taken elsewhere as soon as the necessary arrangements are made.

10.6.2 **In police detention**

Section 118(2) of the Act (see above) provides a definition of when a person is in police detention. The majority of detainees will fall under the category of (a) or (b), which are self-explanatory.

In certain circumstances, detainees may leave the police station, during their period of detention, to assist with the investigation. They will be, of course, in the charge of a constable. Examples of such persons are:

- persons who are assisting the investigating officers with a s. 18 search;
- persons who are accompanying officers to the scene of a crime;
- persons who are accompanying officers to identify premises that have been burgled;
- persons who have been transferred to hospital for an intimate search (e.g. for drugs).

The common feature of the above examples is that evidence is being secured, while the detainee is not at a police station.

Of course, unlike the last example above, some detained persons will be transferred to hospital for medical treatment, which does not form part of the investigative process. Section 41(6) of the Act states that where a person is removed to hospital because of a need for medical treatment, provided they are not interviewed, any time spent at the hospital would not count towards the 'detention clock'.

What this section of the Act fails to establish is whether or not reviews continue to be necessary.

Consider the following:

Case Study

A person was transferred to hospital from police detention, after collapsing in a cell. Following treatment, the person was detained at the hospital for observations overnight. At 4.00am, the custody officer was informed that the detainee could not have committed the offence for which he was arrested.

What safeguards would there be to ensure that the person was released in these circumstances, in accordance with s. 34 of the Act, if no reviews were conducted?

....

The issue of whether or not the person's detention should continue to be reviewed, when he/she has been transferred to hospital from police detention, causes considerable debate.

Section 41(6) of the Act states that where a person is removed to hospital because of a need for medical treatment, provided they are not interviewed, any time spent at the hospital would not count towards the 'detention clock'. The Home Office has rejected amendments to the *Codes of Practice* to clear up this issue on the grounds that:

> Section 41(6) of PACE is clear that all detention and review clocks stop. The Code cannot provide any further clarification than already exists in the Act.

In my view, s. 41(6) of PACE does *not* clarify the position in respect of the review clock and only deals with the detention clock. This section fails to mention reviews, or whether or not they continue to be necessary.

The police have to consider a detainee's right to liberty and security under Article 5 of the European Convention on Human Rights, incorporated in the Human Rights Act 1998, and they should not detain a person without proper grounds, especially as they will almost always be under police guard at a hospital, and not free to come and go as they please. If, as in the example above, a person is eliminated from an enquiry while they are in hospital, without reviews, who would safeguard the person's right to be released promptly, without charge?

There will be other occasions when an arrested person is taken to hospital with an injury before being brought before a custody officer. This is more straightforward—while a person taken to hospital in these circumstances may remain under arrest, their detention would not have been authorised by a custody officer, which is the starting point for the review clock. Such a person is not in police detention—if they were, all the rights/restrictions/powers that would usually apply in such circumstances (e.g. notification of arrest, access to solicitors, appropriate adults and interpreters) should be made available to the suspect and the police alike.

Yet again, I recommend that custody officers consult their own force procedures on both these issues.

10.6.3 **Subject to the investigation of an offence**

Some people will be detained in the custody office, but are not covered by s. 40 because, even though they are (a) in police detention, they are not (b) subject to the investigation of an offence. However, Code C, Note 15B above states that such persons should be 'reviewed periodically as a matter of good practice'(see also *Chief Constable of Cleveland Police* v *McGrogan* [2002] EWCA Civ 86, where the person was detained for a breach of the peace). 'Periodically' is not defined in the *Codes of Practice*; but it would make sense to conduct such reviews at the same intervals as a person who is covered by s. 40.

Examples of people who fall into this category are:

Where a person is:

(a) arrested on warrant having failed to answer bail to appear at court;

(b) arrested under the Bail Act 1976, s. 7(3) for breaching a condition of bail granted after charge;

(c) in police custody for specific purposes and periods under the Crime (Sentences) Act 1997, Sch. 1;

(d) a convicted or remand prisoner being held in a police station on behalf of the Prison Service under the Imprisonment (Temporary Provisions) Act 1980, s. 6;

(e) being detained to prevent them causing a breach of the peace;

(f) being detained at a police station on behalf of the Immigration Service;

(g) being detained by order of the magistrates' court under the Criminal Justice Act 1988, s. 152 (as amended by the Drugs Act 2005) to facilitate the recovery of evidence after being charged with drug possession or drug trafficking and suspected of having swallowed drugs.

Note 15B has cleared up any ambiguity as to who should conduct reviews in relation to detainees falling under the above categories. Such reviews may be conducted by sergeants.

KEYNOTE

Note that a person falling within para. (g) above would not be detained because of an investigation into a new offence; they will have already been charged with the relative offence and their detention will have been ordered by the court to recover evidence only. This extra bullet point has been added to draw attention to the medical risk associated with suspects remanded under s. 152 of the Criminal Justice Act 1988 as amended by s. 8 of the Drugs Act 2005 (see **8.11 Extended detention of suspected drug offenders** above).

Finally, Code C, para. 1.12 makes it clear that even though a person may be in police detention, but not subject to reviews under s. 40 of the Act, the way such people are treated should be of no lower standard than that for other detained people. If in doubt as to whether a person falls within the definition of a detained person, it is suggested that he/she should be afforded all the rights and privileges outlined in the *Codes of Practice*.

10.6.4 **Persons not in police detention**

The final paragraph of s. 118(2)(b) of the Act states that a person who is at a court after being charged is not in police detention for the time that they are in court.

However, some detainees who are taken before the court will return to the station, for example when they have been taken before the magistrates for an application for a warrant to extend detention under s. 43 or s. 44 of PACE. When detainees who fall into this category return to the police station, an inspector should continue to review their detention at nine-hour intervals.

10.7 **Timing of Reviews**

The timing of reviews of police detention are covered by s. 40 of PACE. Section 40(3) sets out the times when reviews must be conducted.

10.7.1 **Legislative provisions**

Section 40(3) PACE

Subject to s. 40(4) . . .

(a) the first review shall be not later than six hours after the detention was first authorised;

(b) the second review shall be not later than nine hours after the first;

(c) subsequent reviews shall be at intervals of not more than nine hours.

Section 40(4) PACE

Reviews may be delayed:

In general, when,

(a) 'It is not practicable to carry out the review';

More specifically when,

(a) (i) The person is being questioned and 'an interruption of the questioning, for the purpose of carrying out the review, would prejudice the investigation' *or*

(ii) 'No review officer is readily available.'

10.7.2 **Reviews brought forward**

It is perfectly acceptable under the Act to bring a review forward to an earlier time, and it may be done for operational reasons. For example, if the review officer is already in the custody office, reviewing another detainee, it makes perfect sense to conduct more than one review at the same time. If the review officer were not allowed to do this, he or she would have to leave the custody office and return several times as the prevailing circumstances demanded.

Another reason for bringing the review forward would be where it can be foreseen that the detained person will be subject of an investigative process, for example, assisting with a s. 18 search, when the review is due. Section 40(3) of the Act enables review officers to do this, as it states reviews shall be conducted 'not later than' six or nine hours (depending on the review), which suggests that reviews may be conducted at any time before the deadline.

> **KEYNOTE**
>
> Where a review has been brought forward for one of the reasons listed, subsequent reviews must take place not more than nine hours after that review was actually conducted and not nine hours after the review was due.

10.7.3 **Delays to reviews**

Wherever there is a delay in complying with any of the provisions of the Act, there is a legal requirement to record those reasons on the custody record. There is one general and two specific occasions when a review may be delayed. These are covered in s. 40(4) of the Act (see above).

Section 40(4)(a)—When it is not practicable to carry out the review

Below are some examples:

• the detained person is the subject of an investigative medical procedure, for example, intimate samples being obtained;

• the detained person is the subject of an intimate search;

• the detained person is assisting with a s. 18 search, when the review is due.

Section 40(4)(b)(i)—Interruption of questioning

This is self-explanatory.

However, if it can be foreseen that the review would coincide with any of the above circumstances, the review should be brought forward.

Section 40(4)(b)(ii)—No review officer is readily available

Below are some examples:

- the review officer, an inspector, is engaged in dealing with a firearms incident when the review is due;
- the review officer, a custody officer, is engaged in 'booking in' several persons when the review is due;
- the review officer, an inspector, is conducting the review of another detainee;
- the reviewing officer reported sick and there was a delay in finding an alternative reviewing officer.

A postponed review must be carried out as soon after the latest period specified as is practicable, and the review officer is required to record the reasons for any postponement in the custody record.

KEYNOTE

Remember that if a review is delayed without a legitimate reason, the subsequent period of detention could be unlawful, until the review is properly conducted.

The case, *Roberts* v *Chief Constable of Cheshire Constabulary* [1999] 1 WLR 662, highlights this issue. In this case, there was a two-hour delay, caused by a miscalculation of when the review was due.

It was held that even though the review was conducted late without good reason, when the review eventually took place, there were still legitimate grounds to detain Roberts. This meant that even though Roberts was unlawfully detained during that two-hour period, the unlawfulness was cured by the subsequent review and any further detention was, in fact, lawful. Damages were only awarded for the unlawful two-hour period. The effect of the *Roberts* case is that if it is discovered that a review has been missed, for whatever reason, there is no requirement for the custody officer or the review officer to release the person from custody, provided grounds still remain for the person's detention to continue. The importance of continuing to review detainees was highlighted in the introduction to this chapter, and the consequences of failing to comply with PACE were outlined. Despite these difficulties, custody officers in a busy custody office will be expected to manage large numbers of detainees, with different Relevant Times and Review Times.

10.8 Reviewing Detainees who are Unfit to be Dealt With

10.8.1 Legislative provisions

Code C, Para. 12.3

Before a detainee is interviewed, the custody officer, in consultation with the officer in charge of the investigation and appropriate health care professionals as necessary, shall assess whether the detainee is fit to be interviewed.

10.8.2 Determining that the detainee is unfit

Often the custody officer will determine that a detained person is not fit to be dealt with, when detention is first authorised. A person may be unfit for several reasons, such as:

- being drunk;
- being under the influence of drugs;
- because of their physical state;
- because of their mental state.

As previously discussed, when conducting the review, the review officer must determine whether or not detention continues to be necessary. Persons who have been arrested for an offence, and have also been declared unfit for one of the reasons listed above, may fall under one of two broad categories:

1. those where there is sufficient evidence to charge (e.g. drunk and disorderly, or s. 5 of the Public Order Act 1986);

2. those who have been arrested for an offence which involves an investigative process (e.g. burglary where the person is under the influence of drink or drugs).

Dealing with situation 1, there may be circumstances when it is necessary to interview a person arrested for s. 5; however, in most cases, these people are detained for the purpose of charge only. Where such a person is unfit to be charged, the custody officer will detain him or her under s. 37(9) of PACE, until a time when the person is fit to be dealt with.

Dealing with situation 2, where an interview, or other investigation is necessary, the custody officer will detain the person under s. 37(2) of the Act. However, in these circumstances, the investigative process to secure and preserve evidence may continue, even though the person is unfit.

We have already discussed the review officer's duties in respect of s. 40 of the Act. Section 40(9) places an additional obligation on the review officer if the person in custody was detained under s. 37(9) (sufficient evidence to charge, but unfit to do so).

Section 40(9) does not state that it is the sole responsibility of the review officer to determine that a person is 'yet in a fit state' to be dealt with. It is simply one of the issues to be checked upon whilst conducting the review. The custody officer has an ongoing responsibility to establish whether a detainee is 'yet in a fit state' to be dealt with. This situation is mentioned in relation to 'Fitness to be Interviewed', in Code C, para. 12.3 above.

(Further guidance is provided in Annex G of the *Codes of Practice*.)

10.9 **Relevant Time Discussed in Depth**

10.9.1 **Legislative provisions**

Section 41 of the Act is dedicated to occasions when people are arrested outside a force area, and how this affects the relevant time. In the vast majority of cases, the relevant time will be the point when a detained person first arrives at a custody office whilst under arrest for an offence. Unfortunately, things get a little complicated when detainees are arrested in other force areas or even abroad. We will examine the principles behind this section.

- Only the police stations in England and Wales are subject to s. 41. For this reason the English/Scottish border is to be treated as a 'point of entry' into England and Wales. This point is highlighted by s. 41(2)(b)(ii).

- All of the police forces in England and Wales are to be treated as separate and individual 'police areas'. This point is highlighted by s. 41(3), (4) and (5).

- The time period of 24 hours features twice in the Act:

  (i)   24-hours Investigation Time—the period in which the police can investigate a crime without applying for an extension to this time.

  (ii) 24-hours Travelling Time—the maximum amount of travelling time permissible to transfer a detainee between any two police areas within England and Wales or to transfer a detainee arrested abroad to any police station within England and Wales, once they have crossed the Scottish border, landed at an airport, or docked at a seaport.

- The basic assumption is that 24 hours is sufficient time to transfer a detainee between any two police areas anywhere within England and Wales and if this period is exceeded, any additional Travelling Time must be deducted from the 24-hour Investigation Time.
- Each police area is allowed a period of 24 hours to investigate their respective matters; and a period of 24 hours Travelling Time, to enable the detainee to be transferred on each and every occasion between different police areas.
- In each of the cases, if he/she is interviewed in the first area about an offence for which he/she is wanted in the second area, the relevant time will commence from the time he/she arrived in the first area.

KEYNOTE

In the case of *DPP* v *Davies* [1992] Crim LR 911, a person underwent a station breath test procedure in one police area (including providing samples), before being transferred to a second area where he was wanted for the offence. This was held not to be an interview for the purposes of the detention clock.

The relevant time marks the start of the 24-hour 'investigation period', but this can be affected by the Travelling Times. In order to fully comprehend the impact that the Travelling Time has on the relevant time, we must first establish when the 24-hour Travelling Time commences.

Consider the following:

Case Study

Detainee arrested by a police force for an offence in its own area, and wanted by the 'home force' for another offence.

CARTER was arrested for taking a conveyance without the owner's consent in the Greater Manchester Police area. After arriving at the custody office, PNC showed that CARTER was wanted for a burglary in Bristol (Avon and Somerset Police area).

....

There are a number of ways in which officers from each police area could deal with this matter, but let us assume that officers from Avon and Somerset wish to question CARTER, in Bristol.

In this scenario, the Manchester officers could detain CARTER for up to 24 hours (or 36 if authorised) to investigate their own offence. In order to transfer CARTER from Manchester to Bristol, a period of 24 hours travel time is allowed between the two police areas. Provided CARTER has not been interviewed about the Bristol offence, and he arrives in Bristol before the end of this period, the Avon and Somerset officers may detain him for a further 24 hours to investigate their burglary.

Because the Manchester officers require time to investigate their own offence, the 24-hour Travelling Time doesn't actually start until CARTER leaves the custody office in Manchester.

Case Study

Detainee arrested by a police force on behalf of the 'home force'.

Officers from Swindon (Wiltshire Police Area) have circulated BROWN as being wanted in their police area for theft. BROWN is stopped by Maidstone officers (Kent Police Area), for a routine check. PNC reveals that BROWN is wanted in Swindon and he is arrested for the theft and taken to the nearest custody office. BROWN is to be transferred to Swindon.

In the second scenario the Maidstone officers have no need to question BROWN and therefore do not require a 24-hour investigation period. Swindon officers will require a period of up to 24-hours Travelling Time plus 24-hours Investigation Time in respect of the Swindon theft.

Because there is no requirement for Maidstone officers to investigate an offence in their own area, provided BROWN is not interviewed about the Swindon offence before he leaves, the 24-hour travelling period commences when the Maidstone officers first arrested BROWN.

Some questions arise out of the above Case Studies:

What if in the first scenario the Manchester officers wanted to apply for a remand in custody for CARTER's involvement in their offence?

Answer: The Bristol officers could submit an application to the magistrates' court in Manchester for CARTER to be transferred to their custody under the Magistrates' Courts Act, 1980 ('three day lie down').

Alternatively, if appropriate, the Bristol officers could request that the police in Manchester release CARTER on bail for the Bristol offence to attend at a police station within the Bristol area at a later date.

NB: If this latter course of action is taken, there is no provision for the 24-hour detention period to restart when CARTER answers bail at Bristol. Only the remaining time of CARTER's initial 24-hour period of detention could be utilised.

What if, in the second scenario, BROWN was arrested for a Kent warrant (failing to appear) and then it was discovered that BROWN was wanted in Swindon?

Answer: In this instance Kent officers would have to obey the instructions of the warrant to take him before the next available court. However, because BROWN is not in detention for an offence, s. 31 of the Act (which requires officers to arrest for further offences prior to release) does not apply. Therefore if BROWN was given bail by the court, Kent officers could then arrest him on behalf of Swindon officers. The 24-hour Travelling Time would, as before, commence at the point of BROWN's arrest after appearing at court.

10.10 **Answering Police Bail**

10.10.1 **Legislative provisions**

Section 47(7) PACE

Where a person who was released on bail subject to a duty to attend at a police station is re-arrested, the provisions of this Part of this Act shall apply to him as they apply to a person arrested for the first time but this sub-section does not apply to a person who is arrested under s. 46A above or has attended a police station in accordance with the grant of bail (and who accordingly is deemed by s. 34(7) above to have been arrested for an offence).

10.10.2 **Detention clock**

The situation relating to reviews and relevant time is not straightforward when it comes to detainees being granted police bail.

As previously discussed, the time spent in police detention is measured by the 'detention clock'. The clock starts at the 'relevant time' and only stops when a detainee is either charged, transferred to hospital, or released before charge, either with or without bail. Therefore, it follows that the detention clock also stops when a person is released on police bail (see **Chapter 16— Bail**).

This section examines what happens to the detention clock, when the person's police bail is cancelled. The detention clock is affected by three different situations:

1. where the person answers bail as directed;
2. where the person fails to answer bail as directed;
3. where the person has been arrested before answering bail.

10.10.3 **When the person answers bail**

When a person has been released on police bail, and returns at the time directed by the custody officer, the clock will recommence when bail is answered, from the point at which it was temporarily halted (s. 47(6)).

Consider the following:

Case Study

FRANCIS was arrested for aggravated burglary and spent 22 hours in police detention, before being released on police bail to allow enquiries to be made. FRANCIS answered bail at the police station at the appointed time; however, at that time, the custody officer was dealing with a vulnerable detainee in the custody office who had tried to commit suicide. Due to the delay, the custody officer re-authorised FRANCIS' detention an hour after she arrived in the foyer of the police station.

In these circumstances, would the hour FRANCIS spent in the police station foyer count towards her detention clock?

....

PACE is not clear on this issue and practices vary around the country, with some forces insisting that the custody officer records the time the person actually arrived at the station and others that the custody officer records the time detention was re-authorised.

On the one hand, it could be said that FRANCIS has complied with the requirements of s. 47(3)(b) of the Act, which is 'to attend at such police station at such time, as the custody officer may appoint'. However, what if FRANCIS had arrived on time, but her legal representative was late and she decided to wait in the foyer until their arrival? Would the answer be different because the person had *chosen* not to present themselves before the custody officer?

Alternatively, what if there was a delay in the police station foyer that was beyond the custody officer's control; for example, it was busy and FRANCIS had to wait 20 minutes to be seen by the station enquiry clerk? Would the clock start when she arrived at the station, when she spoke to the station enquiry clerk or when the custody officer re-authorised detention? How far do you go?

Comparisons may be made to s. 7(2) of the Bail Act 1976, which states that a court may issue a warrant if a person who has been released on bail in criminal proceedings actually answers bail, but subsequently absents himself/herself from the court at any time after he/she has surrendered to custody, and before the court is ready to begin the hearing. What if FRANCIS had decided not to wait for the custody officer and walked away? Could the police have arrested her for failing to answer bail?

Section 47(6) of PACE states that where a person who has been granted bail and either has attended at the police station in accordance with the grant of bail or has been arrested under s. 46A above is detained at a police station, any time during which he or she was in police detention prior to being granted bail shall be included as part of any period which falls to be calculated under this Part of this Act.

As with many such contentious issues, there is no case law and little reference in the Act to guide a custody officer. For example, PACE does not instruct the custody officer to actually record the time of arrival when the person answers police bail (in contrast to the specific definition of when a person is 'at a police station' in Code C, para. 2.1A). Further, the Act does not specifically state that the clock starts when the detainee first arrives at the police station on their return from bail (as opposed to when detention is *first* authorised).

It is my view that in the circumstances described above, FRANCIS was not in police detention while waiting in the foyer; therefore, the time she spent there should not count towards the detention clock and the investigating officer has two hours in which to deal with the detainee (unless s. 42 of PACE applies and detention is extended). If she had walked away before detention was re-authorised, I believe she would not have answered bail and could be arrested. As usual, custody officers should check their own force policy on this issue.

10.10.4 When the person fails to answer bail

When a person is arrested for failing to answer police bail, the detention clock continues from the point where it was halted when the person was released and the existing custody record should be re-opened. The time re-commences when the custody officer re-authorises detention. This situation is similar to when the person actually answered bail above.

10.10.5 When the person is arrested before answering bail

The situation changes when a person is re-arrested, while they are actually on police bail. Where a person is arrested as a result of new evidence, which requires further investigation, the detention clock is re-set to zero and a new custody record should be opened (see s. 47(7) above).

(Section 47(7) refers to s. 46A of the Police and Criminal Evidence Act 1984. Section 46A has been inserted into the Act to provide police officers with a power of arrest for people who fail to answer police bail (a power that did not previously exist).)

(This subject is also covered in more depth in **Chapter 16—Bail**).

10.10.6 Reviewing detainees released on bail

Where a person has been released on police bail and does return to the police station, their 'review clock' carries on in the same manner as the detention clock.

In all other cases mentioned above, the detained person will be treated as if they are in custody for a 'new' offence, and the review should be calculated as normal, from the time that detention is first authorised by the custody officer.

Example

A person has been arrested and has spent eight hours in police detention, before being released on police bail. A review has been conducted by the duty inspector, at six-hours detention time. When the person returns to answer bail, another review will be due seven hours after their detention is once again authorised by the custody officer.

KEYNOTE

Remember!

New Evidence = New Detention Clock = New Review Clock = New Custody Record

10.11 **Summing Up**

Relevant time

The point in time from which the detained person's investigative clock commences, which in most cases lasts no longer than 24 hours (s. 41), but can be extended (see s. 42). The relevant time starts when a detained person arrives at the police station or if they are already at the police station when they are arrested.

'Detention Clock' and 'Review Clock'

The two clocks which run simultaneously whilst a person is in police detention.

- Detention Clock—measures how much investigation time has been used and starts at the relevant time;
- Review Clock—used to calculate when reviews should be carried out and commences when the custody officer first authorises detention.

Reviews (s. 40)

Periodic checks by the appropriate officer (see below) to establish if the arrested person's detention continues to be necessary.

Review officer

- Before charge—Inspector rank or above.

269

- After charge—Custody Officer.

NB. An officer is only a Review Officer at the point in time that the review is being conducted. The officer does not have a continuing responsibility between reviews.

Timing of reviews (s. 40)

- First review—to be conducted no later than six hours after detention is first authorised.
- Subsequent reviews—to be conducted no later than nine hours after the previous review and nine hours thereafter.

Delays to reviews

Three main occasions when a delay is permitted:

- In general—where it is not practicable to carry out the review;
- More specifically—when the detainee is being questioned and to interrupt the interview would prejudice the investigation;
- No Review Officer is 'readily available'.

Persons not in police detention

Where detainees are not under arrest for an offence, e.g. arrested to prevent a Breach of the Peace, failing to comply with bail conditions (s. 7 Bail Act 1976). Also, any detainee taken to court after charge (e.g. an application for a 72-hour remand in police custody under the Magistrates' Courts Act, otherwise known as a 'three day lie down') is no longer in Police Detention.

NB: any detainee taken to court for an application to a magistrate to extend detention under s. 43 or s. 44, remains in Police Detention for the purposes of the Act. Therefore the detention and review clocks keep running.

Persons answering police bail

- Where a person is arrested as a result of new evidence, which requires further investigation, the detention clock is re-set to zero and a new custody record should be opened.
- Where a person is arrested for failing to answer police bail, the detention clock continues from the point where it was halted when the person was released and the existing custody record should be re-opened. The time re-commences when the custody officer re-authorises detention.

LOCAL PROCEDURES

1. Does your force require reviews to be conducted on a detainee who has been held in custody at a hospital?

SPACE FOR NOTES

SPACE FOR NOTES

SPACE FOR NOTES

11

Extending Detention

11.1 **Introduction**

In the previous chapter (**Chapter 10—Reviews and Relevant Time**), we examined s. 41 of the Police and Criminal Evidence Act 1984, which allows a detained person to be kept in police detention for a maximum period of 24 hours, before they must be charged or released. In this chapter we will be examining the issue of detaining a person beyond the initial 24-hour period.

In the majority of cases, where a detained person is brought into police custody, 24 hours will be sufficient time to investigate the offence. But when the Act was drafted, the legislators considered that more time would be required to carry out an effective investigation for a more serious offence.

The Criminal Justice Act 2003 introduced a significant change to s. 42 of PACE, allowing a superintendent to authorise continued detention beyond 24 hours for less serious offences. The change, introduced in January 2004, meant that such detention could be authorised where a person was in custody for an arrestable offence (as opposed to a serious arrestable offence).

The introduction of the Serious Organised Crime and Police Act 2005, and the removal of the terms 'arrestable' and 'serious arrestable offence' from PACE, caused a further change, meaning that a superintendent must now consider whether the detainee has been arrested and detained for an indictable offence.

Higher levels of authority are still required in order to further extend periods of detention. Sections 43 and 44 of the Act require the authority of a magistrate to authorise additional periods of detention, beyond those which may be authorised by a superintendent.

We will be examining each section separately, concentrating on:

- who may authorise extensions to detention;
- under what circumstances they may be authorised; and
- the timing of applications.

Remember that a person's detention must be lawful and failing to follow the provisions of ss. 42, 43 and 44 may impact on the investigation. To deviate from this may render that detention unlawful, which may mean that any interviews conducted, or evidence secured during that period, are deemed inadmissible by the court.

The Human Rights Act 1998

This introduction would not be complete without a mention of the Human Rights Act 1998. As a reminder, Article 5 of the 1998 Act (right to liberty and security) will be of particular relevance when determining whether or not to authorise continued detention, especially in relation to detainees arrested under the Terrorism Act 2000, where detention periods are longer than those under PACE. A breach of the *Codes of Practice* may also be found to be a breach of the detainee's human rights.

As a 'public authority', the magistrates' courts will also have to be mindful of the implications of the 1998 Act, when deciding whether to authorise continued detention.

11.2 **Superintendent's Authority (s. 42)**

When reading this section, and those below relating to s. 43 and s. 44, it must be remembered that once the authority has been granted, there is no obligation on either the superintendent or magistrate to monitor the progress of the enquiry. Their role will be simply to authorise extra periods of detention to facilitate the investigation. There are sufficient provisions in the Act to ensure that the investigation is progressing in a diligent and expedient manner, as monitored by the custody officer and review officer. (See **flow chart 7 in Appendix 1** for an easy guide.)

11.2.1 **Legislative provisions**

Section 42(1) PACE

Under s. 42 of the Act—

Where a police officer of the rank of superintendent or above who is responsible for the police station at which a person is detained has reasonable grounds for believing that—

(a) the detention of that person without charge is necessary to secure or preserve evidence relating to an offence for which he is under arrest or to obtain such evidence by questioning him; and

(b) the offence for which he is under arrest is an indictable offence; and

(c) the investigation is being conducted diligently and expeditiously,

he may authorise the keeping of that person in police detention for a period expiring at or before 36 hours after the relevant time.

Code C, Note for Guidance 15E

The officer responsible for the police station holding the detainee includes:

a superintendent or above who, in accordance with their force operational policy or police regulations, is given that responsibility on a temporary basis whilst the appointed long-term holder is off duty or otherwise unavailable.

Section 42(4) PACE

An authorisation for an extension may not be given:

(a)   more than 24 hours after the relevant time; or

(b)   before the second review of his detention under s. 40 above has been carried out.

Code C, Para. 1.8

If this code requires a person to be given certain information they do not have to be given it if at the time they are incapable of understanding what is said, are violent or likely to become violent or in urgent need of medical attention, but they must be given it as soon as practicable.

11.2.2 **Granting the application**

We will examine the key issues arising out of s. 42. Note for Guidance 15E above clarifies the position in relation to who the 'officer responsible for the police station' is. Some police forces operate night time and weekend coverage at superintendent level, for serious incidents. These officers are often used as authorising officers for PACE requirements in all stations throughout their force area, and not just their own operational stations. These officers may act as authorising officers under PACE.

The Criminal Justice Act 2003 introduced a significant change to s. 42(1) of PACE, allowing a superintendent to authorise continued detention beyond 24 hours for less serious offences. As a result, detention could be authorised where a person was in custody for an arrestable offence (as opposed to a serious arrestable offence). In January 2005, the introduction of the Serious Organised Crime and Police Act 2005 meant the removal of the terms 'arrestable' and 'serious arrestable offence' from PACE. A superintendent must now consider whether the detainee has been arrested and detained for an indictable offence.

As discussed below, these changes should not mean that superintendents will be rushing to authorise extensions beyond 24 hours for relatively minor offences. Indeed, Home Office Circular 60/2003 (introduced as guidance in relation to the changes from the 2003 Act) states that the extension of the detention period for a broader category of offences represents a significant additional power for the police and it should be used sparingly and only where there is full justification. The additional need to consider Article 5 of the European Convention on Human Rights, incorporated in the Human Rights Act 1998 (right to liberty and security), should mean that an authorisation under s. 42(1) will only be granted for less serious offences when it is necessary and proportionate.

The circular makes particular reference to juveniles and other vulnerable people:

> Detaining a juvenile or a mentally vulnerable person for longer than 24 hours without charge will only normally be justifiable where the offence is a serious arrestable offence.

Paragraph 15.2A of the *Codes of Practice* provides further guidance on this issue. This paragraph states that detaining a juvenile or mentally vulnerable person for longer than 24 hours will be dependent on the circumstances of the case and with regard to:

(a) the person's special vulnerability;

(b) the legal obligation to provide an opportunity for representations to be made prior to a decision about extending detention;

(c) the need to consult and consider the views of any appropriate adult; and

(d) any alternatives to police custody.

Prior to the publication of the 2005 edition of the *Codes of Practice*, concern was expressed by a coalition of some children's charities and the Law Society that para. 15.2A is less stringent than the contents of HOC 60/2003 in relation to detaining juveniles and vulnerable persons, in that the Circular makes specific reference to serious arrestable offences (which obviously no longer exist), whereas the above Code is more general in its guidance on these matters. The Home Office deferred the decision at this time, stating that the Code does not dilute this consideration. The matter will be considered for future editions of the *Codes of Practice* and appropriate reference may be made.

Whichever guidance is used, when a superintendent is considering extending the detention of a juvenile or mentally vulnerable person who is detained for an indictable offence, he or she will need to be absolutely certain that his or her actions are both proportionate and justifiable in the circumstances.

278

In all other aspects, s. 42 remains the same, and in order to authorise an extension beyond 24 hours, the superintendent must have reasonable grounds for believing that the detention of that person without charge is necessary to investigate an indictable offence for which the person is under arrest, either by:

• securing or preserving evidence; or

• obtaining such evidence by questioning.

The two terms above are dealt with in depth in **Chapter 2—Detainees— Initial Action**. The terms diligently and expeditiously still apply, even though the superintendent may now authorise detention for an indictable offence and in some respects they take on more significance. For example, theft or shoplifting is an indictable offence, but is a superintendent likely to consider the investigation is being conducted diligently and expeditiously, if asked for an authorisation to extend detention beyond 24 hours for this particular offence? Of course each case will be different, but such a request is highly unlikely to be granted, unless the investigating officer has had exceptional difficulties in interviewing the detainee during the 24-hour period, because the person may be unfit through drink or drugs, or suffering from a mental health problem. It is more likely that where a superintendent is considering offences which are slightly more serious or complicated than shoplifting, such as burglary, robbery or fraud, he or she may consider the application favourably because of the number of witnesses or other detainees who need to be interviewed.

According to the *Oxford English Dictionary*, diligently, in these circumstances, means 'industriously', 'meticulously' and 'conscientiously'; expeditiously means 'speedily' or 'quickly'.

Consider the following:

Case Study

DURANI was arrested for an offence of aggravated burglary. A number of witnesses were spoken to during the first 24 hours of detention and by the time the investigating officers were ready to interview him, DURANI's 24-hour clock was running down quickly. The duty superintendent authorised an extension to his 24-hour detention period, allowing the investigating officer a further nine hours to conduct interviews and research an alibi provided by DURANI. This period was deemed to be sufficient at that time.

However, during this time, a further witness was found and it was decided to hold an identification parade. The superintendent was re-contacted and asked to authorise a further three hours detention to allow the parade to take place.

Would this request be acceptable?

....

The above scenario is quite common and perfectly acceptable under the Act. Authorisation may be given to keep the person in police detention for a period up to 36 hours after the relevant time. The length of time that a superintendent authorises in these circumstances will depend on how much time is actually needed by the investigating officer (bearing in mind the requirement for the investigation to be conducted diligently and expeditiously). Under s. 42(2) of the Act, if the superintendent authorises further detention for a period expiring less than 36 hours after the relevant time, that period may be re-examined and if necessary extended, up to a maximum period of 36 hours after the relevant time (provided the conditions specified in s. 42(1) are still satisfied when he/she gives the new authorisation).

KEYNOTE

The authorisation will extend the person's detention up to 36 hours after the relevant time. This means that regardless of when the authorisation is granted during the first 24 hours, the additional 12 hours (if that amount of time is authorised) commences when the 24-hour period expires.

11.2.3 Timing of the application

The onus will be on the investigating officer to manage the investigation time while the detainee is in custody, as regards such things as preparing for interviews, interviewing and managing forensic issues. Where a person has been detained for a serious offence, the detainee's clock will form part of the investigation strategy and experienced investigators will always have one eye on the detention clock. However, both the custody officer and the reviewing officer also have an important part to play.

During the investigation of more serious offences, Senior Investigating Officers (SIOs) often appoint a 'PACE Officer', who would be responsible for advising on issues such as monitoring detention periods, authorisations, and crucially, the timing of applications. There is a need for all persons involved to think ahead and communicate effectively with all parties involved, if it is likely that the investigation is going to last beyond the first 24 hours. The timing of the application for an extension will become crucial.

KEYNOTE

Issues that need consideration are:

- the application for an extension can take some time, particularly where more than one suspect is involved;
- the superintendent will be speaking to suspects, and possibly their legal representative, before making the decision (see **11.2.4 Detainee's rights** below);
- the need to make sure the superintendent is available to deal with the application in person;
- legal representatives and appropriate adults may need to be contacted and arrangements made for their presence;
- the custody officer may be busy with other detainees;
- detainees may be held in different custody offices;
- the detainee may require a period of rest or medication;
- the detainee may require transferring to another police station or force area (see s. 42(3) of the Act, which advises this must be taken into consideration).

With these and many other issues to consider, there is a definite need to plan ahead and avoid last minute applications.

In addition to the practical issues discussed above, there is a legal reason for considering the timing of applications for detention beyond the 24-hour period. Section 42(4)(a) of PACE (see above) is clear that an extension may not be granted once the 24 hours has expired (even if there would have been sufficient grounds to detain the person). Once the detention clock has expired, the detainee must be released and there is nothing more embarrassing than having to do so in these circumstances, especially if the offence is serious.

Under ss. (4)(b) above, the inspector must have conducted a second review on the detainee, before an extension can be authorised. This does not mean that the detainee has to have been in custody for 15 hours before it can be granted. For example, reviews are often brought forward for various reasons, which means that the second review may have been conducted after the detainee had been in custody for only 12 hours (or less). However, even if the first and second reviews were brought forward for legitimate reasons, it is possible that a superintendent will refuse an authorisation to extend detention for 12 hours, when there are still 10 or more hours remaining from the original 24-hour period. Obviously it will depend on the circumstances, but care should be taken not to abuse the authorities provided by the Act.

11.2.4 **Detainee's rights**

Before determining whether to authorise an extension under s. 42, the officer must give that person or any solicitor representing him/her, who is available at the time when it falls, an opportunity to make representations to him or her about the detention (s. 42(6)). In a Northern Ireland case, it was held that a failure to allow the detainee an opportunity to make representations may affect any subsequent application to the court for a further extension of detention (see *Re Maughan's Application* [1998] N.I. 293, QBD, Crown Side).

It is usual practice to make arrangements for the legal representative to be present when the decision is being made; however, s. 42(6) does not make it mandatory. Alternatively, the solicitor may be made available by telephone to give advice to their client. Again, if the investigation is planned correctly, solicitors may be given advanced notice of the intent to request an extension of detention.

KEYNOTE

Other issues affecting the detained person's rights are:

- representations may be made by the detainee or their legal representative either orally or in writing (s. 42(7));

- if the detained person is likely to be asleep at the latest time when an authorisation of continued detention may take place, the appropriate officer should bring it forward so that the detained person may make representations without being woken up (Code C, Note for Guidance 15C);

- where an officer authorises the keeping of a person in police detention under s. 42, he or she must inform that person of the grounds for his/her continued detention (s. 42(5));

- the superintendent may refuse to hear oral representations from the person in detention if he/she considers that the person is unfit to make such representations by reason of his/her condition or behaviour (s. 42(8));

- a review to decide whether to authorise a person's continued detention under s. 42 must be done in person rather than over the telephone (Code C, Note for Guidance 15F);

- where an officer authorises further detention under s. 42 and at the time the detainee has not yet exercised a right conferred by s. 56 (right to have someone informed), or s. 58 (right to legal advice), the officer shall:

  1. inform him/her of that right;
  2. decide whether he/she should be permitted to exercise it;
  3. record the decision in the custody record; and

---

4. if the decision is to refuse to permit the exercise of the right, record the grounds for the decision in that record.

KEYNOTE

Note that although there is a statutory duty under s. 42(5) to always inform the detained person of the decision to extend their detention, this is not necessary if the person is incapable of understanding what is said (see Code C, para. 1.8 above).

Also, the superintendent may refuse to hear representations from a detained person under s. 42(8) above if he/she considers the person is unfit, because of his/her condition or behaviour.

11.2.5 **Deferred bail**

Under s. 42(10) of the Act, where a person has had their detention extended by a superintendent, they must be released not later than 36 hours after the relevant time (either on bail or without bail), unless they have been charged with an offence, or continued detention has been authorised under s. 43 (application to magistrates).

When a person has been released under s. 42(10), he or she shall not be re-arrested without a warrant for the same offence, unless new evidence justifying a further arrest has come to light since his/her release (s. 42(11)).

On occasion, the investigating officer may decide to release the detained person on deferred bail. Provided there is no serious threat to witnesses or danger that the detainee will re-offend or fail to appear, the use of deferred bail may provide valuable time to the investigation, which might not otherwise be possible when relying on s. 42, s. 43 or s. 44.

The use of deferred bail in circumstances as described above does, however, raise a question. Consider the following circumstances:

Case Study

PORTER was arrested for an offence of deception, where she used several stolen credit cards to obtain £20,000 worth of goods. PORTER's detention was extended by 12 hours when she had been in custody for 20 hours; however, the officer in the case decided that she would be unable to conclude her enquiries for some weeks; there-fore, PORTER was released on deferred bail for four weeks. PORTER had been in cus-tody for 30 hours when she was released.

The question often asked in these circumstances is:

> 'Does a superintendent have to re-authorise the detention time on Porter's return to the station, or does the original authorisation to extend the detention by 12 hours still apply?'

Since neither PACE nor the *Codes of Practice* refer specifically to this issue, police forces are left to their own interpretation. There are two opposite trains of thought:

1. The reason for extending detention should be re-visited and a superintend-ent should re-authorise the extended period of detention, as the circumstances may have changed since the person was released on bail. Since it required an officer of the rank of superintendent to authorise the extension in the first place, the integrity of the investigation could be compromised if an officer of that rank did not question the reason for detention, as the 24 hours have now expired.

2. There is nothing in the Act that states that a superintendent must re-authorise detention at this time. If the original reasons for the extension still apply (i.e. it is an indictable offence; the enquiry is still being conducted diligently and expeditiously; evidence needs to be obtained by questioning or secured and preserved), a superintendent need not re-authorise detention at this time.

In this section, we have concluded that there is no specific obligation on either a superintendent or a magistrate to monitor the progress of an enquiry once a decision has been made to extend detention under ss. 42 or 43. Why then would a superin-tendent have to re-visit this decision, simply because the period of detention has been interrupted by a period of bail? Also, what if the detainee in the scenario had been bailed until the next day for an ID parade because the investigating officer did not wish to use up their clock? Should this be viewed differently from the case of the detainee who is bailed for extensive enquiries?

There are sufficient safeguards in PACE and the *Codes of Practice* to make sure the detainee's detention time is monitored initially by the custody sergeant when the person answers bail and where necessary by the review officer subsequently. My view is that for the above reasons, and the fact that PACE is silent on this issue, a superintendent's authority is not needed at this stage. However, I recommend that custody officers consult their own force policy on this issue.

> **KEYNOTE**
>
> Note that whichever answer is used, the investigating officer in the scenario will only have six hours in which to complete her enquiries.
>
> However, if the superintendent in the scenario had only granted 10 hours extra detention, instead of 12, the investigating officer would have only four hours to complete the enquiries. If further time were required (i.e. the remaining two hours), this would have to be authorised by a superintendent.

11.3 **Warrants of Further Detention (s. 43)**

Where it appears to the investigating officer that 36 hours may not be long enough to conclude their enquiries, they may apply for a warrant of further detention. Under s. 43 and s. 44 of the Act, applications may be made for two further periods of time, both of 36 hours duration. An application must initially be made for a warrant of further detention under s. 43 (taking the maximum detention period up to 72 hours), and then an application for an extension to the warrant of further detention may be made under s. 44 (taking the maximum detention period up to 96 hours). (See **flow chart 8 in Appendix 1** for an easy guide.)

The introduction of the Serious Organised Crime and Police Act 2005 means that, as with an application under s. 42(1) above (superintendent's authority to extend detention), an application under s. 43 or s. 44 of PACE may now be made in relation to any *indictable* offence (as opposed to a serious arrestable offence). However, as discussed in **11.2.2 Granting the application**, the authorisation of additional detention time for minor offences should only be used sparingly, and where there is full justification. As a public authority, the court will need to consider Article 5 of the European Convention on Human Rights, incorporating the Human Rights Act 1998 (right to liberty and security), which should mean that authorisations under s. 43 and s. 44 will only be granted for less serious offences when it is necessary and proportionate.

11.3.1 **Legislative provisions**

Section 43(11)–(12) PACE

A warrant of further detention may be issued for such period as the magistrates' court thinks fit, having regard to the evidence before it; however, this period shall not be longer than 36 hours.

Section 43(5)(b) PACE

Where an application is made, and—

(i) it is not practicable for the magistrates' court to which the application will be made to sit at the expiry of 36 hours after the relevant time; but

(ii) the court will sit during the 6 hours following the end of that period,

the application may be made at any time before the expiry of the said 6 hours.

Code C, Note for Guidance 15D

An application for a warrant of further detention or its extension should be made between 10am and 9pm, and if possible during normal court hours. It will not be practicable to arrange for a court to sit specially outside the hours of 10am to 9pm.

If it appears possible that a special sitting may be needed (either at a weekend, Bank/Public Holiday or on a weekday outside normal court hours but between 10am and 9pm) then the clerk to the justices should be given notice and informed of this possibility, while the court is sitting if possible.

11.3.2 **Applying for warrant of further detention**

Under s. 43(1), a constable may make an application on oath, by laying information before a magistrates' court for a warrant of further detention (see above). The court may issue a warrant, which authorises the keeping of that person in police detention if they are satisfied 'that there are reasonable grounds for believing that the further detention of the person to whom the application relates is justified'.

In other words, if an application is granted at this stage, the detainee may be held up to a maximum of 72 hours (three days) from their relevant time, without being charged.

The court must be provided with a copy of the information from the officer making the application (s. 43(2)), and s. 43(14) sets out what must be contained in the information:

- the nature of the offence for which the person to whom the application relates has been arrested;

- the general nature of the evidence on which that person was arrested;

- what enquiries relating to the offence have been made by the police and what further enquiries are proposed by them;

- the reasons for believing the continued detention of that person to be necessary for the purposes of such further enquiries.

Under s. 43(4), the court must consider similar issues that a superintendent
would have to consider when authorising an extension under s. 42(1), that:

(a) the detention of that person without charge is necessary to secure or preserve evidence relating to an offence for which he/she is under arrest or
to obtain such evidence by questioning him/her;

(b) an offence for which he/she is under arrest is an indictable offence;
and

(c) the investigation is being conducted diligently and expeditiously.

KEYNOTE

Some other issues to note:

- The application must be made before at least two justices of the peace in open
court.
- The detained person must be brought before the court for the hearing.
- The detainee is also entitled to be legally represented at the hearing and, if
he/she is not represented but wishes to be, the court must adjourn the hearing
to obtain representation.
- The detainee may be kept in police detention during the adjournment.

11.3.3 Timing of the application

As with an application under s. 42 of the Act (superintendent's authority), the
timing of the application under s. 43 will be important, and the onus will be
with the investigating officer, liaising with the custody officer, to ensure that
the time is managed efficiently.

An application may be made under s. 43 at any time before the expiry of
36 hours after the relevant time (s. 43(5)(a)). The officer in the case will nat-
urally wish to use as much time from the 36 hours available to him/her (if a
superintendent's extension has been granted), but the facility is available to
take the detainee to court at any time during this initial period of detention.

Consider the following:

Case Study 1

The police are investigating a murder, and the senior investigating officer (SIO) realises early on that 36 hours will not be sufficient, and that an application for extended
detention will almost certainly be required.

Consider the following question:

> If the SIO did take the detainee before court after 12 hours' detention, would 12 hours be lost from the investigation time?

....

The answer to the above question is 'no'; the time would not be lost by taking the detained person to court early. The time periods under s. 42 and s. 43 run consecutively, whenever the extension is granted. The court would merely state that detention expires after 72 hours from the relevant time. This would include the original 24 hours (allowed in all cases), as well as the additional 12 hours that could be granted by a superintendent (even if they were not applied for), as well as the additional 36 hours that could by granted by a magistrate. (However, it should be noted that the magistrates are not obliged to grant the full 36 hours in these circumstances and may decide that the police can make do with less time.)

Consider another example:

Case Study 2

KIM has been arrested for an indictable offence and has been in custody for 26 hours, having had his detention time extended for 12 hours by a superintendent. The time is 4.00pm on Friday, and the next available court is 10.00am tomorrow. The investigating officer has indicated that she will require further time to investigate the offence, and intends applying to the court for a warrant of further detention.

Will it be possible to keep KIM in custody and take him to the next available court tomorrow?

....

In addition to allowing early applications for extensions, s. 43 also allows late applications to be made (see s. 43(5)(b) above).

KIM's current detention time expires at 2.00am, which is 8 hours before the next court sits. Section 43(5)(b) requires the detainee to be in court at most 6 hours after the expiry of the 36-hour period. Therefore, KIM would need to be taken before the magistrates sometime between 2.00am and 8.00am, which is, of course, not possible. KIM must be taken to court now, if an extension is to be granted.

Where a person has been detained under s. 43(5)(b)(ii) above and is awaiting an appearance in court, the custody officer shall make a note in that person's custody record that the 36 hours has expired, and the reason that the person is still in detention.

Further guidance is provided in relation to the timing of an application in Code C, Note for Guidance 15D above.

To further emphasise the need to make the application on time, s. 43(7) states that if it is made after the expiry of 36 hours after the relevant time, and it appears to the magistrates' court that it would have been reasonable for the police to make it before the expiry of that period, the application must be dismissed. This was confirmed in *R v Slough Justices, ex parte Stirling* [1987] Crim LR 576, which centred around a detainee, whose 36-hour period had expired at 12.53pm. The case was not heard by the justices until 2.45pm. The Divisional Court held that the police should have made their application between 10.30am and 11.30am, even though this was before the 36-hour time limit had been reached.

Section 45(2) of PACE provides some limited protection to investigating officers and review officers, where errors are made in relation to the timing of an application for an extension by a superintendent, or warrant for further detention, by stating that:

> Any reference in this Part of this Act to a period of time or time of day shall be treated as approximate only.

However, this will not provide an excuse for delaying an application for more than a few minutes.

KEYNOTE

Where a warrant of further detention has been granted, the person shall be released from police detention, either on bail or without bail, upon or before the expiry of the warrant, unless he/she is charged. Such a person must not be re-arrested without a warrant for the same offence, unless new evidence justifying a further arrest has come to light since his/her release (see s. 43(18)).

11.3.4 Where an application has been refused

Under s. 43(8), where a court is not satisfied that there are reasonable grounds for believing that the further detention is justified, they may either refuse the application, or adjourn the hearing until a time not later than 36 hours after the relevant time. This means that if the officer making the application fails to convince the court that detention is necessary under s. 43, the court may order an adjournment. This could be either to give themselves more time to consider the application, or to order further evidence to be produced by the investigating officer showing that further detention is necessary. The person may be kept in police detention during the adjournment (s. 43(9)), but the case must be heard before the expiry of 36 hours from the relevant time.

If the application is refused outright, the detained person shall forthwith be charged or released, either on bail or without bail (s. 43(15)).

KEYNOTE

Under s. 43(16) if the application is heard, and refused, during the detained person's initial 24-hour detention period, he or she may be returned to police detention and the officer would have to apply to a superintendent for an extension under s. 42 of the Act if necessary.

If the application is heard, and refused, during the detained person's first 36-hour detention period (i.e. following authorisation under s. 42), he or she may be returned to police detention until the end of that period.

In either of the above cases, the detained person may be returned to court for a further application, but only if it is supported by evidence which has come to light since the refusal (see s. 43(17)).

11.4 Extension to Warrant of Further Detention (s. 44)

11.4.1 Applying for an extension

A final application may be made for an extension to the warrant of further detention, under s. 44 of the Act. A successful application will authorise a detention period of up to a further 36 hours, taking the maximum detention period to 96 hours (four days). (See **flow chart 9 in Appendix 1** for an easy guide.)

As with s. 43 above, an application under s. 44 must be made by a constable on oath, by laying information before a magistrates' court for a warrant of further detention. The court may issue a warrant, which authorises the keeping of that person in police detention if they are satisfied that there are reasonable grounds for believing that the further detention of the person to whom the application relates is justified (s. 44(1)).

A warrant of further detention under s. 44 may be issued for such period as the magistrates' court thinks fit, having regard to the evidence before it (s. 44(2)); however, this period shall not be longer than 36 hours, and end later than 96 hours after the relevant time (s. 44(3)).

Section 44(4) of the Act provides that if a court authorises a warrant of further detention for a period of less than the maximum 36 hours, a further application may be made to extend that period, for a period ending before 96 hours after the relevant time.

KEYNOTE

The procedure for making an application under s. 44 is the same as for an application under s. 43, which is described above.

11.4.2 **Timing of the application**

An application for extended detention under this section may only be made when a person has been detained, following a successful application for a warrant of further detention, under s. 43 above. The application must be made before the 36 hours, granted under s. 43, expires.

KEYNOTE

There is no provision under s. 44 to delay the application until a court is sitting in 6 hours time, as with s. 43(5) above. However, the provisions of Code C, Note for Guidance 15D do apply (see **11.3.3 Timing of the application** above, for the full extract from the *Codes of Practice*).

11.4.3 **Where an application has been refused**

Where an application under this section is refused, the person to whom the application relates shall forthwith be charged or released, either on bail or without bail (s. 44(7)). However, a person need not be released if they are already in custody subject to a warrant of further detention (issued under s. 43 above), until the time limit has expired on that particular extension (s. 44(8)). This means that the investigating officer may return the detainee to the police station until this time has expired, unless further information becomes available which is sufficient to return to court and apply again under s. 44.

KEYNOTE

If it is proposed to transfer a person in police detention to a police area other than that in which he/she is detained when the application for a warrant of further detention is made, the court hearing the application shall have regard to the distance and the time the journey would take (s. 45(13)).

The amount of extended detention time that can be authorised and the timing of applications vary according to the section. The table below offers a quick guide:

Maximum Detention Period Authorised	PACE Section	By Whom Authorised?	When may it be Authorised?	Maximum Detention Time (Calculated from Relevant Time)
Initial 24 Hours	s. 37(3) s. 41	Custody Officer	Any time following arrest & arrival at station	24 hours
Additional 12 Hours	s. 42	Superintendent	Any time after second review (see text)	36 hours
Additional 36 Hours	s. 43	Magistrates' court	Any time during first 36 hours of detention	72 hours
Additional 36 Hours	s. 44	Magistrates' court	Any time before the warrant authorised under s. 43 above expires	96 hours

11.5 **Review Officer's Responsibility**

It must be remembered that even though an authorisation may have been granted under either s. 42, s. 43 or s. 44 above, the custody officer and reviewing officer still have a part to play in the person's detention. The person has not yet been charged; therefore, an inspector will be required to continue reviewing detention every 9 hours, applying the criteria set out in s. 40 of the Act (see **Chapter 10—Reviews and Relevant Time**, for an in-depth discussion on this subject).

The custody officer will also have a responsibility to continually monitor the person's detention under s. 34 of the Act. If he or she becomes aware that the grounds for the person's detention have ceased to apply and is not aware of any other grounds to justify continued detention, the custody officer must order the detainee's immediate release from custody.

11.6 **Summing Up**

Superintendent's authorisation (s. 42)

Where a police officer of the rank of superintendent or above who is responsible for the police station at which a person is detained has reasonable grounds for believing that—

(a) the detention of that person without charge is necessary to secure or preserve evidence relating to an offence for which he/she is under arrest or to obtain such evidence by questioning him/her;

(b) an offence for which he/she is under arrest is an indictable offence; and

(c) the investigation is being conducted diligently and expeditiously,

he/she may authorise the keeping of that person in police detention for a period expiring at or before 36 hours after the relevant time.

(s. 42 PACE)

Timing the application

1. The authorisation will extend the person's detention up to 36 hours after the relevant time. This means that regardless of when the authorisation is granted during the first 24 hours, the additional 12 hours (if that amount of time is authorised) commences when the 24-hour period expires.

2. An authorisation for an extension may not be given:

    (a) more than 24 hours after the relevant time; or

(b) before the second review of his/her detention under s. 40 above has been carried out.

(s. 42(4) PACE)

Warrants of further detention (s. 43)

1. A warrant of further detention may be issued for such period as the magistrates' court thinks fit, having regard to the evidence before it; however, this period shall not be longer than 36 hours.

(s. 43(11)–(12) PACE)

2. An application may be made under s. 43 at any time before the expiry of 36 hours after the relevant time.

(s. 43(5)(a) PACE)

3. Where an application is made, and—
    (i) it is not practicable for the magistrates' court to sit at the expiry of 36 hours after the relevant time; but
    (ii) the court will sit during the six hours following the end of that period, the application may be made at any time before the expiry of the six hours.

(s. 43(5)(b) PACE)

Extension to a warrant of further detention (s. 44)

1. An application may be made for an extension to a warrant of further detention, which may be issued for such period as the magistrates' court thinks fit, having regard to the evidence before it. However, this period shall not be longer than 36 hours, and end later than 96 hours after the relevant time.

(s. 44(3) PACE)

2. The application must be made before the 36 hours, granted under s. 43, expires.

Reviews

Even though an authorisation may have been granted under s. 42, s. 43 or s. 44, an inspector will still be required to continue reviewing detention every nine hours, applying the criteria set out in s. 40 of the Act.

LOCAL PROCEDURES

1. When a person has been released on deferred bail, and their detention time has been extended under s. 42 of PACE, does your force require a superintendent to re-authorise the detention time, when a person answers bail?

SPACE FOR NOTES

SPACE FOR NOTES

SPACE FOR NOTES

12

Identification and Samples

12.1 **Introduction**

The legislation governing identification can be found mainly in ss. 61, 62, 63, 64 and 65 of the Police and Criminal Evidence Act 1984, and Code D of the *Codes of Practice*. This chapter concentrates mainly on the powers given to take fingerprints and samples from detainees, and the duties given to authorising officers and custody officers. Code D also deals with identification by witnesses, such as showing photographs, identification parades and group identification; however, these are not dealt with in this book.

Substantial changes have been made to the original legislation, by the Criminal Justice and Public Order Act 1994 and the Criminal Evidence (Amendment) Act 1997. The Anti-Terrorism, Crime and Security Act 2001 has also inserted ss. 54A and 64A into PACE, relating to the areas of examining detainees to establish their identity and taking photographs.

There have been significant changes to this subject, notably in relation to taking intimate samples and other samples without consent. An inspector may now give authorisation, whereas previously, the authority of a superintendent was required.

The section on fingerprints is quite straightforward and deals with the issue of consent and non-consent. The Criminal Justice Act 2003 simplified the power to take fingerprints and non-intimate samples without consent.

Under s. 61 of PACE the police may take fingerprints away from the police station. Section 64A provides similar powers to take photographs of suspects away from the station, while under s. 61A(5) of PACE, officers may take samples of footwear from detainees for identification purposes.

Samples are divided into Intimate Samples (s. 62), and Non-Intimate Samples (s. 63). As with 'intimate searches' (see **Chapter 8—Dealing with Property and Searching**), a greater degree of authority is required to take an 'intimate sample', because of the potential for causing embarrassment to the detained person. Also, some intimate samples may only be taken by a registered medical practitioner, a registered nurse or a registered paramedic.

The Criminal Justice Act 2003 inserted s. 63B into PACE, which allows the police to test detainees for the presence of Class A drugs. This matter is covered in depth in this chapter.

It should be noted that many of the powers given to constables in this chapter have now also been given to detention officers. See **Chapter 1—The Role of the Custody Officer** for the full extent of powers given to detention officers.

The Human Rights Act 1998

Once again, the Human Rights Act 1998 has a part to play in this chapter; specifically Article 3 of the Convention, which states that, 'No one shall be subjected to torture or to inhuman or degrading treatment or punishment.' Although this aspect of the Human Rights Act is presently untested, clearly the police have a duty to rationalise their actions and show that it was necessary, proportional and legal to obtain an intimate sample.

12.2 **Fingerprints**

12.2.1 **Legislative provisions**

Section 61(1) PACE

Except as provided by this section, no person's fingerprints may be taken without the appropriate consent.

Section 61(3) PACE

The fingerprints of a person detained at a police station may be taken without the appropriate consent if—

(a) he is detained in consequence of his arrest for a recordable offence; and

(b) he has not had his fingerprints taken in the course of the investigation of the offence by the police.

Section 61(4) PACE

The fingerprints of a person detained at a police station may be taken without the appropriate consent if—

(a) he has been charged with a recordable offence or informed that he will be reported for such an offence; and

(b) he has not had his fingerprints taken in the course of the investigation of the offence by the police.

Section 61(3A) PACE

Where a person mentioned in para. (a) of ss. (3) or (4) has already had his fingerprints taken in the course of the investigation of the offence by the police, that fact shall be disregarded for the purposes of that subsection if—

(a) the fingerprints taken on the previous occasion do not constitute a complete set of fingerprints; or

(b) some or all of the fingerprints taken on the previous occasion are not of suffi-cient quality to allow satisfactory analysis, comparison or matching (whether in the case in question or generally).

12.2.2 **Taking fingerprints without consent**

Section 61(4) of PACE (see above) remains unchanged. A person's fingerprints may be taken by consent when he/she has been charged or reported for a recordable offence, and the authority of an inspector is not required.

The Criminal Justice Act 2003, Part 1, has extended the circumstances in which the police may take a person's fingerprints without consent, when a person has not been charged with a recordable offence.

Previously, where a person had not been charged with a recordable offence, the authority of an inspector was required, who could only authorise finger-prints to be taken without consent, if he/she had reasonable grounds for sus-pecting the person was involved in a criminal offence and either for believing that his or her fingerprints would tend to confirm or disprove their involve-ment; or to assist in establishing a person's identity.

It can be seen that the above provisions offer far wider powers to the police, who need only be satisfied that the arrested person is detained in consequence of his or her arrest for a recordable offence and that the person has not had his/her fingerprints taken in the course of the investigation of the offence, or if he/she has had fingerprints taken, they were insufficient. (See **flow chart 10 in Appendix 1** for an easy guide.)

The Home Office contends that giving the police this power will: prevent wanted persons from being released through providing a false identity; pre-vent innocent persons being detained for longer than necessary; reduce the risk of harm to officers and detained persons; reduce bureaucracy; make use of new time-saving technology; and improve efficiency through reducing the unnecessary use of police time.

The new powers are simpler, and provide the police with the power to take fingerprints to:

- establish whether they are involved in the specific offence being investig-ated; or
- establish whether they are involved in any other offences; or
- establish their identity.

The police may take fingerprints from all detainees who have been arrested for a recordable offence. It means that the fingerprints of every person who

enters the custody office may be compared instantly against a list of outstanding 'idents', of persons wanted for offences, utilising the National Automated
Fingerprint Identification System (NAFIS).

KEYNOTE

Note a person's fingerprints may only be taken without consent if they are over
10 years of age (see Code D, para. 4.3).

It should be noted that an inspector is no longer required to authorise the
taking of a person's fingerprints without consent—this proviso has been
removed from the new legislation. However, in practice, the custody officer
should be consulted before a decision is made to do so, because while the
power exists for any officer to do so, the custody officer should be aware of
any such issues in the custody office. Officers will also find that it will not
be easy to take quality fingerprints without the person's consent and efforts
should be made to persuade the detainee to give consent to reduce the risk of
injuries.

KEYNOTE

It should be noted that wherever there is a power to take fingerprints without
consent, this may be done by force, by virtue of s. 117 PACE.

12.2.3 Power to re-take fingerprints

Section 61(3A) of PACE was added by the Criminal Justice and Police Act
2001, and provides the police with the power to take fingerprints from a person, where the previous set was rejected by the fingerprint bureau for quality
reasons.

There are further powers under s. 27 of PACE, to require a person to attend
a police station to have their fingerprints taken when the person:

- has not been in police detention and has not had their fingerprints taken
  in the course of the investigation; or

- has had their fingerprints taken in the course of the investigation and
  the fingerprints do not constitute a complete set, or some or all of the
  fingerprints are not of sufficient quality to allow satisfactory analysis, comparison or match.

The arrested person may be required to attend the police station in order to
have his/her fingerprints re-taken. The person should be given at least seven

days notice, and the person requiring him/her to attend may give directions as to the time of day (or between times of day).

> **KEYNOTE**
>
> A constable may arrest without warrant a person who fails to attend as directed under s. 27 above.

12.2.4 Taking fingerprints when a person has been convicted

Under s. 61(6) of PACE, where a person has been

- convicted,
- cautioned,
- warned or reprimanded,

for a recordable offence, their fingerprints may be taken without the appropriate consent. The power under s. 61(6) may be used, for example, where a person has been reported for summons for a recordable offence and has not been in police detention. The requirement may be made within one month of the date of conviction, caution, reprimand or warning, and the person must be given seven days in which to attend the police station. The person may be arrested if they fail to comply with the requirement.

> **KEYNOTE**
>
> The person is required to have admitted the offence for which he or she receives the caution, reprimand or warning.

12.2.5 Where the person's identity is in doubt

Under s. 61(4A) of PACE, fingerprints may be taken from a person without their consent, if they have been bailed to a court or police station, if the person:

- has answered bail for a person whose fingerprints were taken previously and there are reasonable grounds for believing they are not the same person; or
- has answered bail and claims to be a different person from a person whose fingerprints were taken previously.

The authority to take fingerprints without consent under this subsection may be granted either by an inspector, or a magistrate, depending where the person has answered bail. This power to establish a person's identity has also been added by Code D, para. 4.3.

12.2.6 Other powers to take fingerprints

The police and immigration officers have been given further powers to take fingerprints, without consent, from a person who has been detained under the Immigration Act 1971 and the Immigration and Asylum Act 1999. These extensive powers may be found in Code D, para. 4.10–4.14.

KEYNOTE

The powers given to constables to take fingerprints without consent extend to detention officers, who may use force if necessary. Detention officers are also given the power to require a person to attend a police station for their fingerprints to be taken under s. 27 of the Act.

12.3 Taking Fingerprints Away from the Police Station

12.3.1 Legislative provisions

Section 61(6A) PACE

A constable may take a person's fingerprints without the appropriate consent if—

(a) the constable reasonably suspects that the person is committing or attempting to commit an offence, or has committed or attempted to commit an offence; and

(b) either of the two conditions mentioned in subsection (6B) is met.

Section 61(6B) PACE

The conditions are that—

(a) the name of the person is unknown to, and cannot be readily ascertained by, the constable;

(b) the constable has reasonable grounds for doubting whether a name furnished by the person as his name is his real name.

12.3.2 **Background**

Section 117(2) of the Serious Organised Crime and Police Act 2005 inserted subsections (6A) and (6B) into s. 61 of PACE, to allow the police to take fingerprints away from the police station. The background to this power comes from the Home Office research document, *Modernising Police Powers to Meet the Community Needs*, which recommended that the police be given the power to take fingerprints outside the police station for identification purposes, to reduce the number of offenders who escape justice by giving false details and to prevent such people being arrested under s. 24(5)(a) or (b) PACE (name and/or address unknown etc.).

Although the main provisions of the Act commenced on 1 January 2006, as at the most recent Commencement Order, SI 2008/1325, s. 117(2) is not yet in force. Further, the legislation relies on technology which is still not widely available to all forces.

When the powers are fully enacted, police officers, using digital fingerprint readers, can connect remotely to the National Automated Fingerprint Identification System (NAFIS) to check a person's fingerprint impressions with the database.

The legislation should enable—

- a quick and direct route to establish identity;
- a more efficient use of an officer's time;
- increased opportunity to detect crime;
- early warning access for police for suspected or wanted criminals.

Code G, para. 1.3 of the *Codes of Practice* states that the use of the power to arrest must be fully justified and officers exercising the power should consider if the necessary objectives can be met by other, less intrusive means. Therefore, a simple check at the scene may prove the person's identity and remove the necessity of making an arrest.

12.3.3 **Authority to take fingerprints**

Officers will be able to take fingerprints without consent at the scene of the offence. There is no mention in s. 61 of any person having to *authorise* the taking; therefore, the officer dealing may take the decision to take the fingerprints by force if the circumstances allow it (this is in line with the power to take fingerprints at the police station—see **12.2.2 Taking fingerprints without consent** above).

This power will apply to any offence (including summary offences). Therefore, it could apply to a motorist who has been stopped and his or her identity is unknown to, and cannot be readily ascertained by, the constable, or he or she has reasonable grounds for doubting whether a name furnished by the person is his/her real name (see s. 61(6B) above). Fingerprints may be taken where the constable reasonably suspects:

- that the person is committing an offence; *or*
- that the person is attempting to commit an offence; *or*
- that the person has committed or attempted to commit an offence.

KEYNOTE

The power available under s. 61 will be of use at the scene of an offence to establish a person's identity only. The taking of fingerprints by virtue of s. (6A) does not count for any of the purposes of this Act as taking them in the course of the investigation of an offence by the police. Therefore, if the officer decides to arrest a person after confirming their identity, further fingerprint impressions may be taken at the police station, for other purposes, such as investigating a person's involvement in an offence (s. 61(6C) PACE).

Fingerprints taken from a person by virtue of s. 61(6A) above must be destroyed as soon as they have fulfilled the purpose for which they were taken—i.e. *confirming identity at the scene* (s. 64(1BA) PACE).

12.4 **Taking Footwear Impressions**

12.4.1 **Legislative provisions**

Section 61A(1) PACE

Except as provided by this section, no impression of a person's footwear may be taken without the appropriate consent.

Section 61A(2) PACE

Consent to the taking of an impression of a person's footwear must be in writing if it is given at a time when he is at a police station.

Section 61A(3) PACE

Where a person is detained at a police station, an impression of his footwear may be taken without the appropriate consent if—

(a) he is detained in consequence of his arrest for a recordable offence, or has been charged with a recordable offence, or informed that he will be reported for a recordable offence; and

(b) he has not had an impression taken of his footwear in the course of the investigation of the offence by the police.

12.4.2 **Background**

The police have, for a long time, unofficially taken footwear impressions from detainees (usually by seizing their shoes/trainers for evidential purposes). The Home Office research document, *Modernising Police Powers to Meet the Community Needs*, recommended that the police be given formal powers to take footwear impressions for the purposes of identification.

The paper concluded that this is a further important area in relation to identification evidence, in that the police would be able to then take impressions from that footwear and compare them to impressions from a crime scene to seek to prove or disprove involvement in a specific offence.

Section 54(4)(b) of PACE already allowed for footwear to be removed from suspects where they represented relevant evidence. However, while s. 54 legitimises this approach, it can enable the suspect to avoid this identification process by deciding not to wear that footwear again or to destroy it. The taking of footwear impressions overtly without the suspect's consent can overcome this and provide a potential aid to solving future crimes where the culprit might wear the same footwear again.

The Forensic Science Service (FSS) already has a database of footwear impressions taken from crime scenes. These impressions are stored on the Mark Intelligence Index. A separate database is kept of samples from footwear manufacturers. The new power under s. 61A of PACE will build on these facilities.

12.4.3 **Obtaining footwear impressions**

Footwear impressions may be taken either with consent, or without consent under s. 61A(3) above, provided the person has been detained at a police station, after being arrested for, or charged (or reported) with, a recordable offence and he/she has not had an impression taken of his or her footwear in the course of the investigation of the offence by the police.

If the person has already had an impression taken of his or her footwear in the course of the investigation of the offence, a further impression may be taken under s. 61A(3) if the impression of his/her footwear taken previously is either incomplete or not of sufficient quality to allow satisfactory analysis, comparison or matching (see s. 61A(4)).

KEYNOTE

Reasonable force may be used, if necessary, to take a footwear impression from a detainee without consent (see Code D, para. 4.18).

A record must be made, as soon as possible, of the reason for taking a person's footwear impressions without consent. If force is used, a record shall be made of the circumstances and those present (see Code D, para. 4.20).

It should be noted that as with other samples, such as fingerprints and DNA, footwear impressions may be taken and stored when the person has not been arrested, charged or reported for an offence, for elimination purposes, or during a large investigation. In these circumstances, footwear impressions will only be taken if the person consents to them being retained, on the understanding that they will be used:

> only for purposes related to the prevention and detection of a crime, the investigation of an offence or the conduct of a prosecution either nationally or internationally.

In these circumstances, the person will be asked to sign a declaration to the above effect, which will also state that once the person consents to the relevant impression being retained, that consent may not be withdrawn (see Code D, Note for Guidance 4B).

12.4.4 Information to be given to detainee

Under s. 61A(5) of PACE, if an impression of a person's footwear is taken at a police station, whether with or without the appropriate consent:

(a) before it is taken, an officer shall inform the person that it may be the subject of a speculative search; and

(b) the fact that the person has been informed of this possibility shall be recorded as soon as is practicable after the impression has been taken, and if he or she is detained at a police station, the record shall be made on his/her custody record.

If an impression of a person's footwear is taken without the appropriate consent, the person must be told the reason before it is taken, and the reason must be recorded on the custody record as soon as is practicable after the impression is taken. A record must also be made when a person has been informed of the possibility that their footwear impressions may be the subject of a speculative search.

12.5 **Examination to Establish Identity**

This section is grouped together in the *Codes of Practice*, as many of the powers are cross-referenced.

Police officers have the power to search detainees at police stations for identifying marks, features or injuries. The Anti Terrorism, Crime and Security Act 2001 inserted s. 54A(1) into PACE (see below). Details of the powers are also contained in Code D, paras. 5.1–5.11 of the *Codes of Practice*. Section 54 of the original Act provides the power to search detainees and this subject is covered in detail in **Chapter 8—Dealing with Property and Searching**, above. However, the new s. 54A will be dealt with here, as it refers to identification issues.

12.5.1 **Legislative provisions**

Section 54A(1) PACE

Allows a detainee at a police station to be searched or examined or both, to:

(a) establish whether they have any marks, features or injuries that would tend to identify them as a person involved in the commission of an offence and to photograph any identifying marks; *or*

(b) establish their identity.

12.5.2 **Persons involved in the commission of an offence**

A search under s. 54A(1)(a) may be used, for example, when a detained person has been identified by a witness because of a particular feature, such as a tattoo, or a scar, which may be hidden by the detainee's clothing. The search may be carried out without the detainee's consent, if authorised by an officer of at least inspector rank, either:

1. when consent has been withheld; *or*

2. when it is not practicable to obtain consent.

KEYNOTE

Examples of when it would not be practicable to obtain a detainee's consent to a search, examination or the taking of a photograph of an identifying mark include:

- when the person is drunk or otherwise unfit to give consent (if the matter is urgent; otherwise the detainee may be allowed time to recover their fitness); *or*

- when there are reasonable grounds to suspect that if the person became aware a search or examination was to take place or an identifying mark was to be photographed, they would take steps to prevent this happening, e.g. by violently resisting, covering or concealing the mark etc. and it would not otherwise be possible to carry out the search or examination or to photograph any identifying mark; *or*

- in the case of a juvenile, if the parent or guardian cannot be contacted in sufficient time to allow the search or examination to be carried out or the photograph to be taken.

12.5.3 **Establishing identity**

A search under s. 54A(1)(b) above may be used, for example, when a detainee is suspected of giving false details to the custody officer. The search may be carried out without the detainee's consent if authorised by an officer of at least inspector rank, either:

1. when the detainee has refused to identity themselves; *or*

2. when the authorising officer has reasonable grounds for suspecting the person is not who they claim to be.

KEYNOTE

There are several other issues contained in Code D, para. 5 that should be noted; the main ones are listed below:

- Where the detainee is mentally disordered, or mentally vulnerable, consent is only valid if given in the presence of an appropriate adult.

- Where the detainee is a juvenile, consent is only valid if their parent/guardian's consent is also obtained (unless the juvenile is under 14, where the parent/guardian may give consent in their own right).

- These powers do not apply to a detainee who has been brought to a police station to be searched under a stop and search power (Code A).

- Marks, features or injuries may be photographed with the detainee's consent or without their consent if it is withheld or it is not practicable to obtain it.
- A detainee may only be searched, examined and photographed under this section by a police officer of the same sex.
- Authority for the search/examination under s. 54A(i)(a) or (b) of PACE may be given orally or in writing. If given orally, the authorising officer must confirm it in writing as soon as practicable. A separate authority is required for each purpose which applies.
- If a person is unwilling to co-operate sufficiently to enable a search and/or examination to take place or a suitable photograph to be taken, an officer (or detention officer) may use reasonable force to:

  1. search and/or examine a detainee without their consent; and

  2. photograph any identifying marks without their consent.

- The thoroughness and extent of any search or examination must be no more than the officer considers necessary to achieve the required purpose. Any search or examination which involves the removal of more than the person's outer clothing shall be conducted in accordance with Code C, Annex A, para. 11 (conduct of strip searches).
- An intimate search may not be carried out under the powers in s. 54A.

KEYNOTE

Photographs of identifying marks may be used or disclosed only for purposes related to the prevention or detection of crime, the investigation of offences or the conduct of prosecutions by, or on behalf of, police or other law enforcement and prosecuting authorities inside, and outside, the UK.

After being so used or disclosed, the photograph may be retained but must not be used or disclosed except for these purposes (Note for Guidance 5B gives several examples of purposes related to the prevention or detection of crime, the investigation of offences or the conduct of prosecutions—see **12.6.4 Authority to take photographs** below).

12.6 **Photographing Suspects**

12.6.1 **Legislative provisions**

Code D, Para. 5.12

Under PACE, s. 64A, an officer may photograph:

(a) any person whilst they are detained at a police station; and

(b) any person who is elsewhere than at a police station and who has been:

   (i)   arrested by a constable for an offence;

   (ii) taken into custody by a constable after being arrested for an offence by a person other than a constable;

   (iii) made subject to a requirement to wait with a community support officer under para. 2(3) or (3B) of Sch. 4 to the Police Reform Act 2002;

   (iv) given a penalty notice by a constable in uniform under Chapter 1 of Part 1 of the Criminal Justice and Police Act 2001, a penalty notice by a constable under s. 444A of the Education Act 1996, or a fixed penalty notice by a constable in uniform under s. 54 of the Road Traffic Offenders Act 1988;

   (v)   given a notice in relation to a relevant fixed penalty offence (within the meaning of para. 1 of Sch. 4 to the Police Reform Act 2002) by a community support officer by virtue of a designation applying that paragraph to him; or

   (vi) given a notice in relation to a relevant fixed penalty offence (within the meaning of para. 1 of Sch. 5 to the Police Reform Act 2002) by an accredited person by virtue of accreditation specifying that that paragraph applies to him.

Code D, Para. 5.12A

Photographs taken under PACE, s. 64A:

(a) may be taken with the person's consent, or without their consent if consent is withheld or it is not practicable to obtain their consent (see Note 5E); and

(b) may be used or disclosed only for purposes related to the prevention or detection of crime, the investigation of offences or the conduct of prosecutions by, or on behalf of, police or other law enforcement and prosecuting authorities inside and outside the United Kingdom or the enforcement of any sentence or order made by a court when dealing with an offence. After being so used or disclosed, they may be retained but can only be used or disclosed for the same purposes. (See Note 5B.)

12.6.2 **Background**

Before the Anti-Terrorism, Crime and Security Act 2001 inserted s. 64A into PACE, the photograph of an arrested person could only be taken without their consent if they had been charged with, or reported for, a recordable offence, or had been arrested at the same time as other people and a photograph was necessary to establish who was arrested. Section 64A introduced changes to taking photographs of detainees and photographs may now be taken of a detainee with or without their consent, and if necessary by force under Code D, para. 5.14.

More recently, s. 116 of the Serious Organised Crime and Police Act 2005 amended s. 64A of PACE to allow a photograph of an arrested person to be taken away from the police station, under certain conditions, listed in Code D, para. 5.12 above. These changes to s. 64A were brought about as a result of recommendations in the Home Office research document, *Modernising Police Powers to Meet the Community Needs*.

The above document concluded that there was no statutory power to take a photograph of a suspect—excluding surveillance situations—outside the police station. With the increasing Government drive to make use of interventions outside the police station, such as street bail and fixed penalty notices, and the requirement under s. 24(4) of PACE to consider whether, on reasonable grounds, the arrest is *necessary*, it was felt important that the police were given powers to take a visual image of a suspect at the scene of the arrest or intervention. Street bail is covered in depth in **16.8 'Street Bail'**.

12.6.3 **Photographing suspects away from the station**

Under Code D, para. 5.12 above, photographs may be taken of a person who has been arrested for an offence, either at a police station (para. 5.12(a)) or elsewhere than at a police station (para. 5.12(b)). A 'photograph' includes a moving image (s. 64A(6A) PACE). Where a photograph is to be taken under para. 5.12(b), the conditions are that the person has been arrested, taken into custody or simply given a fixed penalty notice in one of the following circumstances:

- *arrested by a constable for an offence*—in these circumstances, it is likely that the constable will deal with the person by making use of an intervention outside the police station, such as street bail or a fixed penalty notice;

- *taken into custody by a constable after being arrested for an offence by a person other than a constable*—in these circumstances, a person is likely to have been arrested by a member of the public, such as a store detective, and again, the constable may intend dealing with the person by making use of one of the above interventions outside the police station;

- *made subject to a requirement to wait with a police community support officer*—in these circumstances, a Police Community Support Officer (PCSO) has reason to believe that a person has committed a relevant offence for which a fixed penalty notice may be issued by him/her, and the person has either failed to give their name and address as above or the PCSO has reasonable grounds for suspecting the name or address is false or inaccurate;

- *given a penalty notice by a constable in uniform*—in these circumstances, a constable in uniform may intend issuing a fixed penalty notice—for a disorder offence, such as being drunk in a highway; for failing to secure regular attendance at school of a registered pupil;

- *given a notice in relation to a relevant fixed penalty offence by a PCSO*—in these circumstances, a PCSO may intend issuing a fixed penalty notice in respect of graffiti or fly-posting, or dog fouling or litter;

- *given a notice in relation to a relevant fixed penalty offence by an accredited person*—in these circumstances, an accredited person may intend issuing a fixed penalty notice in respect of graffiti or fly-posting, or dog fouling, or litter.

KEYNOTE

It should be noted that where a photograph is taken away from the police station under para. 5.12(b) above, all other aspects of the *Codes of Practice* in relation to photographing suspects apply, such as taking the photograph without consent, or the use of force. The remainder of this Code is discussed below.

However, the use of reasonable force to take the photograph of a suspect elsewhere than at a police station must be carefully considered. In order to obtain a suspect's consent and co-operation to remove an item of religious headwear to take their photograph, a constable should consider whether in the circumstances of the situation the removal of the headwear and the taking of the photograph should be by an officer of the same sex as the person. It would be appropriate for these actions to be conducted out of public view (see Code D, Note for Guidance 5F).

12.6.4 Authority to take photographs

Photographs may be taken of a detainee with or without their consent, and if necessary by force under Code D, para. 5.14 (see below), provided the photographs are to be used or disclosed for purposes related to:

- the prevention or detection of crime; *or*
- the investigation of offences; *or*

- the conduct of prosecutions by, or on behalf of, police or other law enforcement and prosecuting authorities inside, and outside, the UK.

Code D, Note for Guidance 5B cites several examples of purposes related to the prevention or detection of crime, the investigation of offences or the conduct of prosecutions:

- checking the photograph against other photographs held in records or in connection with, or as a result of, an investigation of an offence to establish whether the person is liable to arrest for other offences;
- when the person is arrested at the same time as other people, or when it is likely that other people will be arrested, using the photograph to establish who was arrested, at what time and where;
- when the real identity of the person is not known and cannot be readily ascertained or there are reasonable grounds for doubting a name and other personal details given by the person, are their real name and personal details;
- when it appears any identification procedure may need to be arranged;
- when the person's release without charge may be required, and if the release is:
  1. on bail to appear at a police station, using the photograph to help verify the person's identity when they answer their bail and if the person does not answer their bail, to assist in arresting them; or
  2. without bail, using the photograph to help verify their identity/assist in locating them to serve a summons in criminal proceedings;
- when the person has answered to bail at a police station and there are reasonable grounds for doubting they are the person who was previously granted bail, using the photograph to help establish or verify their identity;
- when the person arrested on a warrant claims to be a different person from the person named on the warrant and a photograph would help to confirm or disprove their claim;
- when the person has been charged with, reported for, or convicted of, a recordable offence and their photograph is not already on record as a result of any of the above, or their photograph is on record but their appearance has changed since it was taken and the person has not yet been released or brought before a court.

12.6.5 **Taking photographs without consent**

Under para. 5.12A above, a photograph may be taken of a detainee without their consent either if consent is withheld or it is not practicable to obtain their consent. Note for Guidance 5E provides examples of when it would not be practicable to obtain the person's consent to a photograph being taken, which include:

(a) when the person is drunk or otherwise unfit to give consent;

(b) when there are reasonable grounds to suspect that if the person became aware a photograph, suitable to be used or disclosed for the use and disclosure described in para. 5.6, was to be taken, they would take steps to prevent it being taken, e.g. by violently resisting, covering or distorting their face etc., and it would not otherwise be possible to take a suitable photograph;

(c) when, in order to obtain a suitable photograph, it is necessary to take it covertly; and

(d) in the case of a juvenile, if the parent or guardian cannot be contacted in sufficient time to allow the photograph to be taken.

KEYNOTE

Note that there is no power to arrest a person convicted of a recordable offence solely to take their photograph. The power to take photographs in this section applies only where the person is in custody as a result of the exercise of another power, e.g. arrest for fingerprinting under PACE, s. 27 (see Code D, Note for Guidance 5C).

Further powers are provided to enable the photograph to be taken without consent:

• The officer proposing to take a detainee's photograph may require the person to remove any item or substance worn on, or over, all, or any part of, their head or face. If they do not comply with such a requirement, the officer may remove the item or substance (Code D, para. 5.13).

• If it is established the detainee is unwilling to co-operate sufficiently to enable a suitable photograph to be taken and it is not reasonably practicable to take the photograph covertly, an officer may use reasonable force:

1. to take their photograph without their consent; and

2. for the purpose of taking the photograph, remove any item or substance worn on, or over, all, or any part of, the person's head or face which they have failed to remove when asked (Code D, para. 5.14).

• For the purposes of this Code of Practice, a photograph may be obtained without the person's consent by making a copy of an image of them taken at any time on a camera system installed anywhere in the police station (Code D, para. 5.15).

KEYNOTE

There will be occasions when a person is at a police station voluntarily and not detained, but there are reasonable grounds for suspecting their involvement in a criminal offence. The provisions of s. 54A and s. 64A will still apply to those people, but with some modifications. Force may not be used to search and/or examine the person to discover whether they have any marks, or establish their identity. Neither may force be used to take photographs of the person or of any identifying marks (see Code D, paras. 19–21).

12.6.6 Information to be given

Code D, para. 5.16 states that when a person is photographed under the provisions of para. 5.12, or their photograph obtained as in para. 5.15, they must be informed of the:

(a) purpose of taking the photograph;

(b) grounds on which the relevant authority, if applicable, has been given; and

(c) purposes for which the photograph may be used, disclosed or retained.

This information must be given before the photograph is taken, *unless* the photograph is to be taken covertly or obtained as in para. 5.15 above, in which case the person must be informed as soon as practicable after the photograph is taken or obtained.

12.6.7 Documentation

Under Code D, para. 5.17, a record must be made when a detainee is searched, examined, or a photograph of the person, or any identifying marks found on them, are taken. The record must include the:

(a) identity of the officer carrying out the search, examination or taking the photograph;

(b) purpose of the search, examination or photograph and the outcome;

(c) detainee's consent to the search, examination or photograph, or the reason the person was searched, examined or photographed without consent.

If force is used when searching, examining or taking a photograph in accordance with this section, a record shall be made of the circumstances and those present (see para. 5.18).

317

12.7 **Intimate Samples**

12.7.1 **Legislative provisions**

Section 62(1)(a) PACE

An intimate sample may only be taken from a person in police detention if a police officer of at least the rank of inspector authorises it to be taken, and consent is given.

Section 62(1A) PACE

An intimate sample may be taken from a person who is not in police detention, if a police officer of at least the rank of inspector authorises it to be taken and consent is given.

Section 62(2) PACE

An inspector may only give an authorisation under s. 62(1) or s. 62(1A) above if he has reasonable grounds for believing the sample will tend to confirm or disprove involvement of the person from whom the sample is to be taken in a recordable offence.

12.7.2 **Intimate samples defined**

The definition for 'intimate samples' may be found in s. 65 of the 1984 Act, which states:

'intimate sample' means—

- a sample of blood, semen or any other tissue fluid, urine or pubic hair;
- a dental impression;
- a swab taken from any part of a person's genitals, or from a person's body orifice other than the mouth.

12.7.3 **Authorisation to obtain an intimate sample**

Previously, the person was required to be in custody for a serious arrestable offence. This was amended in s. 54 of the Criminal Justice and Public Order Act 1994, to include those people involved in recordable offences.

An inspector may give an authorisation under s. 62(1) or 62(1A) orally or in writing but, if it is given orally, it must be confirmed in writing as soon as is practicable (s. 62(3)).

Where it is proposed to take an intimate sample, and the appropriate authorisation has been given, before any intimate sample is taken, Code D, para. 6.8 states that the person must be informed:

(a)   of the reason for taking the sample;

(b)   of the grounds on which the relevant authority has been given;

(c)   that the sample or information derived from the sample may be retained and subject of a speculative search (see Note 6E), unless their destruction is required as in Annex F, Part A.

Note for Guidance 6E and Annex F, Part A deal with fingerprints, footwear impressions and DNA samples, which are not covered in this section.

The officer informing the person of the authorisation, and the grounds for giving it, need not be the officer who actually authorised it. However, under s. 62(6), the officer must state the nature of the offence in which it is suspected that the person from whom the sample is to be taken has been involved.

12.7.4 Obtaining the appropriate consent

Code D, para. 6.3 states that before a suspect is asked to provide an intimate sample, they must be warned that if they refuse without good cause, their refusal may harm their case if it comes to trial. Note for Guidance 6D states that the following form of words may be used:

> You do not have to provide this sample/allow this swab or impression to be taken, but I must warn you that if you refuse without good cause, your refusal may harm your case if it comes to trial.

If the suspect is in police detention and not legally represented, they must be reminded of their entitlement to have free legal advice. If the person is attending a station voluntarily, their entitlement to free legal advice must also be explained to them.

The detainee must give the appropriate consent, and it must be given in writing; there is no power to take an intimate sample from a detained person by force.

In *R v Smith* (1985) 81 Cr App R 286, the person refused to supply a sample of hair. It was held that it was proper for the court to draw appropriate inferences in these circumstances. Since this case, the *Codes of Practice*, Code D, para. 6.3 has been introduced, which states that a person must be warned that if they refuse to provide an intimate sample, their refusal may harm their case if it comes to trial. Under s. 63 of the Act, a hair sample can be taken from a suspect without his/her consent (see **12.8 Non-Intimate Samples** below).

Intimate samples may be taken for elimination purposes with the consent of the person concerned (Code D, Note for Guidance 6C).

12.7.5 **Written record**

Under s. 62(7), if an intimate sample is taken from a person, the information below must be recorded, as soon as is practicable after the sample is taken:

- the relevant authority;
- the grounds for giving the authorisation;
- the fact that the appropriate consent was given in writing;
- that a warning was given;
- that the detainee was informed that the sample may be subject of a speculative search;
- that they were reminded of their entitlement to have free legal advice.

> **KEYNOTE**
>
> The information referred to above may be recorded in the custody record if the person is in police detention. If the information is not recorded in a detainee's custody record, a note in this record should state where it is recorded, alongside an entry stating that a sample has been taken.

12.7.6 **Obtaining an intimate sample**

Generally, an intimate sample, other than a sample of urine, may only be taken from a person by a registered medical practitioner, a registered nurse or a registered paramedic. However, dental impressions have been added to the list of intimate samples, and these may only be taken by a registered dentist (s. 62(9)).

> **KEYNOTE**
>
> It should be noted that only the sample that was authorised may be taken. Therefore, if the investigating officer requires further samples to be taken, new authorisation must be given for each one.

Code D, para. 6.9 deals with those occasions when clothing needs to be removed in circumstances likely to cause embarrassment to the person. In these situations, no person shall be present:

- of the opposite sex who is not a registered medical practitioner or registered healthcare professional; or
- whose presence is unnecessary.

If the detainee is a juvenile, mentally disordered or mentally vulnerable person, *and* that person specifically requests the presence of an appropriate adult of the opposite sex who is readily available, this may be permitted.

In the case of a juvenile, this is also subject to the overriding proviso that such a removal of clothing may take place in the absence of the appropriate adult only if the juvenile signifies, in the appropriate adult's presence, that they prefer the adult's absence and the adult agrees.

12.8 **Non-Intimate Samples**

12.8.1 **Legislative provisions**

Section 63(1) PACE

Except as provided by this section, a non-intimate sample may not be taken from a person without the appropriate consent.

Section 63(2A)–(2C) PACE

A non-intimate sample may be taken from a person without the appropriate consent if two conditions are satisfied:

- that the person is in police detention in consequence of his arrest for a recordable offence; and
- that—

  (a) he has not had a non-intimate sample of the same type and from the same part of the body taken in the course of the investigation of the offence by the police, *or*

  (b) he has had such a sample taken but it proved insufficient.

Section 63(3) PACE

A non-intimate sample may be taken from a person without the appropriate consent if—

(a) he is being held in custody by the police on the authority of a court; and

(b) an officer of at least the rank of inspector authorises it to be taken without the appropriate consent.

Section 63(3A) PACE

A non-intimate sample may also be taken from a person (whether or not he is in police detention or held in custody by the police on the authority of a court) without the appropriate consent, if—

(a) he has been charged with a recordable offence or informed that he will be reported for such an offence; and

(b) either he has not had a non-intimate sample taken from him in the course of the investigation of the offence by the police, or he has had a non-intimate sample taken from him but either it was not suitable for the same means of analysis or, though so suitable, the sample proved insufficient.

Section 63(4) PACE

An officer may only give an authorisation under ss. (3) above if he has reasonable grounds—

(a) for suspecting the involvement of the person from whom the sample is to be taken in a recordable offence; and

(b) for believing that the sample will tend to confirm or disprove his involvement.

12.8.2 **Non-intimate samples defined**

The definition for 'non-intimate samples' may also be found in s. 65 of the 1984 Act, which states:

'non-intimate sample' means—

• a sample of hair other than pubic hair [and includes hair plucked from the root];

• a sample taken from a nail or from under a nail;

• a swab taken from any part of a person's body other than a part from which a swab taken would be an intimate sample;

• saliva;

- a skin impression which means any record, other than a fingerprint, which is a record, in any form and produced by any method, of the skin pattern and other physical characteristics or features of the whole, or any part of, a person's foot or of any other part of their body.

12.8.3 **Obtaining non-intimate samples without consent**

From the above list, the majority of non-intimate samples taken from detainees are DNA samples. Unlike intimate samples above, under s. 63 of PACE, a non-intimate sample may be taken from a person in police detention without their consent. In addition, a non-intimate sample may also be taken from a person who is not in police detention.

The Criminal Justice Act 2003, Part 1, extended the circumstances in which the police may take non-intimate samples without consent, as it has with taking fingerprints without consent (see **12.2 Fingerprints**, above). The powers have been extended mainly so that more DNA samples are taken, to provide the police with more opportunities to detect crime. The new powers mean that the authorising officer need only be satisfied that the arrested person is detained in consequence of his arrest for a recordable offence and that the person had not had a non-intimate sample taken in the course of the investigation of the offence, or that a sample was taken, which proved to be insufficient.

As with the taking of fingerprints, previously, an inspector was required first to believe that the person had been involved in a criminal offence, and secondly that the taking of a non-intimate sample would confirm or disprove their involvement. Authority from an inspector is no longer required.

The new powers are simpler, and provide the police with the power to take a non-intimate sample to:

- establish whether they are involved in the specific offence being investigated; *or*
- establish whether they are involved in any other offences.

The police may take non-intimate samples from all detainees who have been arrested for a recordable offence, to be compared to those samples on the National DNA Database.

Where a sample is taken from a person without the appropriate consent, the person must be told the reason before the sample is taken and the reason shall be recorded as soon as practicable after the sample is taken (s. 63(8A)).

Consent to the taking of a non-intimate sample must be given in writing (s. 63(2)). There is no provision under s. 63 for a court to draw inferences from the refusal to supply a non-intimate sample. Since there is a power to take it without consent, by force if necessary (Code D, para. 6.7), the detainee does not have the option to refuse.

KEYNOTE

It should be noted that wherever there is a power to take a non-intimate sample without consent, this may be done by force, by virtue of s. 117 PACE.

If force is used, a record shall be made of the circumstances and those present. If written consent is given to the taking of a sample or impression, the fact must be recorded in writing (Code D, para. 6.10).

12.8.4 Other powers to obtain non-intimate samples without consent

A non-intimate sample may also be taken from a person without the appropriate consent, if he/she has been convicted of a recordable offence.

There is a power to direct a person to attend a police station to provide a non-intimate sample, where that person has not previously been in police detention, or where the person has not had a sample taken during the course of the investigation, or where the sample taken has proved insufficient (see s. 63A(4)).

The above power may be exercised within a month of the person being charged with a recordable offence, or within a month of the police being informed that the sample was insufficient.

As with taking fingerprints, the person should be given seven days' notice to attend the police station, and a constable may arrest a person who fails to attend as directed.

KEYNOTE

A sample may be 'insufficient' under s. 63(3A) above because of its quantity or quality, or because it has been lost, contaminated or damaged, as a result of an earlier unsuccessful analysis (see Code D, Note for Guidance 6B).

KEYNOTE

Note that a detention officer may exercise the same powers as a constable to take a non-intimate sample without consent, and to direct a person to attend the station for a sample to be taken (see Chapter 1—The Role of the Custody Officer for full details of the powers given to a detention officer).

12.8.5 **Custody record**

Section 63(8) requires a record to be made of the authorisation and the grounds for giving it (as in s. 62(7) above).

If a non-intimate sample is taken from a person detained at a police station, the matters relating to the taking of the sample shall be recorded in the custody record (s. 63(9)).

12.8.6 **Obtaining a non-intimate sample**

Because of the type of samples involved, there is no requirement for a registered medical practitioner to take a non-intimate sample. They may be taken by a police officer (of the opposite sex if necessary); however, where clothing is likely to be removed, Code D, para. 6.9 above will apply (see **12.7.6 Obtaining an intimate sample**, above).

Further guidance is provided in the *Codes of Practice*, Code D, Note for Guidance 6A. Where hair samples are taken for the purpose of DNA analysis (rather than for other purposes such as making a visual match) the suspect should be permitted a reasonable choice as to what part of the body he wishes the hairs to be taken from. When hairs are plucked they should be plucked individually unless the suspect prefers otherwise and no more should be plucked than the person taking them reasonably considers necessary for a sufficient sample.

> **KEYNOTE**
>
> Further information on samples, relating to 'speculative searches' and 'destruction of samples' may be found in s. 63A of PACE (as amended by the Criminal Justice and Police Act 2001, s. 81) and s.64 of PACE respectively.

12.9 **Vulnerable People**

12.9.1 **Legislative provisions**

Section 65 PACE

In the case of a person over the age of 17, that person may consent to a sample being taken himself. In the case of a person under the age of 17:

- if the person is between the ages of 14 years and 17 years (a young person), the consent of that person and his parent or guardian;
- if the person is under the age of 14 years (a child), the consent of his parent or guardian only.

Code D, Para. 2.12

If any procedure in this Code requires a person's consent, the consent of a mentally disordered or otherwise mentally vulnerable person is only valid if given in the presence of the appropriate adult.

12.9.2 **Appropriate consent**

Section 65 above gives a specific definition of 'appropriate consent', relating to young persons and children. Where a juvenile is in the care of the local authority or voluntary organisation, consent may be given by a member of that authority or organisation who is representing his/her interests (see Code D, Note for Guidance 2A).

Additional protection is given to other vulnerable persons, in Code D, para. 2.12 of the *Codes of Practice*. As discussed above, generally, if the provision of a sample is likely to involve the removal of clothing in circumstances likely to cause embarrassment, no person of the opposite sex who is not a medical practitioner or nurse shall be present. However, a juvenile or a 'mentally disordered' or 'mentally handicapped' person may specifically request the presence of an appropriate adult of the opposite sex who is readily available (see Code D, para. 6.9).

> **KEYNOTE**
>
> In the case of a juvenile, the overriding proviso is that removal of clothing may take place in the absence of the appropriate adult only if the person signifies in the presence of the appropriate adult that he/she prefers the search to be done in his/her absence and the appropriate adult agrees.

> **KEYNOTE**
>
> Code D, Note for Guidance 2B offers advice in relation to people who are seriously visually impaired or unable to read. The Note for Guidance suggests that such people, quite rightly, may be unwilling to sign police documents. Representatives may be asked to sign on their behalf, which should protect the interests of both the individual and the police.

12.10 **Testing for Presence of Class A Drugs**

12.10.1 **Legislative provisions**

Code C, Para. 17.2

A sample of urine or a non-intimate sample may be taken from a person in police detention for the purpose of ascertaining whether he has any specified Class A drug in his body only where they have been brought before the custody officer and:

(a) either the arrest condition (see para. 17.3), or the charge condition (see para. 17.4), is met;

(b) the age condition (see para. 17.5), is met;

(c) the notification condition is met in relation to the arrest condition, the charge condition or the age condition, as the case may be. (Testing on charge and/or arrest must be specifically provided for in the notification for the power to apply. In addition, the fact that testing of under-18s is authorised must be expressly provided for in the notification before the power to test such persons applies.) (See para. 17.1); and

(d) a police officer has requested the person concerned to give the sample (the request condition).

Code C, Para. 17.3

The arrest condition is met where the detainee:

(a) has been arrested for a trigger offence (see Note for Guidance 17E), but not charged with that offence; or

(b) has been arrested for any other offence but not charged with that offence and a police officer of inspector rank or above, who has reasonable grounds for suspecting that their misuse of any specified Class A drug caused or contributed to the offence, has authorised the sample to be taken.

Code C, Para. 17.4

The charge condition is met where the detainee:

(a) has been charged with a trigger offence; or

(b) has been charged with any other offence and a police officer of inspector rank or above, who has reasonable grounds for suspecting that the detainee's misuse of any specified Class A drug caused or contributed to the offence, has authorised the sample to be taken.

Code C, Para. 17.5

The age condition is met where:

(a)   in the case of a detainee who has been arrested but not charged as in para. 17.3, they are aged 18 or over;

(b)   in the case of a detainee who has been charged as in para. 17.4, they are aged 14 or over.

12.10.2 **Notification to police forces by the Secretary of State**

One of the purposes of the power provided by para. 17 of Code C is to assist the police in monitoring drug misuse in their area. The information will also be of use to the courts when deciding whether or not to grant bail to a detainee. Also, because emphasis should also be placed on rehabilitation, the information should also be of use to drug referral agencies.

Code C, para. 17.1 applies only in selected police stations in police areas, where the provisions for drug testing under s. 63B of PACE (as amended by s. 5 of the Criminal Justice Act 2003 and s. 7 of the Drugs Act 2005) are in force and in respect of which the Secretary of State has given a notification to the relevant chief officer of police that arrangements for the taking of samples have been made. This notification represents authority for the relevant force or area to undertake the drug testing.

Drug testing falls into two age categories, detainees under 14 and detainees under 18. The notification will outline which category the force is allowed to test. Currently, drug testing for those aged 14 to 17 applies only in the Cleveland, Greater Manchester, Humberside, Merseyside, Metropolitan Police District, Nottinghamshire, and West Yorkshire police areas.

Drug testing may take place for detainees over 18 in Avon and Somerset, Bedfordshire, Cambridgeshire, Cleveland, Devon and Cornwall, Greater Manchester, Gwent, Humberside, Lancashire, Leicestershire, Merseyside, Metropolitan Police District, Northumbria, North Wales, Nottinghamshire, South Wales, South Yorkshire, Staffordshire, Thames Valley, West Midlands, and West Yorkshire.

The scheme may cover either an entire police area, or particular stations within a police area, and notification will be sent by the Secretary of State outlining which particular type of testing the police station or force is expected to undertake, under the following categories:

(a) persons in respect of whom the arrest condition is met;

(b) persons in respect of whom the charge condition is met;

(c) persons who have not attained the age of 18.

(See **flow chart 11 in Appendix 1** for an easy guide.)

12.10.3 **Categorising detainees**

Code C, para. 17.2 above allows for either a sample of urine, or another non-intimate sample to be taken from a detainee who falls within one of the categories listed. This does not, therefore, allow the police to take blood, which is an intimate sample (see **12.7.2 Intimate samples defined** and **12.8.2 Non-intimate samples defined** for a full list of these samples).

Under para. 17.2(c), the sample may only be taken from the detainee if he or she is in police detention in either a police station or a police area which is authorised (by virtue of a notification from the Secretary of State). Once this is established, consideration must be given as to which category he or she falls within, under para. 17.2(a). Either the detainee will not have been charged with an offence (and falls within the requirements of para. 17.3), or he/she will have been charged with an offence (and falls within the requirements of para. 17.4). These paragraphs are dealt with separately below. Under para. 17.2(b), consideration must be given to the detainee's age. This paragraph is also dealt with below.

Under para. 17.2(d), before a sample can be taken, a police officer must make a request to the person concerned to give the sample (the request condition). Paragraph 17.6 provides detailed information as to what the person should be told—see **12.10.7 Information to be given to the detainee** below.

12.10.4 **Arrest condition (Code C, para. 17.3)**

Where a person has been arrested, but has not yet been charged with an offence, a sample may be taken under para. 17.3(a) if he or she has simply been arrested for one of the trigger offences listed in Note for Guidance 17E below. There is no requirement under this paragraph for the officer making the request to have reasonable grounds for suspecting that the detainee is under the influence of, or has misused, a Class A drug, or that such a drug caused or contributed to the offence.

Practically speaking, if it seems likely that a person arrested for one of the listed offences is going to be detained for a lengthy time, the sample may be taken early on in their detention time, rather than waiting until they have been charged and the effects of the Class A drug have diminished.

Paragraph 17.10 deals with circumstances in which the custody officer has decided to release a person on bail without charge, for whom the arrest condition is met. In these cases, the person may continue to be detained after the decision is made to bail that person, to enable a sample to be taken. However, detention in these circumstances must not go beyond 24 hours from the relevant time (as defined in s. 41(2) of PACE). There may be practical issues to consider if this happens, because the detention clock will still be running, which may have an effect on the person's detention time when he or she returns to answer bail.

What would happen if a person has been arrested for a trigger offence where there is insufficient evidence to charge them, but then arrested for a different offence not covered by this *Code*?

Consider the following:

Case Study

MELLOR has been arrested on suspicion of an offence of robbery, where he approached the victim in the street, threatened them with a knife and stole their mobile telephone. It has been decided that MELLOR should be released on bail for identification procedures, and he has not been asked to provide a sample under para. 17.3(a).

Prior to MELLOR's release, the investigating officer has informed the custody officer that he is wanted for an offence of criminal damage to a neighbour's fence.

Under what authority could MELLOR be asked to provide a sample, bearing in mind he was about to be released for the trigger offence?

....

The circumstances above are covered specifically in Code C, para. 17.11, which states that where a person has been detained, and the arrest condition is met, but not the charge condition, and whose release would be required before a sample can be taken had they not continued to be detained as a result of being arrested for a further offence which does not satisfy the arrest condition, he or she may have a sample taken at any time within 24 hours after the arrest for the offence that satisfies the arrest condition.

Only one sample may be taken from the person during the same continuous period of detention. For example, if a sample is taken from a person during the period before they are charged, there is no power to take a further sample if the person is subsequently charged with a trigger offence (see para. 17.9).

Home Office Circular 28/2007 amended the list of trigger offences (superseding HOC 42/2004) due to the changes created by the Fraud Act 2006. The trigger offences are listed in Code C, Note for Guidance 17E and are those which would generally be linked to people with addictions who commit acquisitive crime in order to buy drugs.

They are as follows:

1. Offences under the following provisions of the Theft Act 1968:

    - s. 1 (theft);
    - s. 8 (robbery);
    - s. 9 (burglary);
    - s. 10 (aggravated burglary);
    - s. 12 (taking motor vehicle or other conveyance without authority);
    - s. 12A (aggravated vehicle-taking);
    - s. 22 (handling stolen goods);
    - s. 25 (going equipped for stealing, etc.).

2. Offences under the following provisions of the Misuse of Drugs Act 1971, *only* if committed in respect of a specified Class A drug:

    - s. 4 (restriction on production and supply of controlled drugs);
    - s. 5(2) (possession of a controlled drug);
    - s. 5(3) (possession of a controlled drug with intent to supply).

3. Offences under the following provisions of the Fraud Act 2006:

    - s.1 (fraud);
    - s.6 (possession etc. of articles for use in frauds);
    - s.7 (making or supplying articles for use in frauds).

3A. An offence under section 1(1) of the Criminal Attempts Act 1981 if committed in respect of an offence under:

    (a) any of the following provisions of the Theft Act 1968:

    - s.1 (theft);
    - s.8 (robbery);
    - s.9 (burglary);
    - s.22 (handling stolen goods);

    (b) s.1 of the Fraud Act 2006 (fraud).

4. Offences under the following provisions of the Vagrancy Act 1824:

    - s.3 (begging);
    - s.4 (persistent begging).

Under para. 17.3(b), a sample may be taken from a person who has been arrested for any other offence, but has not been charged. However, there is a condition attached to this power, which is that an officer of inspector rank or above must have reasonable grounds for suspecting that their misuse of any specified Class A drug caused or contributed to the offence.

If a sample is taken following authorisation by an officer of the rank of inspector or above, the custody record must be endorsed with the authorisation and the grounds for suspicion, the fact that a warning was given of the consequences of failing to provide the sample and the time of charge or, where the arrest condition is being relied upon, the time of arrest (see para. 17.12).

KEYNOTE

It is worth noting that when a person has been arrested but not charged for a trigger offence, the authority to request a sample lies with a constable, whereas an inspector must authorise a sample to be taken when a person has been arrested for any other offence.

12.10.5 Charge condition (Code C, para. 17.4)

Where a person has been arrested and has been charged with an offence, a sample may be taken under para. 17.4(a) if he or she has been charged with one of the trigger offences listed above. Again, there is no requirement under this paragraph for the officer making the request to have reasonable grounds for suspecting that the detainee is under the influence of, or has misused, a Class A drug, or that such a drug caused or contributed to the offence.

Under para. 17.4(b), a sample may be taken from a person who has been charged with any other offence. As with para. 17.3(b) above, there is a condition attached to this power, which is that an officer of inspector rank or above must have reasonable grounds for suspecting that their misuse of any specified Class A drug caused or contributed to the offence.

Again, it should be noted that when a person has been charged with a trigger offence, the authority to request a sample lies with a constable, whereas an inspector must authorise a sample to be taken when a person has been charged with any other offence.

A detainee from whom a sample may be taken may be detained for up to six hours from the time of charge if the custody officer reasonably believes the detention is necessary to enable a sample to be taken (see para. 17.10).

KEYNOTE

Authorisation by an officer of the rank of inspector or above within para. 17.3(b) or 17.4(b) may be given orally or in writing but, if it is given orally, it must be confirmed in writing as soon as practicable (para. 17.8).

12.10.6 **Age condition (Code C, para. 17.5)**

Paragraph 17.5 deals with two categories of detainees; those who are 18 years of age or over and those who are 14 years of age or over. A sample may not be taken from a person who is under the age of 14, under this Code.

Paragraph 17.5(a) effectively lays down the condition that where a detainee has been arrested, but not charged (as in para. 17.3), a sample may not be taken unless he or she has reached the age of 18 years. Under para. 17.5(b), any person over the age of 14 may be asked for a sample, provided he or she has been charged with an offence (as in para. 17.4). Of course, this will only be the case if the notification condition is met (under para. 17.1) and either the police station or police area has been authorised by the Secretary of State.

12.10.7 **Information to be given to the detainee**

Under para. 17.6, before requesting a sample from the person concerned, an officer must:

(a) inform them that the purpose of taking the sample is for drug testing under PACE. This is to ascertain whether they have a specified Class A drug present in their body;

(b) warn them that if, when so requested, they fail without good cause to provide a sample, they may be liable to prosecution;

(c) where the taking of the sample has been authorised by an inspector or above in accordance with para. 17.3(b) or 17.4(b) above, inform them that the authorisation has been given and the grounds for giving it.

Note for Guidance 17A gives advice about the wording that should be used, when warning a person who is asked to provide a sample in accordance with para. 17.6(b) above. The following form of words may be used:

> You do not have to provide a sample, but I must warn you that if you fail or refuse without good cause to do so, you will commit an offence for which you may be imprisoned, or fined, or both.

The detainee must also be reminded of the following rights, which may be exercised at any stage during the period in custody:

- the right to have someone informed of their arrest;
- the right to consult privately with a solicitor and that free independent legal advice is available; and
- the right to consult the *Codes of Practice*.

In the case of a person who has not attained the age of 17, the making of the request for a sample under para. 17.2(d) above, the giving of the warning and the information under para. 17.6 above and the taking of the sample, may not take place except in the presence of an appropriate adult (para. 17.7).

Note for Guidance 17G states that an appropriate adult in para. 17.7 above means the person's:

(a) parent or guardian or, if they are in the care of a local authority or voluntary organisation, a person representing that authority or organisation; or

(b) a social worker of, in England, a local authority or, in Wales, a local authority social services department; or

(c) if no person falling within (a) or (b) above is available, any responsible person aged 18 or over who is not a police officer or a person employed by the police.

KEYNOTE

Under Code C, para. 17.20, the following must be recorded in the custody record:

(a) that the requirement to attend an initial assessment has been imposed; and

(b) the information, explanation, warning and notice given in accordance with paras. 17.17 and 17.19.

12.10.8 Obtaining the sample

Under Code C, para. 17.13, a sample may only be taken by a prescribed person. The Police and Criminal Evidence Act 1984 (Drug Testing of Persons in Police Detention) (Prescribed Persons) Regulations 2001 (SI 2001 No. 2645) describe a prescribed person as:

(a) a police officer;

(b) a person employed by a police authority or police force whose contractual duties include taking samples for the purpose of testing for the presence of specified Class A drugs;

(c) a person employed by a contractor engaged by a police authority or police force whose duties include taking samples for the purpose of testing for the presence of specified Class A drugs.

(A 'contractor' means any person or body obliged, under any of the terms of a contract with a police authority or a police force, to provide, when required, the service of taking samples for the purpose of testing for the presence of specified Class A drugs.)

> **KEYNOTE**
>
> Force may not be used to take any sample for the purpose of drug testing (see Code C, para. 17.14).

Under s. 63C(1) of PACE, inserted by the Criminal Justice and Court Services Act 2000, a person guilty of refusing to provide a sample shall be liable on summary conviction to imprisonment for a term not exceeding three months, or to a fine not exceeding level 4 on the standard scale, or to both.

> **KEYNOTE**
>
> Code C, Annex K makes provisions allowing the police to conduct an x-ray of a detainee or an ultrasound scan to be carried out on them, where there are reasonable grounds for believing the person has swallowed a Class A drug which he/she was in possession of with intent to supply it to someone else. Annex K is dealt with in more depth in **8.10 X-rays and Ultrasound Scans**.

12.10.9 Action after the sample has been taken

Any sample taken may not be used for any purpose other than to ascertain whether the person concerned has a specified Class A drug present in his or her body. The sample can be disposed of as clinical waste unless it is to be sent for further analysis in cases where the test result is disputed at the point when the result is known, or where medication has been taken, or for quality assurance purposes (see Code C, para. 17.16).

> **KEYNOTE**
>
> Samples, and the information derived from them, may not be subsequently used in the investigation of any offence or in evidence against the persons from whom they were taken (see Code C, Note for Guidance 17D).
>
> Also, Code D, Note for Guidance 6F states that samples of urine and non-intimate samples taken in accordance with ss. 63B and 63C of PACE may not be used for identification purposes in accordance with this Code.

12.10.10 When the test is positive

Code C, para. 17.17 states that under the provisions of Part 3 of the Drugs Act 2005, where a detainee (who is a person who has reached the age of 18) has tested positive for a specified Class A drug under s. 63B of PACE, a police officer may, at any time before the person's release from the police station, impose a requirement on the detainee to attend an initial assessment of their drug misuse by a suitably qualified person and to remain for its duration.

The officer must, at the same time, impose a *second* requirement on the detainee to attend and remain for a follow-up assessment (previously, the detainee was only required to attend one assessment). The officer must inform the detainee that the second requirement will cease to have effect if, at the initial assessment, they are informed that a follow-up assessment is not necessary.

When imposing a requirement to attend both the initial assessment and the follow-up assessment, the police officer must inform the person of the time and place at which the assessment is to take place and explain that this information will be confirmed in writing. The detainee must be warned that he or she may be liable to prosecution for failing without good cause to attend either assessment and remain for the duration (see para. 17.18).

The officer must then hand a notice to the detainee which confirms the appointment and repeats the above warning (para. 17.19). Under para. 17.20, the fact that the requirement to attend an initial assessment and a follow-up assessment has been imposed, and the information, explanation, warning and notice given in accordance with paras. 17.17 and 17.19, must all be recorded on the custody record.

Finally, where a notice is given in accordance with para. 17.19, a police officer can give the person a further notice in writing which informs the person of any change to the time or place at which the initial assessment is to take place and which repeats the warning referred to in para. 17.18 (see para. 17.21).

12.11 **Summing Up**

Fingerprints

May be taken without consent:

Before Charge when:

1. The person is detained in consequence of his arrest for a recordable offence; and he/she has not had his/her fingerprints taken in the course of the investigation, or he/she has had his/her fingerprints taken and they are insufficient.

(s. 61(3) PACE)

After Charge when:

2. The person has been charged with or reported for a recordable offence, and

   (a) he/she has not had his/her fingerprints taken in the course of the investigation of the offence by the police *or*

   (b) the fingerprints do not constitute a complete set, or some or all of the fingerprints are not of sufficient quality.

(s. 61(4) PACE)

3. Where a person has been convicted, cautioned, warned or reprimanded, for a recordable offence.

(s. 61(6) PACE)

Taking fingerprints away from the police station

A constable may take a person's fingerprints away from the police station without the appropriate consent if he/she reasonably suspects that the person is:

• committing or attempting to commit an offence, or has committed or attempted to commit an offence; and

• the name of the person is unknown, and cannot be readily ascertained, or

• the constable has reasonable grounds for doubting whether a name furnished by the person as his name is his real name.

(s. 61(6A) & 61(6B) PACE)

(It should be noted that even though this power commenced on the 1 January 2006, it relies on technology that is not widely available at this time. As a result, s. 117(2) of the 2005 Act was not in force at the time of writing this book.)

Taking footwear impressions

Where a person is detained at a police station, an impression of his footwear may be taken with or without the appropriate consent if:

• he/she is arrested and detained for a recordable offence, or has been charged with a recordable offence, or informed that he/she will be reported for a recordable offence; and

- he/she has not had an impression taken of his/her footwear in the course of the investigation of the offence by the police.

(s. 61A(3) PACE)

Reasonable force may be used, if necessary, to take a footwear impression from a detainee without consent.

(Code D, para. 4.18)

Examination to establish identity

A detainee at a police station may be searched or examined or both, to:

(a)   establish whether they have any marks, features or injuries that would tend to identify them as a person involved in the commission of an offence and to photograph any identifying marks; or

(b)   establish their identity.

May be done without consent, with the authority of an inspector and force may be used.

(s. 54A(1) PACE)

Photographing suspects

An officer may, with or without consent, photograph:

- any person whilst they are detained at a police station; and
- any person who is elsewhere than at a police station and who has been:—

   (i)   arrested by a constable for an offence; or

   (ii)   taken into custody by a constable after being arrested for an offence by a person other than a constable; or

   (iii)   made subject to a requirement to wait with a community support officer; or

   (iv)   given a penalty notice by a constable in uniform for certain specified offences; or

   (v)   given a penalty notice by a PCSO for certain specified offences; or

   (vi)   given a penalty notice by an accredited person for certain specified offences.

(s. 64A PACE and Code D, para. 5.12A)

'Intimate sample'

A sample of blood, semen or any other tissue fluid, urine or pubic hair; a dental impression; a swab taken from any part of a person's genitals, or from a person's body orifice other than the mouth.

(s. 65 PACE)

Authorisation for intimate sample

An intimate sample may be taken only when a police officer of at least the rank of inspector authorises it to be taken, and the appropriate consent is given in writing.

There is no power to obtain an intimate sample by force.

(s. 62(1)(a) PACE)

An officer may only give an authorisation to obtain an intimate sample if he/she has reasonable grounds—

- for suspecting the involvement of the person from whom the sample is to be taken in a recordable offence; and
- for believing that the sample will tend to confirm or disprove his or her involvement in such an offence.

(s. 62(2) PACE)

Refusal to provide intimate sample

If a person refuses to provide an intimate sample, his/her refusal may harm his/her case if it comes to trial. He or she must be warned of this fact before the sample is taken.

'Non-intimate sample'

A sample of hair other than pubic hair [and includes hair plucked from the root]; a sample taken from a nail or from under a nail; a swab taken from any part of a person's body other than a part from which a swab taken would be an intimate sample; saliva; a footprint or a similar impression of any part of a person's body other than a part of his hand; a skin impression other than a fingerprint.

(Code D, para. 6.3)

Consent—non-intimate sample

A non-intimate sample may be taken from a person without the appropriate consent (using reasonable force if necessary) if—

- he/she is in police detention, or is being held in custody by the police on the authority of a court; and

- an officer of at least the rank of inspector authorises it to be taken without the appropriate consent; or

- he/she has been charged with a recordable offence or reported for such an offence; and

- either he/she has not had a non-intimate sample taken from him in the course of the investigation of the offence by the police, or

- he/she has had a non-intimate sample taken from him/her but either it was not suitable for the same means of analysis or, though so suitable, the sample proved insufficient.

(s. 63(3) PACE)

Vulnerable people

- If the person is between the ages of 14 years and 17 years (a young person), consent must be obtained from that person and his/her parent or guardian;

- if the person is under the age of 14 years (a child), the consent must be obtained from his/her parent or guardian only;

- where the consent of a mentally disordered or otherwise mentally vulnerable person is required, this will only be valid if given in the presence of the appropriate adult.

Testing for presence of Class A Drugs

A sample of urine or non-intimate sample may be taken from a person in police detention to ascertain if he/she has any specified Class A drug in his/her body only where they have been brought before the custody officer and:

- either the arrest condition or the charge condition is met; and

- the age condition is met; and

- the notification condition is met in relation to the arrest condition, the charge condition, or the age condition, as the case may be.

(Code C, para. 17.2)

The arrest condition is met where the detainee has been arrested for:

- a trigger offence, but not charged; or

- any other offence but not charged and an inspector has authorised the sample to be taken where he/she has reasonable grounds to suspect the detainee's misuse of any specified Class A drug caused/contributed to the offence.

(Code C, para. 17.3)

The charge condition is met where the detainee has been charged with:

- a trigger offence; or
- any other offence and an inspector has authorised the sample to be taken where he/she has reasonable grounds to suspect the detainee's misuse of any specified Class A drug caused/contributed to the offence.

(Code C, para. 17.4)

The age condition is met in the case of a detainee who has been:

- arrested but not charged and they are aged 18 or over;
- charged and they are aged 14 or over.

(Code C, para. 17.5)

Force may not be used to take any sample for the purpose of drug testing.

(Code C, para. 17.14)

LOCAL PROCEDURES

1. Has your police area or police station received notification from the Secretary of State to apply the provisions for drug testing under s. 63B of PACE (as amended by s. 5 of the Criminal Justice Act 2003 and s. 7 of the Drugs Act 2005)?

SPACE FOR NOTES

341

SPACE FOR NOTES

SPACE FOR NOTES

Dealing with Legal Representatives

13.1 **Introduction**

Legal representation appears in many sections of PACE and the *Codes of Practice* and there is some overlap with other chapters, for example, **Chapter 6—The Detainee's Entitlements** (which deals with on-call solicitors and commencing an interview without a solicitor being present), and **Chapter 18—Interviewing** (which deals with interviews themselves).

This chapter concentrates on the role of the solicitor throughout the custody procedure, and identifies the behaviour that the custody officer should expect from defence solicitors when they arrive at the custody office. Also, in this chapter we identify who may actually act as a solicitor, and the role of accredited and probationary representatives (also known as legal representatives or clerks).

Note that legal representatives are considered to be 'solicitors' in the *Codes of Practice*. Therefore, unless otherwise stated, solicitors in this chapter include any person representing a detainee at a police station.

13.2 **Who May Act as a 'Solicitor'?**

13.2.1 **Legislative provisions**

Code C, Para. 6.12

'Solicitor' in this Code means:

- a solicitor who holds a current practising certificate;
- an accredited or probationary representative included on the register of representatives maintained by the Legal Services Commission.

Code C, Para. 6.12A

An accredited or probationary representative sent to provide advice by, and on behalf of, a solicitor shall be admitted to the police station for this purpose unless an officer of inspector rank or above considers such a visit will hinder the investigation and directs otherwise.

Hindering the investigation does not include giving proper legal advice to a detainee as in Note 6D. Once admitted to the police station, paras. 6.6 to 6.10 apply.

Code C, Para. 6.13

In exercising their discretion under para. 6.12A, the officer should take into account in particular:

- whether:
  - the identity and status of an accredited or probationary representative have been satisfactorily established;
  - they are of suitable character to provide legal advice, e.g. a person with a criminal record is unlikely to be suitable unless the conviction was for a minor offence and not recent;
- any other matters in any written letter of authorisation provided by the solicitor on whose behalf the person is attending the police station. [See Note 6F].

Code C, Para. 6.14

If the inspector refuses access to an accredited or probationary representative or a decision is taken that such a person should not be permitted to remain at an interview, the inspector must notify the solicitor on whose behalf the representative was acting and give them an opportunity to make alternative arrangements. The detainee must be informed and the custody record noted.

13.2.2 **Solicitors**

In general, solicitors acting on behalf of detainees at police stations operate in a three-tier system:

- qualified solicitors and trainees;
- accredited representatives;
- probationary representatives.

Any of the above group may represent a detainee at a police station; the latter two groups may do so on a solicitor's behalf. In this section, the role of accredited representatives and probationary representatives is examined in more depth than the role of the qualified solicitor.

13.2.3 **Accredited representatives**

Accredited representatives (also known as legal representatives) are people who act on behalf of defence solicitors, when defending suspects at police stations. According to the definition of a 'solicitor' in para. 6.12 above, they should be viewed as solicitors, which means they have the same right to view the custody record and represent the detainee in all aspects of their detention.

Accredited representatives are increasingly used by solicitors for call-outs to police stations, instead of a solicitor who will eventually represent the client in court. They have the same authority as a solicitor to act on behalf of a detainee at a police station.

13.2.4 **Probationary representatives**

Probationary representatives should be viewed as trainee accredited representatives (or legal executives). As with accredited representatives, probationary representatives are 'sent' to the police station by solicitors, to act on behalf of their clients. They are also covered by the definition of a 'solicitor' in para. 6.12 above.

13.2.5 **Exclusion of accredited and probationary representatives**

There is a power to exclude accredited or probationary representatives from the police station; however, it should be noted that Code C, para. 6.12A also states that such a person shall be admitted to the police station, unless the requirements of that paragraph apply.

In **Chapter 6—The Detainee's Entitlements**, it was acknowledged that a detainee has a fundamental human right to be legally represented, and that any denial of these rights may only be authorised under the Police and Criminal Evidence Act 1984, or the *Codes of Practice*. Inspectors who authorise the exclusion of a legal representative must bear in mind this fact. In any case, if a particular legal representative is excluded, the detainee is still entitled to representation by another solicitor from the same firm (see para. 6.14 above).

Paragraph 6.12A above does not give specific advice on what would represent a hindrance to an investigation, but it does not include giving proper legal advice to a detainee. Some guidance is provided in para. 6.13, which states that the authorising officer may take into account:

- whether the identity and status of the person has been satisfactorily established; *or*
- whether they are of unsuitable character to provide legal advice (e.g. a person with a criminal record would not be—except where the offence was a minor offence and not recent).

The inspector may also take into account any written letter of authorisation provided by the solicitor on whose behalf the person is attending the police station (presumably this applies only to confirming the identity and status of the person).

The above list does not include a lack of qualifications or experience as a reason to exclude a legal representative. However, what if the person has a complete lack of understanding of custody procedure? Such a person may hinder the investigation, which might give grounds for their exclusion. One would hope that a solicitor would not send such a person to a police station in any event.

> **KEYNOTE**
>
> Note that once an accredited or probationary representative has been admitted to the police station, paras. 6.6 to 6.10 will apply (which includes the detainee being entitled to consult with a solicitor and have him/her present at an interview).
>
> The accredited or probationary representative may then only be excluded after being allowed entry if para. 6.9 applies (i.e. that he/she was disruptive in the interview—see **13.7 Removing a Solicitor from an Interview**, below).

Consider the following:

Case Study

PEARSON is a senior partner in a firm of solicitors. He has recently employed his son-in-law, HEMBURY, as a probationary representative, with a view to training him for accreditation. However, PEARSON was unaware that HEMBURY had a recent conviction for theft.

HEMBURY shadowed another accredited representative for six months at police stations in his local area, until he was given the all clear to attend on his own. One day, he attended a police station he had not been to before, but unfortunately for him, he was recognised by the officer who had arrested him for the theft.

The officer informed the duty inspector of HEMBURY's convictions, and his intention to represent a client, and the inspector made the decision to exclude him from the custody office. The duty inspector contacted PEARSON's firm, suggesting that an alternative legal representative be sent.

What would happen if PEARSON kept HEMBURY in the firm, but only allowed him to work in the area near his home, where he would not be recognised?

....

What is clear from Code C is that when a person is excluded from a police station, they are not automatically excluded from all police stations, or even from returning to the same station on a different day. This may cause practical problems for the local police, as they would need to send a notice to all the custody offices in the area that a person had been excluded from entering the police station. But, can the police authorise a 'blanket ban' on a person entering police stations?

The simple answer is 'no'. This issue was examined in the case of *R* v *Chief Constable of Avon and Somerset, ex parte Robinson* [1989] 1 WLR 793, 2 All ER 15. In this particular case, it was held that guidance by chief officers as to the suitability of certain clerks could be sent to other officers to be considered, but the ultimate decision should rest with individual inspectors, based on their knowledge of the person. This decision was followed in *R* v *Chief Constable of Northumbria, ex parte Thompson* [2001] 4 All ER 354, where the Court of Appeal held that a blanket ban was unlawful and each case should be taken on its own merits.

Therefore, if the person in the scenario did continue to attend police stations, he would need to be excluded each time by an inspector. This situation is catered for in Note for Guidance 6F above. If the firm or solicitor fails to take action, and persists in sending accredited or probationary representatives who are unsuited to provide legal advice (within the definition under para. 6.13 above), a superintendent should be informed, who may take the matter up with the Law Society.

13.3 **Understanding the Role of Solicitors**

13.3.1 **Legislative provisions**

Code C, Note for Guidance 6D

A detainee has a right to free legal advice and to be represented by a solicitor. The solicitor's only role in the police station is to protect and advance the legal rights of their client. On occasions, this may require the solicitor to give advice which has the effect of the client avoiding giving evidence which strengthens a prosecution case.

13.3.2 **'Them and us'**

Because the criminal justice system in England and Wales is essentially adversarial, there will invariably be a 'them and us' mentality between the police and legal representatives. On the one hand, police officers may view legal representatives as a hindrance, or a 'necessary evil' (and may try to influence the custody officer into thinking the same way).

On the other hand, defence solicitors may view the police with suspicion, expecting them to be difficult to deal with and secretive about their client. Many solicitors may also be of the opinion that police officers have a lack of understanding of legislation and their role in the criminal justice system.

This is not to say that all police officers have the view expressed above, or that all legal representatives are disruptive and think the police are idiots.

Another view is that a detainee at a police station may only be a client to one or other of the sides in the justice system. This view is somewhat reinforced by Code C, Note for Guidance 6D above, which refers to a solicitor 'protecting and advancing' the legal rights of their client. Note for Guidance 6D also identifies that the solicitor may be required to give advice which has the effect of the client avoiding giving evidence which strengthens a prosecution case. This commonly occurs where a solicitor identifies that the prosecution case is weak, and advises the client to make no comment in the interview.

So where does the custody officer fit into this system? The custody officer, of course, must act impartially and he or she should be performing a similar role to the solicitor. The custody officer, if they are doing their job properly, will also be protecting the legal rights of the detainee.

KEYNOTE

If a solicitor arrives at the station to see a detainee, he/she must be informed of the solicitor's attendance, whether or not they are being interviewed and asked if they would like to see the solicitor (unless Annex B applies and authorisation has been given by a superintendent for the detainee to be held without access to legal advice). This applies even if the detainee has declined legal advice or, having requested it, subsequently agreed to be interviewed without receiving advice. The solicitor's attendance and the detainee's decision must be noted in the custody record (see Code C, para. 6.15).

13.3.3 The solicitor's objectives

A legal representative is required to act in the best interests of their client. Custody officers should expect a forceful approach by the solicitor, on behalf of their client.

At the custody office, this will mean representing their client in the following terms:

- by viewing the custody record on arrival at the station (to ensure that the detainee's legal rights and the *Codes of Practice* have been complied with);
- by making representations to the custody officer in relation to PACE issues contained in the custody record;
- by seeking information from the arresting officer as to the circumstances of the arrest (while at the same time testing the strength of police evidence);
- by attempting to persuade the custody officer that an interview is unnecessary (possibly in an attempt to prevent the detainee from incriminating himself/herself);

- by advising their client prior to interview of their rights (including the right to silence);
- by representing the client at an interview;
- by representing their client in respect of charging (including attempts to persuade the custody officer that there is insufficient evidence against their client);
- by representing their client in respect of bail issues (by suggesting alternatives to remands in custody).

We will be dealing with most of these subjects in this chapter, but what is obvious from the above list is that the solicitor's objectives at the custody office will be in direct conflict with those of the investigating officer.

13.4 **Access to the Custody Record**

13.4.1 **Legislative provisions**

Code C, Para. 2.4

A solicitor or appropriate adult must be permitted to consult a detainee's custody record as soon as practicable after their arrival at the station and at any other time whilst the person is detained. Arrangements for this access must be agreed with the custody officer and may not unreasonably interfere with the custody officer's duties.

Code C, Para. 2.4A

When a detainee leaves police detention or is taken before a court they, their legal representative or appropriate adult shall be given, on request, a copy of the custody record as soon as practicable. This entitlement lasts for 12 months after release.

Code C, Para. 2.5

The detainee, appropriate adult or legal representative shall be permitted to inspect the original custody record after the detainee has left police detention provided they give reasonable notice of their request. Any such inspection shall be noted in the custody record.

351

13.4.2 **When access to custody records must be given**

The provisions of paras. 2.4–2.5 above ensure that transparency is maintained. This allows the detainee, his/her appropriate adult or the legal representative to establish whether or not the police have complied with PACE and the *Codes of Practice* in respect of the detention period.

The provisions are self-explanatory and do not require extensive debriefing. They fall into the following categories:

- the appropriate adult or solicitor may consult the custody record as soon as practicable after they have arrived at the station;
- the appropriate adult or solicitor may consult the custody record at any other time whilst the person is detained;
- the detainee, appropriate adult or solicitor may request a copy of the custody record up to 12 months after their release;
- the detainee, appropriate adult or legal representative may inspect the original custody record any time after the detainee has left police detention (provided they give reasonable notice of their request).

KEYNOTE

Note that when the detainee is in police detention, access to the custody record by the appropriate adult or solicitor may not unreasonably interfere with the custody officer's duties.

13.5 **Initial Disclosure to Solicitors**

13.5.1 **Information to be given**

It must be remembered that as soon as the solicitor walks into the custody office, he or she will be doing everything possible to seek information which will assist the detainee. The police and the solicitor must work together to ensure that all the information given is correct. However, the custody officer should avoid discussing anything at this point, other than what is contained in the custody record, and issues relating to PACE.

It will be for the investigating officer to disclose further information to the solicitor, prior to interview. We examined the issue of what the investigating officer should disclose in **2.4 What else must be recorded on the custody record?** Nevertheless, it is worth re-capping at this point. There is no specific requirement under PACE, or the Criminal Justice and Public Order Act 1994, for the police to disclose information to the legal representative (other than allowing him/her to see the custody record under para. 2.4 above).

However, if the detainee were to make no comment in interview, he/she may claim that there had not been full disclosure prior to interview, thus depriving the solicitor of the ability to give appropriate advice to the client, and that the court should not draw any inference from this silence.

This issue was examined in *R* v *Argent* [1997] Crim LR 346, where the court did not accept that an inference could not be drawn because there had not been full disclosure at the interview.

The investigating officer will need to strike a balance between providing enough information to the solicitor to allow him/her to properly represent the client, and providing the detainee with a ready-made defence prior to the interview.

KEYNOTE

Custody officers and investigating officers should be advised that any information given to the solicitor prior to interview will be passed on to the client. Occasionally, officers may be tempted to disclose information, and ask the solicitor to keep it to themselves.

To do this would be naïve, as the solicitor is under a general duty to inform their client what they have been told and to represent their interests fully.

13.6 **The Solicitor's Role in an Interview**

13.6.1 **Legislative provisions**

Code C, Note for Guidance 6D

The solicitor may intervene in order to seek clarification, challenge an improper question to their client or the manner in which it is put, advise their client not to reply to particular questions, or if they wish, to give their client further legal advice.

This section deals with the role of the solicitor in the interview itself. Some solicitors do not get involved at all in the interview, while others play a very active role, offering advice to their clients and objecting to questions put by the interviewing officers. Note for Guidance 6D above shows that some involvement is allowed, such as:

- clarifying questions put by the interviewing officers;
- challenging improper questions;

- advising the detainee that he/she may remain silent;
- offering legal advice.

Sometimes the solicitor may behave in a manner which goes beyond that which is allowed under Note for Guidance 6D above. This issue is dealt with below in **13.7 Removing a Solicitor from an Interview**. But there may also be implications for the detainee if the solicitor fails to intervene on behalf of their client.

Consider the following:

Case Study

MILLER was arrested for an offence of murder. He was interviewed several times in the presence of a solicitor and later admitted the offence. He was later charged, and at the subsequent court case was found guilty.

MILLER appealed against his conviction, on the grounds that the confession was obtained unfairly and that the interview was oppressive. The prosecution maintained that MILLER was represented in the interview by a solicitor, and that his rights would have been protected because of the solicitor's presence.

MILLER's appeal was successful and the conviction quashed.

How legitimate was the prosecution's claim in respect of the defence solicitor's presence?

....

The above circumstances are based around a case dealt with by the Court of Appeal in the rather infamous case of *R* v *Miller* [1993] Crim LR 361. Stephen Miller and his two co-defendants were convicted originally on the strength of his confession, which the Court of Appeal found oppressive. Lord Chief Justice Taylor said at the appeal:

> Short of physical violence, it was hard to conceive of a more hostile approach by officers to a suspect. The solicitor who sat in the interviews seemed to have done that and little else. It seemed that his presence might actually have rendered a disservice since the officer might have taken the view that unless and until the solicitor intervened, they could not be criticised for going too far.

The Law Society expects a defence solicitor to vigorously protect the rights of their clients, something which clearly did not happen in the case above. Obviously not all interviews will follow the same course as the one in *Miller*, but interviewing officers should not be surprised when defence solicitors take an active part on behalf of their client.

13.7 **Removing a Solicitor from an Interview**

13.7.1 **Legislative provisions**

Code C, Para. 6.9

The solicitor may only be required to leave the interview if their conduct is such that the interviewer is unable properly to put questions to the suspect. See Notes 6D and 6E.

Code C, Note for Guidance 6D

Paragraph 6.9 only applies if the solicitor's approach or conduct prevents or unreasonably obstructs proper questions being put to the suspect or the suspect's response being recorded. Examples of unacceptable conduct include answering questions on a suspect's behalf or providing written replies for the suspect to quote.

Code C, Para. 6.10

If the interviewer considers a solicitor is acting in such a way, they will stop the interview and consult an officer not below superintendent rank, if one is readily available, and otherwise an officer not below inspector rank not connected with the investigation. After speaking to the solicitor, the officer consulted will decide if the interview should continue in the presence of that solicitor. If they decide it should not, the suspect will be given the opportunity to consult another solicitor before interview continues and that solicitor given an opportunity to be present at the interview. See Note 6E.

Code C, Para. 6.11

The removal of a solicitor from an interview is a serious step and, if it occurs, the officer of superintendent rank or above who took the decision will consider if the incident should be reported to the Law Society. If the decision to remove the solicitor has been taken by an officer below superintendent rank, the facts must be reported to an officer of superintendent rank or above who will similarly consider whether a report to the Law Society would be appropriate. When the solicitor concerned is a duty solicitor, the report should be both to the Law Society and to the Legal Services Commission.

Code C, Note for Guidance 6E

An officer who takes the decision to exclude a solicitor must be in a position to satisfy the court the decision was properly made. In order to do this they may need to witness what is happening.

13.7.2 **When to remove a solicitor from an interview**

There is a contrast between the powers to remove a solicitor from an interview under para. 6.9 above and the powers to exclude an accredited representative under para. 6.12A (see **13.2.5 Exclusion of accredited and probationary representatives**, above). A solicitor may only be removed from an interview because of their behaviour at the time, whereas an accredited legal representative may only be excluded from entering the police station because of their training or character.

It should be noted that although the detainee is entitled to have a solicitor present during an interview, it is the detainee's entitlement and not the solicitor's; the solicitor could not therefore claim damages against the police for their refusal to allow access to a client (see *Rixon* v *Chief Constable of Kent, The Times*, 11 April 2000).

Further, in *Coyle* v *Reid* [2000] N.I. 7, the court found in favour of the police, when a solicitor claimed that her rights had been interfered with, when she was ejected from the custody office by force. The solicitor was removed when she insisted on being present when police were attempting to obtain a DNA sample from her client, who had indicated that he would resist.

Nevertheless, as para. 6.11 identifies, the removal of a solicitor from an interview is a serious step and the decision should not be taken lightly. Before making a decision, the authorising officer may need to witness the behaviour, which may be done by listening to the tape of the interview. As Note for Guidance 6E above points out, any decision to remove a solicitor from the interview may have to be defended in court at some future date.

Note for Guidance 6D above gives examples as to when a solicitor's conduct may be seen as improper:

- when the solicitor's approach or conduct prevents or unreasonably obstructs proper questions being put; *or*
- when the solicitor's approach or conduct prevents or unreasonably obstructs the suspect's response being recorded; *or*
- when the solicitor answers questions on a suspect's behalf; *or*
- when the solicitor provides written replies for the suspect to quote.

KEYNOTE

Note that a solicitor may advise more than one client in an investigation if they wish and any question of a conflict of interest is for the solicitor to identify under their professional code of conduct. If, however, waiting for a solicitor to give advice to one client may lead to unreasonable delay to the interview with another, the provisions of para. 6.6(b) may apply (and the interview may be conducted without the solicitor being present—see **Chapter 6—The Detainee's Entitlements** and Code C, Note for Guidance 6G).

Consider the following:

Case Study

SHAH is in custody for assaulting his partner and is due to be interviewed about the offence. He has consulted with his solicitor, who has advised him to make no comment during the interview.

When the interview commences, SHAH makes no comment to several questions put to him; however, the officer persists and after a while, SHAH begins to answer some of the questions. His solicitor intervenes at this point, advising SHAH not to answer any more questions. This happens on a few occasions and eventually, the interviewing officer stops the interview and approaches the custody officer, asking for the solicitor to be removed.

Does the solicitor's behaviour amount to a breach of the *Codes of Practice* in these circumstances?

....

Remember that Note for Guidance 6D is in two parts, and a solicitor's conduct will not be seen as improper if he or she is merely clarifying questions put by the interviewing officers, challenging improper questions, or advising the detainee that he/she may remain silent or offering legal advice. If the detainee indicated to the solicitor prior to interview that he intended to remain silent, the solicitor may feel that any change of mind, such as in the circumstances above, has occurred due to duress and may advise their client accordingly, whether the interviewing officer likes it or not.

This is of course a fine line, and solicitors must make sure that their approach does not amount to an obstruction of proper questions being put to the detainee, as they may not be able to claim that they are acting in accordance with the *Codes of Practice*.

Paragraph 6.10 does not define when a superintendent may be 'readily available', but it can be assumed that if the interview has to be delayed unnecessarily to await the arrival of a superintendent, the views of an inspector should be sought.

In determining whether or not a solicitor should be removed, the superintendent or inspector is expected to speak to the solicitor involved. This will provide the solicitor with the opportunity to explain their conduct. The officer may decide to warn the solicitor about their conduct and allow the interview to continue in their presence. In these circumstances, the officer must make clear what is expected of the solicitor in the interview, and that if the interview is disrupted further, he or she may be removed.

If the decision is made to remove a solicitor from an interview, this should be noted in the interview record (see Code C, para. 6.17).

KEYNOTE

Even if para. 6.9 above is applied, and the solicitor is removed from an interview, the detainee is still entitled to representation from another solicitor (see para. 6.10 above).

13.8 Objections to Charging and Bailing Suspects

In general, objections from solicitors are likely to come after interview, when the decision is to be made as to whether a detainee should be charged and bailed to court. Obviously, the solicitor's objectives will be to try to persuade the custody officer that either:

1. there is insufficient evidence to charge the detainee, or
2. if the detainee is charged, he or she should be released on bail.

The legislative provisions of charging and detention after charge are dealt with in depth in **Chapter 14—Charging Suspects** and **Chapter 15—Continued Detention After Charge** respectively. In this section, we will examine the issues of dealing with objections from solicitors when it comes to making decisions in these two areas. Experienced custody officers will be aware that some solicitors will play a more rigorous role in defending their clients than others. Also, there may be a history of disagreements between a custody officer and a particular solicitor. Custody officers should ensure they do not let any of these things affect their independence and professional behaviour.

Section 37(7) of PACE makes it clear that it is the custody officer's decision as to whether a detainee will be charged with an offence. In making their decision, the custody officer may hear representations from either the detainee or their solicitor (but this is not mandatory).

When it comes to making a decision about bailing or remanding a suspect under s. 38 of PACE, the custody officer will need to take any representations from the solicitor or the detainee into account. Although there is nothing in PACE stating this is required, the general view is that when the custody officer is considering further detention after charge, he/she will effectively be conducting a review of the person's detention, which does require the reviewing officer to listen to any representations from the detainee, the appropriate adult, or legal representative.

In most circumstances, the custody officer will hear applications for continued detention from the investigating officer, followed by objections from the detainee or his/her solicitor. The custody officer will then make his/her decision and inform all parties.

If the custody officer makes the decision to detain a person following charge, he/she should expect the solicitor to ask for an explanation as to which part of s. 38(1) is being applied. It is therefore important that the custody officer understands fully the implications of this section, to be able to give a rational explanation of his/her decision. The solicitor then is likely to argue that the continued detention is unnecessary, as the detainee may be released on bail, with conditions, instead. At this point, custody officers can be under intense pressure, which may come from the investigating officer, the legal representative, appropriate adult and even the detainee. Additionally, there may be more than one detainee involved in the decision.

Other external matters may also affect the decision-making process, such as the number of other detainees in custody and even whether or not the custody officer is tired or hungry.

It is essential that important decisions are not made hastily and the following provides some practical tips to custody officers:

- Decisions do not need to be instantaneous—if the person has been charged, their detention clock has stopped ticking. Take time to consider what has been said—even ask the solicitor to come back in 10 minutes when you have reviewed all the evidence.
- Try to avoid being 'ambushed' by the investigating officer. Examine the status of all your detainees before charge to try to anticipate what charges are likely to be proposed, and whether or not applications for further detention may be made.
- Speak to the investigating officer before charge—find out what their intentions are and offer guidance.
- If the detainee is charged, and a remand application is anticipated, instruct the investigating officer to produce a 'remand package' which sets out all the requirements under s. 38(1) PACE—i.e. PNC printouts and intelligence checks, which identify the detainee's previous offending history, or witness statements and other evidence outlining the current allegation.
- Be certain that you are aware of your powers—get the books out if necessary.
- Display leadership qualities—the custody officer is in charge. You may even decide to authorise further detention based on what you know, even when

there is no application by the investigating officer (see **Chapter 15—Continued Detention After Charge**, which identifies clearly that the decision whether or not to grant bail is the custody officer's).

- Display confidence and record decisions rationally.
- Most of all, be firm but fair with all parties.

There are no definitive right or wrong answers to dealing with objections from solicitors, but by displaying the above qualities, custody officers can make their job easier. He or she will appear more professional and gain the respect of colleagues and legal representatives whom they will have to deal with again in the future.

13.9 **Summing Up**

Who may act as a 'solicitor'

'Solicitor' in this Code means:

- a solicitor who holds a current practising certificate;
- an accredited representative included on the register of representatives maintained by the Legal Services Commission.

(Code C, para. 6.12)

Legal representatives

Accredited representatives (also known as legal representatives) may act on behalf of defence solicitors, when defending suspects at police stations. They should be viewed as solicitors and have the same right to view the custody record and represent the detainee in all aspects of their detention.

Probationary representatives should be viewed as trainee accredited representatives (or legal executives). They have the same authority as an accredited representative to represent a detainee.

Exclusion from the police station

If an officer of inspector rank or above considers that the presence of an accredited or probationary representative at the station will hinder the investigation, that person may be prevented from entering the station.

Note:

- hindering the investigation does not include giving proper legal advice to a detainee;
- hindering the investigation does include:

- where the identity and status of the person has not been satisfactorily established; *or*
- where the person is of unsuitable character to provide legal advice (e.g. a person with a criminal record—except where the offence was minor offence and not recent).

(Code C, paras. 6.12A and 6.13)

Understanding the role of solicitors

The solicitor's only role in the police station is to protect and advance the legal rights of their client. This may require the solicitor to give advice which has the effect of the client avoiding giving evidence which strengthens a prosecution case.

(Code C, Note for Guidance 6D)

Access to the custody record

- The appropriate adult or solicitor may consult the custody record as soon as practicable after they have arrived at the station.
- The appropriate adult or solicitor may consult the custody record at any other time whilst the person is detained.
- The detainee, appropriate adult or solicitor may request a copy of the custody record up to 12 months after the detainee's release.
- The detainee, appropriate adult or legal representative may inspect the original custody record any time after the detainee has left police detention (provided they give reasonable notice of their request).

(Code C, paras. 2.4–2.5)

The solicitor's role in an interview

The solicitor may intervene in an interview, in order to:

- clarify questions put by the interviewing officers;
- challenge improper questions;
- advise the detainee that he/she may remain silent;
- offer legal advice.

Conduct of the solicitor in an interview

1. The solicitor may be required to leave the interview if:
   - their conduct is such that the interviewer is unable properly to put questions to a suspect; *or*

- their approach or conduct prevents or unreasonably obstructs the suspect's response being recorded; *or*
- they answer questions on a suspect's behalf; *or*
- they provide written replies for the suspect to quote.

If a solicitor is acting in such a way, the interview should be stopped and the interviewer should consult an officer not below superintendent rank, if one is readily available, and otherwise an officer not below inspector rank not connected with the investigation, who will decide if the interview should continue in the presence of that solicitor.

2. The suspect will be given the opportunity to consult another solicitor if his/her solicitor is removed.

3. The officer who took the decision will consider if the incident should be reported to the Law Society.

4. If the decision to remove the solicitor has been taken by an officer below superintendent rank, the facts must be reported to an officer of superintendent rank, who will consider whether a report to the Law Society would be appropriate.

5. An officer who takes the decision to exclude a solicitor must be in a position to satisfy the court the decision was properly made.

SPACE FOR NOTES

SPACE FOR NOTES

SPACE FOR NOTES

Charging Suspects

14.1 **Introduction**

A shorter chapter, but nevertheless important. There are other topics in this book which link to the subject of charging a detainee, such as continued detention and release on bail. These matters are covered in depth in **Chapter 15—Continued Detention After Charge** and **Chapter 16—Bail**. Also, in **Chapter 2—Detainees—Initial Action** we examined certain aspects of s. 37 of PACE, including the power to detain a person until there is sufficient evidence to charge him/her.

However, in this chapter, we will be discussing the process from the time the decision is made to actually charge the suspect, up to the point where the custody officer has to make a decision as to whether or not the person will be detained after charge, or released on bail. This chapter makes it clear that the custody officer is the person responsible for making the decision as to whether a detainee is to be charged with an offence. We will also examine the procedure for charging and cautioning a detainee and what should be recorded when a person has been charged.

There are certain circumstances when a person may be interviewed after charge—this subject is also examined in depth in this chapter. Advice is also given to investigating officers when a detainee issues a prepared statement, after being charged with an offence.

The Government drive to improve the failings in the criminal justice system to 'narrow the justice gap' means that under the Criminal Justice Act 2003, some of the decisions in relation to charging suspects are taken away from the custody officer, and given to the Crown Prosecution Service, who will advise on appropriate charges.

Also, the police will be given the power to administer 'conditional cautions', which are aimed at rehabilitation of offenders who have committed minor offences, and introducing a reparation scheme for victims.

The Human Rights Act 1998

Article 5, para. 2 of the 1998 Act states that:

> Everyone who is arrested shall be informed promptly, in a language which he understands, of the reasons for his arrest and of any charge against him.

Obviously the custody officer's actions will be dictated largely by the requirements of PACE and the *Codes of Practice*; however, there are requirements under the Human Rights Act 1998 above to inform the detainee 'promptly' of the charge against him/her.

366

14.2 **Making the Decision to Charge the Suspect**

14.2.1 **Legislative provisions**

Code C, Para. 16.1

When the officer in charge of the investigation reasonably believes there is sufficient evidence to provide a realistic prospect of the detainee's conviction they shall, without delay, inform the custody officer who will be responsible for considering whether the detainee will be charged.

Section 37(7) PACE

Subject to s. 41(7) below, if the custody officer determines that he has before him sufficient evidence to charge the person arrested with the offence for which he was arrested, the person arrested—

(a) shall be released without charge and on bail for the purpose of enabling the Director of Public Prosecutions to make a decision under s. 37B below;

(b) shall be released without charge and on bail but not for that purpose;

(c) shall be released without charge and without bail, or

(d) shall be charged.

Section 37(7A) PACE

The decision as to how a person is to be dealt with under subsection (7) above shall be that of the custody officer.

14.2.2 **Duties of the investigating officer**

Consider the following:

Case Study

DC SETHI has arrested BRIGGS, who was found in possession of a video stolen from a burglary approximately a month ago. When interviewed, BRIGGS denied committing the burglary, stating that he had bought the video recorder in a pub. Following the interview, DC SETHI returned to the custody officer, stating, 'Sarge, I've decided to charge him with burglary.'

....

Who does have the authority to decide whether or not the detainee should be charged with a particular offence? Would a charge of burglary be correct in these circumstances, or would a charge of handling stolen goods be more appropriate?

Section 37(7A) of PACE and Code C, para. 16.1 above make it clear that the decision-maker at this stage is the custody officer, and not the investigating officer, or any other person. As to which offence the detainee should be charged with, significant changes have been made to this decision-making process, with the introduction of Sch. 2 to the Criminal Justice Act 2003, and the requirement for the police to seek advice from the Crown Prosecution Service (CPS), in respect of appropriate charges. These matters are dealt with in depth below in **14.2.3 Statutory Charging**.

KEYNOTE

If the person arrested is not in a fit state to be dealt with under ss. (7) above, he/she may be kept in police detention until he/she is (see s. 37(9) PACE).

Once the interviewing officer realises there is a realistic prospect of conviction, questioning in relation to that offence should cease. Similarly, if the custody officer determines that there is sufficient evidence to charge the suspect, he/she should not allow a further interview.

The issue of whether there is sufficient evidence to charge (or provide a realistic prospect of the detainee's conviction) has attracted much attention in the courts. In *D* v *HM Advocate* (2000) *The Times*, 14 April, it was held that where there there is sufficient evidence to charge, a delay in bringing charges may be seen to be unreasonable under Article 6 of the European Convention on Human Rights.

Where there is more than one suspect for an offence, it will be perfectly legitimate for the police to hold all suspects until they have been interviewed to determine what evidence exists against all or some of them (see *Clarke* v *Chief Constable of North Wales* (2000) *The Independent*, 22 May).

It is also lawful to detain a person when there is sufficient evidence to charge, if there is a conflict between accounts given by the suspect and a witness, while awaiting a witness statement—even if the statement needs to be translated into English (see *R* v *Chief Constable of Hertfordshire, ex parte Wiles* [2002] EWHC 387 (Admin)).

KEYNOTE

In *R (on the application of G) v Chief Constable of West Yorkshire and the DPP* [2008] EWCA Civ 28, the Court of Appeal held that a custody officer who detained a juvenile for three hours pending advice from the CPS on the appropriate charge was acting unlawfully. Once the decision was made to charge, the detainee should have been charged. However, this case pre-dates s. 11 of the Police and Justice Act 2006, which came into force on 15 January 2007, and introduced statutory charging and compulsory pre-charge advice from the CPS in certain cases.

Custody officers are justified in detaining a person whilst awaiting a charging decision from the CPS provided they follow the DPP Guidelines, which are dealt with below in **14.2.3 Statutory charging**.

It is still possible that claims for damages may be made from other suspects who were kept in police detention, pending a decision from the CPS, before the above date.

This issue is often complicated when defence solicitors, in order to prevent their client from being interviewed, claim that he or she will make no comment and that the custody officer should charge the detainee immediately. Several cases have examined this issue, but there still appears to be some disagreement as to when questioning should actually cease.

For example, in *R v Pointer* [1997] Crim LR 676, the detainee made no comment during interview. In the subsequent trial, the interviewing officer admitted that before he interviewed the suspect, he believed there was sufficient evidence for a successful prosecution (the standard required under the old *Codes of Practice*). The court held that while it was appropriate to give the suspect the opportunity to say something during the interview, the questioning should cease once the suspect indicated he/she did not want to answer questions.

On the other hand, in *R v McGuiness* [1999] Crim LR 502, it was claimed that the court should not draw inferences from the detainee's silence during interview, as the police had sufficient evidence to prosecute before the interview commenced. The Court of Appeal rejected this submission, on the grounds that if the police had to charge a suspect every time there was a prima facie case, the police would lose the opportunity to interview the suspect and for the suspect to put forward an explanation, which may even prove his/her innocence. The court went further to state that any explanation or lack of one should be a factor in the decision as to whether there was sufficient evidence for a prosecution to succeed.

Custody officers should take into account both of the above decisions, but in the absence of any defining judgment, the *McGuiness* case would appear to be the most sensible option.

KEYNOTE

Note that the interviewing officer must also be satisfied that he/she has asked the detainee all the questions relevant to obtaining reliable information about the offence, including allowing the suspect to make an innocent explanation (see Code C, para. 11.6(a)).

KEYNOTE

When a person is detained in respect of more than one offence, it is permissible to delay bringing him/her before the custody officer until there is sufficient evidence to charge in respect of all offences (see Code C, para. 16.1).

14.2.3 Statutory charging

Schedule 2 of the Criminal Justice Act 2003 amended s. 37(7) of PACE, making it a statutory responsibility for the police, in certain circumstances, to seek advice from the Director of Public Prosecutions (DPP) in respect of certain charges (though, in practice, this advice will be provided by the Crown Prosecution Service (CPS)).

Statutory charging is embedded in all 42 Local Criminal Justice Boards and is intended to:

- improve file timeliness and quality;
- ensure that the right decisions are made at the right time for the police, witnesses, victims and courts;
- reduce the number of cracked and ineffective trials;
- improve conviction rates/guilty pleas, ultimately narrowing the justice gap.

In order to facilitate efficient and effective early consultations and make charging decisions, Crown Prosecutors are deployed, as Duty Prosecutors on a locally agreed basis, to provide guidance and make charging decisions. This service is complemented by a centrally managed out-of-hours duty prosecutor arrangement to ensure a continuous 24-hour service known as CPS Direct.

Previously under s. 37(7), where a custody officer determined there was sufficient evidence to charge a suspect, the custody officer was required to charge the person, or release them without charge, either on bail or without bail. Under the amended version of s. 37(7), where a custody officer determines there is sufficient evidence to charge, the detainee must either be:

- released without charge and on bail for the purpose of enabling the CPS to make a charging decision;

- released without charge and on bail but not for that purpose (i.e. because there is sufficient evidence to meet the threshold test—but further evidence is required—for example, awaiting the results of forensic evidence);

- released without charge and without bail (i.e. because there is insufficient evidence to meet the threshold test—and further enquiries are required); or

- charged with an offence.

Section 37(7B) states that where a person is released under subsection (7)(a) above, it shall be the duty of the custody officer to inform the person that he/she is being released to enable the CPS to make a decision. Where the CPS notifies a custody officer that there is insufficient evidence to charge, or that there is sufficient evidence to charge, but a person should not be charged or given a caution (possibly because it is not in the public interest to proceed), the custody officer must give a written notice outlining that the detainee is not to be prosecuted (s. 37B(5) PACE).

Under s. 37(8), where a person is released under subsection (b) or (c) and at the time of release a decision as to whether he/she should be prosecuted has not been taken, it shall be the duty of the custody officer to inform the person.

14.2.4 **Director of Public Prosecution's guidance in respect of charging**

Section 37A(1) states that the DPP may issue guidance to enable custody officers to decide how detainees should be dealt with under s. 37(7). According to s. 37A(3), custody officers must take this guidance into account in deciding how persons should be dealt with under this section. *The Guidance to Police Officers and Crown Prosecutors Issued by the Director of Public Prosecutions under s37A of the Police and Criminal Evidence Act 1984* was produced in January 2005 and applies in those Local Criminal Justice Board Areas where approval has been granted by the Home Office for the scheme to take place.

Under s. 2 of the Guidance (*Key Provisions and Principles*), the CPS will determine whether a person is to be charged in all indictable only, either way, or summary offences, and will make charging decisions following a review of evidence in those cases. However, there will be some cases where the police can proceed to charge, without advice from the CPS (see **14.2.6 Charging by the police** below).

The CPS will provide guidance and advice to investigators throughout the investigative and prosecuting process. This may include advice on lines of enquiry, evidential requirements and assistance in any pre-charge procedures. Crown Prosecutors are expected to be pro-active in identifying, and where possible, rectifying evidential deficiencies and in bringing to an early conclusion those cases that cannot be strengthened by further investigation.

Where necessary, pre-charge bail arrangements will be utilised to facilitate the evidence gathering, including, in appropriate cases, all the key evidence on which the prosecution will rely, prior to the charging decision being taken (s. 37(7)(a) and s. 47(1A) PACE) (see **Chapter 16—Bail** for a full discussion on issues relating to bail).

Where Crown Prosecutors decide that a person should be cautioned but it proves not to be possible to give the person such a caution (for example, if the detainee refuses to accept it), the person must be charged with the offence (s. 37B(7) PACE).

> **KEYNOTE**
>
> It should be noted that where the CPS make a decision as to whether a person should be charged with an offence or given a caution, conditional caution, a reprimand or final warning, the custody officer *must* follow that decision (s. 37B(6) PACE).

14.2.5 **Application of the Threshold Test by a custody officer**

The CPS will be responsible for the decision to charge and the specifying or drafting of the charges in all indictable only, either way or summary offences, but *only* where a custody officer determines that the Threshold Test is met. If the custody officer determines that the offence is one which is listed in the Guidance, the person may be charged or cautioned by the police without reference to a Crown Prosecutor (as to which, see **14.2.6 Charging by the police** below).

In applying the Threshold Test, the custody officer will require an overall assessment of whether, in all the circumstances of the case, there is at least a reasonable suspicion against the person of having committed an offence (in accordance with Article 5 of the European Convention on Human Rights) and that at that stage it is in the public interest to proceed. The evidential decision in each case will require consideration of a number of factors including: the evidence available at the time and the likelihood and nature of further evidence being obtained; the reasonableness for believing that evidence will become available; the time it will take and the steps being taken to gather it; the impact of the expected evidence on the case, and the charges the evidence will support.

If the matter passes the Threshold Test, then the custody officer may decide to charge (if he/she is the relevant charging authority), detain the person for charging, if CPS are the charging authority, or release the individual without charge either to obtain CPS advice or to obtain further evidence (or to release the detainee without charge and without bail—but these cases are likely to be rare).

14.2.6 **Charging by the police**

The police may determine the charge in the following cases:

(i)   Any offence under the Road Traffic Act or any other offence arising from the presence of a motor vehicle, trailer or pedal cycle on a road or other public place,
      except where (and the charge must therefore be determined by the CPS):

- the circumstances have resulted in the death of any person; *or*

- there is an allegation of dangerous driving; *or*

- the allegation is one of driving whilst disqualified and there has been no admission in a PACE interview to both the driving and the disqualification; *or*

- the statutory defence to being in charge of a motor vehicle (unfit through drink or drugs or excess alcohol) may be raised under ss. 4(3) or 5(2) of the Road Traffic Act 1988; *or*

- there is an allegation of the unlawful taking of a motor vehicle or the aggravated unlawful taking of a motor vehicle (unless the case is suitable for disposal as an early guilty plea in the magistrates' court).

(ii) Any offence of absconding under the Bail Act 1976 and any offence contrary to s. 5 of the Public Order Act 1986 and any offence under the Town Police Clauses Act 1847, the Metropolitan Police Act 1839, the Vagrancy Act 1824, the Street Offences Act 1959, under s. 91 of the Criminal Justice Act 1967, s. 12 of the Licensing Act 1872, any offence under any bylaw and any summary offence punishable on conviction with a term of imprisonment of 3 months or less.

The police may determine the charge in any either way or summary offences where it appears to the custody officer that a guilty plea is likely and that the case is suitable for sentencing in the magistrates' court, but excluding those specified in Annex A to Guidance (see **14.2.8 When the police may not charge** below). If the custody officer is uncertain whether a case falls under this category, early consultation with the CPS should be undertaken to clarify whether the charging decision is one that should be made by the CPS or the police.

KEYNOTE

Sections 75 to 97 of the Criminal Justice Act 2003 introduced a statutory exception to the rule against double jeopardy. Schedule 5 to the 2003 Act lists a series of 'qualifying offences' to which these provisions apply; they are all serious offences, which in the main carry a maximum sentence of life imprisonment.

Section 76 allows a prosecutor to apply to the Court of Appeal for an order to quash the person's acquittal for a 'qualifying offence', and therefore re-try the case.

When a person is arrested under the provisions of the 2003 Act, the detention provisions of PACE are modified and make an officer of the rank of *superintendent* or above, who has not been directly involved in the investigation, responsible for determining whether the evidence is sufficient to charge (Code C, Note for Guidance 16AA).

14.2.7 **Requirement for early consultations**

Where it appears likely that a charge will be determined by the CPS, custody officers must direct investigating officers to consult a Duty Prosecutor as soon as is practicable after a person is taken into custody. This will enable early agreement to be reached as to evidential requirements and, where appropriate, for any period of bail to be determined.

Early consultation with the CPS will allow the early identification of weak cases and those where the charging decision may be made upon consideration of limited information.

In referrals where the police do not wish to proceed in any indictable only case in which the Threshold Test is met and in which an investigating or supervisory officer decides that he does not wish to proceed with a prosecution, the case must be referred to the CPS to confirm whether or not the case is to proceed. Early consultation in such a case may allow the investigation and preparation of case papers to be curtailed unless the complexity or sensitivity of the case determines otherwise.

Where, in any case, it appears that there is manifestly no evidence and the Threshold Test is not met in respect of a detained person, the custody officer need not refer the case to a Crown Prosecutor before releasing that person, whether on bail or otherwise.

In any case where the Guidance requires charges to be determined by the CPS and a custody officer concludes that the Threshold Test is met, the custody officer will ensure that the case is referred to a Crown Prosecutor as soon as is practicable, or, where the person is suitable for bail, release the person detained on pre-charge bail, with or without conditions, in accordance with s. 37(7)(a) above.

14.2.8 **When the police may not charge**

There are some offences or circumstances, which must always be referred to the CPS for early consultation and charging decision—*whether admitted or not*—

- offences requiring the Attorney-General's or Director of Public Prosecution's consent;
- any indictable only offence;
- any either way offence triable only on indictment due to the surrounding circumstances of the commission of the offence, or the previous convictions of the person;
- offences under the Terrorism Act 2000, the Prevention of Terrorism Act 2005 or any other offence linked with terrorist activity;
- offences under the Anti-terrorism, Crime and Security Act 2001;
- offences under the Explosive Substances Act 1883;
- offences under any of the Official Secrets Acts;
- offences involving any racial, religious or homophobic aggravation;
- offences classified as domestic violence;
- offences under the Sexual Offences Act 2003 committed by or upon persons under the age of 18 years;
- offences involving Persistent Young Offenders, unless chargeable by the police;
- offences arising directly or indirectly out of activities associated with hunting wild mammals with dogs under the Hunting Act 2004;
- the following specific offences:
  - wounding or inflicting grievous bodily harm, contrary to s. 20 of the Offences Against the Person Act 1861;
  - assault occasioning actual bodily harm, contrary to s. 47 of the Offences Against the Person Act 1861;
  - violent disorder, contrary to s. 2 of the Public Order Act 1986;
  - affray, contrary to s. 3 of the Public Order Act 1986;
  - offences involving deception, contrary to the Theft Acts 1968 & 1978;
  - handling stolen goods, contrary to s. 22 of the Theft Act 1968.

KEYNOTE

It should be noted that where the charges or joint charges to be preferred against one or more persons include a combination of offences, some of which may be determined by the police, and others that must be determined by the CPS, the custody officer shall refer all charges to a Crown Prosecutor for determination.

14.2.9 **Emergency cases—expiry of PACE time limits**

In cases where the charging responsibility lies with the CPS, and it is proposed to withhold bail for the purposes of making an application to a court for a remand in custody (or for bail conditions that may only be imposed by a court), but it proves not to be possible to consult with a Crown Prosecutor in person or by telephone before the expiry of any PACE custody time limit, a custody officer may proceed to charge, but only on the authority of a duty inspector. The duty inspector shall note the custody record and MG3 to confirm that it is appropriate to charge under this emergency provision. The case must be referred to the CPS as soon as is practicable for authority to proceed with the prosecution.

14.2.10 **Police action post referral and escalation procedure**

In any case where the Threshold Test is met and the case has been referred to the CPS for a charging decision, and the decision is to charge, caution, obtain additional evidence or take no action, the police will not proceed in any other way without first referring the matter back to the CPS.

Where in any case an investigating or custody officer is not in agreement with the charging decision, the report requirements, or any diversion proposal of the CPS and wishes to have the case referred for further review, the case must be referred to the BCU Crime Manager (normally Detective Chief Inspector), or appointed Deputy, for consultation with a CPS Unit Head, or appointed Deputy for resolution. If further escalation is required, the involvement of the Divisional Commander and the Level E Unit Head or Chief Crown Prosecutor should be obtained. Procedures should be in place for this review to be conducted.

14.2.11 **Continued detention when the decision has been made to charge**

Normally, where the custody officer determines that there is sufficient evidence to charge a detainee, that person should be charged without delay. However, under the guidelines relating to pre-charge advice, the custody officer may have made that decision, but is waiting for the outcome of advice from the CPS. The inevitable delay caused by such cases is catered for in Code C, Note for Guidance 16AB, which states that a custody officer who determines in accordance with that Guidance that there is sufficient evidence to charge the detainee, may detain that person for no longer than is reasonably necessary to decide how that person is to be dealt with under PACE, s. 37(7)(a) to (d). This will include, where appropriate, consultation with the CPS. However, it should be noted that this Code does not enable the police to extend any statutory time limits under PACE (e.g. s. 42—24-hour extension), in order to await the advice.

Paragraph 16AB also states that where, in accordance with the Guidance, the case is referred to the CPS for a decision, the custody officer should ensure that an officer involved in the investigation sends to the CPS such information as is specified in the Guidance (presumably to ensure that some quality control is maintained over the process).

14.2.12 **Alternative options to charging the suspect**

Under Code C, Note for Guidance 16A, the custody officer must take into account alternatives to prosecution under the Crime and Disorder Act 1998. Juvenile detainees may be given reprimands and final warnings, whereas persons aged 18 or older may receive a 'simple caution' (see HO circular 30/2005 for full details).

The 'Guidance to Police Officers and Crown Prosecutors' issued by the Director of Public Prosecutions under s. 37A of the Police and Criminal Evidence Act 1984, states that where the police consider that the Threshold Test is met in a case, other than an indictable only offence, and determine that it is in the public interest instead to administer a simple caution, or to administer a reprimand or final warning in the case of a youth, the police may issue that caution, reprimand or final warning as appropriate, without referring the case to a Crown Prosecutor. However, the investigating officer may wish to consult with the CPS in respect of any case in which it is proposed to deal with a person by way of a caution, reprimand or final warning.

Where a conditional cautioning scheme is in force locally and the police wish to conditionally caution any person for an offence, the custody officer *must* refer the case to the CPS for a decision (see **14.2.13 Conditional cautions** below for full details of this scheme).

With the pressure on police forces to achieve targets and in particular sanctioned detections, custody officers may often be asked to consider cautioning detainees as an alternative option to charging, where the evidence is weak. Quite often, defence solicitors may offer such a 'deal' to avoid their client receiving a conviction in court and a criminal record.

What must be remembered is that the custody officer must be satisfied that the person admits their guilt. A number of cases have been taken to the Court of Appeal, whereby individuals have received cautions and subsequently challenged the process.

In one such case, *R (on the application of W)* v *Chief Constable of Hampshire Constabulary* [2006] EWHC 1904 (Admin), the defendant was arrested for a sexual assault on a female in a night club and subsequently received an adult caution. W appealed against the caution on the grounds that he had not made a clear admission to the offence. When the court heard the interview, it agreed that W had not made a clear and reliable admission, which would have justified him being formally cautioned, and the caution was quashed.

In another case, the Divisional Court quashed a caution because a number of reasonable lines of enquiry had not been made while the suspect had been in custody for 17 hours; for instance, the police had failed to take a statement from the victim's friend, or obtain CCTV that was available, or fully investigate the victim's injuries. The court also considered that the suspect's admission was ambiguous (see *Omar* v *Chief Constable of Bedfordshire Constabulary* [2002] EWHC 3060 (Admin)).

Two cases concerned themselves with interviews, prior to cautions being administered. In one, *DPP* v *Ara* [2001] EWHC 493 (Admin), the court examined the issue of disclosure and found that while it was not binding, there may be a general need for the police to make some disclosure to a suspect's legal representative in order that he/she can advise on whether a caution should be accepted. In another case, it was held that it was not always necessary for the suspect to be interviewed or to show that the admission had been obtained in circumstances which satisfied the *Codes of Practice* (see *R* v *Chief Constable of Lancashire Constabulary, ex parte Atkinson* [1998] EWHC 145 (Admin)). However, the court did advise that police officers would be well advised to take precautions that would satisfy Code C and it would be both fairer and more reliable for a formal interview to take place.

It should also be remembered that custody officers may also have the detainee reported by summons for offences, as charging a person is only one method of compelling a person to appear in court. For example, the detainee may be elderly, or ill, and provided the custody officer feels that conditional or unconditional bail is not necessary, he or she may follow this course of action.

KEYNOTE

In the future, persons may be charged whilst in police detention, or in accordance with s. 29 of the Criminal Justice Act 2003 (*charging by post*) when it is brought into force.

Also, Penalty Notices may be used for offences of disorder and other anti-social behaviour. While these notices are essentially designed for issue out on the streets (to ensure officers spend more time on patrol), they may also be issued at the custody office as an alternative to charging a suspect.

14.2.13 **Conditional cautions**

As an alternative to being charged with a minor offence, under s. 22(3) of the Criminal Justice Act 2003, an offender may be given a caution with a condition (or conditions) attached. Section 22(3) has been amended by s. 17 of the Police and Justice Act 2006 in that it will allow financial penalties (amongst other provisions) to be part of a conditional caution; however this amendment has yet to be brought into force.

Conditional cautions, are those which have one or more of the following objects—

1. facilitating the rehabilitation of the offender;

2. ensuring that the offender makes reparation for the offence;

3. punishing the offender.

The Crown Prosecution Service's *Director's Guidance on Conditional Cautioning* states:

> Conditional cautions are intended to be a swift and effective means of dealing with straightforward cases where the offender is willing to admit the offence and to agree to comply with specified conditions. The disposal should only be used where it provides an appropriate and proportionate response to the offending behaviour.

Annex A of the above Guidance contains examples of offences that will be suitable for a conditional caution. They include—

(a) summary only offences, such as common assault, assaulting/obstructing a police officer, ss. 4, 4A and 5 of the Public Order Act 1986, prostitution and kerb crawling, unlawful taking of a motor vehicle and interference with vehicles, or

(b) either way offences and attempts to commit these offences, such as theft, fraud, handling, criminal damage and possession of any class of drug (consistent with personal use).

A conditional caution will *not* be suitable where a person has committed—

(a) an offence under the Road Traffic Act 1988 and the Road Traffic Offenders Act 1988, or

(b) an indictable only offence or one classified as hate crime, including any racially or religiously aggravated offence, any offences involving homophobic or transphobic aggravation, disability hate crime and domestic violence.

Conditional cautions may be administered by an authorised person, who may be a constable, an investigating officer (i.e. a person designated as an investigating officer under s. 38 of the Police Reform Act 2002), or any person authorised by the relevant prosecutor.

The caution may be given to a person aged 18 or over, if each of the requirements below is satisfied:

• there is sufficient evidence that the offender has committed an offence;

• the relevant prosecutor decides:

(a)   that there is sufficient evidence to charge the offender with the offence, and

(b)   that a conditional caution should be given to the offender in respect of the offence.

Also that—

- the offender admits the offence;

- the authorised person explains the effect of the conditional caution to the offender and warns him/her that failure to comply with any of the conditions attached to the caution may result in them being prosecuted for the offence;

- the offender signs a document containing details of the offence, an admission of guilt, consent to being given the conditional caution, and the conditions attached to the caution.

KEYNOTE

Although conditional cautions only apply to offenders over the age of 18, Sch. 9 of the Criminal Justice and Immigration Act 2008 amends the Crime and Disorder Act 1998, to make provision for the giving of youth conditional cautions to children and young persons under the age of 16, provided the Secretary of State makes such an order.

When the full provisions of s. 22 are in force, a conditional caution may include the imposition of a financial penalty, which must not exceed one quarter of the amount of the maximum fine for which a person is liable on summary conviction of the offence, or £250, whichever is the lower. Alternatively, the conditions may require the person to attend at a specified place at a specified time (possibly to complete a specified activity which does not exceed 20 hours).

The Police and Justice Act 2006 inserted s. 24A into the Criminal Justice Act 2003. Again, when these provisions are fully in force, under s. 24A(1), if a constable has reasonable grounds for believing that the offender has failed, without reasonable excuse, to comply with any of the conditions attached to the conditional caution, he/she may arrest him or her without warrant. A person arrested under this section must be—

(a)   charged with the offence in question,

(b)   released without charge and on bail to enable a decision to be made as to whether he should be charged with the offence, or

(c)   released without charge and without bail (with or without any variation in the conditions attached to the caution).

A person may be kept in police detention to allow for the above decision to be made, but this decision must be made as soon as practicable. This detention time includes time to allow an investigation as to whether the offender failed without reasonable excuse to comply with any of the conditions.

KEYNOTE

The *Director's Guidance on Conditional Cautioning* states that where an offender fails to comply with the conditions of a caution, it will be for a Crown Prosecutor to determine whether to commence proceedings, or whether any reasons for non-compliance amount to a reasonable excuse, or to impose new conditions.

14.3 **Charging and Cautioning the Suspect**

14.3.1 **Legislative provisions**

Code C, Para. 16.3

When a detainee is charged they shall be given a written notice showing the particulars of the offence, the officer's name and the case reference number. As far as practicable, the particulars of the offence shall be stated in simple terms, but they shall show the precise offence in law with which the detainee is charged.

14.3.2 **Written notice**

When the detainee is charged, he or she must be told what the charge is, and given a written notice (charge sheet), with the details of the particular offence, and the Act and section he/she is alleged to have contravened.

Many custody officers insist on the full details of the charge being read out to the detainee; however, you will note from Code C, para. 16.3 above that this is unnecessary. The detainee need only be told in simple terms the details of the allegation (e.g. you are charged with theft/criminal damage etc.). They will be able to see the precise details of the offence from the charge sheet.

The charge sheet must contain details of the officer's name and the case reference number, unless the detainee is to be charged with an offence which is either:

(a)   linked to investigating terrorism; *or*

(b)   one which would lead the officer to reasonably believe that recording or disclosing their name might put them in danger.

381

Where a person is charged with an offence named above, only the officer's warrant number need be endorsed on the charge sheet (Code C, para. 2.6A).

> **KEYNOTE**
>
> The purpose of para. 2.6A(b) above is to protect officers investigating organised crime, where particularly violent suspects may be charged with offences, when there is reliable information that those arrested or their associates may threaten or harm those involved. Where there is doubt, an officer of above inspector rank should be consulted (see Code C, Note for Guidance 2A).

14.3.3 The caution

Under Code C, para. 16.2, when a person has been charged with an offence, they must immediately be cautioned in the following terms:

> You do not have to say anything. But it may harm your defence if you do not mention now something which you later rely on in court. Anything you do say may be given in evidence.

Under the Criminal Justice and Public Order Act, 1994 (s. 34, 36 and 37), as amended by s. 58 of the Youth Justice and Criminal Evidence Act 1999, courts may draw an adverse inference from a person's failure or refusal to say anything about their involvement in an offence, either:

- when they are interviewed; *or*
- when they are charged or informed they may be prosecuted for the offence.

It is important, therefore, that when the detainee is cautioned after charge, the correct wording above is used and the person is told that their defence may be harmed if they attempt to rely on something which they had an opportunity to mention either in the interview or when being charged. A failure to warn the detainee in the correct manner may affect the court's ability to draw inferences from silences.

14.4 Written Statements

14.4.1 Legislative provisions

Code C, Para. 16.4

If, after a detainee has been charged with or informed they may be prosecuted for an offence, an officer wants to tell them about any written statement or interview with another person relating to such an offence, the detainee shall either be handed a true copy of the written statement or the content of the interview record brought to their attention. Nothing shall be done to invite a reply except to:

(a)   caution the detainee, 'You do not have to say anything, but anything you do say may be given in evidence'; and

(b)   remind the detainee about their right to legal advice.

14.4.2 **Disclosing written statements**

Code C, para. 16.4 above allows the investigating officer to disclose written statements or the contents of an interview with another detainee after the person has been charged with an offence. Generally, this may be an admission by a co-accused, or further evidence contradicting the detainee's account during an interview. This material would represent an opportunity for the detainee to consider their position before they reply to the charge that has been put to them. You should note that the officer handing over the statement/content of an interview must not invite a response. He or she must merely caution the detainee and remind him/her of their right to legal advice.

Under Code C, Annex C 1(b)(i), if the detainee fails or refuses to say anything about the documents shown to him or her, the court may not draw an adverse inference from this failure or refusal. You will note that the caution under para. 16.4 above is different from the one used in ordinary cases, under para. 16.2 (which includes a reference to adverse inferences being drawn).

KEYNOTE

In relation to written statements, if the detainee:

- cannot read, the document should be read to him/her;
- is a juvenile, mentally disordered or otherwise mentally vulnerable, the appropriate adult should be given a copy, or the interview record brought to their attention (see Code C, para. 16.4A).

KEYNOTE

Note that adverse inferences may not be drawn even when a detainee has asked to be legally represented, and a decision has been made to conduct the interview without a solicitor being present (see Chapter 6—The Detainee's Entitlements for a full discussion on these powers).

14.5 **Interviews after Charge**

14.5.1 **Legislative provisions**

Code C, Para. 16.5

A detainee may not be interviewed about an offence after they have been charged with, or informed they may be prosecuted for it, unless the interview is necessary:

- to prevent or minimise harm or loss to some other person, or the public;
- to clear up an ambiguity in a previous answer or statement;
- in the interests of justice for the detainee to have put to them, and have an opportunity to comment on, information concerning the offence which has come to light since they were charged or informed they might be prosecuted.

Generally, once a person has been charged, or informed they may be prosecuted for an offence further questions may not be put to them about the offence. However, there are certain circumstances when this is permissible.

Under Code C, para. 16.5, a detainee may be interviewed after he/she has been charged/informed they may be prosecuted for an offence if one of the three circumstances listed above applies. We will examine the requirements individually:

1. In the first set of circumstances above, no mention is made of how serious the harm or loss to a person or the public must be. Therefore provided a person is likely to suffer some loss, this section would appear to apply.

2. In the second set of circumstances, the person may be interviewed to clear up an ambiguity to answers or a statement they may have made.

   One example could be where a detainee has been provided with a written statement under para. 16.4 above, and has made a comment which requires clarification.

   Alternatively, a person may have been charged and has provided a prepared written statement in response to the charge. The investigating officer may feel that there is some ambiguity in the statement, which requires exploration in an interview. (This issue is dealt with in more depth below in **14.6.2 Prepared statement.**)

3. In the third set of circumstances above, the information must have come to light since the person was charged or informed they might be prosecuted, and the investigating officer believes it is necessary in the interests of justice to allow the detainee to comment on the information.

KEYNOTE

What if the detainee refuses to be interviewed, or refuses to answer questions that are put to him/her after being charged?

In these circumstances, adverse inferences may not be drawn from any refusal or failure to answer questions put to them (see Code C, Annex C 1(b)(ii)).

14.6 **Recording the Detainee's Responses**

14.6.1 **Responses after charge**

Quite simply, a record must be made of anything that the detainee says when he or she is charged with an offence (Code C, para. 16.8). The purpose of this paragraph is obviously to allow the court to hear the detainee's response to being charged, whether in the form of an admission or denial, or even mitigation. However, even if the detainee says something totally unconnected to the case, this must still be recorded. Paragraph 16.8 doesn't actually say where the response must be recorded, but common practice is to write down anything said on the charge sheet.

KEYNOTE

Note—Code C, para. 16.9 deals with questions put to a detainee after charge, during an interview. Under this paragraph, the questions and answers should be recorded during the interview, and the record should be signed by the detainee. However, if the interview is audibly recorded or visually recorded, the normal procedure covered by Codes E and F will apply (i.e. a transcript or summary of the interview may be prepared for the court).

14.6.2 **Prepared statement**

Consider the following:

Case Study

PC CARTWRIGHT has arrested TAYLOR for an offence of burglary of a dwelling. TAYLOR's fingerprints were found inside the house. During interview, TAYLOR made no comment and did not account for the presence of his fingerprints at the burglary. Following the interview, TAYLOR was charged with burglary; he made no reply in response to the charge, but his solicitor handed to PC CARTWRIGHT a piece of paper, containing an apparently innocent explanation of how his fingerprints were found at the scene of the burglary.

What action should PC CARTWRIGHT take in respect of this document?

....

Prepared statements can often be viewed by officers as a defence tactic to frustrate an inquiry. But let's look at the situation logically, taking into account what we have learned in this chapter.

First, any written statement such as this should be retained, as it would be a documentary exhibit. (If the detainee makes a verbal prepared statement, this response should be recorded in accordance with Code C, para. 16.8 above.)

Clearly, in the set of circumstances given, the detainee failed during the interview to give a satisfactory account of his presence at the scene of the burglary. The written statement handed over by the solicitor will obviously lead the investigating officer to want to ask further questions of the detainee. Can this be done?

You will recall that we examined this topic earlier in this chapter, in 14.5 **Interviews after Charge**. Generally, under Code C, para. 16.5, a detainee may not be interviewed about an offence after they have been charged with, or informed they may be prosecuted for, it. However, as discussed above, there are circumstances when a person may be interviewed in this way. One of the reasons that it may be done is:

Where the interview is necessary:

> in the interests of justice for the detainee to have put to them, and have an opportunity to comment on, information concerning the offence which has come to light since they were charged or informed they might be prosecuted.

It is clear that the officer in the set of circumstances above would be entitled to re-interview the detainee regarding new information that came to light after he was charged, even though the information came from the detainee himself.

In the scenario, the detainee made no comment in the first interview. Remember, if the detainee refuses to comment in the re-interview after charge, the court may not draw any adverse inferences from this silence (Code C, Annex C 1(b)(ii)).

KEYNOTE

The issue of prepared statements was examined by the Court of Appeal in the case of *R v Ali (Sarfraz) and others* [2001] EWCA Crim 863. During interview, the defendant remained silent, but handed over a prepared statement. In the original case, the judge allowed the jury to draw adverse inferences from the defendant's silence. He subsequently appealed, on the grounds that he had been advised by his solicitor to remain silent.

The Appeal Court found in favour of the defendant, as he had, in fact, disclosed material facts relating to his defence, an alibi in the prepared statement. The jury should therefore not have been allowed to draw adverse inferences from his silence.

KEYNOTE

Remember, if presented with a prepared statement after charge—written or otherwise—the following advice should be given to the investigating officer:

- don't just accept the statement;
- take time to read the contents (or review notes if it was verbal);
- look for new information or ambiguities;
- interview again where necessary;
- challenge the contents of the statement where necessary;
- take charge of the situation.

14.7 **Vulnerable Detainees**

Note that if the detainee is a juvenile, mentally disordered or otherwise mentally vulnerable, any action taken under paras. 16.2–16.5 above must be conducted in the presence of the appropriate adult, if they are at the police station. If they are not at the police station, the provisions must be complied with again in their presence when they arrive (Code C, para. 16.6).

The issue of charging vulnerable detainees is dealt with in more depth above in **Chapter 7—Vulnerable People and Appropriate Adults.**

14.8 **Summing Up**

The investigating officer's responsibilities

1. When the officer in charge of the investigation reasonably believes there is sufficient evidence to provide a realistic prospect of the detainee's conviction they shall, without delay, inform the custody officer who will be responsible for considering whether the detainee will be charged.

2.   The above may be delayed when a person is detained in respect of more than one offence, until the above conditions are satisfied in respect of all offences.

(Code C, para. 16.1)

Custody officers as decision-makers

If the custody officer determines that there is sufficient evidence to charge a detainee, the person shall be either:

*   released without charge and on bail for the purpose of enabling the CPS to make a decision; or
*   released without charge and on bail but not for that purpose; or
*   released without charge and without bail; or
*   charged.

(s. 37(7) PACE)

The decision as to how a person is to be dealt with under subsection (7) above shall be that of the custody officer.

(s. 37(7A) PACE)

Pre-charge advice

The CPS will determine whether a person is to be charged in all indictable only, either way or summary offences, and will make charging decisions following a review of evidence in those cases. However, there will be some cases where the police can proceed to charge, without advice from the CPS—generally where there is likely to be a guilty plea, or where the person has been arrested for certain specified offences.

Charging the suspect

1.   When a detainee is charged they shall be given a written notice showing the particulars of the offence.
2.   As far as practicable, the particulars of the offence shall be stated in simple terms, but they shall show the precise offence in law with which the detainee is charged.

(Code C, para. 16.3)

Written statements

1.   After a detainee has been charged with or informed they may be prosecuted about an offence, the officer may tell them about any written statement or interview with another person relating to such an offence.

2. The detainee shall either be handed a true copy of the written statement or the content of the interview record brought to their attention. Nothing shall be done to invite a reply except to caution the detainee, and remind him/her about their right to legal advice.

(Code C, para. 16.4)

Interviews after charge

A detainee may not be interviewed about an offence after they have been charged with, or informed they may be prosecuted for it, unless the interview is necessary:

*   to prevent or minimise harm or loss to some other person, or the public;
*   to clear up an ambiguity in a previous answer or statement;
*   in the interests of justice for the detainee to have put to them, and have an opportunity to comment on, information concerning the offence which has come to light since they were charged or informed they might be prosecuted.

(Code C, para. 16.5)

Note that where a person is interviewed in the circumstances above, adverse inferences may not be drawn from any refusal or failure to answer questions put to them.

(Code C, Annex C 1(b)(ii))

Prepared statements

Where the officer in the case is presented with a prepared statement by a detainee after he/she has been charged with an offence, the following advice should be followed:

*   don't just accept the statement;
*   take time to read the contents (or review notes if it was verbal);
*   look for new information or ambiguities;
*   interview again where necessary.

SPACE FOR NOTES

SPACE FOR NOTES

15

Continued Detention After Charge

15.1 **Introduction**

The decision to deny a person's liberty can be a stressful experience for the custody officer. In this chapter, we will examine in depth the power, under s. 38 of the Police and Criminal Evidence Act 1984, which allows a custody officer to authorise a person's continued detention after he or she has been charged with an offence. This power is also affected by Code C, para. 16 of the *Codes of Practice*.

When deciding whether or not to authorise a person's continued detention after charge, custody officers will often be faced with opposition from defence solicitors, appropriate adults, the detainee and even sometimes their own colleagues. This chapter attempts to offer some practical advice to custody officers when faced with these decisions. In the end, the custody officer will have to use a mixture of firmness, common sense and practical application of the legislation.

We will also be examining the effects of s. 25 of the Criminal Justice and Public Order Act 1994, which provides that in certain circumstances, custody officers and the courts have an obligation not to grant bail to detainees.

Lastly, we will be examining the effect of s. 38(6) of the Act, which requires a juvenile detainee, in certain circumstances, to be transferred to the care of the local authority when bail has been denied.

The Human Rights Act 1998

As with the previous chapter, custody officers will need to consider Article 5 of the Human Rights Act 1998 (right to liberty and security). Once again, provided custody officers comply with PACE and the *Codes of Practice*, the human rights of the individual should be protected.

This chapter contains specific references to the 1998 Act, in **15.2.9 The Human Rights Act 1998**, which deals with the general grounds where refusal of bail will be considered appropriate under the European Convention, and **15.5.2 Requirement to take the detainee to court**, which deals with the requirement to take a detainee to court 'promptly'.

15.2 **Detention after Charge**

Before the custody officer makes the decision to charge a suspect with an offence, he or she will already have considered s. 37(7) of PACE, which determines that if the custody officer determines that there is sufficient evidence to charge a detainee, the person shall be either released without charge and on bail for the purpose of enabling the CPS to make a decision, released without charge and on bail but not for that purpose, released without charge and without bail or charged. This matter is dealt with in depth in **Chapter 14—Charging Suspects**.

The current chapter deals with situations where the decision has been reached to charge the suspect (either by the custody officer or the CPS), and the custody officer intends detaining the person further, under s. 38 of PACE.

The first presumption under s. 38(1) of PACE is that where a person has been charged, he or she is entitled to be released with or without bail. There are circumstances where a person is not entitled to bail, depending on the offence that they have been charged with. These circumstances are dealt with below in **15.3 Restriction on Granting Bail**.

However, the detainee may be kept in custody after charge if any of the requirements in s. 38(1)(a) below apply. There is no need for the custody officer to apply more than one of the reasons before making this decision. Of course, if more than one of the requirements in this subsection do apply, the decision for the custody officer will be easier.

15.2.1 **Legislative provisions**

Section 38(1) PACE

Where a person arrested for an offence otherwise than under a warrant endorsed for bail is charged with an offence, the custody officer shall (subject to s. 25 of the Criminal Justice and Public Order Act 1994), order his release from police detention, either on bail or without bail, unless—

(a)   if the person arrested is not an arrested juvenile—

   (i)   his name or address cannot be ascertained or the custody officer has reasonable grounds for doubting whether a name or address furnished by him as his name or address is his real name or address;

   (ii)   the custody officer has reasonable grounds for believing that the person arrested will fail to appear in court to answer to bail;

   (iii)   in the case of a person arrested for an imprisonable offence, the custody officer has reasonable grounds for believing that the detention of the person arrested is necessary to prevent him from committing an offence;

   (iiia)   except in a case where (by virtue of subs. (9) of s. 63B below) that section does not apply, the custody officer has reasonable grounds for believing that the detention of the person is necessary to enable a sample to be taken from him under that section;

   (iv)   in the case of a person arrested for an offence which is not an imprisonable offence, the custody officer has reasonable grounds for believing that the detention of the person arrested is necessary to prevent him from causing physical injury to any other person or from causing loss of or damage to property;

(v) the custody officer has reasonable grounds for believing that the detention of the person arrested is necessary to prevent him from interfering
with the administration of justice or with the investigation of offences or
of a particular offence; or

(vi) the custody officer has reasonable grounds for believing that the detention of the person arrested is necessary for his own protection.

15.2.2 **The custody officer's duties**

We examined the subject of charging a detainee in the previous chapter. Once
the detainee has been charged, the custody officer will have to decide whether
to keep the person in police detention until the next available court, or release
them on bail.

However, custody officers are likely to face pressure from the officer in the
case, the defendant and their solicitor, and sometimes senior officers, when
it comes to deciding whether or not a person is to be bailed, or kept in police
detention following charge.

Section 38(1)(a) above lists the reasons a custody officer must consider,
before denying bail to an arrested person who is not a juvenile. Section
38(1)(b) deals with juvenile detainees, and this chapter examines this issue
below in **15.6 Juvenile Detainees**. Section 25 of the Criminal Justice and Public Order Act 1994, which is referred to above, is also dealt with in this chapter,
below in **15.3 Restriction on Granting Bail**.

Section 38(1)(a)(iiia) was inserted by the Criminal Justice and Court Services Act 2000, s. 57(3)(a) and was later replaced by s. 5(2) of the Criminal
Justice Act 2003. This subsection allows police officers to test detainees for the
presence of Class A drugs, in certain circumstances. The custody officer may
authorise continued detention for up to six hours after charge, for the provision of the sample. This matter is dealt with fully, in **Chapter 12—Identification and Samples**.

The other aspects of s. 38(1) above are examined below. When considering
whether or not to grant bail to a detainee, the custody officer should follow
the same criteria as a magistrate, when they are deciding whether or not to
remand a person in custody.

The factors to be taken into account are contained in Schedule 1, Part I,
para. 9 of the Bail Act 1976; they are as follows:

- the nature and seriousness of the offence and the probable method of dealing with the offender for it;
- the character, antecedents, associations and community ties of the accused;

- his or her record for having answered bail in the past (or failed to answer bail); and
- the strength of the evidence put forward.

As discussed in **Chapter 14—Charging Suspects** above, Sch. 2 of the Criminal Justice Act 2003 amended s. 37(7) of PACE, to compel the police, in certain circumstances, to seek advice from the CPS on decisions relating to charging suspects. But what about decisions in respect of remanding a detainee, or releasing them on bail, after charge? Section 4 (Decisions Ancillary to the Charging Decision) of the *Guidance to Police Officers and Crown Prosecutors Issued by the Director of Public Prosecutions under s. 37A of the Police and Criminal Evidence Act 1984*, produced in January 2005, makes it clear that this decision still remains with the custody officer, but offers the following guidance:

> Whilst decisions to detain or bail persons are exclusively matters for a custody officer, where it appears that a person in police detention should not be released and should be detained for the purposes of an application being made to a court for a remand in custody, including short periods in police custody for the purpose of enquiries into other offences, the custody officer may wish to consult a Duty Prosecutor to confirm that any proposed application for a remand in custody or the imposition of bail conditions which can only be imposed by a court is justified in accordance with the Bail Act 1976, is proportionate, is likely to be ordered by the court and that sufficient detail to support any such application is recorded on the MG7.

15.2.3 **When the name and address cannot be ascertained**

Under s. 38(1)(a)(i) above, the person may be further detained, either:

- if their name and address cannot be ascertained; *or*
- if the custody officer has reasonable grounds for doubting the truthfulness of the name and address given by the detainee.

Note that there is no mention of the detainee refusing to provide their name and address. There may be situations where a detainee has refused to provide such information, but the custody officer actually knows who the detainee is. In these circumstances, the name and address may have been 'ascertained' and the detainee may be entitled to bail.

The custody officer's 'reasonable grounds for doubting' the name and address furnished will be a subjective test, which the custody officer will have to justify in writing.

KEYNOTE

This subsection may also apply where a person has been arrested under s. 24(5)(a) or (b) of PACE, and the custody officer has reasonable grounds for doubting the name and/or address given by the detainee. In this case, the detainee may be detained until the next available court.

15.2.4 When the detainee may fail to appear at court

The custody officer must have reasonable grounds for believing that the person may fail to appear. Evidence that the detainee has failed to appear in court in the past is useful in order to implement s. 38(1)(a)(ii) and custody officers often rely on information from the Police National Computer (PNC) to assist with their decision-making process. However, conflict often arises in this area when the detainee has not failed to appear recently. Defence solicitors will often argue that a failure to appear several years ago does not automatically give the custody officer the grounds to reasonably suspect that it may happen again this time.

There is no definite answer to this problem and custody officers will need to evidence their reasonable grounds; however, a failure to appear in the past may be sufficient to satisfy the custody officer that the grounds exist.

The detainee may also be of no fixed abode, which would mean that he/she would be untraceable if he/she failed to appear, which would almost certainly provide the custody officer with reasonable grounds to authorise continued detention after charge.

15.2.5 When detention is necessary to prevent a further offence

Evidence to detain a person under ss. (iii) above may also be provided by the PNC. The custody officer will need to examine the detainee's previous offending history in order to decide whether there are reasonable grounds to believe that if he/she were to be released on bail, further offences may be committed. The custody officer should take into account the offence for which the detainee has been charged on this occasion. For example, if the detainee only has previous convictions for shoplifting, and has been arrested and detained for a burglary, it would be difficult to justify further detention to prevent him/her from committing further burglaries. However, each case has to be taken on its merits.

KEYNOTE

It should be noted that this section only applies to imprisonable offences committed by the detainee.

15.2.6 When detention is necessary to prevent injury, loss or damage

Where the custody officer believes that the detainee must be prevented from causing physical injury to any other person or from causing loss of or damage to property, statements from the investigating officer and witnesses may provide the necessary grounds.

KEYNOTE

It should be noted that this section applies to non-imprisonable offences committed by the detainee.

15.2.7 To prevent interference with the administration of justice

Section 38(1)(a)(v) is generally utilised when the custody officer has reasonable grounds for believing that the detainee may intimidate witnesses. Again, the custody officer must rationalise their decision in writing. Evidence of the detainee's behaviour towards witnesses in the present or past cases would be useful, preferably by way of a statement.

15.2.8 For the detainee's own protection

In some cases, the detainee may require protection from himself or herself, for example, where a detainee is mentally vulnerable. Otherwise, the detainee may need protection from the public, such as in the case of a sex offender, where there may be anger within the community towards that person.

15.2.9 The Human Rights Act 1998

The European Court has identified four general grounds where refusal of bail will be considered appropriate under the Convention. Under our own Human Rights Act 1998, courts in England and Wales are under an obligation to consider decisions made in the European Court; therefore, these four grounds provide useful guidance to custody officers when making decisions to authorise continued detention. The areas referred to under the Convention are:

1. fear of absconding;

2. interference with the course of justice;

3.   the prevention of crime;

4.   the preservation of public order.

It may be seen that these grounds are similar to those contained in s. 38(1)(a). The only issue that appears to be missing is the 'preservation of public order', although this could be covered by s. 38(1)(a)(iv), if the offence were serious enough.

   The European Court of Human Rights has found that the seriousness of the offence alone is not a sufficient reason to detain a person on the grounds that they are likely to abscond (*Yagci and Sargin* v *Turkey* [1995] 17 EHRR 60). This case demonstrates that custody officers need to apply s. 38(1) of PACE strictly when determining whether or not to detain a person after charge.

   It should be remembered that custody officers have the ability under s. 3 of the Bail Act 1976 to either issue Bail Conditions, or demand sureties from the detainee (these issues are dealt with in more depth in **Chapter 16—Bail**). These are viable alternatives to detaining a person after charge and should form part of the decision-making process; for example, could the detainee be prevented from failing to appear, from committing further offences, or from interfering with justice by imposing conditions?

   The custody officer's decision to deny bail was tested in the case of *Gizzonio* v *Chief Constable of Derbyshire* [1998] *The Times*, 29 April, where it was claimed that the custody officer had acted unlawfully, by refusing bail for charges which the police did not eventually pursue. The court dismissed the claim in favour of the custody officer on this occasion, as it had been the intention of the police to prosecute at the time the detainee was charged.

15.3 **Restriction on Granting Bail**

Much has been made in this book of the application of the Human Rights Act 1998 to individuals who are in police detention. The Criminal Justice and Public Order Act 1994, however, requires custody officers and courts to consider other needs when detainees have been charged or convicted with more serious offences.

   Of course individual rights are important, but the Human Rights Act 1998 deals with a balance of the individual's needs, versus the needs of the public at large. Criticism is often aimed at the courts or police when a person charged with a serious offence is allowed to re-offend whilst on bail.

   Section 25 of the Criminal Justice and Public Order Act 1994 places the emphasis firmly on the needs of the public, and demands that those involved in the criminal justice system justify their actions when releasing certain detainees charged with serious offences into the community. The requirements under s. 25 of the Act apply equally to custody officers and the court, where a person has been charged with an offence and bail is being considered.

The section also applies to a court, where the person has been convicted of an offence, and the court is considering the issue of bail. We will deal with the custody officer's duties in this section.

15.3.1 **Legislative provisions**

Section 25(1) Criminal Justice and Public Order Act 1994

A person who in any proceedings has been charged with or convicted of an offence to which this section applies, in circumstances to which it applies, shall be granted bail in those proceedings only if the court or, as the case may be, the constable considering the grant of bail is satisfied that there are exceptional circumstances which justify it.

Section 25(2) Criminal Justice and Public Order Act 1994

This section applies, subject to subsection (3) below, to the following offences:

- murder/attempted murder;
- manslaughter;
- rape/attempted rape.

Section 25(3) Criminal Justice and Public Order Act 1994

This section applies to a person charged with or convicted of any such offence only if he has been previously convicted by or before a court in any part of the United Kingdom of any such offence or of culpable homicide, if he was then sentenced to imprisonment or, if he was then a child or young person, to long-term detention under any of the relevant enactments.

15.3.2 **Authorising continued detention**

As discussed above, generally, detainees have a right to bail after they have been charged with an offence. However, under s. 25(1) of the Criminal Justice and Public Order Act 1994 above, there is a presumption that certain people, in restricted circumstances, will not be entitled to bail.

The custody officer will have to justify why he/she has granted bail to a person covered by this Act and section. This is obviously a move away from s. 38(1) above, where the custody officer has to justify refusal of bail. The custody officer is required to detain any person to whom this section applies; unless he/she is satisfied there are exceptional circumstances which justify granting bail.

It's unsurprising that the restrictive nature of s. 25(1) has been challenged in court as being a breach of Article 5 of the Human Rights Act 1998. In *O v Harrow Crown Court: in re O (application for a writ of Habeas Corpus)* [2006] UKHL 42, the appellant challenged the fact that he was remanded in custody for a period of 22 months until his trial, with bail being refused under s. 25. The court dismissed the appeal, citing that there was a strong case to refuse bail in this particular case and that s. 25 placed the burden on the detained person to prove that he/she should be released, which *O* had been unable to do.

In order to implement s. 25(1), the custody officer must first consider the offence that has been committed. It can be seen from s. 25(2) that this legislation is aimed at protecting the public from persons who are suspected of committing more serious offences.

Under s. 25(3), the custody officer must also take into account the offending history of the person charged. This section will not apply to all persons charged with offences listed above. It will only apply to detainees who have been convicted of an offence listed in s. 25(2) or culpable homicide and as a result, were sentenced to a term of imprisonment; or as a child or young person, convicted of an offence listed in s. 25(2) and sentenced to long-term detention as a result.

In all of the circumstances above, the detainee must have been convicted or sentenced 'by or before a court in any part of the United Kingdom'.

KEYNOTE

Note that this section also applies to a person who has been convicted of an offence, when they are appealing against the conviction or sentence (s. 25(4)).

15.4 **Other Matters Affecting Refusal of Bail**

15.4.1 **Legislative provisions**

Section 38(3) PACE

Where a custody officer authorises a person who has been charged to be kept in police detention, he shall, as soon as practicable, make a written record of the grounds for the detention.

Section 40(3) PACE

Subject to subsection (4) below—

(a) the first review shall be not later than six hours after the detention was first authorised;

(b) the second review shall be not later than nine hours after the first;

(c) subsequent reviews shall be at intervals of not more than nine hours.

15.4.2 **Written records**

According to s. 38(3), the decision to authorise continued detention after charge must be recorded on the custody record. It is possible that the custody officer will authorise continued detention for more than one reason, under s. 38(1) above. If this is the case, each reason must be recorded on the custody record.

Under s. 38(4), the written record must be made in the presence of the person charged. Additionally, under s. 38(5), the custody officer must inform the detainee of the grounds for his/her detention, unless:

at the time when the written record is made, the person is:

(a) incapable of understanding what is said to him/her; *or*

(b) violent or likely to become violent; *or*

(c) in urgent need of medical attention.

15.4.3 **Reviews after charge**

Once the decision has been made to authorise continued detention, the detainee will still have to be reviewed after charge by the custody officer (s. 40(1)(a) PACE). The issue of conducting a review is dealt with in more depth in **Chapter 10—Reviews and Relevant Time.**

The timing of the reviews for custody officers are outlined in s. 40(3) of PACE above, and are the same as those that relate to an inspector's review before charge. However, in practice, when a custody officer authorises continued detention after charge, he or she will effectively be carrying out a review. This means that all subsequent reviews should be conducted at nine-hourly intervals after the detainee has been charged.

As the reviewing officer, the custody officer must consider the same issues as an inspector would have, when conducting the review before charge. Review officers should follow this practical checklist at every review stage:

• enquire into the reasons for detention;

• determine if detention is still necessary;

- remind the detainee of entitlement to free legal advice;
- allow representations to be made;
- note any comment made;
- record the decision in the presence of the detainee.

Besides the issues above, **Chapter 10—Reviews and Relevant Time**, above, contains extensive guidance in relation to conducting reviews, for example:

- when reviews may be delayed;
- when reviews may be brought forward;
- reviews of detainees unfit to be dealt with.

This section should be read in conjunction with **Chapter 10—Reviews and Relevant Time**.

15.5 **Attendance at Court**

15.5.1 **Legislative provisions**

Section 46(2) PACE

If the person charged is to be brought before a magistrates' court for the petty sessions area in which the police station at which he was charged is situated, he shall be brought before such a court as soon as is practicable and in any event not later than the first sitting after he is charged with the offence.

Section 46(4) PACE

If the person charged is to be brought before a magistrates' court for a petty sessions area, other than that in which the police station at which he was charged is situated, he shall be removed to that area as soon as is practicable and brought before such a court as soon as is practicable after his arrival in the area and in any event not later than the first sitting of a magistrates' court for that area after his arrival in the area.

15.5.2 **Requirement to take the detainee to court**

Under s. 46(2) above, when a person has been charged with an offence, and has been kept in police detention (or detained by a local authority), that person must be taken before a magistrates' court not later than the first sitting after he/she has been charged with the offence.

If no magistrates' court for that area is due to sit either on the day on which he/she is charged or on the next day, the custody officer for the police station at which he/she was charged shall inform the clerk to the justices for the area that there is a person in the area to whom s. 46(2) above applies (s. 46(3)).

It will often be a matter for the custody officer to liaise with the clerk of the court to ensure that the detainee is placed on the court list for the magistrates to hear the case. Very often, if the detainee is charged and kept in custody during the daytime, provided the court list is not too full, he/she may be taken before the court immediately. If the court is too busy, however, the person may need to be detained overnight until the next available court.

The European Convention on Human Rights states that an arrested person must be brought promptly before a competent legal authority. The term 'promptly' is not defined; however, in the case of *Brincat* v *Italy* [1992] 16 EHRR 591, the detainee was held for four days before being brought before the court, which was considered to be too long. Of course, in this country, the requirement to comply with PACE means that extended detention should comply with European legislation (however, for a further discussion on this matter, see **9.2.2 Arrested for an offence and then found to be wanted on warrant**).

15.5.3 Delay in taking the detainee to court

Section 46(4) above deals with circumstances in which a person may have been arrested and charged in one petty sessions area, for an offence committed in another area. The case should be heard where the offence took place.

However, what if the detainee has been arrested in one petty sessions area, but is wanted for offences in another petty sessions area?

Consider the following:

Case Study

ROBBINS has been arrested for shoplifting in Cardiff. Later, in the custody office, it was discovered that he was wanted for similar offences by officers in Swansea and Bridgend Police Stations. All three stations are in the same police area, South Wales Police, and the custody officer has contacted the relevant stations to inform them that ROBBINS is in custody. ROBBINS has refused to tell the officers where he lives and has been listed as of no fixed abode for bail purposes.

How should the police proceed with the investigation for all three offences?

....

Provided there is sufficient evidence to charge him for all three offences, it is likely that the detainee will be kept in custody for court after charge.

Very often, travelling offenders may be arrested in a police area and found to be wanted in other areas. Where the offence was committed in a different force area, the investigating officers would have the luxury of transferring the detainee between forces in order to investigate their own offences (see **Chapter 10— Reviews and Relevant Time**, for further details). However, where a person has been arrested for several offences within the same force area, but in separate petty sessions areas, the investigating officers will often only have the minimum 24-hour detention period in which to deal with the detainee (assuming that an authorisation has not been granted to extend detention).

Returning to s. 46(4) above, where a person charged is to be brought before a magistrates' court for a petty sessions area, 'other than that in which the police station at which he/she was charged is situated', that person must be:

removed to that area as soon as is practicable and brought before such a court as soon as is practicable after his/her arrival in the area.

Assuming the detainee in the scenario is charged with all three offences of theft, he could be taken to court in the Cardiff area first, and then transferred to courts in the other areas as soon as is practicable. The detainee would then have to be taken before the court in each area 'not later than the first sitting of a magistrates' court for that area after his/her arrival in the area'.

If no magistrates' court for that area is due to sit either on the day on which the detainee arrives in the area, or on the next day,

the detainee should be taken to a police station in the area and the custody officer at that station should inform the clerk to the justices for the area that there is a person in the area to whom ss. (4) applies, (s. 46(5)).

KEYNOTE

Section 46(6) and (8) of PACE places the responsibility firmly with the clerk of the court to arrange a sitting, where one is not available. The custody officer's responsibility is only to inform the clerk of the court that a detainee is required to attend court (see *R* v *Avon Magistrates, ex parte Broome* [1988] Crim LR 618).

KEYNOTE

Nothing in this section requires a person who is in hospital to be brought before a court if he/she is not well enough (see s. 46(9)).

15.6 **Juvenile Detainees**

15.6.1 **Legislative provisions**

Section 38(1)(b) PACE

Where a person arrested for an offence otherwise than under a warrant endorsed for bail is charged with an offence, the custody officer shall order a detainee's release from police detention, either on bail or without bail, unless—

(a)   if the person is an arrested juvenile—

  (i)   any of the requirements of s. 38(1)(a) is satisfied; *or*

  (ii)   the custody officer has reasonable grounds for believing that he ought to be detained in his own interests.

Code C, Para. 16.7

Where a juvenile is charged with an offence and the custody officer authorises their continued detention after charge, the custody officer must try to make arrangements for the juvenile to be taken into the care of a local authority to be detained pending appearance in court unless the custody officer certifies it is:

- impracticable to do so; *or*
- in the case of a juvenile of at least 12 years old, no secure accommodation is available and there is a risk to the public of serious harm from that juvenile.

Code C, Note for Guidance 16D

Except as in para. 16.7, neither the juvenile's behaviour nor the nature of the offence provides grounds for the custody officer to decide it is impracticable to arrange the juvenile's transfer to local authority care. Similarly, the lack of secure local authority accommodation does not make it impracticable to transfer the juvenile.

Code C, Note for Guidance 16D

The availability of secure accommodation is only a factor in relation to a juvenile aged 12 years or over when the local authority accommodation would not be adequate to protect the public from serious harm from them.

15.6.2 **Additional grounds for detaining juveniles**

All of the requirements we examined in s. 38(1)(a) apply to both adults and juveniles (see s. 38(1)(b)(i)). Section 38(1)(a) of PACE is dealt with in depth above in **15.2 Detention after Charge**.

Section 38(1)(b)(ii) provides the custody officer with an additional reason to detain a juvenile person after he/she has been charged. A juvenile detainee may be kept in custody after charge, when the custody officer 'has reasonable grounds for believing that he ought to be detained in his own interests'.

Note that the juvenile may either be detained under s. 38(1)(a) or s. 38(1)(b). There is no requirement for the custody officer to consider both of these subsections before making the decision to keep a juvenile in detention after charge.

The intention of this subsection is to ensure that custody officers take into consideration a juvenile detainee's welfare. Juvenile detainees may be vulnerable to homelessness or to committing further offences, if released on bail. This section allows a custody officer to detain a juvenile to prevent such things happening.

15.6.3 **Release of juvenile detainees to local authority care**

We have discussed in the section above that a custody officer may authorise continued detention for a juvenile detainee under s. 38(1) of PACE, in the same way as an adult detainee.

However, s. 38(6) of the Act recognises that it may not be appropriate to detain a juvenile, possibly overnight, in a police cell or detention room. Code C, para. 16.7 above explains the situation in more depth than s. 38(6) and we will concentrate on the wording of this paragraph. (See **flow chart 12 in Appendix 1** for an easy guide.)

Under Code C, para. 16.7 (and s. 38(6)), a juvenile who is charged and detained under s. 38(1) must be transferred to the care of the local authority for the remainder of their detention, unless one of the conditions below applies.

This requirement often causes confusion amongst custody officers, and frustration amongst investigating officers. It must be remembered that when a juvenile detainee is transferred to the local authority under this section, they have still been remanded in custody and must appear in court the next day. The only difference is that the juvenile will not be detained in a police cell or detention room.

The custody officer must consider this issue in a step-by-step process. First, he or she must be certain that there is a good enough reason to detain the juvenile after charge under s. 38(1) of PACE. If there is not, the juvenile should be released, on bail or otherwise, in the same manner as any detainee. It is only when the custody officer is satisfied that the continued detention of a juvenile is necessary that para. 16.7 (and s. 38(6)) is activated.

In order to authorise continued detention at the police station, and not transfer the person to local authority care, once the custody officer is satisfied that further detention is necessary under s. 38(1), he or she must certify that it is either:

- impracticable to do so; *or*
- in the case of a juvenile of at least 12 years old, no secure accommodation is available and there is a risk to the public of serious harm from that juvenile.

If neither of the above conditions applies, the juvenile must be transferred to local authority care.

We will now examine some of the key points of para. 16.7 above, namely:

- 'impracticable to do so';
- 'secure accommodation';
- 'risk of serious harm';
- 'juveniles under 12 years of age'.

Impracticable to do so

As discussed above, in order to reach this stage of the decision-making process, the custody officer will already have determined that there are sufficient grounds to detain the juvenile under s. 38(1) of PACE (the first stage in the process). The second stage of this process is for the custody officer to determine whether or not it is practicable to transfer the detainee to local authority care.

So what does impracticable mean?

Code C, Note for Guidance 16D offers an explanation of this term; however, this Note for Guidance merely informs us when it will not be impracticable to transfer a juvenile to local authority care. It is left for the custody officer to interpret when it will be impracticable to make the transfer.

The juvenile's behaviour and the nature of the offence will not have a bearing on whether the custody officer decides that it is impracticable to transfer the juvenile. The offence and the juvenile's behaviour in relation to that offence will be relevant when the custody officer is considering detaining the juvenile further because of a lack of secure accommodation and this is looked at below.

When considering whether or not it is impracticable to transfer the juvenile, the custody officer should consider such things as:

- the availability of a member of the youth offending team to collect the juvenile (for example in some areas, this facility is not available after normal working hours);
- inclement weather;
- the court is not ready to accept the juvenile detainee—i.e. a hearing has been arranged for the afternoon court and the detainee is having a meal.

There may be many other reasons why it is impracticable to transfer the juvenile detainee, but it is clear from Note for Guidance 16D above that the custody officer should not be considering the availability of secure accommodation at this moment.

The only consideration at this stage is whether or not it is physically impracticable to transfer the juvenile, regardless of their age or the offence they have committed.

If a custody officer considers it is impracticable to transfer the juvenile to local authority care, the juvenile may be detained in the custody office. In *R (on the application of M)* v *Gateshead Metropolitan Borough Council* [2006] EWCA Civ 221, the applicant applied for judicial review of the failure of a local authority to provide secure accommodation as requested by the police. The police made the request at 0020 hrs and the detainee was due to appear in court the following morning. The local authority was unable to provide accommodation and the detainee was held in police detention until court. *M* claimed that the local authority was under a duty to provide accommodation in these circumstances and that the subsequent detention was unlawful.

The court held that it was unrealistic to expect local authorities to be able to guarantee that they would provide secure accommodation whenever a request was received under s. 38(6) and in this case, given the time when the request was made, it was wholly impracticable to consider providing accommodation and the local authority was not in breach of its duty in failing to provide secure accommodation.

KEYNOTE

If it is impracticable for a juvenile to be transferred to local authority care because no one is available to collect him/her during the night, consideration should be given to transferring the detainee in the morning when someone does become available.

Secure accommodation/Risk of serious harm

These two considerations go hand in hand and represent the third phase of the custody officer's decision-making process. If the custody officer has decided that it is appropriate to detain the juvenile under s. 38(1), and then considers that it would be practicable to transfer the detainee to local authority care (i.e. there is someone available to collect him/her), the detainee may still be kept at the police station only if:

> the juvenile is at least 12 years old, no secure accommodation is available and there is a risk to the public of serious harm from that juvenile.

So what is secure accommodation?

Most local authorities offer some kind of juvenile accommodation, for both those with a history of offending, or those with family problems. However, this accommodation will not usually be secure, in that the juvenile may walk out at any time. Secure accommodation would be a place where a juvenile may be held until the next available court, to prevent them from re-offending.

Many authorities do not have the provision of secure accommodation, which means that if it is necessary to transfer a juvenile, they will have to negotiate for a spare place outside the juvenile's area. However, it is often the case that such accommodation will not be available at short notice. The custody officer will have to liaise with a member of their local youth offending team to establish whether it is available or not.

When will the public be at risk of serious harm?

It must be remembered that this section is not designed to prevent all persistent juvenile offenders from committing further offences. Whatever the offending history of the juvenile, if they have not been charged with an offence which would cause the custody officer to believe that serious harm would come to a member of the public, they should be handed over to the local authority (unless it is impracticable to do so). However, where a juvenile over 12 has been charged with an offence, which would cause the custody officer to believe that if the juvenile was not detained in secure accommodation, the public would be at risk of serious harm, that juvenile may be further detained under this section.

The type of offences that should be considered here are:

- robbery;
- aggravated burglary;
- rape;
- aggravated vehicle taking;
- grievous bodily harm.

Obviously the above list is not exhaustive and some juveniles will be charged with even more serious offences than those above. It will be a subjective test for the custody officer, who will have to make a balanced decision based on the offence charged, and the nature of the serious harm feared (see *R* v *Croydon Crown Court, ex parte G* [1995] *The Times*, 3 May).

KEYNOTE

It should be noted that although the offences listed above are of a more serious nature, the juvenile may be responsible for a relatively minor offence (e.g. theft), but may have been responsible for threatening a witness with a knife, which would give rise to the fear that serious harm may come to the public.

It is not the offence that matters but the conduct of the juvenile, together with the matter of whether secure accommodation is available.

KEYNOTE

The obligation to transfer a juvenile detainee to local authority accommodation applies as much to a juvenile charged during the daytime as to a juvenile to be held overnight, subject to the requirement to bring the juvenile before a court under PACE s. 46 (see Code C, Note for Guidance 16D).

Juveniles under 12 years of age

Where a custody officer has authorised the continued detention of a juvenile who is under 12 years of age, that person must be transferred to local authority care, whatever offence has been committed. A juvenile detainee under 12 years of age may only be detained in a police cell/detention room under s. 38(1) if it is impracticable to transfer him or her to local authority care.

15.6.4 **Other matters relating to juvenile detainees**

Appearance in court

The local authority must ensure that the detainee appears in the next available court. In fact, once the juvenile has been transferred to the care of the local authority, the custody officer will cease to have any PACE responsibility for him/her (s. 39(4)).

KEYNOTE

It will be the responsibility of the local authority to ensure that the juvenile attends the next available court (see s. 39(5) PACE).

Written record

Under s. 38(7) of PACE, the custody officer must produce a certificate of the decision made under ss. (6) above in respect of an arrested juvenile who has been detained in a police station and not transferred to the local authority. The certificate should outline the offence that the detainee has been charged with, and the reasons for not transferring him/her. The certificate must be produced to the court before which the juvenile is first brought.

Juveniles arrested for breaching bail or for failing to appear in court

This has proved to be something of a grey area, when it comes to interpreting the requirement to transfer a juvenile detainee to local authority care. Custody officers are advised to consult with their own force policy, in case local arrangements are in place.

Consider the following:

Case Study

TAYLOR was arrested for breaching her bail, when she was found in breach of her curfew. The custody officer has decided to detain her until the next available court.

What should the custody officer now do, in respect of transferring TAYLOR to local authority care?

....

In order to answer the question posed in the scenario, we must return to s. 38(6)) above, and Code C, para. 16.7, which state that:

> Where a juvenile is charged with an offence and the custody officer author-
> ises their continued detention after charge, the custody officer must try to
> make arrangements for the juvenile to be taken into the care of a local
> authority to be detained pending appearance in court.

The key word in s. 38(6) above is 'charged'. The Bail Act 1976 provides the power for a constable to arrest a person without warrant who is in breach of their bail conditions (this power is discussed in more depth in **Chapter 16—Bail**). Once a person has been arrested under this Act, he/she must be brought before a magistrate in the petty sessions area where he/she was arrested as soon as practicable and in any event within 24 hours (s. 7(4)(a)). There is no requirement to charge a person arrested for breach of bail before taking them to court.

Since s. 38(6) of PACE only deals with people who have been charged with offences, it does not apply to people arrested under the Bail Act for breach of bail. Therefore there will be no requirement to transfer a juvenile detainee to local authority care.

However, it should be noted that in some force areas, detainees are charged with breaching their bail. In these cases, s. 38(6) would apply (unless it is impracticable to transfer the detainee for one of the reasons dealt with above).

A similar situation arises with juvenile detainees, who have been arrested for a fail to appear warrant. Again, the police are only required to bring the detainee before the next available court, under the terms of the warrant. There is no requirement to charge a detainee who has been arrested for failing to appear. However, this is not to say that a person cannot be charged, as there is a specific offence of failing to appear under s. 5.6 of the Bail Act 1976. If a juvenile detainee is charged with this offence, s. 38(6) will apply, but if they are not, this section will not apply.

KEYNOTE

Where a detainee has been arrested and charged for an offence, and is also being held in police detention for breach of bail conditions, s. 38(6) will apply, as if they have been charged with an offence.

15.7 **Summing Up**

Detention after charge

Continued detention may be authorised for the following reasons:

- if the detainee's name and address cannot be ascertained; or
- if the custody officer has reasonable grounds for doubting the truthfulness of the name and address given by the detainee.

(s. 38(1)(a)(i) PACE)

- for his/her own protection; or
- to prevent him/her from causing physical injury to any other person or from causing loss of, or damage to property.

(s. 38(1)(a)(ii) PACE)

Where the custody officer believes:

- that the person arrested will fail to appear in court to answer to bail; or
- that his/her detention is necessary to prevent him/her from interfering with the administration of justice or with the investigation of offences or of a particular offence.

(s. 38(1)(a)(iii) PACE)

The Human Rights Act 1998

Four general grounds where refusal of bail will be considered appropriate under the European Convention:

1. fear of absconding;
2. interference with the course of justice;
3. the prevention of crime;
4. the preservation of public order.

Restriction on granting bail

Where a person has been charged with:

- murder/attempted murder;
- manslaughter;
- rape/attempted rape,

and he or she has a previous conviction for such an offence, the custody officer *or* court must detain that person without bail, unless they can justify not doing so.

(s. 25(3) Criminal Justice and Public Order Act 1994)

Attendance at court

The detainee must be taken before a magistrates' court not later than the first sitting after he/she has been charged with the offence.

(s. 46(2) PACE)

Additional grounds for detaining juveniles

A juvenile detainee may be kept in custody after charge, when the custody officer has reasonable grounds for believing that he/she ought to be detained in his own interests.

(s. 38(1)(b)(ii) PACE)

Release of juvenile detainees to local authority care

Where a juvenile is charged with an offence and the custody officer authorises their continued detention after charge, arrangements must be made for the juvenile to be taken into the care of a local authority to be detained pending appearance in court unless the custody officer certifies it is:

- impracticable to do so; *or*

- in the case of a juvenile of at least 12 years old, no secure accommodation is available and there is a risk to the public of serious harm from that juvenile.

(s. 38(6) PACE)

LOCAL PROCEDURES

1. Does the local authority in your area have secure accommodation to detain a juvenile pending a court case?

2. Does your force require a juvenile arrested for breach of bail to be charged before attending court?

SPACE FOR NOTES

SPACE FOR NOTES

SPACE FOR NOTES

16

Bail

16.1 **Introduction**

In **Chapter 15—Continued Detention After Charge**, we examined the grounds for refusing bail, under s. 38(1) of the Police and Criminal Evidence Act 1984. In this chapter, we will be looking at the powers to grant bail, which originate from the Bail Act 1976.

This chapter deals with the powers given to custody officers and the courts to grant bail in criminal proceedings. Custody officers will generally release people on bail before charge, to return to a police station (deferred bail), or after charge to a magistrates' court. The court will generally release a person on bail either to return to the magistrates' court, or to Crown Court.

Bail may be granted unconditionally or conditionally and we will be examining the impact of these powers on the custody officer and the courts. We will also review the types of conditional bail that may be granted, and how officers may check that conditions are being complied with.

The Bail Act 1976 provides that people who either fail to answer bail, or breach their conditions of bail, may be arrested. We will be examining the powers of arrest given to police officers, and the duties given to custody officers to ensure the detainee attends court within the specified time limits.

The chapter also examines the powers given to custody officers and the courts to require sureties and security from the detainee or others, to ensure they attend court as directed.

Finally, Home Office schemes to reduce crime amongst young offenders, through electronic monitoring and intensive supervision programmes, will be reviewed.

The Human Rights Act 1998

Custody officers and courts need to consider Article 5 of the Human Rights Act 1998 (right to liberty and security), to ensure that detainees are not given erroneous bail conditions or where sureties are demanded that they are reasonable. Provided custody officers comply with PACE and the *Codes of Practice*, and they and the courts apply the Bail Act 1976 correctly, the human rights of the individual should be protected.

16.2 **Granting Bail**

16.2.1 **Legislative provisions**

Section 1(1) PACE

In this Act 'bail in criminal proceedings' means—

(a) bail grantable in or in connection with proceedings for an offence to a person who is accused or convicted of the offence; or

(b) bail grantable in connection with an offence to a person who is under arrest for the offence or for whose arrest for the offence a warrant (endorsed for bail) is being issued.

Section 47(3) PACE

Subject to s. 47(4) below in this Part of this Act references to 'bail' are references to bail subject to a duty—

(a) to appear before a magistrates' court at such time and such place; or

(b) to attend at such police station at such time, as the custody officer may appoint.

16.2.2 **Bail in criminal proceedings**

Under the Bail Act 1976, custody officers and the courts will be concerned with granting 'bail in criminal proceedings'. The meaning of 'bail in criminal proceedings' is defined in s. 1(1) of the Bail Act 1976 above. Section 1(1) deals with bail relating to criminal offences (as opposed to civil wrongs), and is applicable to any current law, including common law (s. 1(2)).

It should be noted that s. 1(1) applies

whether the offence was committed in England or Wales or elsewhere, and whether it is an offence under the law of England and Wales, or of any other country or territory (s. 1(5)).

KEYNOTE

There is no power to bail a detainee who has been detained for a breach of the peace, since the person was not arrested for a criminal offence (see *Williamson* v *Chief Constable of West Midlands, The Times*, 11 March 2003).

16.2.3 **Power to grant bail**

Section 47(3) of PACE provides the authority for custody officers to bail a detainee either to the magistrates' court, or to a police station. The custody officer will appoint the time and date for the detainee to answer bail.

Under s. 47(4) of the Act, where a custody officer has granted bail to a person subject to a duty to appear at a police station, the custody officer may give notice in writing to that person that his/her attendance at the police station is not required.

A detainee may be released:

- either on conditional or unconditional bail to return to a police station (known as deferred bail);
- on unconditional bail from a police station to a court;
- on conditional bail from a police station to a court.

These issues are dealt with in this chapter.

16.3 **Bail to Appear at a Police Station**

16.3.1 **Legislative provisions**

Section 37B PACE

Where a person is released on bail under s. 37(7)(a) above, an officer involved in the investigation of the offence shall, as soon as practicable, send to the Director of Public Prosecutions such information as may be specified under s. 37A above.

Section 47(2) PACE

Nothing in the Bail Act 1976 shall prevent the re-arrest without warrant of a person released on bail subject to a duty to attend at a police station if new evidence justifying a further arrest has come to light since his release.

Section 47(7) PACE

Where a person who was released on bail subject to a duty to attend at a police station is re-arrested, the provisions of this Part of this Act shall apply to him as they apply to a person arrested for the first time but this sub-section does not apply to a person who is arrested under s. 46A above or has attended a police station in accordance with the grant of bail (and who accordingly is deemed by s. 34(7) above to have been arrested for an offence).

16.3.2 **Detainees released on deferred bail**

As discussed in **14.2.3 Statutory charging** above, under s. 37(7) of PACE, if the custody officer determines that he has before him or her sufficient evidence to charge the person arrested with the offence for which he/she was arrested, the person:

(a) shall be released without charge and on bail for the purpose of enabling the Director of Public Prosecutions to make a decision under s. 37B below;

(b) shall be released without charge and on bail but not for that purpose;

(c) shall be released without charge and without bail; *or*

(d) shall be charged.

The decision to bail the detainee may be as a result of consultation with the CPS (s. 37(7)(a) above), or because the custody officer determines that even though there is sufficient evidence to charge, further enquiries are required (s. 37(7)(b) above). These matters are discussed in depth in **14.2.3 Statutory charging** above. Under s. 37(7)(a) or (b) above, the custody officer is likely to be bailing the detainee to return to the police station, which may be for one of the following reasons:

• further witnesses need to be interviewed;

• the detainee has provided details of an alibi witness who is unavailable;

• advice needs to be taken from the CPS;

• results are pending from a blood sample provided for a breath test offence.

The *Guidance to Police Officers and Crown Prosecutors Issued by the Director of Public Prosecutions under s. 37A of the Police and Criminal Evidence Act 1984,* produced in January 2005, deals with practical issues in respect of bail. Paragraph 8.5 of the Guidance states that in any case where this Guidance requires charging decisions to be made by the CPS and the required information is not then available, custody officers will release those persons suitable for bail (with or without conditions as appropriate) to allow for consultation with the CPS and the submission of an evidential report for a charging decision (MG3) in accordance with this Guidance.

The period of bail should be such as to allow the completion of the investigation, submission of a report to a Crown Prosecutor for a Charging Decision (MG3), for the person to be charged, and for early disclosure of the evidence and any unused material prior to the first appearance.

KEYNOTE

There are no restrictions on the length of time a person is bailed, nor are there restrictions on the number of times a person can be re-bailed. For example, the person may have been released on deferred bail to await results of a blood sample and there is some delay. However, the police and the CPS have targets on bringing offenders to justice speedily. This is particularly true in relation to persistent young offenders (PYOs). Ultimately, the custody officer will have to justify this decision to re-bail someone.

16.3.3 **Powers of arrest for persons released on deferred bail**

Police officers are provided with powers of arrest relating to people released on deferred bail, where that person has:

(a)   failed to answer bail as directed; or

(b)   been arrested before answering bail—because of new evidence.

The Police and Criminal Evidence Act 1984 provides two distinct powers of arrest in relation to the above two situations and these are dealt with separately below. Police officers also have powers of arrest under PACE, to deal with people who have breached conditions of bail, as well as other powers under the Bail Act 1976, and these are dealt with later in this chapter.

We should examine the above two circumstances first:

(a) Where the person fails to answer deferred bail

Quite simply, whatever the reason for releasing a detainee on deferred bail, he or she must surrender at the appointed time and place. A person who fails to appear as directed by the custody officer may be arrested without warrant (s. 46A(1) PACE). The power of arrest does not apply, when a person is merely 'suspected' of failing to appear, however reasonable the suspicion.

As discussed in **14.2.3 Statutory charging** above, in some circumstances, detainees must now be released on bail under s. 37(7)(a) of PACE, to allow the police time to consult with the CPS in respect of the appropriate charge. During this period, the CPS are required, under s. 37B(4), to give the police a written notice of their decision. Where a person has been arrested for failing to answer deferred bail, under s. 46A(1), and the CPS have not yet provided that written notice, the custody officer must consider whether or not it is appropriate to charge the detainee, or to release them either on bail or without bail. The decision as to which action is most appropriate will be the custody officer's (see s. 37C).

Where a person has been arrested on reasonable grounds of having broken any of the conditions of bail, or for failing to surrender to bail at the police station, and a custody officer concludes that the person should be detained in custody for the purpose of an application to the court for a remand in custody, the custody officer *must* consult with the CPS for a decision as to whether to charge with the offence for which the person had previously been released on bail or with any other offence or whether the person should be released without charge either on bail or without bail.

However, where it has proved not to be possible to consult with the CPS in person or by telephone before the expiry of any PACE custody time limit and it is proposed to withhold bail for the purposes of an application for a remand into custody (or for bail conditions that may only be imposed by the court), the custody officer may proceed to charge, but only on the authority of a duty inspector, who must note the decision on the custody record and MG3 to confirm that it is appropriate to charge under the emergency provisions. The case must be referred to a Crown Prosecutor as soon as is practicable for authority to proceed with the prosecution (see the *Guidance to Police Officers and Crown Prosecutors Issued by the Director of Public Prosecutions under s. 37A of the Police and Criminal Evidence Act 1984*).

KEYNOTE

It should be noted that where a person has been circulated on PNC for failing to answer police bail, and the person is arrested in another force area, the relevant time starts when the person arrives at the first police station in that area.

Also, there is no power of entry to premises to arrest a person for failing to answer police bail.

The person who fails to appear will also commit an offence under s. 6(1) of the Bail Act 1976, if he/she fails to appear 'without reasonable cause'. This issue is dealt with in more depth below in **16.6 Failing to Surrender to Custody**.

(b) New evidence

As discussed above, a detainee may be released on deferred bail because there is insufficient evidence to charge him or her in the first instance. However, new evidence may 'come to light' while they are still on bail, before they are due to return to the police station. Section 47(2) of PACE above allows for a detainee to be re-arrested if new evidence 'justifying a further arrest' comes to light during this time.

Consider the following:

Case Study

MARIO was arrested for rape. He was in custody for a total of 30 hours, having had his detention time extended to 36 hours by a superintendent.

He was interviewed, but denied the offence, stating that he had never met the victim. The victim failed to identify him on an ID parade and he was later released on deferred bail, after providing a DNA sample.

Eventually, the results of MARIO's DNA sample provided a positive match with samples taken from the victim during the medical examination.

1.   What options are available to the investigating officers to re-arrest MARIO?
2.   What effect will the re-arrest have on his detention clock?

....

First, it should be noted that with the advances in forensic science, in most cases DNA samples may be 'fast tracked' to the forensic science laboratory, which could have produced a result while the detainee was still in custody. However, for the purposes of our scenario, we will assume the person has been released on deferred bail.

To answer question 1 in the scenario, s. 47(2) of PACE applies in these circumstances. The detainee has been released on deferred bail, as there is insufficient evidence to charge him. The result of the DNA test would represent 'new evidence which has come to light since his release'. This new evidence would 'justify a further arrest' in accordance with s. 47(2) above.

There are two issues that emerge from s. 47(2) above that are important and should be noted by custody officers:

1.   The evidence must be new and must have been 'unavailable' to the investigating officers while the detainee was still in custody. The importance of this fact will become clear when we examine the answer to the second question in the scenario.

2.   The new arrest must be justified. For example, what if the detainee in the scenario had been arrested for driving whilst under the influence of drugs and a sample of blood had been sent off for analysis? If the result of the test were positive, it would certainly represent 'new' evidence, as the positive blood sample may prove the offence against the detainee. However, would this justify the re-arrest of a person due to answer bail for the offence?

While the power exists to re-arrest a person under this section, custody officers should also bear in mind the impact of the Human Rights Act 1998, in respect of a person's right to freedom. Would such an arrest be necessary or proportionate? Probably not. On the other hand, the custody officer should be able to argue justification in a case as serious as rape. Once again, a sensible approach is required, taking each case on its own merit.

We will now turn to question 2 in the above scenario. We will assume that the decision has been taken to re-arrest the detainee who was suspected of a rape, because of the new evidence, before his deferred bail date is due. What effect will this re-arrest have on his original detention clock, bearing in mind that his overall time in detention was 30 hours?

The simple answer is none. The answer to this question can be found in s. 47(7) of PACE above. Where a person is arrested utilising the power under s. 47(2), 'the provisions of this Part of this Act shall apply to him as they apply to a person arrested for the first time'. In other words, they become a 'new detainee', the detention clock is re-set to zero. The effect of s. 47(7) above is that the investigating officers will have at least a further 24 hours in which to investigate the new evidence while the detainee is in custody.

The significance of this new investigation was referred to above, when we were examining the issue of evidence that had come to light since the detainee was released on bail. It should be remembered that the detention clock is only 're-set' in these circumstances because there is new evidence available in the case which merits further investigation.

KEYNOTE

Remember!

New Evidence = New Detention Clock = New Review Clock

= New Custody Record

What if the information about the DNA had been available to the officers when the suspect was in custody originally, and he was released on bail for other reasons? Unless any other new evidence came to light when he was on bail, the officers would have had to wait for him to return on the given date and would have had only six hours of detention time left for the investigation.

In summary, the purpose of s. 47(2) is first to allow the detainee to be re-arrested if further investigation is necessary, but also, to protect him/her from being held in police detention for longer than necessary, when no new evidence is available justifying further detention.

KEYNOTE

It should be noted that if there is new evidence and an arrest is justified, the officers should not wait for the detainee to answer bail if they do need the clock set back to zero.

Once the detainee arrives at the police station (comes over the threshold) he/she has answered his/her bail and the original clock is re-activated. The best opinion is that you cannot then arrest for an offence for which the person is already detained and re-set the clock (s. 47(6)). This is a problem that custody officers face on a fairly frequent basis.

This matter is also dealt with in **Chapter 10—Reviews and Relevant Time**, in respect of reviewing a detainee who has been released on deferred bail.

16.3.4 **Custody records**

In **Chapter 10—Reviews and Relevant Time**, we discussed that the detention clock is affected by three different situations:

1. where the person answers bail as directed;
2. where the person fails to answer bail as directed;
3. where the person has been arrested before answering bail.

The situation is the same in respect of custody records. Where a person either answers bail as directed, or fails to answer bail as directed (as in situations 1 and 2 above), their detention time continues from the point where it was halted when the person was released and the existing custody record should be re-opened.

Where a person is arrested before answering bail (as in situation 3 above), the detention clock is re-set to zero and a new custody record should be opened.

When a person has been released on bail and re-attends the police station as directed, the custody officer must consider s. 37(1) of the Act, to determine whether or not he/she has sufficient evidence to charge the detainee, or whether further detention is necessary for other reasons.

Under s. 37(2) of PACE above, the custody officer must re-authorise detention either to:

• secure or preserve evidence relating to the offence; or
• obtain such evidence by questioning him/her.

These terms are examined in depth in **Chapter 2—Detainees—Initial Action**. The custody officer must record the decision in writing in the custody record.

16.4 **Bail to Appear in Court**

16.4.1 **Legislative provisions**

Section 47(3A) PACE

Where a custody officer grants bail to a person subject to a duty to appear before a magistrates' court, he shall appoint for the appearance—

(a) a date which is not later than the first sitting of the court after the person is charged with the offence; or

(b) where he is informed by the clerk to the justices for the relevant petty sessions area that the appearance cannot be accommodated until a later date, that later date.

16.4.2 **Arranging a court appearance**

Custody officers and the courts may release a person either on unconditional or conditional bail. The following section deals mainly with the legislation as it applies to a custody officer, but you should bear in mind the courts have similar powers.

The wording of s. 47(3A) tends to suggest that all people will be bailed to the next available court, unless the clerk of the court instructs otherwise. However, in reality, most petty sessions areas will insist on a longer bail date.

16.5 **Conditional Bail**

16.5.1 **Legislative provisions**

Section 3A(5) Bail Act 1976

Where a constable grants bail to a person no conditions shall be imposed under subs. (4), (5), (6) or (7) of s. 3 of this Act unless it appears to the constable that it is necessary to do so for the purpose of preventing that person from—

(a) failing to surrender to custody; or

(b) committing an offence while on bail; or

(c) interfering with witnesses or otherwise obstructing the course of justice, whether in relation to himself or any other person.

Section 3A Bail Act 1976

1. Section 3 of this Act applies, in relation to bail granted by a custody officer under part IV of the Police and Criminal Evidence Act 1984 in cases where the normal powers to impose conditions of bail are available to him, subject to the following modifications.
2. Subsection (6) does not authorise the imposition of a requirement to reside in a bail hostel or any requirement under para. (d) or (e).

Section 47(1A) PACE

The normal powers to impose conditions of bail shall be available to him where a custody officer releases a person on bail under ss. 37 or 38(1).

Section 3A(4) Bail Act 1976

Where a custody officer has granted bail in criminal proceedings he or another custody officer serving at the same police station may, at the request of the person to whom it was granted, vary the conditions of bail and in doing so he may impose conditions or more onerous conditions.

Section 7(3)(b) Bail Act 1976

A person who has been released on bail in criminal proceedings and is under a duty to surrender into the custody of a court may be arrested without warrant by a constable—

if the constable has reasonable grounds for believing that that person is likely to break any of the conditions of his bail or has reasonable grounds for suspecting that that person has broken any of those conditions.

16.5.2 **Powers to grant conditional bail**

The courts may grant conditional bail, under s. 3(6) of the Bail Act 1976. Changes to PACE by s. 27(1)(b) of the Criminal Justice and Public Order Act 1994 and more recently, Sch. 6 to the Police and Justice Act 2006, mean that the police have the same powers as the courts to impose bail conditions in relation to all types of police bail, including—

- bail to court from a police station;
- bail to a police station to allow further enquiries/evidence to be gathered;
- bail to a police station for pre-charge advice;
- bail to a police station where bail has been granted away from the station (see **16.8 'Street bail'** below for the full provisions of these powers).

KEYNOTE

Where a custody officer determines that deferred bail is required in pre-charge advice cases, it may be necessary to consult with the CPS on the appropriate conditions, although ultimately, the decision still remains with the custody officer (see the *Guidance to Police Officers and Crown Prosecutors Issued by the Director of Public Prosecutions under s. 37A of the Police and Criminal Evidence Act 1984*).

A custody officer may only grant conditional bail in order to ensure that the person:

- surrenders to custody; *or*
- does not commit offences while on bail; *or*
- does not interfere with witnesses or otherwise obstruct the course of justice.

The custody officer would also have to consider the above requirements under s. 38 of PACE, when deciding whether or not to detain a person after charge. The issue is discussed in more depth in **Chapter 15—Continued Detention After Charge**, but it is clear that imposing bail conditions should be viewed as an alternative to authorising detention after charge. When a court issues bail conditions, it must consider the same requirements as in s. 3A(5) above (s. 3(6) of the Bail Act 1976). Subsections 3(4), 3(5) and 3(7) referred to above relate to the release of a person on bail with sureties under the original Act. This matter is dealt with below in **16.7 Sureties and Security**.

The table below is a summary of the type of conditions often issued by custody officers, under s. 3A(5) above, to ensure a person complies with his/her bail. The list is not exhaustive, and custody officers and courts are capable of coming up with many other innovative and imaginative bail conditions to ensure compliance by a detainee, such as, not to enter licensed premises, not to drive a motor vehicle or not to be a passenger in a motor vehicle.

Provided the custody officer or the court can justify a particular condition, there is no actual limit as to the kind of condition that may be imposed.

Condition	Preventative Measure
To report to his/her local police station (daily, weekly or at other intervals)	• committing an offence while on bail • failing to surrender to custody
Not to enter a certain area or building, or to go within a specified distance of a specified address	• interfering with witnesses • otherwise obstructing the course of justice
Not to contact (whether directly or indirectly) the victim of the alleged offence and/or any other probable prosecution witness	• interfering with witnesses • otherwise obstructing the course of justice
To surrender his/her passport	• failing to surrender to custody
A curfew between set times (i.e. when it is thought the accused might commit offences or come into contact with witnesses)	• committing an offence while on bail • interfering with witnesses • otherwise obstructing the course of justice

16.5.3 **Doorstepping powers**

The matter of checking whether or not a person is complying with his/her bail conditions can be contentious. Many defendants and their legal representatives have sought to argue that police officers attending a person's home address, to check whether or not they are complying with their conditions, is incompatible with their human rights. The matter was clarified with the following advice in Home Office Circular 61/2002:

> Courts and the public need to know that if bail is granted with a condition to be at home on curfew the police can check the person is at home where they are supposed to be.

The CPS and Home Office issued guidance to clarify this and encourage the use of such checks. The guidance states that:

- magistrates should continue to issue curfew conditions in cases where it is proportionate and appropriate; and
- the curfew condition should state that the defendants are required to present themselves at the door when a uniformed officer comes to check.

The guidance ensures that strong measures are also in place to prevent re-offending on bail for those people who are not eligible for secure remand.

Although the above advice only mentions magistrates, presumably, the intention is that the same positive stance would apply where a custody officer has issued a bail condition.

KEYNOTE

Note that the defendant is required to present himself/herself at the door when a uniformed officer attends to check.

It should also be noted that a balance of needs should be struck in respect of individuals' human rights. For example, does the above guidance allow an officer to call on a person at 4.00 am to check their curfew? There may sometimes be circumstances where it is necessary to do so, but the officers should remember the human rights tests of necessity and proportionality.

16.5.4 When a custody officer cannot grant conditional bail

While s. 3A(5) above identifies when a custody officer can issue bail conditions, s. 3A(2) above states that a custody officer cannot do so in certain circumstances. The powers under this section are available only to the courts, who may impose additional conditions, that the defendant:

- makes himself/herself available for the purpose of making a report to assist the court in dealing with the offence;
- attends an interview with an authorised advocate or authorised litigator;
- resides in a bail hostel;
- complies with an electronic monitoring programme;
- undergoes examination by two medical practitioners for the purpose of enabling reports to be prepared.

16.5.5 Varying or changing bail conditions

A person who has been released on conditional bail may, occasionally, make a request for the conditions to be varied. For example, a person may have conditions to reside at a particular address and is moving house. It would not be unreasonable to allow a variation in these circumstances.

However, the request does not have to be granted. What if the person has bail conditions not to approach witnesses, and their intention is to move to an address closer to those people? In those circumstances, would it be appropriate not to authorise a change in the conditions? As usual, it will be for the custody officer to decide, taking into account the nature of the offence, the rights of the detainee and the risk to witnesses.

A request to vary bail conditions may be made either to a court (under s. 3(8) of the original Act), or to a custody officer (under s. 3A(4) above). In either case, the court or the custody officer may decide to impose more onerous conditions if it is felt justified. Where a custody officer has been asked to vary conditions, whatever the decision, he/she must record the fact that a request was made, his or her decision, and the reasons for it, on the original custody record.

Under s. 3A(4) above, there is no requirement for the defendant to return to the same custody officer, to have his/her bail conditions varied. However, the custody officer must be from the police station where the defendant was initially bailed.

The same applies when the defendant applies to a court for a variation. He/she must apply to the court that imposed the conditions, but not necessarily to the same magistrate or judge.

Where a custody officer varies bail conditions, he/she may only do so if it appears that it is necessary to prevent that person from—

(a) failing to surrender to custody; *or*

(b) committing an offence while on bail; *or*

(c) interfering with witnesses or otherwise obstructing the course of justice.

Where a person is released on street bail subject to conditions, the conditions may be varied by a custody officer at the police station at which the person is required to attend. The custody officer may vary or rescind any of those conditions, or impose further conditions.

KEYNOTE

Where a detainee has been released on conditional bail from the court, only the court may alter or vary the conditions.

Where a detainee has been released on conditional bail by a custody officer, that officer, or any other at the station where bail was granted, may alter or vary the conditions.

KEYNOTE

It should be noted that where a person has been released on deferred bail under s. 37(7)(a) (awaiting decision from the CPS), the custody officer has the authority under s. 37D(1) to amend the time or date at which the person is to attend the police station to answer bail. The custody officer must give the person a notice in writing outlining that the time has been changed (s. 37D(2)).

If the person is on conditional bail, the exercise of the power under subsection (1) above will not affect any of the conditions (see s. 37D(3)).

16.5.6 Failing to comply with bail conditions

There are four general powers to arrest a person who fails to comply with conditional bail:

1. where a person has been charged and released on conditional bail by a custody officer to appear in court;
2. where a person has appeared in court, and the court has decided to release that person on conditional bail;
3. where a person has not been charged, and has been released on conditional bail by a custody officer to return to a police station;
4. where a person has been released on bail elsewhere than at a police station, to a police station.

In circumstances 1 and 2 above, the custody officer and court will rely on the power granted under the Bail Act 1976. Under s. 7(3)(b) of the 1976 Act, where a person has been released on bail in criminal proceedings by a custody officer (to appear in court), or by the court, a constable may arrest that person without warrant when he/she has reasonable grounds for believing that the person:

- is likely to break any conditions of bail; *or*
- has broken, any conditions of bail.

In circumstances 3 and 4, a constable may arrest that person without warrant *only* when he/she has reasonable grounds for believing that the person:

- has broken any conditions of bail.

KEYNOTE

There is no requirement for the constable to be in uniform to exercise any of the above powers.

Consider the following:

Case Study

CHRISTOU was on bail from the magistrates' court for assaulting his ex-partner, SALLY. He was given bail conditions not to go within 100 metres of SALLY.

The day before he was due to appear in court, CHRISTOU saw SALLY in a shopping centre in a different area from where he was arrested. He approached her, trying to talk to her. A police officer was passing by and after speaking to SALLY, the officer arrested CHRISTOU for breaching his bail conditions. He was arrested at 3.30pm.

CHRISTOU was detained to appear before court the next day, for breaching his bail.

1. Which court should CHRISTOU be sent to (i.e. the area in which he was arrested, or the area from which he was bailed)?
2. How long do the police have, in which to transfer CHRISTOU to court?

....

To answer question 1 in the scenario first, where a person has been arrested for breaching their bail conditions, he or she must be taken to a court in the petty sessions area in which he/she was arrested (s. 7(4)(a) of the Bail Act 1976).

However, there is an exception to the above rule. Where the person is arrested within 24 hours of the time appointed for him/her to surrender to custody, which is the case in the scenario, he/she must be brought before the court at which he/she was to have so surrendered (s. 7(4)(b)). In reckoning the 24-hour period, no account is to be taken of Christmas Day, Good Friday or any Sunday (s. 7(4)).

Therefore, the custody officer in the scenario must make arrangements for CHRISTOU to be taken before the court at which he is due to appear the next day.

In relation to the second question in the above scenario, s. 7(4)(a) requires the person to be brought before the court within 24 hours of being arrested. Therefore, in the scenario, the custody officer should ensure that CHRISTOU appears before the court before 3.30pm the next day. The case of *R* v *Governor of Glen Parva Young Offender Institution, ex parte G (a minor)* [1998] QB 887 should be noted. The detainee must be brought before a justice of the peace within 24 hours of being arrested, not just to the court precincts or cells. If a detainee is not brought before a justice of the peace within 24 hours, the court will have no jurisdiction to remand him or her for the breach of bail.

Where a person has been arrested on reasonable grounds of having broken any of the conditions of bail, or for failing to surrender to bail at the police station, and a custody officer concludes that the person should be detained in custody for the purpose of an application to the court for a remand in custody, the custody officer *must* consult with the CPS for a decision as to whether to charge with the offence for which the person had previously been released on bail or with any other offence or whether the person should be released without charge either on bail or without bail.

However, where it has proved not to be possible to consult with the CPS in person or by telephone before the expiry of any PACE custody time limit and it is proposed to withhold bail for the purposes of an application for a remand into custody (or for bail conditions that may only be imposed by the court), the custody officer may proceed to charge, but only on the authority of a duty inspector, who must note the decision on the custody record and MG3 to confirm that it is appropriate to charge under the emergency provisions. The case must be referred to a Crown Prosecutor as soon as is practicable for authority to proceed with the prosecution (see the *Guidance to Police Officers and Crown Prosecutors Issued by the Director of Public Prosecutions under s. 37A of the Police and Criminal Evidence Act 1984*).

When a person has been released on bail under s. 37(7)(a) of PACE, to allow the police time to consult with the CPS in respect of the appropriate charge, the CPS are required, under s. 37B(4), to give the police a written notice of their decision during the period of bail. Where a person has been arrested for failing to appear under s. 46A(1) and the CPS have not provided that written notice, the custody officer must consider whether or not it is appropriate to charge the detainee, or to release them either on bail or without bail. The decision as to which action is most appropriate will be the custody officer's. If there is insufficient evidence to charge the detainee at this time, and the custody officer decides to release the person on bail, that person *must* be given the same conditions which applied immediately before his/her arrest (see s. 37C PACE).

KEYNOTE

Note that there is no requirement for a police officer to attend court to give evidence of a breach of bail, as the person will not have been arrested for an 'offence' (see *R* (*DPP*) v *Havering Magistrates' Court* [2001] 1 WLR 805).

16.5.7 Criminal offences

The circumstances in the scenario above are quite straightforward, but what would happen if it is discovered that the detainee is wanted for a criminal offence as well as the breach of bail? Custody officers often find that their hands are tied when this happens.

The requirement to place the detainee before the court within 24 hours is absolute. Generally, the police will attempt to deal with the detainee for the criminal offence in time to take him/her to court to answer the breach of bail. However, this is not always possible and often, the breach of bail matter will be lost, in favour of the criminal offence.

Experience shows that people arrested for breaching their bail are very rarely remanded by the courts. Detainees are often either released with more stringent conditions or the same ones. Sometimes the court will even give the detainee less stringent bail conditions. In any case, the view often taken amongst police officers is that where a person is arrested for breaching their bail, the only punishment they will receive is a night in the cells.

At least the breach of bail may provide the custody officer with grounds to believe that the detainee will commit offences while on bail, which means he or she may be detained for the next available court in respect of the criminal offence.

Another option for dealing with a detainee in these circumstances would be to place him/her before court for the breach of bail, and arrest him/her after the hearing (if the person is released) for the criminal offence. This is not ideal; however, under these circumstances the police are not required to arrest a person before his/her release to court because he/she will not be covered by s. 31 of PACE (which requires a person to be arrested before release, when he/she is in custody for an offence, and would be liable for arrest for another offence if released from custody—breach of bail is not an offence).

Of course, if the person is remanded in custody by the court, the police would have to bring the detainee to a police station from prison on a production order.

As usual, there will be no absolute right or wrong answer and the custody officer will have to use an element of common sense when reaching their decision.

16.6 **Failing to Surrender to Custody**

16.6.1 **Legislative provisions**

Section 6(1) Bail Act 1976

If a person who has been released on bail in criminal proceedings fails without reasonable cause to surrender to custody he shall be guilty of an offence.

Section 7(1) Bail Act 1976

If a person who has been released on bail in criminal proceedings and is under a duty to surrender into the custody of a court fails to surrender to custody at the time appointed for him to do so the court may issue a warrant for his arrest.

Section 7(3)(a) Bail Act 1976

A person who has been released on bail in criminal proceedings and is under a duty to surrender into the custody of a court may be arrested without warrant by a constable—

if the constable has reasonable grounds for believing that that person is not likely to surrender to custody.

16.6.2 **Offence of failing to surrender to custody**

Where a person fails to surrender to custody as directed, he or she will commit an offence under s. 6(1) of the Bail Act 1976 above. This offence under s. 6(1) applies either when a person fails to appear at a police station, or at a court.

A person may have 'reasonable cause' for failing to surrender as directed, which would provide them with a defence to this offence. However, even if the person has a 'reasonable cause' for failing to surrender to custody, if he or she

fails to surrender to custody at the appointed place as soon after the appointed time as is reasonably practicable he/she shall be guilty of an offence, (s. 7(3)(a)).

In other words, it is not enough for the detainee simply to fail to surrender, even if they had reasonable cause to do so. They must surrender as soon as is reasonably practicable after the appointed time, and the onus is on the defendant to do so.

KEYNOTE

A failure to give the person granted bail in criminal proceedings a copy of the record of the decision shall not constitute reasonable cause for that person's failure to surrender to custody (see s. 6(4) of the Bail Act 1976).

As a custody officer, there were a few occasions when I forgot to give the defendant a copy of the bail sheet with the reminder of the court date. On each occasion, I managed to get the copy to the detainee's solicitor. Presumably, telling the detainee to appear in court at a certain time and date will be enough.

The burden of proof in relation to showing 'reasonable cause' is a matter for the accused, who need only show, on the balance of probabilities, that he/she had a reasonable cause (s. 6(3)).

16.6.3 **Failing to appear in court**

Where a person fails to appear, the court may issue a warrant for their arrest. The warrant may be executed by a constable arresting the detainee, to secure his/her attendance before the court. Two types of warrant may be issued:

- warrants which are backed for bail; *or*
- warrants which are not backed for bail.

A warrant which is backed for bail will instruct the custody officer to bail the defendant to appear before the next available court. A warrant which is not backed for bail will instruct the custody officer to detain the person, and to take him/her before the next available court.

Under s. 7(2) of the Bail Act 1976, the court may also issue a warrant if a person who has been released on bail in criminal proceedings actually answers bail, but subsequently absents himself/herself from the court at any time after he/she has surrendered into custody, and before the court is ready to begin or to resume the hearing of the proceedings.

KEYNOTE

In *R* v *Casim Scott* [2007] EWCA Crim 2757, the defendant was convicted of failing to appear in court, having overslept and arriving 30 minutes late for court. The defendant appealed against the conviction on the grounds that the judge had a reviewable discretion not to prosecute for this offence and that the actions were unreasonable and draconian. The Appeal Court held that there might be circumstances where a late arrival would be so marginal that to charge a s. 6 offence would be unreasonable but those instances would be rare. The court dismissed the appeal, citing that the failure of defendants to arrive on time had consequences for all court users and impacted on victims, witnesses and others. If a culture of delay were tolerated, the effects would be cumulative and affect the administration of justice overall.

A warrant will not be issued under this subsection where that person is absent in accordance with leave given to him/her by or on behalf of the court.

16.6.4 **Additional power of arrest**

A further power of arrest is granted under s. 7(3)(a) of the Bail Act 1976 above. Under this subsection, a person may be arrested by a constable who

> has reasonable grounds for believing that that person is not likely to surrender to custody.

This will be a subjective test for the constable, who will have to provide evidence as to why he/she believed that the defendant was unlikely to surrender to custody. A similar power exists under s. 7(3)(b) of the Act, where a person may be arrested who is likely to break any conditions of court bail (see **16.5.2 Powers to grant conditional bail** above).

KEYNOTE

Note that the power mentioned in s. 7(3)(a) of the Bail Act 1976 above only applies to a person who has been bailed to a court. Therefore, if an officer believes a person who is released on deferred bail is not likely to appear, there is no similar preventative power of arrest. The power to arrest in these circumstances only applies where the person has failed to appear (see **16.3.3 Powers of arrest for persons released on deferred bail** above).

16.7 **Sureties and Security**

This section deals with occasions where a person known to the accused may act as a surety, in order to secure his/her attendance in court, and secondly, where the accused provides his/her own security for the same reason.

Sureties and security may be seen as an alternative to remanding a defendant in custody or releasing him/her with bail conditions, although there is nothing preventing a custody officer or a court using bail conditions and surety or security as a means of ensuring the person surrenders to custody as required.

16.7.1 **Legislative provisions**

Section 3(4) Bail Act 1976

A person granted bail in criminal proceedings may be required before release on bail to provide one or more sureties to secure his surrender to custody.

Section 7(3)(c) Bail Act 1976

A person who has been released on bail in criminal proceedings and is under a duty to surrender into the custody of a court may be arrested without warrant by a constable—

- in a case where that person was released on bail with one or more surety or sureties; *or*

- if a surety notifies a constable in writing that that person is unlikely to surrender to custody and that for that reason the surety wishes to be relieved of his obligations as a surety.

16.7.2 **Sureties**

Before releasing a person on bail, the custody officer or court has the discretion to require a person to provide one or more sureties, under s. 3(4) of the Bail Act 1976. The purpose of requiring a surety in this manner is to ensure that the person surrenders to custody.

KEYNOTE

Where the detainee is a juvenile detainee, the parent or guardian consenting to be a surety cannot be bound for a sum of more than £50.00 (s. 3(7) Bail Act 1976).

As the power applies both to custody officers and courts, and it is intended to ensure a person surrenders to custody, it may be used either when a person is being bailed to court, or to a police station (on deferred bail) (s. 43(2) Magistrates' Courts Act 1980).

The powers for custody officers and the courts to apply securities are similar to those discussed in **16.5.2 Powers to grant conditional bail** above.

KEYNOTE

Sureties can only be applied where it is believed the accused may:

(a) fail to surrender to custody; *or*

(b) commit an offence while on bail; *or*

(c) interfere with witnesses or otherwise obstruct the course of justice.

(See Sch. 1, Part I Bail Act 1976.)

KEYNOTE

There is no power to take sureties or security from a person who has been released on street bail to attend a police station. See **16.8 'Street Bail'** for the full provisions of these powers.

16.7.3 **Taking sureties**

Section 8 of the Bail Act 1976 contains details of how to judge the suitability of a person acting as surety. The custody officer or the court may take into account the surety's:

- financial resources;
- character and previous convictions;
- relationship to the person for whom he/she stands surety.

Section 8(4) of the Act lists those people who may accept a surety's recognisance, namely:

- a justice of the peace;
- a justices' clerk;
- a police officer who is above the rank of inspector, or who is in charge of a police station;
- the governor of a prison or remand centre where the accused is being held;
- an officer of the Crown Court.

16.7.4 **Failing to surrender when subject of a surety**

Section 7(3)(c) of the Bail Act 1976 requires the surety to notify a constable in writing that the accused is unlikely to appear to answer bail (and that he/she no longer wishes to act as surety).

Where a constable receives such information, the accused may be arrested without warrant.

KEYNOTE

Where a person fails to surrender to custody, the person acting as surety is likely to forfeit all or part of any recognisances which he/she stood surety. In order to avoid losing the recognisance, the surety will have to show that he or she took 'reasonable steps', which could include co-operating with the police under s. 7(3)(c).

Where a surety has taken all reasonable steps to ensure the appearance of an accused, it was held that the recognisance should not to be forfeited (see *R v York Crown Court, ex parte Coleman* [1987] 86 Cr App R 151).

KEYNOTE

There is no requirement to prove that the surety was in any way involved in the defendant's failure to appear (see *R* v *Warwick Crown Court, ex parte Smalley* [1987] 1 WLR 237).

16.7.5 **Security**

A custody officer or a court may require the defendant himself/herself to provide their own security, before releasing that person on bail (s. 3(5) of the Bail Act 1976). As in the case of sureties, the custody officer or court must believe that the accused may:

(a)   fail to surrender to custody; *or*

(b)   commit an offence while on bail; *or*

(c)   interfere with witnesses or otherwise obstruct the course of justice.

The defendant may be required to deposit a sum of money or valuable item before being granted bail. If the person fails to appear, the security may be forfeited, unless he/she is able to show there was a reasonable cause for the failure (s. 5(7)–(9) of the Bail Act 1976).

KEYNOTE

The loss incurred by the complainant should not be a factor when considering the amount of security set (see *Neumeister* v *Austria* [1968] 1 EHRR 91).

16.8 **'Street Bail'**

16.8.1 **Legislative provisions**

Section 30A PACE

1.   A constable may release on bail a person who is arrested or taken into custody in the circumstances mentioned in s. 30(1).

2.   A person may be released on bail under subsection (1) at any time before he arrives at a police station.

3.   A person released on bail under subsection (1) must be required to attend a police station.

Section 30B PACE

---

1. Where a constable grants bail to a person under s. 30A, he must give that person a notice in writing before he is released.

2. The notice must state—

    (a) the offence for which he was arrested; and

    (b) the ground on which he was arrested.

16.8.2 **Key aims**

Section 4 of the Criminal Justice Act 2003 inserted ss. 30A–30D into PACE. A constable is no longer obliged to take every arrested person directly to a police station, as per the requirement in s. 30(1) of PACE (for full details of this requirement see **1.3.2 Designated police stations**).

The legislation provides a constable with the power to grant an arrested person immediate bail from the scene of arrest. The provisions of this section are described in Home Office Circular 61/2003.

The powers came into effect on 20 January 2004. Commonly referred to as 'street bail', the key aims are to:

- enable officers to remain on patrol for longer periods and raise visibility;
- give officers greater flexibility to decide how best to use their time and organise their casework;
- remove the need for suspects to be taken to a police station only to be bailed on arrival;
- maintain the safeguards and protections for those granted street bail.

KEYNOTE

Sch. 6 to the Police and Justice Act 2006 provides the police with powers to impose bail conditions on persons who have been bailed under this section. See **16.5.2 Powers to grant conditional bail** for more details of these powers.

A notice must be given to a person granted street bail, which should include the conditions of bail, the fact that the bail conditions may be varied and details of the police station at which a request to vary the conditions may be made. It is proposed that a custody officer at that station, or a magistrate, may vary those conditions on request.

444

The amendments also provide a power of arrest where a constable has reasonable grounds for suspecting that the person has broken any of the conditions of bail. A person arrested under this power must be taken to a police station as soon as practicable after the arrest.

The constable will not be allowed to impose conditions which include the taking of a recognisance, security or surety or a requirement to reside in a bail hostel.

16.8.3 **'Street bail' in practice**

'Street bail' enables front-line officers to apply their discretion at the point of arrest. The general idea of this new power is that a constable on patrol may arrest a person and if appropriate, bail them to a police station pending further enquiries into the case, so that the arrested person may be dealt with expeditiously when they are actually in custody.

There are four key considerations:

- the nature of the offence;
- the ability to progress the investigation at the station;
- confidence in the suspect answering bail;
- the level of awareness and understanding of the procedure by the suspect.

These points will be examined individually:

The nature of the offence

This power will be used mainly for offences at the lower end of the scale, such as theft (shoplifting), minor criminal damage, minor public order offences and possibly minor assaults. The arresting officer will need to consider whether or not evidence will be lost by bailing a person at this point, such as recovery of stolen property from house searches, or interference with witnesses.

The ability to progress the investigation at the station

This requirement links in with the point made above, which is to remove the need for suspects to be taken to a police station only to be bailed on arrival, although how often this actually happens is in question. There will be occasions, however, when a person is brought to the station and witnesses are unavailable to make statements, meaning that the detainee is held in detention while officers make those enquiries, and may be released on bail without being interviewed. The power to bail a person at the scene will at least give the officer time to make those enquiries without using time from the detention clock.

Confidence in the suspect answering bail

If the offence is of a serious nature, or the person is known to fail to appear, officers should avoid using the power to bail from the scene unless they can be certain the person will appear. Also, the officer will need to be certain about the identity of the arrested person, and that he/she has provided a suitable address for bail.

The level of awareness and understanding of the procedure by the suspect

A person who is considered mentally disordered or otherwise mentally vulnerable, or is under the influence of drink or drugs, should not be bailed using this power. The arresting officer must be certain that the arrested person understands why they have been arrested, and the fact that they must answer bail at a certain time and date.

KEYNOTE

There is no power to impose conditions of bail at this point; therefore, if the detainee is likely to interfere with witnesses, commit further offences, or fail to appear, the officer should not use this power at the point of arrest (see s. 30A(4)).

Consider the following:

Scenario 1

An officer has been searching for a person for an offence of making off without payment for petrol. The person is traced to an address in another police area and local officers attend to arrest him. The arrested person may be bailed to the investigating officer's police station, by virtue of s. 30A(5) of PACE, which states:

> The police station which the person is required to attend may be any police station.

Scenario 2

During a busy shift, an officer arrests five juvenile shoplifters. When she contacts the control room, she is told that there is only room in the custody office for two of them, and she will have to take the others to another designated police station five miles away. The detainees may be bailed to appear at the officer's own police station at a convenient time.

KEYNOTE

Although the Act does not prevent a juvenile being bailed without the presence of an appropriate adult, the officer must bear in mind the ability of the person to understand the requirement to attend a police station as discussed above. In practical terms, it may be better to take the juveniles home and bail them in the presence of an appropriate adult.

Scenario 3

An officer attends a neighbour dispute, where one neighbour has been accused of deliberately damaging a fence belonging to the other. The damage is of minimal value. There is an independent witness to the incident, but this person has gone away for the weekend. Provided the officer is satisfied that there will be no recurrence of the incident, the arrested person may be bailed to attend the police station when the witness has returned and a statement has been taken.

KEYNOTE

Remember that officers may still use their discretion as to whether a person is arrested or not. For some incidents, such as the one above, proceeding by way of summons may still be a more appropriate option. Each case will have to be taken on its merits.

16.8.4 **Bail notice**

The arrested person must be given a written notice, which must inform him/her of the requirement to attend a police station. The notice should specify the police station which he is required to attend and the time when he is required to attend. If the notice does not include the information mentioned above, the person must subsequently be given a further notice in writing which contains that information.

The key to providing the above details will be the ability to liaise with the custody officer from the scene of the incident, to arrange a time which is convenient for the custody officer, as well as the arresting officer and the detainee.

More than one notice may be given to the detainee relating to changes in the bail requirements. Also, the detainee should be given written notice if he/she is no longer required to answer bail.

16.8.5 Failure to answer bail

Under s. 30D(1), a constable may arrest without a warrant a person who—

(a)   has been released on bail under s. 30A subject to a requirement to attend a specified police station; but

(b)   fails to attend the police station at the specified time.

A person arrested under subsection (1) above must be taken to a police station as soon as practicable after the arrest. The person may be taken to the police station specified in the original notice (or one specified in any renewed notice), or any other police station.

An arrest under this section is to be treated as an arrest for an offence (see s. 30D(4)).

16.9 **Summing Up**

Failure to appear when released on deferred bail

A person who fails to appear as directed by the custody officer may be arrested without warrant.

(s. 46A PACE)

Re-arrest of detainee released on deferred bail

1.   Nothing in the Bail Act 1976 shall prevent the re-arrest without warrant of a person released on bail subject to a duty to attend at a police station if new evidence justifying a further arrest has come to light since his/her release.

(s. 47(2) PACE)

2. When a person who has been released on deferred bail is arrested for new evidence, the custody officer will open a new custody record and the detention clock is re-set to zero.

(s. 47(7) PACE)

When a person either answers bail as directed, or fails to answer bail

Where a person either answers bail as directed, or fails to answer bail as directed, their detention time continues from the point where it was halted when the person was released and the existing custody record should be re-opened (although custody officers should consult their own force policy in relation to this issue).

Granting conditional bail

(a) A custody officer or court may only grant conditional bail, when it appears to him/her that it is necessary to do so for the purpose of preventing the detainee from—

   (i)   failing to surrender to custody; *or*

   (ii)   committing an offence while on bail; *or*

   (iii) interfering with witnesses or otherwise obstructing the course of justice, whether in relation to himself/herself or any other person.

(s. 3A(5) Bail Act 1976)

(b) A custody officer has the normal powers to impose conditions of bail for a person released for pre-charge advice, to prevent the suspect from committing any of the above acts.

(s. 47(1A) PACE)

Bail conditions that may only be granted by courts

Only a court may issue conditions to ensure that a defendant:

* makes himself/herself available for the purpose of making a report to assist the court in dealing with the offence;
* attends an interview with an authorised advocate or authorised litigator;
* resides in a bail hostel;
* complies with an electronic monitoring programme;
* undergoes examination by two medical practitioners for the purpose of enabling reports to be prepared.

(s. 3(6) Bail Act 1976)

Varying bail conditions

Where a custody officer has granted bail in criminal proceedings he/she or another custody officer serving at the same police station may, at the request of the person to whom it was granted, vary the conditions of bail and in doing so he/she may impose conditions or more onerous conditions.

(s. 3A(4) Bail Act 1976)

Power to arrest a person released on bail with conditions

(a) Where a person has been released on bail in criminal proceedings by a custody officer (to appear in court), or by the court, a constable may arrest that person without warrant when he/she has reasonable grounds for believing that the person:

- is likely to break any conditions of bail; *or*
- has broken any conditions of bail.

Where a person has been released on bail for CPS advice, a constable may arrest that person without warrant *only* when he/she has reasonable grounds for believing that the person:

- has broken any conditions of bail.

(b) Where a person has been arrested for breach of conditions when on deferred bail, the custody officer *must* consult with the CPS for a decision as to whether to charge with the offence for which the person had previously been released on bail or with any other offence or be released without charge either on bail or without bail.

Taking a detainee to court who has been arrested for breach of bail conditions

A person who has been arrested for breaching their bail conditions must be taken to a court within 24 hours of being arrested, in the petty sessions area in which he/she was arrested, unless the person has been arrested within 24 hours of the time appointed for him/her to surrender to custody, in which case—he/she must be brought before the court at which he/she was to have so surrendered.

Note that the person will only be 'before the court' when they appear before the magistrate/judge (i.e. they will not be 'before the court' when in the court cells).

(s. 7(4)(a)–(b) Bail Act 1976)

Failure to give bail form

A failure to give the person granted bail in criminal proceedings a copy of the record of the decision shall not constitute reasonable cause for that person's failure to surrender to custody.

(s. 6(4) Bail Act 1976)

Power to arrest a person who is not likely to appear in court

A person who has been released on bail in criminal proceedings and is under a duty to surrender into the custody of a court may be arrested without warrant by a constable if the constable has reasonable grounds for believing that that person is not likely to surrender to custody.

(s. 7(3)(a) Bail Act 1976)

Sureties

1. Sureties can only be applied where it is believed the accused may:

    (a)   fail to surrender to custody; *or*

    (b)   commit an offence while on bail; *or*

    (c)   interfere with witnesses or otherwise obstruct the course of justice.

(Sch. 1, Part I Bail Act 1976)

2. The custody officer or the court may take into account the surety's:

    • financial resources;

    • character and previous convictions;

    • relationship to the person for whom he/she stands surety.

(s. 8 Bail Act 1976)

'Street bail'

A constable may release on bail a person who is arrested or taken into custody at any time before he/she arrives at a police station.

(s. 30A PACE)

Where a constable grants bail to a person under section 30A, he must give that person a notice in writing before he is released, which must state—

• the offence for which he was arrested; *and*

• the ground on which he was arrested.

(s. 30B PACE)

A constable may arrest without warrant a person who fails to answer bail.

(s. 30D PACE)

LOCAL PROCEDURES

1. Does your force require a new custody record to be opened when a person has failed to answer bail, and has been re-arrested?

SPACE FOR NOTES

SPACE FOR NOTES

SPACE FOR NOTES

17

Terrorism Act 2000 Detainees

17.1 **Introduction**

In the first and second editions of this book, issues relating to terrorist detainees were dealt with in several different chapters, as and when the provisions of the Terrorism Act 2000 (TACT) related to those in PACE and the Codes of Practice. However, these provisions are now brought together in one chapter for ease of reference, as well as to highlight the importance of this subject.

Most custody officers are unlikely to experience being in charge of terrorist suspects detained under TACT. Detainees who have been arrested as a result of in particular pre-planned operations are generally taken to the more secure Paddington Green Police Station, London. However, increasingly, local forces find themselves in the position of having to deal with terrorist suspects in more spontaneous circumstances and each force is required to identify a suitable designated police station to do so.

It is therefore important that all custody officers familiarise themselves with the legislative requirements under the 2000 Act and the implications of holding terrorist suspects in police cells.

This chapter will concentrate on the initial detention issues, such as access to legal advice and being held incommunicado, followed by reviews, relevant times and extending detention. We will also deal with charging suspects and obtaining samples, comparing issues under TACT to those under PACE.

The legislative provisions in this chapter will feature a mixture of the Schedules contained in the Terrorism Act 2000 and Code H of the PACE *Codes of Practice*, which relate specifically to suspects detained under TACT. It should be noted that that much of the guidance in Code H mirrors that contained in Code C of the *Codes of Practice*, relating to PACE prisoners. This chapter focuses on those paragraphs that relate specifically to TACT detainees.

The Human Rights Act 1998

Article 5 of the 1998 Act (right to liberty and security) will be of particular relevance when determining whether or not to authorise continued detention in relation to detainees arrested under the Terrorism Act 2000, where detention periods are longer than those under PACE. A breach of the *Codes of Practice* may also be found to be a breach of the detainee's human rights.

As a 'public authority', the magistrates' courts will also have to be mindful of the implications of the 1998 Act, when deciding whether to authorise continued detention.

17.2 **Custody Offices**

Police forces are required to nominate at least one secure custody office which may be used in the event of a pre-planned TACT arrest in their area. Custody officers should be specifically trained in the handling of such detainees.

The custody office must be designed to minimise the risk relating to forensic issues—for example, it is suggested that if the area is in close proximity to a firearms range, there may be a danger of cross-contamination from firearms residue. If there is time, cells should be searched, forensically cleaned and sealed prior to the detainee's arrival. Also, the detainee should be forensically examined by an expert as soon as practicable and it is recommended that a person's hands should be secured in appropriate bags if it is suspected that they have been handling explosives.

In the event of a TACT arrest, custody offices should be dedicated to these detainees only. This may cause practical problems of transferring other detainees out of the custody office. However, it is important to remember that the custody officer in these circumstances is likely to be under considerable pressure to get things right and should be allowed the space and time to do so. If there is more than one detainee, there may be a requirement to house them in different custody offices, unless there is a guarantee that they can be separated sufficiently so that they cannot communicate with each other. The force's own Special Branch and the Anti-Terrorist Branch of the Metropolitan Police are likely to be involved at this stage and will be able to give specialist advice.

Clearly, the risk posed by a TACT detainee is likely to be high. Custody officers must ensure that the risk assessment is completed as soon as practicable after the detainee's arrival (see **Chapter 3—Safer Detention** for risk assessments).

17.3 **Defining 'Terrorism' and 'Terrorists'**

A 'terrorist' is defined, under s. 40(1) of the Terrorism Act 2000, as a person who—

(a) has committed an offence under any of ss. 11, 12, 15 to 18, 54 and 56 to 63; *or*

(b) is or has been concerned in the commission, preparation or instigation of acts of terrorism.

There are a number of offences listed in the Terrorism Act 2000, from being a 'member of a proscribed organisation' (s. 11), to 'directing activities of organisation concerned in acts of terrorism' (s. 56). The sections listed above may be found in the original Act.

> **KEYNOTE**
>
> A person will have been 'concerned in the commission, preparation or instigation of acts of terrorism' if they have been, either before or since the passing of the Act, concerned in the commission, preparation or instigation of acts of terrorism within the meaning given by the Act (see above).

17.4 **Entitlements**

As with a detainee under PACE, a person detained under the Terrorism Act 2000 will have the same entitlement to have a friend, relative or person who is likely to take an interest in their welfare, informed of their arrest (para. 5). Such a detainee will also have the right to consult a solicitor as soon as is reasonably practicable, privately and at any time (para. 6). Where a detained person is transferred from one police station to another, he/she may exercise the above rights when he/she arrives at the police station to which he/she is transferred.

Note that, as with PACE, a TACT detainee must sign the custody record as to whether they would like legal advice, or someone informed of their detention. However, Code H, para. 2.8 of the *Codes of Practice*, allows for the identities of custody staff and investigating officers to be protected in cases linked to the investigation of terrorism, or where they are likely to be placed in danger.

17.4.1 **Legislative provisions**

Schedule 8, Para. 9(1) Terrorism Act 2000

A direction under this paragraph may provide that a detained person who wishes to exercise the right under para. 7 may consult a solicitor only in the sight and hearing of a qualified officer.

Schedule 8, Para. 8(1) Terrorism Act 2000

Subject to sub-para. (2), an officer of at least the rank of superintendent may authorise a delay—

(a) in informing the person named by a detained person under para. 6;

(b) in permitting a detained person to consult a solicitor under para. 7.

Schedule 8, Para. 8(4) Terrorism Act 2000

An officer may only authorise a delay under para. 8(1) above if he has reasonable grounds for believing that informing the named person of the detention, or the exercise of the right to legal advice, will have any of the consequences specified in sub-para. (4) below.

Those consequences are—

(a) interference with or harm to evidence of an indictable offence;

(b) interference with or physical injury to any person;

(c) the alerting of persons who are suspected of having committed an indictable offence but who have not been arrested for it;

(d) the hindering of the recovery of property obtained as a result of an indictable offence or in respect of which a forfeiture order could be made under s. 23;

(e) interference with the gathering of information about the commission, preparation or instigation of acts of terrorism;

(f) the alerting of a person and thereby making it more difficult to prevent an act of terrorism; and

(g) the alerting of a person and thereby making it more difficult to secure a person's apprehension, prosecution or conviction in connection with the commission, preparation or instigation of an act of terrorism.

17.4.2 **Private access to a solicitor**

The right to consult privately with a solicitor under PACE is fundamental. However, para. 9 of the Terrorism Act 2000 allows, in certain circumstances, for a 'qualified officer' to be present during the consultation between the detainee and his/her legal representative.

A direction may only be authorised under this paragraph by an officer of at least the rank of Commander or Assistant Chief Constable, if he or she has reasonable grounds for believing that, unless the direction is given, the exercise of the right by the detained person will have any of the consequences specified in para. 8(4) (see **17.4.1 Legislative provisions** above), or the consequence specified in para. 8(5)(c) (which refers to the proceeds of crime).

A 'qualified officer' means a police officer who—

(a) is of at least the rank of inspector;

(b) is of the uniformed branch of the force of which the officer giving the direction is a member; and

(c) in the opinion of the officer giving the direction, has no connection with the detained person's case.

Human Rights Act 1998

Home Office Circular 42/2003 has been produced, because of concern over the implications of para. 9 of the Terrorism Act 2000, and the possible consequences of violating a person's human rights.

The circular cites the case of *Brennan v The United Kingdom*, which was held in the European Court of Human Rights in Strasbourg on 16 October 2001. The court was ruling on a provision under s. 45 of the Northern Ireland (Emergency Provisions) Act 1991 (which is similar to para. 9 above—consultation in the presence of a qualified person).

The circumstances surrounding the original case were that Brennan had been arrested in Northern Ireland under s. 14 of the Prevention of Terrorism (Temporary Provisions) Act 1989, by police officers investigating the murder of a former member of the Ulster Defence Regiment. Authorisation was given to delay access to his solicitor for the first 48 hours of his detention and when he was subsequently allowed to consult with his solicitor, it was in the presence of a police officer.

Brennan took his claim to the European Court on two counts:

1. that his human rights had been interfered with by denying him access to a solicitor for 48 hours;

2. that his human rights had further been interfered with by denying him access to private consultation with his solicitor.

The court ruled that, in relation to his first claim, there had been no violation of his human rights. However, the court found that the presence of a police officer within hearing during the applicant's first consultation with his solicitor would have inhibited Mr Brennan from speaking openly to his solicitor and given him cause to hesitate before addressing important questions in the case against him. This, the court decided, was an infringement of his right to 'defend himself in person or through legal assistance' and that there had been, in that respect, a violation of ECHR Article 6(3)(c), read together with Article 6(1).

Home Office Circular 42/2003 states that the judgment in Brennan does not mean that application of the restriction permitted under para. 9 of Sch. 8 to the Terrorism Act 2000 cannot take place. However, it does emphasise the fact that there will only be limited circumstances where this power can be exercised compatibly with Article 6 and that there must be a thorough assessment of those circumstances and of proportionality before it is applied.

Primarily, this assessment must be against the test contained in para. 9(3):

> that the officer issuing the direction must have reasonable grounds for believing, that unless a direction is given, the exercise of the right to speak to a solicitor in private would result in the consequences laid out in para. 8(4) of Schedule 8.

(as to which, see **17.4.1 Legislative provisions** above)

Significantly, in *Brennan*, the court found no reason to doubt that the restriction had been imposed in good faith. However, it could equally find no compelling reason arising in the case to warrant the imposition of the restriction.

The Circular concludes by emphasising that the restriction should only be used in exceptional circumstances, after a careful assessment encompassing applicability and proportionality. This will involve a balance between the necessity of applying the restriction, against the effect on the suspect. In all cases, the authorising officer must bear in mind that improper use of the restriction may lead to any subsequent trial being ruled unfair and/or to further challenges under the European Convention on Human Rights (ECHR).

17.4.3 **Delaying entitlements**

Paragraph 8(1) above provides that a superintendent may authorise a delay:

- in notifying a person of the detainee's arrest; *or*
- in access to legal advice.

Where a delay is authorised as above, the detainee must be allowed to exercise his/her rights not later than 48 hours beginning with the time of his/her arrest (as opposed to 36 hours where a person has been detained under PACE (as to which, see **6.8 Delay in Access to Legal Advice**)). An officer may only authorise a delay under para. 8(1) above if he/she has reasonable grounds for believing that informing the named person of the detention, or the
exercise of the right to legal advice, will have any of the consequences specified in sub-para. (4) (see **17.4.1 Legislative provisions** above).

Subsections (a) to (d) above are similar to those under Annex B, whereas subsections (e) to (g) are specific only to those persons detained under TACT, and who fall within the definition of a 'terrorist' outlined above.

If an authorisation under para. 8(1) is given orally, the person giving it shall confirm it in writing as soon as is reasonably practicable (para. 8(6)). Where authorisation under para. 8(1) is given, the detained person shall be told the reason for the delay as soon as is reasonably practicable and the reason shall be recorded as soon as is reasonably practicable (para. 8(7)). Where the reason for authorising delay ceases to exist, there may be no further delay in permitting the exercise of the right in the absence of a further authorisation under para. 8(1) (para. 8(8)).

> **KEYNOTE**
>
> Note that under Code H, para. 5.6, the detainee shall be given writing materials, on request, and allowed to telephone one person for a reasonable time. Either or both of these privileges may be denied or delayed if an officer of inspector rank or above considers sending a letter or making a telephone call may result in the consequences in Annex B, paras. 1 and 2 (delays under TACT, Sch. 8), particularly in relation to the making of a telephone call in a language which an officer listening to the call does not understand.

17.5 Reviews

17.5.1 Legislative provisions

Schedule 8, Para. 24(2)–(3) Terrorism Act 2000

In the case of a review carried out within a period of 24 hours beginning with the time of arrest, the review officer shall be an officer of at least the rank of inspector.

In the case of any other review, the review officer shall be an officer of at least the rank of superintendent.

Schedule 8, Para. 21(2)–(3) Terrorism Act 2000

The first review shall be carried out as soon as is reasonably practicable after the time of the person's arrest. Subsequent reviews shall be carried out at intervals of not more than 12 hours.

Code H, Note for Guidance 14B

A review officer may authorise a person's continued detention only if satisfied that it is necessary—

(a) to obtain relevant evidence whether by questioning him/her or otherwise;

(b) to preserve relevant evidence;

(c) while awaiting the result of an examination or analysis of relevant evidence;

(d) for the examination or analysis of anything with a view to obtaining relevant evidence;

(e) pending a decision to apply to the Secretary of State for a deportation notice to be served on the detainee, the making of any such application, or the consideration of any such application by the Secretary of State;

(f) pending a decision to charge the detainee with an offence.

Code H, Para. 14.1

The powers and duties of the review officer are in the Terrorism Act 2000, Sch. 8, Part II. See Notes 14A and 14B. A review officer should carry out his duties at the police station where the detainee is held, and be allowed such access to the detainee as is necessary for him to exercise those duties.

17.5.2 **Review officer**

Where a person has been arrested under the Terrorism Act 2000, the review officer for the first 24 hours will be an inspector who is not directly involved in the case. When a period of 24 hours since the detainee's arrest has expired, the review officer will be a superintendent not directly involved in the case.

The provisions of PACE, s. 40A allowing telephone reviews do not apply to reviews under the Terrorism Act 2000, Sch. 8, Part II in terrorism cases (see **10.5.8 Telephone reviews and video conferencing** for further provisions relating to s. 40A). Irrespective of whether the reviewing officer is an inspector or a superintendent, a review under TACT must be done in person.

17.5.3 **Timing of reviews**

Paragraph 21(1) of Sch. 8 to the Act requires a detainee to be reviewed periodically. Under para. 21(2) above, an inspector will review a detainee as soon as is reasonably practicable after the time of the person's arrest. Presumably this review will normally take place when the detainee arrives at the custody office.

Further reviews are due at 12-hour intervals—but because of para. 24(3) above, an inspector will only be required to review the detainee until 24 hours after their arrest. The duties will then be passed on to the superintendent.

17.5.4 Grounds for continued detention

The Terrorism Act 2000 provides additional grounds for detaining a person (see Code H, Note for Guidance 14B above). The additional reasons for detention centre around applying for and making decisions in relation to deportation notices under the Immigration Act 1971. Note for Guidance 14B above refers to 'relevant evidence'. This means evidence which relates to the commission of offences under s. 40 of the Terrorism Act 2000.

Under s. 41(4) of the Terrorism Act 2000, if on a review of a person's detention under Part II of Sch. 8, the review officer does not authorise continued detention, the person shall be released, unless detained in accordance with s. 41(5) or 41(6) (pending the application for an extension of detention), or under any other power.

17.5.5 Hearing representations

Before determining whether to authorise a person's continued detention, a review officer shall give either the detained person, appropriate adult or a solicitor representing him/her, who is available at the time, an opportunity to make written or oral representations about the detention (see Sch. 8, para. 26(1)–(2)).

A review officer may refuse to hear oral representations from the detained person if he/she considers that he/she is unfit to make representations because of his/her condition or behaviour (Sch. 8, para. 26(3)).

> **KEYNOTE**
>
> Code H, para. 14.2 states that for the purposes of reviewing a person's detention, no officer shall put specific questions to the detainee:
>
> - regarding their involvement in any offence; or
> - in respect of any comments they may make:
>   - when given the opportunity to make representations; or
>   - in response to a decision to keep them in detention or extend the maximum period of detention.
>
> Such an exchange could constitute an interview. In these circumstances, a detainee should be cautioned before questions about an offence are put to him or her (see Code H, para.10.1).

Written records must be made of all decisions in relation to reviews in the presence of the detainee, unless he/she is incapable of understanding what is said, violent or likely to become violent, or in urgent need of medical attention (Sch. 8, para. 28). These provisions obviously mirror those in PACE.

> **KEYNOTE**
>
> Where a review officer authorises continued detention, he/she shall inform the detained person—
>
> (a) of any of his/her rights under paras. 6 and 7 which he/she has not yet exercised; and
> (b) if the exercise of any of his/her rights under either of those paragraphs is being delayed in accordance with the provisions of para. 8, of the fact that it is being delayed.
>
> (see Sch. 8, para. 27(1))

17.6 **Extending Detention**

This area of legislation has received much attention since the suicide bomb attacks in London tube stations. An extended period of detention was provided for under the Terrorism Act 2000 of a maximum time of 14 days. Following the attacks in London, the Home Office attempted to extend this period originally to 60 days; however, this was defeated in the House of Lords. The general consensus was that 14 days was insufficient time in order to deal with complex cases relating to the detention of terrorist suspects; however, the Lords challenged the Home Office to show it was necessary to extend this period to 60 days.

During the passage through Parliament of the Terrorism Act 2006, the Government agreed to produce a Code of Practice for the detention of terrorist suspects arrested under s. 41 of the Terrorism Act 2000, before commencing the provisions of the 2006 Act that would extend the maximum period of pre-charge detention from 14 days to 28 days. Home Office Circular 23/2006 (Detention of Terrorist Suspects under Section 41 of the Terrorism Act 2000), published in July 2006, introduced a new Code H to the PACE *Codes of Practice* to outline these provisions.

But this was not the end of the matter. There was a provision attached to the above changes, which meant that the 28-day detention limit would lapse after one year. It was presumed that the Government would be in a position to pass this legislation during this period, but it was not to be. In July 2007, The Terrorism Act 2006 (Disapplication of Section 25) Order 2007 (SI 2007/2181) was implemented in order to extend the provision of a 28-day detention limit until July 2008, unless a further order is made.

In January 2008, the Government published its Counter-Terrorism Bill. The purpose of the Bill, amongst other things, is to make further provision about the detention and questioning of terrorist suspects and the prosecution and punishment of terrorist offences. The Bill proposes to extend the maximum period of detention to 42 days, in seven-day blocks, with provisions after 28 days from the relevant time have elapsed for the Secretary of State to inform Parliament as soon as practicable. This Bill, which proposed to extend the maximum period of detention to 42 days, has been rejected by the House of Lords, therefore, the maximum permissible dentention period under the Terrorism Act remains at 28 days for the time being.

17.6.1 Legislative provisions

Section 41(3) Terrorism Act 2000

Subject to s. 41(4) to (7), a person detained under this section shall (unless detained under any other power) be released not later than the end of the period of 48 hours beginning—

(a) with the time of his arrest under this section; *or*

(b) if he was being detained under Schedule 7 when he was arrested under this section, with the time when his examination under that Schedule began.

Code H, Para. 14.3

If detention is necessary for longer than 48 hours, a police officer of at least superintendent rank, or a Crown Prosecutor, may apply for warrants of further detention under the Terrorism Act 2000, Schedule 8, Part III.

17.6.2 Basic period of detention

In contrast to people who have been detained for offences under PACE (where a person's basic period of detention is 24 hours), s. 41(3) of the Terrorism Act 2000 above allows for a person being dealt with under that Act to be detained for a basic period of up to 48 hours, beginning either:

- with the time of their arrest; *or*
- with the time that a person's examination began under Sch. 7 of the Act.

KEYNOTE

Note, Sch. 7 relates to the examination and detention of people at ports and border controls, who are suspected of being concerned in the commission, preparation or instigation of acts of terrorism.

17.7 Warrants of Further Detention

17.7.1 Legislative provisions

Code H, Note for Guidance 14C

Applications for warrants to extend detention beyond 48 hours may be made for periods of 7 days at a time, up to a maximum period of 28 days from the time of arrest (or if a person was being detained under TACT Schedule 7, from the time at which the examination under Schedule 7 began).

Applications may be made for shorter periods than 7 days, which must be specified. The judicial authority may also substitute a shorter period if it feels a period of 7 days is inappropriate.

17.7.2 **Application for a warrant of further detention**

Application may be made to extend a person's detention under TACT, beyond the initial 48 hours. Applications may be made for *maximum* periods of seven days at a time, depending on the view of the judicial authority.

Previously, only a superintendent could make such an application, but this has now been extended to Crown Prosecutors.

Generally, applications for warrants that would take the total period of detention up to 14 days or less should be made to a judicial authority, meaning a District Judge (Magistrates' Court) designated by the Lord Chancellor to hear such applications (Code H, Note for Guidance 14D).

Any application for a warrant which would take the period of detention *beyond* 14 days from the time of arrest (or if a person was being detained under TACT Sch. 7, from the time at which the examination under Sch. 7 began), must be made to a High Court Judge (Code H, Note for Guidance 14E).

However, Note for Guidance 14F states that if an application has been made to a High Court judge for a warrant which would take detention beyond 14 days, and the High Court judge instead issues a warrant for a period of time which would *not* take detention beyond 14 days, further applications for extension of detention must also be made to a High Court judge, regardless of the period of time to which they refer.

17.7.3 **Notice of rights**

Under Note for Guidance 14G, a notice must be given to the detained person if a warrant is sought for further detention. This must be provided before the judicial hearing of the application for that warrant and must include:

(a) notification that the application for a warrant has been made;

(b) the time at which the application was made;

(c) the time at which the application is to be heard;

(d) the grounds on which further detention is sought.

A notice must also be provided each time an application is made to extend an existing warrant.

When an application for a warrant of further or extended detention is sought under this Act, the detained person and their representative must be informed of their rights in respect of the application, which include:

(a) the right to a written or oral notice of the warrant;

(b) the right to make oral or written representations to the judicial authority about the application;

(c) the right to be present and legally represented at the hearing of the application, unless specifically excluded by the judicial authority;

(d) their right to free legal advice.

(Code H, para. 14.4)

17.7.4 **Timing of the application**

As with an application for a warrant of further detention under ss. 43 or 44 of PACE, the timing of an application under the Terrorism Act 2000 needs to be thought out carefully. Paragraph 30(1) states that the application for further detention has to be made either during the initial period of detention, i.e. 48 hours, or within six hours of the end of that period.

Therefore, if a person's initial 48 hours is due to expire in the middle of the night, the superintendent will have to make the application during the initial 48 hours, unless there is a court sitting within six hours of the end of that period (i.e. first thing in the morning).

KEYNOTE

It should be noted that the provisions of Code C, Note for Guidance 15D (which states that an application for a warrant of further detention under s. 43 and s. 44 of PACE should normally be made between the hours of 10 am to 9 pm), do not appear to apply to applications for similar extensions under the Terrorism Act 2000. Theoretically, such an application may be made at any time of the day or night.

KEYNOTE

For the purposes of Sch. 8, an application for a warrant is made when written or oral notice of an intention to make the application is given to a judicial authority (see para. 30(3)).

It would seem that the paragraph in the Keynote above has been introduced to allow for the fact that the detainee may be delayed in court cells, waiting for the application to be made, or may not be present at the hearing (see para. 33(3) below).

The judicial authority hearing an application will dismiss the application if he/she considers that it would have been reasonably practicable to make it during the initial 48 hours (para. 30(2)).

17.7.5 **Court hearings**

Under Sch. 8, para. 32(1) of TACT, a judicial authority may issue a warrant of further detention only if satisfied that:

(a) there are reasonable grounds for believing that the further detention of the person to whom the application relates is necessary to obtain relevant evidence whether by questioning him or otherwise to preserve relevant evidence; and

(b) the investigation in connection with which the person is detained is being conducted diligently and expeditiously.

'Relevant evidence' means, in relation to the person to whom the application relates, evidence which:

- relates to his/her commission of an offence under any of the provisions mentioned in s. 40(1)(a); *or*
- indicates that he is a person falling within s. 40(1)(b).

Under Sch. 8, para. 33(1) of TACT, the detainee is entitled to make oral or written representations at a hearing and be legally represented. Paragraph 33(2) requires the judicial authority to adjourn the hearing of an application to enable the person to whom the application relates to obtain legal representation where:

- he is not legally represented; *and*
- he is entitled to be legally represented; *and*
- he wishes to be so represented.

However, an officer may apply for an order, under TACT Sch. 8, para. 34, to withhold specified information on which he intends to rely when applying for a warrant of further detention. This application may be made orally or in writing. The most appropriate method of application will depend on the circumstances of the case and the need to ensure fairness to the detainee.

In addition, under para. 32(3), a judicial authority may exclude any of the following persons from any part of the hearing:

(a) the person to whom the application relates;

(b) anyone representing him.

The subsection above differs greatly from an application under s. 43 or s. 44 of PACE, where the application must be made in open court, and the accused must be allowed to be present and legally represented. Under the Terrorism Act 2000, the presence of the detainee at the court may cause a substantial risk to national security.

The issue of whether the detained person and his solicitor should be present at a hearing to determine whether or not to extend a period of detention under the Terrorism Act 2000 Sch. 8, paras. 31 to 34, and para. 36 was examined in *Christopher Owen Ward* v *Police Service of Northern Ireland* [2007] UKHL 50.

In this case, the claimant challenged the judge's use of the power conferred by para. 33(3) in excluding the detained person from court while establishing whether the test for an extension had been met. This was the third request for an extension by the police, who wished to interview Ward about five outstanding topics. The judge wished to be satisfied that the topics were new and had agreed to exclude Ward and his solicitor from the hearing for 10 minutes so that the matter could be explored in detail in their absence. The extension had been granted without Ward or his solicitor being informed of what had transpired during their absence. Ward claimed that, in excluding him from the proceedings, the judge had acted outside the powers conferred on him by Sch. 8, para. 33.

It was held that the judge had acted legally in doing so and that the police were under no general duty to disclose their case to the defence at an application hearing to extend detention.

KEYNOTE

Where facilities exist, hearings relating to extension of detention may take place using video conferencing facilities provided that the requirements set out in Sch. 8 are still met.

However, if the judicial authority requires the detained person to be physically present at any hearing, this should be complied with as soon as practicable.

(Code H, Note for Guidance 14I)

17.8 **Transfer of Detained Persons to Prison**

17.8.1 **Legislative provisions**

Code H, Para. 14.5

Where a warrant is issued which authorises detention beyond a period of 14 days from the time of arrest (or if a person was being detained under TACT Schedule 7, from the time at which the examination under Schedule 7 began), the detainee must be transferred from detention in a police station to detention in a designated prison as soon as is practicable, unless:

(a) the detainee specifically requests to remain in detention at a police station and that request can be accommodated; or

(b) there are reasonable grounds to believe that transferring a person to a prison would:

    (i)   significantly hinder a terrorism investigation;

    (ii) delay charging of the detainee or his release from custody; or

    (iii) otherwise prevent the investigation from being conducted diligently and expeditiously.

17.8.2 **Transferring the detainee**

The transfer to prison of a detainee under this Code is intended to ensure that individuals who are detained for extended periods of time are held in a place designed for longer periods of detention than police stations. Prison will provide detainees with a greater range of facilities more appropriate to longer detention periods. However, under para. 14.5 above, it is recognised that there may be occasions when it is unsuitable to do so because it may harm the investigation. Note that the detainee may choose not to be transferred also.

If any of the grounds in (b)(i) to (iii) above are relied upon, these must be presented to the judicial authority as part of the application for the warrant that would extend detention beyond a period of 14 days from the time of arrest (or if a person was being detained under TACT Sch. 7, from the time at which the examination under Sch. 7 began).

> **KEYNOTE**
>
> If a person remains in detention at a police station under a warrant of further detention as described at s. 14.5, they must be transferred to a prison as soon as practicable after the grounds at (b)(i) to (iii) of that paragraph cease to apply (Code H, para. 14.6). (See **flow chart 13 in Appendix 1** for an easy guide).

Code H, para. 14.7 states that the police should maintain an agreement with the National Offender Management Service (NOMS) that stipulates named prisons to which individuals may be transferred under this section. This should be made with regard to ensuring detainees are moved to the most suitable prison for the purposes of the investigation and their welfare, and should include provision for the transfer of male, female and juvenile detainees.

Police should ensure that the Governor of a prison to which they intend to transfer a detainee is given reasonable notice of this. Where practicable, this should be no later than the point at which a warrant is applied for that would take the period of detention beyond 14 days.

The *Codes of Practice* relating to the transfer of detainees to prison place a duty on the custody officer and the investigation team to provide as much information as necessary to enable the relevant prison authorities to provide appropriate facilities to detain an individual. This should include, but not be limited to:

- medical assessments;
- security and risk assessments;
- details of the detained person's legal representatives;
- details of any individuals from whom the detained person has requested visits, or who have requested to visit the detained person.

KEYNOTE

Under para. 14.10, where a detainee is to be transferred to prison, the custody officer should inform the detainee's legal adviser beforehand that the transfer is to take place (including the name of the prison) and make all reasonable attempts to inform family or friends who have been informed previously of the detainee's detention and the person who was initially informed of the detainee's detention when it was first authorised.

Where a person has been transferred to a designated prison, he or she will no longer be subject to the PACE *Codes of Practice*; their detention will instead be governed by the terms of Sch. 8 and Prison Rules (Code H, para. 14.8). Code H will re-apply if a detained person is transferred back from prison detention to police detention. The police have a responsibility to give notice to the prison Governor as soon as possible of any decision to transfer a detainee from prison back to a police station.

KEYNOTE

Note that any transfer between a prison and a police station should be conducted by police, and Code H will apply during the period of transit in respect of the conditions of detention. There is no requirement to provide such things as bed linen or reading materials for the journey between prison and police station.

17.9 **Charging Detainees**

Code H, para. 15.1 states that the charging of a person detained under TACT is covered by PACE. Any charge under the Act will be for a criminal offence and all the usual conditions will apply in respect of cautioning and providing the detainee with a copy of the charge (except that the document will not contain the identity of the person charging or the officer in the case—see Code H, para. 2.8).

However, it should be noted that there is no provision for bailing a person under TACT (Code H, para. 1.6). Therefore, detainees must either be released without charge or detained under the Act. Of course, it may be appropriate for the Secretary of State to make a control order against the individual under s. 1(2)(b) of the Prevention of Terrorism Act 2005 when he or she is released. Alternatively, it may be possible for the police to continue with another relevant offence under PACE, in which case, the normal PACE conditions of charging and bailing apply.

17.10 **Identification and Samples**

Many of the powers to obtain fingerprints, non-intimate samples and intimate samples under the Terrorism Act 2000 mirror those under ss. 61, 62 and 63 of PACE. The main difference between the two Acts is the fact that authorisations under TACT must be granted by a superintendent, whereas authorisations under PACE may be granted by inspectors.

The main powers to take samples under Sch. 8 of TACT are:

- Fingerprints or non-intimate samples may be taken from the detained person only if they are taken by a constable with the appropriate consent given in writing, or without that consent (para. 10(2)–(3)).

- Fingerprints or a non-intimate sample may be taken from the detained person without the appropriate consent only if—

  (a) he/she is detained at a police station and a police officer of at least the rank of superintendent authorises the fingerprint or sample to be taken; or

  (b) he/she has been convicted of a recordable offence and, where a non-intimate sample is to be taken, he was convicted of the offence on or after 10 April 1995 (para. 10(4)).

- An intimate sample may be taken from the detained person only if—

  (a) he/she is detained at a police station;

  (b) the appropriate consent is given in writing;

  (c) a police officer of at least the rank of superintendent authorises the sample to be taken; and

  (d) subject to para. 13(2) and (3), the sample is taken by a constable (para. 10(5)).

- Subject to para. 10(6A), an officer may give an authorisation under sub-para. (4)(a) or (5)(c) only if—

  (a) in the case of a person detained under s. 41 of TACT, the officer reasonably suspects that the person has been involved in an offence under any of the provisions mentioned in s. 40(1)(a), and the officer reasonably believes that his fingerprints or sample will tend to confirm or disprove his involvement; *or*

  (b) in any case, the officer is satisfied that the taking of the fingerprints or sample from the person is necessary in order to assist in determining whether he/she falls within s. 40(1)(b) (para. 10(6)).

- An officer may also give an authorisation under sub-para. (4)(a) for the taking of fingerprints if—

  (a) he/she is satisfied that the fingerprints of the detained person will facilitate the ascertainment of that person's identity; and

  (b) that the person has refused to identify himself or herself, or the officer has reasonable grounds for suspecting that the person is not who he/she claims to be (para. 10(6A)).

- Where appropriate written consent to the taking of an intimate sample from a person under para. 10 or 12 is refused without good cause, in any proceedings against that person for an offence—the court or jury, in determining whether to commit him/her for trial, or whether there is a case to answer, or whether that person is guilty of the offence charged, may draw such inferences from the refusal as appear proper (para. 13(1)).

- An intimate sample other than a sample of urine or a dental impression may be taken under para. 10 or 12 only by a registered medical practitioner acting on the authority of a constable (para. 13(2)).

- An intimate sample which is a dental impression may be taken under para. 10 or 12 only by a registered dentist acting on the authority of a constable (para. 13(3)).

KEYNOTE

The provisions of s. 63B of the Police and Criminal Evidence Act 1984 (testing persons for the presence of Class A drugs) do not apply to people detained under TACT. Guidance on these provisions can be found in **Chapter 12—Identification and Samples**.

17.11 **Documentation**

Code H, para. 14 contains the provisions for recording activity for TACT detainees and generally mirrors PACE. It is the responsibility of the officer who gives any reminders as at para. 14.4 (see **17.7.3 Notice of rights** above) to ensure that these are noted in the custody record, as well any comments made by the detained person upon being told of those rights.

The grounds for, and extent of, any delay in conducting a review shall be recorded and any written representations shall be retained. Also, a record shall be made as soon as practicable about the outcome of each review or determination whether to extend the maximum detention period without charge or an application for a warrant of further detention or its extension.

Any decision not to transfer a detained person to a designated prison under para. 14.5 must be recorded, along with the reasons for this decision. If a request under para. 14.5(a) is not accommodated, the reasons for this should also be recorded (see **17.8.1 Legislative provisions** above).

17.12 **Summing Up**

Entitlements

1. A direction may be given by a Commander or an Assistant Chief Constable, that a detained person who wishes to exercise the right under para. 7 may consult a solicitor only in the sight and hearing of a qualified officer.

(Schedule 8, para. 9(1), Terrorism Act 2000)

2. A 'qualified officer' means a police officer who is a uniformed inspector, who has no connection with the detained person's case.

3. A superintendent may either authorise a delay:

    *   in notifying a person of the detainee's arrest; *or*

    *   in access to legal advice;

    of a period not longer than 48 hours beginning with the time of his/her arrest (as opposed to 36 hours where a person has been detained under PACE).

(Schedule 8, para. 8(1), Terrorism Act 2000)

4. Authorisation may be given if the consequences are likely to lead to the provisions of Annex B, *or:*
    interference with the gathering of information about the commission, preparation or instigation of acts of terrorism;

    *   the alerting of a person and thereby making it more difficult to prevent an act of terrorism; *and*

- the alerting of a person and thereby making it more difficult to secure a person's apprehension, prosecution or conviction in connection with the commission, preparation or instigation of an act of terrorism.

Reviews

1. In the case of a review carried out within a period of 24 hours beginning with the time of arrest, the review officer shall be an officer of at least the rank of inspector. In the case of any other review, the review officer shall be an officer of at least the rank of superintendent.

(Schedule 8, para. 24(2)–(3))

2. The first review shall be carried out as soon as is reasonably practicable after the time of the person's arrest. Subsequent reviews shall be carried out at intervals of not more than 12 hours.

(Schedule 8, para. 21(2)–(3))

3. Irrespective of whether the reviewing officer is an inspector or a superintendent, a review under TACT must be done in person.

(Code H, para. 14.1)

Extending detention

1. A person detained under TACT shall (unless detained under any other power) be released not later than the end of the period of 48 hours beginning—

    (a) with the time of his arrest under this section; *or*

    (b) if he was being detained under Schedule 7 when he was arrested under this section, with the time when his examination under that Schedule 7 began.

(Section 41(3) Terrorism Act 2000)

2. If detention is necessary for longer than 48 hours, a police officer of at least superintendent rank, or a Crown Prosecutor, may apply for warrants of further detention under the Terrorism Act 2000, Sch. 8, Part III.

(Code H, para. 14.3)

Warrants of further detention

1. Applications for warrants to extend detention beyond 48 hours may be made for periods of seven days at a time, up to a maximum period of 28 days from the time of

arrest (or if a person was being detained under TACT Sch. 7, from the time at which the examination under Sch. 7 began).

Applications may be made for periods shorter than seven days, which must be specified. The judicial authority may also substitute a shorter period if it feels a period of seven days is inappropriate.

(Code H, Note for Guidance 14C)

2. Generally, applications for warrants that would take the total period of detention up to 14 days or less should be made to a judicial authority (a District Judge designated by the Lord Chancellor).

(Code H, Note for Guidance 14D)

3. An application which would take the period of detention *beyond* 14 days from the time of arrest must be made to a High Court Judge.

(Code H, Note for Guidance 14E)

4. A judicial authority may exclude the following persons from the hearing:

    (a) the person to whom the application relates;

    (b) anyone representing him.

(Schedule 8, para. 33(3) Terrorism Act 2000)

Transfer of detained persons to prison

Where a warrant is issued which authorises detention beyond a period of 14 days from the time of arrest, the detainee must be transferred from police detention to a designated prison as soon as is practicable, unless:

(a) the detainee specifically requests to remain in detention at a police station and that request can be accommodated; or

(b) there are reasonable grounds to believe that transferring a person to a prison would:

    (i) significantly hinder a terrorism investigation;

    (ii) delay charging of the detainee or his release from custody; or

    (iii) otherwise prevent the investigation from being conducted diligently and expeditiously.

(Code H, para. 14.5)

Identification and samples

1. Generally powers to take samples are the same as under PACE. However, under the Terrorism Act 2000, authorisations to take samples may only be given by a superintendent, whereas under PACE they may be granted by an inspector.

2. There are no powers to test a TACT detainee for the presence of Class A drugs (under s. 63B of the Police and Criminal Evidence Act 1984).

LOCAL PROCEDURES

1. Does your force have a designated, secure custody office, which may be used in the event of TACT arrests in their area?

2. Are custody officers specifically trained in the handling of such detainees?

3. Do you have a custody office designed to minimise the risk relating to forensic issues?

SPACE FOR NOTES

SPACE FOR NOTES

SPACE FOR NOTES

18

Interviewing

18.1 **Introduction**

The subject of interviews is covered in Code C, paras. 11 and 12 of *Codes of Practice*. Paragraph 11 relates mainly to conducting the interviews themselves, whereas para. 12 deals with custody officers' duties. This chapter will concentrate mainly on para. 12.

The interview is an important part of the custody process and custody officers and investigating officers must abide by the *Codes of Practice*, to ensure that vital admissions or inferences are not lost. Therefore, custody officers must understand the process surrounding these *Codes*.

This chapter will also examine the relationship between custody officers and medical healthcare professionals and the type of advice custody officers can expect to be given.

Paragraph 12 deals with interviewing vulnerable suspects, which inevitably means there will be some overlap between subjects, particularly with **Chapter 7—Vulnerable People and Appropriate Adults**. Where there is an overlap, chapters have been cross-referenced. The issue of 'Rest Periods' actually started in **Chapter 5—Conditions of Detention**, so it is easy to see the close relationship between the various *Codes of Practice*.

It should also be noted that **Chapter 6—The Detainee's Entitlements** deals with the subject of authorisation to interview without a solicitor; again there is an overlap with this chapter.

The overall message from this chapter is that once again, the custody officer has to strike the right balance between the detainee's welfare considerations and the needs of the investigating officer. If this balance is struck, there should be no reason for interviews to be excluded at court hearings for being inadmissible because of a lack of consideration for the detainee's needs.

The Human Rights Act 1998

This chapter deals mainly with interviewing and the role of the custody officer in assessing when a person may be fit for interview. The interview itself will not be conducted by the custody officer; however, it is worth noting that the human rights of a detainee may be interfered with if an interview is considered to be excessively oppressive.

Article 3 of the 1998 Act deals with inhuman or degrading treatment or punishment, which may be apparent in an oppressive interview. However, with audibly recorded interviews, one would hope that such issues are rare these days. Of course, if a custody officer authorises the interview of a detainee who is unfit, or rest periods are interfered with, that person's human rights may still be affected if correct procedure is not followed.

18.2 **The Role of the Custody Officer**

18.2.1 **Legislative provisions**

Code C, Para. 12.1

If a police officer wishes to interview, or conduct enquiries which require the presence of a detained person, the custody officer is responsible for deciding whether to deliver him into his custody.

18.2.2 **The custody officer as a manager**

The custody officer is in overall charge of managing the custody office. This includes deciding when to deliver the detainee for interview.

Code C, para 12.1 above is clear in relation to who is the decision-maker in the custody office. The custody officer will often need to be firm with the investigating officer, so that a balance is reached between what is best for the detainee and what is best for the investigation.

18.3 **Fitness to be Interviewed**

18.3.1 **Legislative provisions**

Code C, Para. 12.3

Before a detainee is interviewed the custody officer, in consultation with the officer in charge of the investigation and appropriate health care professionals as necessary, shall assess whether the detainee is fit enough to be interviewed. This means determining and considering the risks to the detainee's physical and mental state if the interview took place and determining what safeguards are needed to allow the interview to take place (see Annex G). The custody officer shall not allow a detainee to be interviewed if the custody officer considers it would cause significant harm to the detainee's physical or mental state. Vulnerable suspects listed at para. 11.18 shall be treated as always being at some risk during an interview and these persons may not be interviewed except in accordance with paras. 11.18 to 11.20.

Code C, Para. 11.18(b)

The following persons may not be interviewed unless an officer of superintendent rank or above considers delay will lead to the consequences in paras. 11.1(a)–(c), and is satisfied the interview would not significantly harm the person's physical or mental state:

(b) a person who, at the time of the interview, appears unable to:

  • appreciate the significance of questions and their answers; *or*

  • understand what is happening because of the effects of drinks drugs or any illness, ailment or condition.

18.3.2 **Initial consultation**

Most of the people detained in a custody office will automatically be declared fit for interview by the custody officer and will present no particular problems. However, some detainees will be unfit on their arrival, because of either drink or drugs, or their mental state. People who are unfit will normally be identified as such when they first arrive, and it will be for the custody officer to determine when they become fit and ready to be interviewed (see Code C, para. 12.3 above). (See **flow chart 14 in Appendix 1** for an easy guide.)

In determining whether a person is fit for interview, the custody officer may consult with the investigating officer and, in most cases, speak to the detainee. If there are still doubts about the detainee's fitness, the custody officer should consult with the appropriate healthcare professional. This is particularly important if the person has been unfit for some time. Some force areas have a rule that if a person is still unfit after six hours' detention, a healthcare professional should be consulted anyway.

The purpose of the consultation is to assess whether there would be a 'risk to the detainee's physical and mental state', if the interview were to take place. If a risk is identified, an action plan must be worked out to minimise any risk to the detainee.

The overriding aim of para. 12.3 is to ensure that custody officers do not allow a detainee to be interviewed, if the custody officer considers it would cause 'significant harm to the detainee's physical or mental state'.

The provisions of Annex G and paras. 11.18 to 11.20 deal with interviewing vulnerable suspects. For further details see **18.3.3 Interviewing vulnerable suspects** and **18.4 Annex G** below.

18.3.3 **Interviewing vulnerable suspects**

Once again, there is some overlap between chapters. **Chapter 7—Vulnerable People and Appropriate Adults** deals with para. 11.18, subs. (a) and (c) (interviews with vulnerable detainees without an appropriate adult being present).

However, para. 11.18(b) above relates to interviewing 'people who appear unable to understand what is happening because of the effects of drink, drugs or any illness, ailment or condition'.

KEYNOTE

Note that only a superintendent may authorise an interview in the above circumstances.

The authorising officer must be satisfied that the interview 'would not significantly harm the person's physical or mental state' and that a delay will lead to one of the consequences in Code C, para. 11.1, the wording of which should now be familiar:

'...the consequent delay would be likely to:

(a) lead to:

- interference with, or harm to, evidence connected with an offence;

- interference with, or physical harm to, other people;

- serious loss of, or damage to property;

(b) lead to alerting other people suspected of committing an offence but not yet arrested for it;

(c) hinder the recovery of property obtained in the consequence of the commission of an offence.'

In reaching a decision whether or not an interview should take place in these circumstances, the superintendent should consider the provisions of Code C, Annex G, which are discussed below.

18.4 **Annex G**

18.4.1 **Legislative provisions**

Code C, Annex G, para. 2

A detainee may be at risk in an interview if it is considered that:

(a) conducting the interview could significantly harm the detainee's physical or mental state;

(b) anything the detainee says in the interview about their involvement or suspected involvement in the offence about which they are being interviewed might be considered unreliable in subsequent court proceedings because of their physical or mental state.

Code C, Annex G, para. 7

The role of the healthcare professional is to consider the risks and advise the custody officer of the outcome of that consideration. The healthcare professional's determination and any advice or recommendations should be made in writing and form part of the custody record.

Code C, Annex G, para. 8

Once the healthcare professional has provided that information (in Code C, Annex G. para. 7 above), it is a matter for the custody officer to decide whether or not to allow the interview to go ahead and if the interview is to proceed, to determine what safeguards are needed.

Code C, Annex G, para. 6

When healthcare professionals identify risks they should be asked to quantify the risks. They should inform the custody officer:

- whether the person's condition:
  - is likely to improve
  - will require or be amenable to treatment, and
- indicate how long it may take for such improvement to take effect.

18.4.2 Assessing the detainee

Code C, Annex G contains general guidance to help police officers and healthcare professionals assess whether a detainee might be at risk in an interview. Code C, Annex G, para. 2 (see above) reinforces that a failure by the custody officer, or investigating officer, to abide by the *Codes of Practice* may lead to the interview being considered 'unreliable in subsequent court proceedings'. This, of course, may affect the whole outcome of the case.

In assessing whether the detainee is fit to be interviewed, the following must be considered:

(a) how the detainee's physical or mental state might affect their ability to understand the nature and purpose of the interview, to comprehend what is being asked and to appreciate the significance of any answers given and make rational decisions about whether they want to say anything;

(b) the extent to which the detainee's replies may be affected by their physical or mental condition rather than representing a rational and accurate explanation of their involvement in the offence;

(c) how the nature of the interview, which could include particularly probing questions, might affect the detainee.

If in any doubt, the custody officer must seek advice from the appropriate healthcare professional (see **18.4.3 The role of the healthcare professional** below).

18.4.3 **The role of the healthcare professional**

Healthcare professionals perform an increasingly vital role in relation to a person's detention. Apart from determining a person's physical state to be held in a custody office, the healthcare professional is integral to the decision-making process as to when a person will be deemed fit to be interviewed. Code C, Annex G offers considerable guidance to both custody officers and healthcare professionals on their respective roles.

Healthcare professionals should advise on the need for an appropriate adult to be present, whether re-assessment of the person's fitness for interview may be necessary if the interview lasts beyond a specified time, and whether a further specialist opinion may be required. It is intended that the relationship between the custody officer and the healthcare professional be one of consultation. However, the custody officer will be the eventual decision-maker (see Code C, Annex G, para. 8 above). The custody officer (or superintendent if the interview is urgent) should consider the advice from the healthcare professional and make an informed decision on whether to allow an interview to take place.

> **KEYNOTE**
>
> Any decision made, whether by a healthcare professional or police officer, must be recorded in the custody record (see Code C, Annex G, para. 7 above). The healthcare professional should write their own determination in the record or countersign the entry (see **3.5.1 Recognising 'at risk' detainees**, for the advice contained in Home Office Circular 28/2002 in respect of this issue).

One of the issues that will be of most concern to investigating officers is when the detainee will be fit for interview. Often, there will be a race against the clock and the custody officer will require firm guidance from the healthcare professional. Code C, Annex G, para. 6 above identifies what advice custody officers should expect from medical experts.

As well as being unfit for interview through drink or drugs, the detainee may also be unfit because of medication they have taken.

Consider the following:

Case Study

THOMAS was arrested on suspicion of murdering his wife, during a drunken domestic argument. THOMAS is an alcoholic and when he arrived at the custody office, he was extremely drunk. It was also believed that he had taken drugs before his arrest.

THOMAS was unfit for interview for the first 10 hours of his detention time and the custody officer contacted a police doctor to assess his condition. When he was examined, THOMAS declared that he usually took heavy doses of medication for his alcohol and drug addictions.

When he was eventually sober, the doctor prescribed medication for THOMAS. However, his legal representative now claimed that THOMAS was unfit for interview because of the medication.

....

In these circumstances, the custody officer will face pressure from the investigating officers, who will want to interview the detainee, as well as the legal representative, who may wish to delay the interview.

The custody officer will have to consult with all parties to make sure a balance is reached between what is best for the investigation, and what is best for the detainee. Any interview may be considered inadmissible if the detainee is unfit (unless Code C, para. 11.1 applies; see above).

In the above case study, the investigating officers will be able to apply for a superintendent's authority to extend detention, under s. 42 of PACE, to allow time for the detainee to be declared fit for interview.

Previously, the investigating officer would have encountered difficulties, if the detainee had been in custody for a less serious offence. However, applications may be made for an extension of detention under s. 42(1) of PACE in respect of any indictable offence. Details of these provisions can be found in **Chapter 11—Extending Detention.**

To ensure that the power under s. 42(1) is not abused, the *Codes of Practice* have been amended to protect the detainee's basic human rights and ensure that a delay under this section is only authorised for more serious offences. Code C, para. 5.7A states:

> any delay or denial of the rights in this section should be proportionate and should last no longer than necessary.

The circumstances in the case would probably meet the requirements under para. 5.7A above, and s. 42(1)(c) that the investigation was being conducted diligently and expeditiously. It is hardly the investigating officer's fault that the detainee is in such a condition.

KEYNOTE

Prior to the implementation of the Criminal Justice Act 2003, which provided that the superintendent's authority applied to all arrestable offences (of course, this has now been superseded by the Serious Organised Crime and Police Act 2005 referred to above), the Joint Home Office/Cabinet Office Review of PACE found that the initial period of 24 hours failed to provide sufficient investigative time because of delays elsewhere in the custody process. The review cited examples, such as obtaining the services of an appropriate adult, police surgeon, interpreter or solicitor, or where the suspect is initially unfit for interview because of intoxication through alcohol or drugs.

In its 'Options Proposed', the review recommended extending the maximum time for detention without charge from 24 to 36 hours for any arrestable offence (now indictable offence), to stop the custody clock as and when delays occurred and to re-start it when the delay ended. This would have the effect of extending the person's detention time by the time spent during the delay, which could later be added to the detainee's initial 24 hours detention time, thereby extending the period by that amount.

The first option described above was obviously accepted; however, the second option of stopping the clock was not.

Another option that could be considered is to have an appropriate healthcare professional present during the interview, in order to constantly monitor the person's condition and how it is being affected by the interview. This advice is contained in Code C, Annex G, para. 8.

Alternatively, the custody officer could consider bailing a detainee who may be considered to be fit to understand the bail procedure, if not questions in an interview; however, there is no guarantee that the person will answer bail in a sober condition, which would take us back to square one.

18.5 **Rest Periods**

18.5.1 **Legislative provisions**

Code C, Para. 12.2

In any period of 24 hours a detained person must be allowed a continuous period of at least 8 hours for rest, free from questioning, travel or any interruption by police officers in connection with the investigation concerned.

The period may not be interrupted or delayed, except:

(a)   when there are reasonable grounds for believing not delaying or interrupting the period would:

   (i)   involve a risk of harm to people or serious loss of, or damage to property;

   (ii)   delay unnecessarily the person's release from custody;

   (iii)   otherwise prejudice the outcome of the investigation;

(b)   at the request of the detainee, their appropriate adult or legal representative;

(c)   when a delay or interruption is necessary in order to:

   (i)   comply with the legal obligations and duties arising under s. 15;

   (ii)   to take action required under s. 9 or in accordance with medical advice.

18.5.2 **Continuous period of rest**

Code C, para. 12 deals with interviewing detained persons in police stations. This section also provides information about rest periods for detained persons (see para. 12.2 above), and therefore their welfare. Once again, the correct application of this section is crucial to the protection of a detainee's welfare, as well as their human rights.

Consider the following:

Case Study 1

PEARSON was arrested at 11.00pm for an offence of GBH, following a possible stabbing of a person outside a public house. He had been drinking heavily, and the custody officer temporarily withheld notifying him of his rights, as he was incapable of understanding. The custody officer also determined that PEARSON was unlikely to be fit for interview for some time and he was placed in a cell at 11.45pm.

What should be considered, in order to comply with the *Codes of Practice* relating to rest periods?

....

Custody officers should take care when deciding to 'bed down' detainees for the night, when they are as intoxicated as PEARSON clearly was in the case study. The temptation would be simply to allow the detainee to 'sleep off' the effects of the alcohol for the whole night. However, the balance must be met between allowing a completely uninterrupted period of rest, and ensuring the detainee is 'roused' regularly during the night.

KEYNOTE

Annex H of Code C now contains a Detained Persons Observation List—this issue is discussed in depth, in **Chapter 5—Conditions of Detention**.

Also, para. 12.2 above uses the term 'rest' and not sleep. This is important, as it is not necessary for the detainee to be asleep during his/her designated period of rest. Therefore, neither a detainee nor his/her solicitor may refuse to undergo an interview because the detainee chose not to sleep during that period.

The prime consideration of the custody officer should be the welfare of the detained person in these circumstances.

Returning to the scenario:

Case Study 2

The injured person was in hospital being treated for his injuries. The investigating officer intended going off duty at midnight, to return at 8.00am. She asked the custody officer if PEARSON could be ready for interview at that time. Because PEARSON was heavily intoxicated, the custody officer considered it necessary to call a police doctor. The doctor confirmed that PEARSON was fit to be detained, but unfit for inter-view. The doctor determined that PEARSON should be visited and roused at 30-minute intervals for at least two hours and then woken to be re-assessed.

How do the instructions from the doctor affect the request by the officer in the case to have the detainee ready for interview at 8.00am?

....

The custody officer may have arrived at this course of action without the need to consult a doctor, but whoever made the decision, there may be some impact on the designated period of rest and the subsequent interview/investigation process.

The effect of the doctor's decision was that PEARSON's period of rest would have been constantly interrupted for at least two hours during the night, in order to visit and rouse him. Also, after a two-hour period, PEARSON would have been woken and his condition re-assessed.

According to para. 12.2, there will be no need to allocate the detainee a fresh period of rest if he/she is being roused in order to comply with medical advice (see below for the situation when a fresh period of rest must be allocated). However, in the scenario, it is obvious that PEARSON's sleep pattern was interrupted while he was being roused, and it would be worth taking this into account when calculating the rest period.

As to when the detainee will be fit enough for interview, each case should be taken on its own merits. If the detainee is in custody for a simple offence that requires no interview the next day, these interruptions will pose no particular prob-lem. But if he/she is to be interviewed about a complicated or serious matter, it may be worth taking into account the fact that the rest period was interrupted con-stantly and possibly deferring the interview to a later time than requested by the arresting officer, to make sure the detainee is fully rested.

Returning to the scenario:

Case Study 3

At 1.30am, the investigating officer returned to the custody office and stated that the injured person had undergone surgery where it was discovered that he had actu-ally been shot and not stabbed as originally thought. Also, information had been received from a witness who saw PEARSON enter a school playing field after the shooting and immediately prior to his arrest. The investigating officer believed that PEARSON might have hidden a firearm in the field. A search team had failed to find the weapon because of the dark conditions, and the officer in the case requested that he be allowed to interview PEARSON in order to establish where the weapon was.

Considering PEARSON may still have been unfit for interview, and was undergoing a period of rest, what should the custody officer consider now?

1.   What enquiries may be carried out immediately?

2. When does the need to question the detainee during his period of rest become an issue?

....

Irrespective of whether or not he was undergoing a period of rest, there was a strong case for the investigating officer to conduct an 'urgent interview' with PEARSON, provided the appropriate authority was obtained (see **18.3.3 Interviewing vulnerable suspects**, above).

If we assume for the purposes of this scenario that permission was granted to conduct an urgent interview, what effect will the decision have had on PEARSON's period of rest? The presence of a firearm in a school playing field clearly represented a 'risk of harm to persons', and the interruption of the rest period was reasonable. However, how would the custody officer decide when it would be appropriate to conduct further interviews with PEARSON, once the danger from the firearm has been averted?

The answer to this question can be found in Code C, para. 12, which states that where a period of rest is interrupted in accordance with para. 12(a) (see above), a fresh period must be allowed. This is in contrast to the situation referred to in Case Study 2, when a fresh period of rest was not required when the detainee was being roused during the night.

The custody officer will now have to allocate PEARSON a fresh period of rest, taking account of the interruption from the interview. As to when the detainee will be fit, the sensible course of action would be for the custody officer to consult with the interviewing officer and the detainee's solicitor to come to a satisfactory conclusion. It makes little sense to prejudice the investigation by allowing the defence to call into question the validity of the interview because of sleep deprivation. Also, if detention time becomes an issue, it is likely that the period may be extended beyond 24 hours by a superintendent.

18.5.3 **Further interruption of rest periods**

A detainee's rest period may also be interrupted for the reasons outlined in Code C, para. 12.2(b)–(c) above. They fall under three categories:

- at the detainee's own request (or at the request of their appropriate adult or legal representative);
- in order to carry out duties under s. 40 and s. 42 of PACE (reviews and extensions of detention);
- in order to carry out duties under para. 9 of the *Codes of Practice* (clinical care of the detainee, visits and rousing detainees, medical advice).

KEYNOTE

Note that interruptions under para. 12.2 (b) and (c) do not require a fresh period of rest to be allowed.

Consider the following:

Case Study

PARKS has been arrested for an assault occasioning actual bodily harm. It is midnight and the custody officer has authorised detention to obtain evidence by questioning and to secure and preserve evidence. The injured person has attended the hospital but has not been detained. At 0030 hrs, the arresting officer, who is due to complete her tour of duty at 0100 hrs, states that she intends completing her enquiries at 0900 hrs and requests that the detainee be 'bedded down' for the night to allow him a period of uninterrupted rest.

What should the custody officer do in relation to this request?

....

Custody officers are faced with many different reasons for 'bedding down' a detainee at this time of the night, such as a lack of resources to deal with the case, a reluctance from the arresting officer to work overtime, no overtime has been authorised, and so it goes on. While all of these excuses may be genuine, none would justify the custody officer extending the detainee's detention until the following morning.

Under para. 12.2(ii), a person must be allowed a period of uninterrupted rest unless it would delay unnecessarily the person's release from custody. Quite simply, a detainee's period of rest may be interrupted if it means they are likely to be released from custody sooner.

In the circumstances given, if the custody officer is satisfied that the detainee should be interviewed about the offence now, he or she should not authorise continued detention until the next morning. If there are no other officers available to deal with the detainee, the custody officer should consider releasing the detainee on bail, provided his identity has been confirmed and it would not prejudice the enquiry.

Normally, the eight-hour period of rest referred to in para. 12.2 above commences from the time of a person's arrival at the station, unless the person has attended the station voluntarily.

18.6 **Other Matters Concerning Interviews**

There are some matters contained in Code C, para. 12 which directly affect the custody officer's duties relating to interviews—these matters will be examined in this final section.

18.6.1 **Legislative provisions**

Code C, Para. 12.5

A suspect whose detention without charge has been authorised under PACE, because the detention is necessary for an interview to obtain evidence of the offence for which they have been arrested, may choose not to answer questions but police do not require the suspect's consent or agreement to interview them for this purpose.

18.6.2 **Consent to interview**

It may seem odd, but the police do not need a person's consent to interview them, where their detention without charge has been authorised.

Code C, para. 12.5 also states that if a suspect takes steps to prevent themselves being questioned or further questioned, e.g. by refusing to leave their cell to go to a suitable interview room or by trying to leave the interview room, 'they shall be advised their consent or agreement to interview is not required'. The suspect should be cautioned and informed if they fail or refuse to co-operate, the interview may take place in the cell and that their failure or refusal to co-operate may be given in evidence. The suspect shall then be invited to co-operate and go into the interview room. Usually, in order to conduct a cell interview, the officer should take a portable tape recorder with them. This practice will provide better evidence of non-compliance than contemporaneous notes. Of course, if the cell is fitted with CCTV monitoring equipment and sound, all the better. See Code E, para. 3.4 for further advice.

18.6.3 **Welfare issues relating to interviews**

These are quite straightforward and can be summarised as follows:

- As far as practicable interviews shall take place in interview rooms which are adequately heated, lit and ventilated (Code C, para. 12.4).
- People being questioned or making statements shall not be required to stand (Code C, para. 12.6).

- Breaks from interviewing should be made at recognised meal times or at other times that take account of when an interviewee last had a meal. Short refreshment breaks shall be provided at approximately two-hour intervals (Code C, para. 12.8).
- Meal breaks should normally last at least 45 minutes and shorter breaks after two hours should last at least 15 minutes (Code C, Note for Guidance 12B).
- If there is a short interview, and another short interview is contemplated, the length of the break may be reduced if there are reasonable grounds to believe this is necessary to avoid any of the consequences in para. 12.8(i) to (iii) (Code C, Note for Guidance 12B).
- The interviewer has discretion to delay a break if there are reasonable grounds for believing it would:
    (i) involve a:
        - risk of harm to people;
        - serious loss of, or damage to, property;
    (ii) unnecessarily delay the detainee's release;
    (iii) otherwise prejudice the outcome of the investigation.
    (Code C, para. 12.8)
- If the interviewer delays a break in accordance with para. 12.8 above, and prolongs the interview, a longer break should be provided.
    (Code C, Note for Guidance 12B)

18.6.4 Documentation relating to interviews

Again, documentary issues are quite straightforward:

- Any decision to delay a break in an interview must be recorded, with reasons, in the interview record (Code C, para. 12.12).
- A record must be made of the:
    - time a detainee is not in the custody of the custody officer, and why;
    - reason for any refusal to deliver the detainee out of that custody.
    (Code C, para. 12.10)
- A record shall be made of:
    - the reasons it was not practicable to use an interview room; and
    - any action taken as in para. 12.5 (refusal to be interviewed).
    (Code C, para. 12.10)

18.7 **Summing Up**

Fitness to be interviewed

The custody officer has the responsibility for assessing whether a detainee is fit enough to be interviewed.

(Code C, para. 12.3)

Interviewing vulnerable suspects

A person who, at the time of the interview, appears unable to appreciate the significance of questions and their answers, or understand what is happening because of the effects of drinks drugs or any illness, ailment or condition may not be interviewed unless an officer of superintendent rank or above considers delay will lead to the consequences in paras. 11.1(a)–(c), and is satisfied the interview would not significantly harm the person's physical or mental state.

(Code C, para. 11.18(b)

Code C, para. 11.1 states:

'... the consequent delay would be likely to:

(a)   lead to:

    – interference with, or harm to, evidence connected with an offence;

    – interference with, or physical harm to, other people;

    – serious loss of, or damage to property;

(b)   lead to alerting other people suspected of committing an offence but not yet arrested for it;

(c)   hinder the recovery of property obtained in the consequence of the commission of an offence.'

The role of the healthcare professional

The role of the healthcare professional is to consider the risks and advise the custody officer of the outcome of that consideration. The healthcare professional's determination and any advice or recommendations should be made in writing and form part of the custody record.

(Code C, Annex G, para. 7)

Rest periods

In any period of 24 hours a detained person must be allowed a continuous period of at least eight hours for rest, free from questioning, travel or any interruption by police officers in connection with the investigation concerned.

The period may be interrupted or delayed when there are reasonable grounds for believing not delaying or interrupting the period would:

(i)   involve a risk of harm to people or serious loss of, or damage to, property;

(ii) delay unnecessarily the person's release from custody;

(iii) otherwise prejudice the outcome of the investigation.

(Code C, para. 12.2)

Cell interviews

Where a suspect is in detention without charge, his/her consent is not required to interview them. Cell interviews may be conducted for this purpose.

(Code C, para. 12.5)

SPACE FOR NOTES

SPACE FOR NOTES

SPACE FOR NOTES

Appendix 1

Flow Charts

1. Taking an Arrested Person to a Non-Designated Police Station

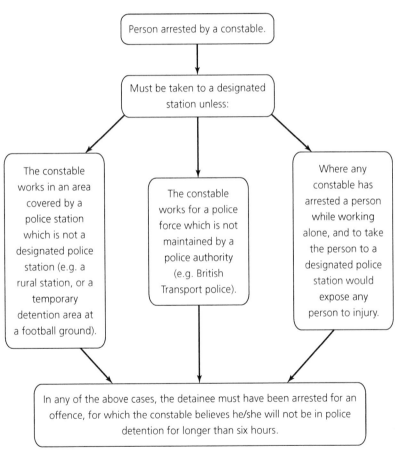

Person arrested by a constable.

Must be taken to a designated station unless:

The constable works in an area covered by a police station which is not a designated police station (e.g. a rural station, or a temporary detention area at a football ground).

The constable works for a police force which is not maintained by a police authority (e.g. British Transport police).

Where any constable has arrested a person while working alone, and to take the person to a designated police station would expose any person to injury.

In any of the above cases, the detainee must have been arrested for an offence, for which the constable believes he/she will not be in police detention for longer than six hours.

(See p. 10)

2. Sufficient Evidence to Charge (s. 37(7))

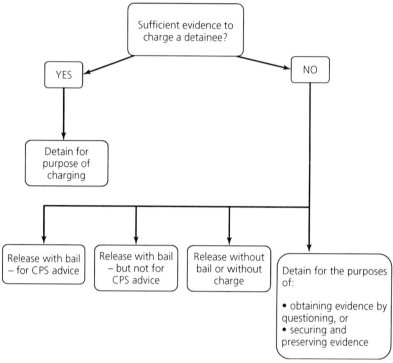

(See p. 28)

3. When Medical Attention Should be Arranged

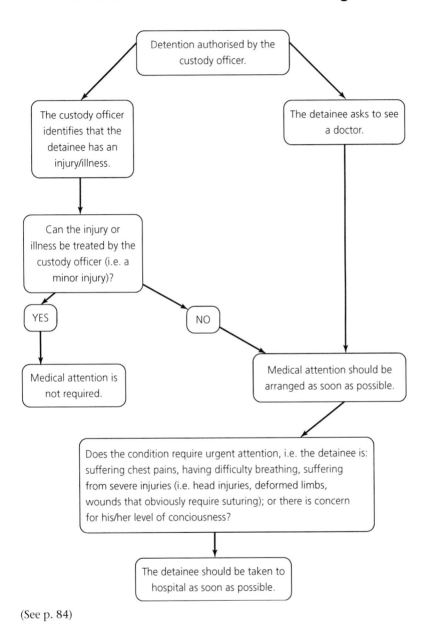

Detention authorised by the custody officer.

The custody officer identifies that the detainee has an injury/illness.

The detainee asks to see a doctor.

Can the injury or illness be treated by the custody officer (i.e. a minor injury)?

YES

NO

Medical attention is not required.

Medical attention should be arranged as soon as possible.

Does the condition require urgent attention, i.e. the detainee is: suffering chest pains, having difficulty breathing, suffering from severe injuries (i.e. head injuries, deformed limbs, wounds that obviously require suturing); or there is concern for his/her level of conciousness?

The detainee should be taken to hospital as soon as possible.

(See p. 84)

4. Delay in Notification of Arrest/Access to Solicitor (Annex B)

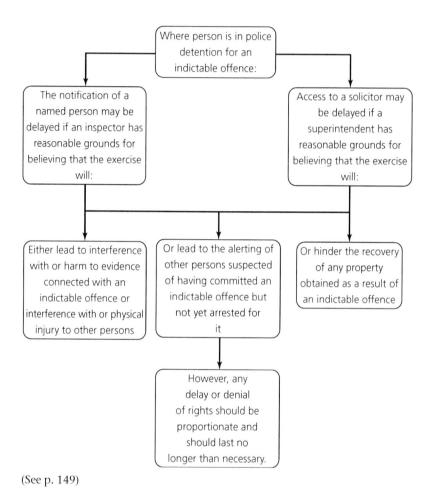

Where person is in police detention for an indictable offence:

The notification of a named person may be delayed if an inspector has reasonable grounds for believing that the exercise will:

Access to a solicitor may be delayed if a superintendent has reasonable grounds for believing that the exercise will:

Either lead to interference with or harm to evidence connected with an indictable offence or interference with or physical injury to other persons

Or lead to the alerting of other persons suspected of having committed an indictable offence but not yet arrested for it

Or hinder the recovery of any property obtained as a result of an indictable offence

However, any delay or denial of rights should be proportionate and should last no longer than necessary.

(See p. 149)

506

5. Authorising an Intimate Search

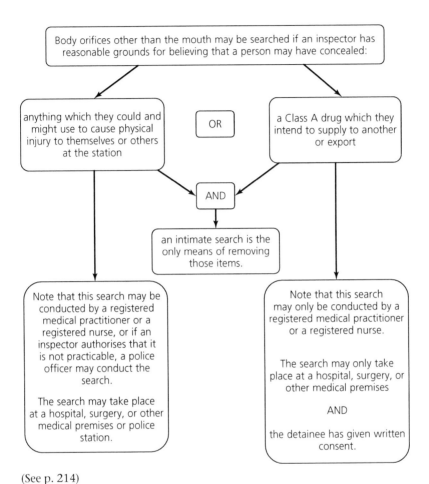

(See p. 214)

6. X-rays and Ultrasound Scans

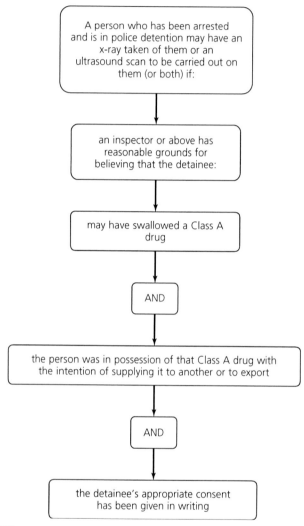

A person who has been arrested and is in police detention may have an x-ray taken of them or an ultrasound scan to be carried out on them (or both) if:

an inspector or above has reasonable grounds for believing that the detainee:

may have swallowed a Class A drug

AND

the person was in possession of that Class A drug with the intention of supplying it to another or to export

AND

the detainee's appropriate consent has been given in writing

(See p. 221)

7. Superintendent's Authority to Extend Detention (s. 42)

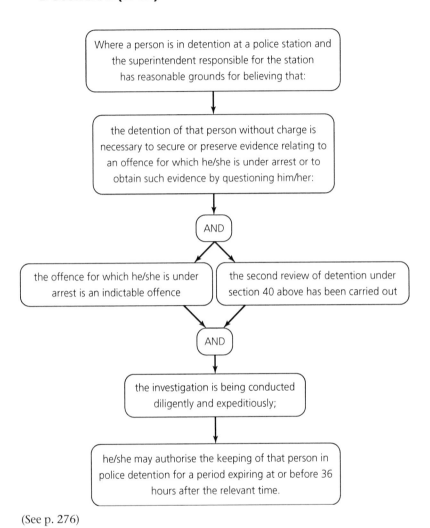

Where a person is in detention at a police station and the superintendent responsible for the station has reasonable grounds for believing that:

the detention of that person without charge is necessary to secure or preserve evidence relating to an offence for which he/she is under arrest or to obtain such evidence by questioning him/her:

AND

the offence for which he/she is under arrest is an indictable offence

the second review of detention under section 40 above has been carried out

AND

the investigation is being conducted diligently and expeditiously;

he/she may authorise the keeping of that person in police detention for a period expiring at or before 36 hours after the relevant time.

(See p. 276)

8. Warrant of Further Detention (s. 43)

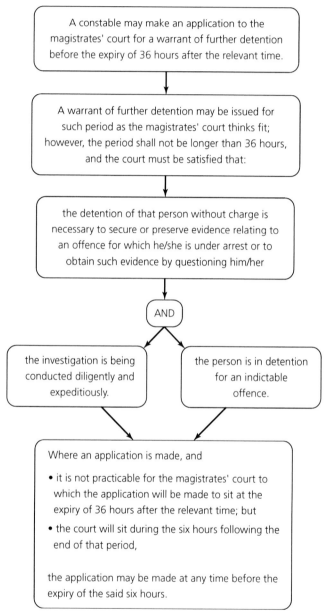

A constable may make an application to the magistrates' court for a warrant of further detention before the expiry of 36 hours after the relevant time.

A warrant of further detention may be issued for such period as the magistrates' court thinks fit; however, the period shall not be longer than 36 hours, and the court must be satisfied that:

the detention of that person without charge is necessary to secure or preserve evidence relating to an offence for which he/she is under arrest or to obtain such evidence by questioning him/her

AND

the investigation is being conducted diligently and expeditiously.

the person is in detention for an indictable offence.

Where an application is made, and

• it is not practicable for the magistrates' court to which the application will be made to sit at the expiry of 36 hours after the relevant time; but

• the court will sit during the six hours following the end of that period,

the application may be made at any time before the expiry of the said six hours.

(See p. 285)

510

9. Extension to Warrant of Further Detention (s. 44)

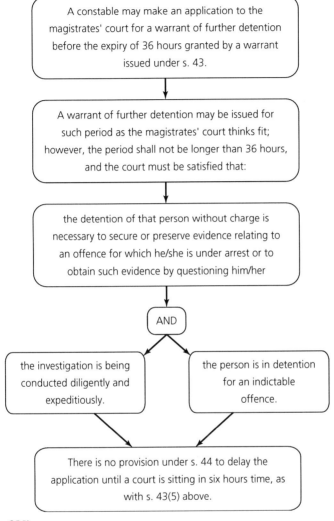

A constable may make an application to the magistrates' court for a warrant of further detention before the expiry of 36 hours granted by a warrant issued under s. 43.

A warrant of further detention may be issued for such period as the magistrates' court thinks fit; however, the period shall not be longer than 36 hours, and the court must be satisfied that:

the detention of that person without charge is necessary to secure or preserve evidence relating to an offence for which he/she is under arrest or to obtain such evidence by questioning him/her

AND

the investigation is being conducted diligently and expeditiously.

the person is in detention for an indictable offence.

There is no provision under s. 44 to delay the application until a court is sitting in six hours time, as with s. 43(5) above.

(See p. 290)

10. Taking Fingerprints Without Consent (s. 61)

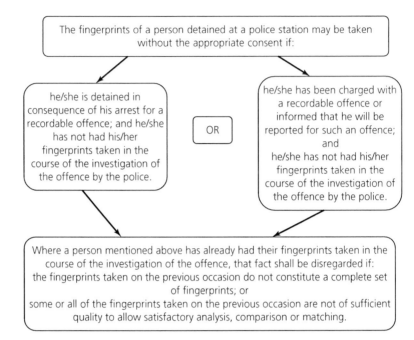

The fingerprints of a person detained at a police station may be taken without the appropriate consent if:

he/she is detained in consequence of his arrest for a recordable offence; and he/she has not had his/her fingerprints taken in the course of the investigation of the offence by the police.

OR

he/she has been charged with a recordable offence or informed that he will be reported for such an offence; and he/she has not had his/her fingerprints taken in the course of the investigation of the offence by the police.

Where a person mentioned above has already had their fingerprints taken in the course of the investigation of the offence, that fact shall be disregarded if:
the fingerprints taken on the previous occasion do not constitute a complete set of fingerprints; or
some or all of the fingerprints taken on the previous occasion are not of sufficient quality to allow satisfactory analysis, comparison or matching.

NOTE – A constable may also take a person's fingerprints without consent away from the police station if he/she reasonably suspects a person is committing or attempting to commit an offence; or has committed or attempted to commit an offence; and the person's name and address is unknown, and cannot be readily ascertained, or there are reasonable grounds for doubting whether the name and address are correct.

(See p. 301)

11. Testing for Presence of Class A Drugs (s. 63B)

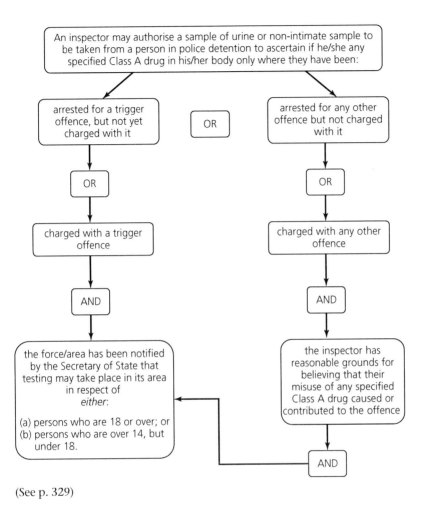

An inspector may authorise a sample of urine or non-intimate sample to be taken from a person in police detention to ascertain if he/she any specified Class A drug in his/her body only where they have been:

arrested for a trigger offence, but not yet charged with it

OR

arrested for any other offence but not charged with it

OR

OR

charged with a trigger offence

charged with any other offence

AND

AND

the force/area has been notified by the Secretary of State that testing may take place in its area in respect of *either*:

(a) persons who are 18 or over; or
(b) persons who are over 14, but under 18.

the inspector has reasonable grounds for believing that their misuse of any specified Class A drug caused or contributed to the offence

AND

(See p. 329)

513

12. Transfer of Juvenile Detainees to Local Authority Care (s. 38(6))

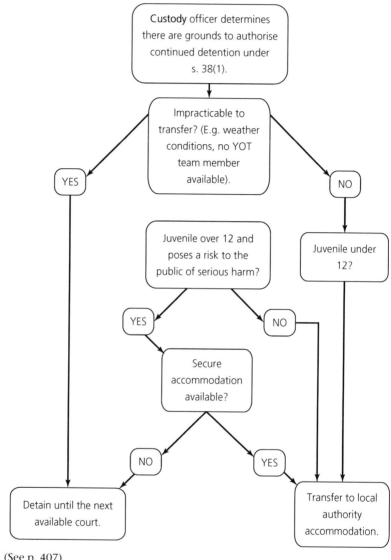

(See p. 407)

13. Transfer of Persons Detained under TACT to Prisons (Code H, para. 14.5)

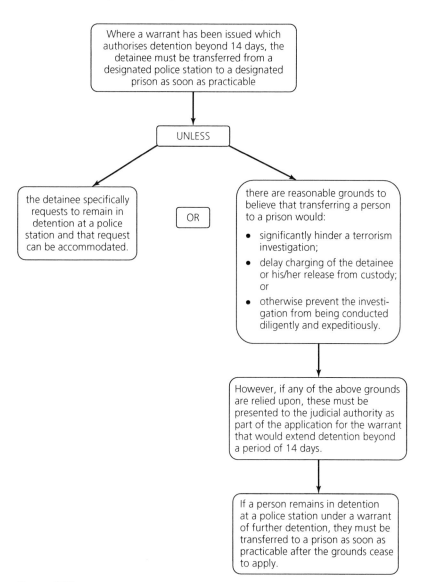

Where a warrant has been issued which authorises detention beyond 14 days, the detainee must be transferred from a designated police station to a designated prison as soon as practicable

UNLESS

the detainee specifically requests to remain in detention at a police station and that request can be accommodated.

OR

there are reasonable grounds to believe that transferring a person to a prison would:

- significantly hinder a terrorism investigation;
- delay charging of the detainee or his/her release from custody; or
- otherwise prevent the investigation from being conducted diligently and expeditiously.

However, if any of the above grounds are relied upon, these must be presented to the judicial authority as part of the application for the warrant that would extend detention beyond a period of 14 days.

If a person remains in detention at a police station under a warrant of further detention, they must be transferred to a prison as soon as practicable after the grounds cease to apply.

(See p. 472)

14. Fitness to be Interviewed (Code C, para. 11.18(b))

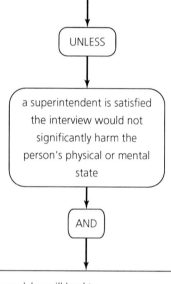

A person who appears unable to appreciate the significance of questions and their answers, or understand what is happening because of the effects of drink, drugs or any illness, ailment or condition, may not be interviewed

UNLESS

a superintendent is satisfied the interview would not significantly harm the person's physical or mental state

AND

that any delay will lead to:

– interference with, or harm to, evidence connected with an offence;
– serious loss of, or damage to, property;
– alerting other people suspected of committing an offence but not yet arrested for it;
– hindering the recovery of property obtained in the consequence of the commission of an offence.

(See p. 485)

Appendix 2

Home Office Circulars

Home Office Circular 13/2002—Deaths in Police Custody

1. This circular advises chief officers of new categories for the reporting of deaths of members of the public during or following police contact.

2. These guidelines replace the chief officer letter of 5 February 1996 which revised the categories of deaths in police custody in an attempt to ensure a distinction between those where there was direct contact with the police and those where it was less immediate.

3. Despite our best efforts at presentation, the whole set of deaths has still often been wrongly viewed as a homogeneous group when described in our annual statistical bulletin. The previous data can be misinterpreted to imply that the number of persons dying 'in custody' is much higher than is actually the case. There is also a clear inconsistency with the figures published by the Police Complaints Authority (PCA) who report separately, for example, deaths arising from road traffic incidents and shootings by the police. The divergence between the Home Office and PCA statistics is a regular cause of confusion and presentational difficulties.

4. Therefore, following a process of consultation, we have decided to introduce four specific categories covering deaths of members of the public during or following contact with the police. Full details are attached at Annex A. The revised categories have been agreed with ACPO, the Police Complaints Authority and the Police Staff Associations, and are as follows:

- *Fatal road traffic incidents involving the police*

This will include people who die in road accidents whilst attempting to avoid arrest and people who die in road traffic accidents involving the police. We currently include in our statistics cases where people die in road accidents whilst attempting to avoid arrest. This category can be difficult to define, particularly as it is sometimes doubtful whether those involved in the accident were aware of being pursued. Such incidents should be clearly distinguished from deaths in custody, while broadening the category to cover all fatal traffic incidents involving on duty police personnel will provide a more comprehensive picture.

This category does not affect the existing arrangements for reporting road traffic deaths to HM Inspectorate of Constabulary.

- *Fatal shooting incidents involving the police*

This will only include people who die where police officers fire the fatal shots. We currently include in our statistics deaths resulting from shooting incidents where police fire the fatal shots. These are not really deaths in police custody in any reasonable sense of the term and a separate category is warranted (shooting incidents where a person shoots himself, or another, whilst police officers are in attendance will be recorded under the category *'deaths during or following other types of contact with the police'* below).

- *Deaths in police custody*

This will include people who die who have been arrested or otherwise detained by the police and deaths occurring whilst a person is being arrested or taken into detention.

One important type of death to be retained within this category is where the person dies in or on the way to hospital following or during transfer from police detention. Many of those suffering injuries or other medical problems whilst in police custody are rightly moved to hospital, but it would distort the statistics if subsequent deaths were not recorded as taking place 'in custody'.

We are also including circumstances where the person dies after leaving police detention and there is a link between that detention and their death. These cases are small in number but frequently contentious. For example, where a person sustains a head injury prior to detention and a lack of care by police staff contributes to their death.

- *Deaths during or following other types of contact with the police*

This will include people who die during or after some form of contact with the police which did not amount to detention and there is a link between that contact and the death. For example, where the person is actively attempting to evade arrest and the death occurs otherwise than as the result of a road traffic accident, or where there is a siege situation or ambush and the person shoots himself or another.

The categories of deaths to be reported exclude:

- Those attending police stations as innocent visitors or witnesses who are not suspects;
- Those which occur in a police vehicle which is being used as an ambulance to transport a dying person to hospital quickly, but not under the circumstances described under the category *'Deaths in police custody'*;
- Those where police attend the scene of an incident where a person, who has not been detained, has received fatal injuries.

5. The revised definition should be used from 1 April 2002. Revised forms covering the details to be reported to the Home Office when there is a death of a member of the public during or following police contact are attached to this circular at Annex B. Part 1a has been introduced in line with the Race

Relations (Amendment) Act 2000. These forms are available electronically from John Unwin or Ann Carter.

john.unwin@homeoffice.gsi.gov.uk
ann.carter@homeoffice.gsi.gov.uk

6. Enquiries about this circular should be addressed to John Unwin/Ann Carter, Police Leadership and Powers Unit, 5th Floor, 50 Queen Anne's Gate, London SW1H 9AT (telephone 020 7273 2663/2698).

Annex A
Report of the Death of a Member of the Public During or Following Police Contact

Please read these notes carefully before completing a Part 1 report. Complete a Part 2 report and submit to the Home Office within 48 hours of the conclusion of the Inquest.

Definition of a Death of a Member of the Public During or Following Police Contact

A Part 1 report should be submitted to the Home Office within 48 hours of a death occurring in the following circumstances:

CATEGORY 1

Fatal road traffic incidents involving the police

This definition covers all deaths of members of the public resulting from road traffic incidents involving the police, both where the person who dies is in a vehicle and where they are on foot.

CATEGORY 2

Fatal shooting incidents involving the police

This definition covers circumstances where police fire the fatal shots.

CATEGORY 3

Deaths in or following custody

This definition covers the deaths of persons who have been arrested or otherwise detained by the police. It also includes deaths occurring whilst a person is being arrested or taken into detention. The death may have taken place on police, private or medical premises, in a public place or in a police or other vehicle.

Deaths in the following circumstances are amongst those covered by the definition:

- where the person dies in or on the way to hospital (or some other medical premises) following or during transfer from police detention;
- where the person dies after leaving police detention and there is a link between that detention and the death;

- where the person is being detained for the purposes of exercising a power to stop and search;
- where the death is of a child or young person detained for their own protection;
- where the person is in the care of the police having been detained under the Mental Health Act 1983;
- where the person is in police custody having been arrested by officers from a police force in Scotland exercising their powers of detention under section 137(2) of the Criminal Justice and Public Order Act 1994;
- where the person is in police custody having been arrested under section 3(5) of the Asylum and Immigration Appeals Act 1993;
- where the person is in police custody having been served a notice advising them of their detention under powers contained in the Immigration Act 1971;
- where the person is a convicted or remanded prisoner held in police cells on behalf of the Prison Service under the Imprisonment (Temporary Provisions) Act 1980.

CATEGORY 4

Deaths during or following other types of contact with the police

This definition covers circumstances where the person dies during or after some form of contact with the police which did not amount to detention and there is a link between that contact and the death.

Examples of deaths which would be covered by the definition are as follows:

- where the person is actively attempting to evade arrest and the death occurs otherwise than as the result of a road traffic incident;
- where there is a siege situation, including where a person shoots himself, or another, whilst police are in attendance;
- where a person is present at a demonstration and is struck by a police baton and subsequently dies.

Deaths which follow police contact but which are not linked to that contact would not be covered. For example:

- Those attending police stations as innocent visitors or witnesses who are not suspects;
- Those which occur in a police vehicle which is being used as an ambulance to transport a dying person to hospital quickly, but not under the circumstances described under the category 'Deaths in police custody';
- Those where police attend the scene of an incident where a person, who has not been detained, has received fatal injuries.

Notes

- The above categorisations cannot be considered completely exhaustive. Cases will still have to be considered individually to decide whether and how they should be recorded;
- The term 'police' includes police civilians as well as police officers;
- Deaths involving off-duty police personnel are not included.

Home Office Circular 32/2000—Minimum Standards for Risk Assessing Detainees

This Circular sets out minimum standards for risk assessment procedures to be applied to all detainees coming into police custody. It also introduces a *new version of the Prisoner Escort Record (PER) Form* and revised arrangements for its use. The form has been revised in the light of operational experience and is intended to be easier to interpret and complete. Its use will now be limited to occasions where a detainee is moved between locations and that will vastly reduce the number of forms which have to be completed.

Risk assessment

2 There is increasing recognition of the importance of conducting effective risk assessment in relation to all detainees entering police custody. Such procedures are essential to ensuring the safety and well-being of both detainees and police staff. Individual forces will have their own procedures but the *guidance at Annex A* covers the key risk factors which should be considered in every assessment and the key questions which should be asked of every detainee.

Revised PER Form and associated guidance

3 *The revised version of the PER Form is at Annex B* and *guidance on its completion at Annex C.*

Purpose of the PER

4 The main purpose of the PER is to ensure that whenever a detainee is moved between locations, those escorting and receiving the detainee are provided with all necessary information about them, particularly in relation to any risks or vulnerabilities they may present. It also enables a record of the detainee's movements and of any relevant incidents occurring during transit to be maintained.

5 The PER is not intended to serve as the primary record of detainee risk assessment. All persons entering police custody should be subject to a structured process of risk assessment as referred to above. That process will inform the completion of the PER, but should be documented as part of the detainee's main custody record.

When should a PER be completed?

6 A PER should be completed whenever a detainee—irrespective of age or reason for detention—is to be escorted from a police station to another location, whether to court, to another police station or another agency, eg Health

Authorities, Social Services, HM Customs & Excise, Immigration Authorities, etc.

NB It will no longer be a requirement that a PER should be originated in respect of every detainee held in custody at a police station.

7 The only circumstances in which a form need not be originated prior to a move are where the detainee is in transit and a form has already been completed by another police officer, the prisoner escort service or the prison service. However, in such circumstances the existing form should be reviewed and, if necessary, updated.

Handling the PER

8 The original version of the PER was an A3 form with a top copy and five self-carbonising copies below that. The police will be expected to use the new version of the PER in A4 format—Parts A and B will be separate documents. However, the prison and escort services will be using an A3 format of the new PER. The escort services may, in addition, use A4 format Part B forms when collecting detainees from the police.

9 The police requirement will usually be confined to Part A, because they will be handing over to escort service staff to deal with the transfer. In such circumstances, the police will need to generate four copies of the completed Part A. One will be retained at the police station and the remaining three (including the top copy) passed to the escort staff, who will link them with a Part B form. Escort staff will, in due course, provide their own Part B forms. However, in the early stages of implementation of the new form and procedures, the police will be required to provide Part B forms. This period should not last more than a few months.

10 Copies of Part A forms may be produced by computer, by photocopying the original or by using pre-printed carbonised versions—this will be for individual forces to decide. Whichever method is used, one copy must be retained by the police.

11 Whichever format of PER is used, the top copies of Parts A and B must travel with the detainee at all times. Staff passing the detainee on to others taking responsibility for custody should always retain a copy of the PER for their own records.

Generating PER Forms

12 The form and guidance will be sent to forces using e-mail and/or computer disks to assist in generating copies of Parts A and B of the PER Form. Colour versions in line with the example at Annex B should be used where possible, but black and white versions can be used where that is the most practical alternative.

Introducing the new arrangements

13 The old arrangements are covered by Home Office Circular 50/1998. The revised PER Form can be introduced as soon as suitable in-force briefing has been completed. However, the current requirement to complete a PER Form for every detainee held at a police station must not be removed until the Chief Officer is satisfied that risk assessments in line with Annex A to this Circular are being carried out in respect of all such detainees and documented in their custody records.

Lay Visitors

14 In accordance with current guidelines concerning access to police records and/or documents, Lay Visitors do not have right of access to records other than the custody record itself. Although a PER Form will be completed using information wholly or mainly drawn from the custody record, it remains a separate document and as a consequence Lay Visitors have no right of access. The Home Office-led Working Group on Lay Visitors may consider this issue and, if so, will issue revised guidance in due course.

Further information

15 If you or your staff require any further information in relation to this Circular, please contact: Paul Douglas on 020 7273 3890 or John Woodcock on 020 7273 4124 (Fax number: 020 7273 2703).

16 Alternatively, both can be contacted by e-mail:
paul.douglas@homeoffice.gsi.gov.uk or *john.woodcock@homeoffice.gsi.gov.uk*.

Annex A

Risk Assessment of Persons Entering Police Custody

1 All persons entering police custody should be assessed to consider whether they are likely to present specific risks, either to staff or to themselves

2 Such assessments are primarily the responsibility of the custody officer, but it will frequently be necessary to consult others such as the arresting officer and the police surgeon.

3 The results of risk assessments should be incorporated in detainees' custody records. Such recording procedures should refer specifically to each risk category included in paragraph 5 and to the responses to the questions in paragraph 6. The record should highlight identified risks in such a way as to be obvious to all those responsible for the detainee's custody. Details of such risks should be given and reports attached where appropriate. Where no specific risks are identified by the assessment, that should be noted in the custody record.

4 Risk assessment is an ongoing process and assessments must always be subject to review where circumstances change. Where the circumstances of risk in relation to a detainee change, a new PER Form must be completed.

5 Specific risk categories which must always be considered are as follows. *Further details relevant to each category are in the guidance at Annex C* which covers the completion of the PER Form.

Much of that guidance is equally applicable to the documenting of risks in the custody record.

Medical/Mental Condition
Medication Issued
Special Needs
First Aid Given
Violence
Conceals Weapons
Escape Risk
Hostage Taker
Stalker/Harasser
Racial Motivation
Sex Offence
Drug/Alcohol Issues
Suicide/Self-Harm
Injuries
Vulnerable
Force/Restraint Used
CS Spray Used.

6 The following questions must be asked of every person entering police custody.

i   Do you have any illness or injury?
ii   Have you seen a doctor or been to a hospital for this illness/ injury?
iii Are you taking or supposed to be taking any tablets/ medication?
iv   What are they? What are they for?
v   Are you suffering from any mental health problems or depression?
vi   Have you ever tried to harm yourself?

7 It is the custody officer's responsibility to determine the response to any specific risk assessment. For example, in terms of calling the police surgeon or instigating extra levels of monitoring or observation.

Annex C

Completing the Prisoner Escort Record (PER) Form

Part A

1 At a police station, the PER should be completed by or under the supervision of the custody officer. The following guidance is intended to assist with that process and works through the form in order.

Overall Risk Assessment

2 One of the boxes at the top of the form must be ticked to indicate either 'Risk' or 'No Known Risk'. This should be done after the detailed consideration of Risk Categories in the box below has been completed.

Prisoner Not for Release

3 This box is generally for use by the Prison Service, but should be ticked by the police where it is clear that the detainee should not be released from custody in any circumstances. For example, where the detainee is a serving prisoner who is temporarily in police custody. In such cases the reason should be stated in the space provided.

Personal Details

4 Surname, forenames, known aliases and date of birth should be entered, as should details of sex and ethnicity. The 5-box ethnicity classification is in accord with the main categories within the 2001 Population Census system. The 'Mixed' box is to be used for persons who are of mixed racial background, eg White and Asian. The 'Chinese/Other' box is to be used for persons who come from one ethnic group other than White, Black or Asian.

5 Where the detainee has a PNC ID number, that should be included in the space provided. Prison number is primarily a matter for the Prison Service, but there may be occasions when it is known to the police officer completing the form. Where the detainee is under the age of 18, the box provided should be ticked to highlight that fact.

Escort Details

6 This section should be completed with the details available prior to the detainee's departure on escort.

Risk Categories

7 These are divided into three sets—Medical, Security and Other. That reflects the fact that in prisons the responsibility for assessing specific sets of risks is clearly divided between different groups of staff. The form allows for that. However, a police officer filling in the PER only has to sign the Risk Categories

box once, using the box identified for 'police use only' within this section of the form.

8 The officer completing the PER must consider the individual risk categories in turn and tick the box against each category that applies. Whenever a box is ticked, additional details should be entered in the 'Further information about risk' section and reports attached where appropriate. (It may be necessary to continue 'Further Information' on a separate report which must then be attached to the Part A.) If no known risks in a specific set are identified, the officer should tick the 'No Known Risk' box at the bottom of the relevant column. Once the assessment is completed the officer should sign and date the box identified for police use and then reflect the assessment by ticking either the 'Risk' or 'No Known Risk' box at the top of the form.

9 In completing the PER, the responsible officer will often be drawing from the structured risk assessment that should be carried out in respect of all detainees entering police custody (see *Annex A*). S/he may also need to liaise with medical personnel and other colleagues such as the arresting officer.

Medical Risks

Medical/Mental Condition

10 Where the custody officer is aware that there may be medical risks to record, this should normally be done in consultation within the relevant medical, psychiatric or healthcare staff. It will not be normal practice to record information about medical conditions on the face of the PER, unless that is essential to ensure the health and safety of the detainee or others. For example, it will not be appropriate to record the fact that a detainee may be HIV positive, since escorts will assume this may apply to any detainee in their charge. However, communicable diseases should be recorded to safeguard others who may come into contact with the detainee.

11 Confidential medical information should generally be attached to the PER in a sealed envelope, marked with an indication of its contents, that can be opened in an emergency. However, it is important that essential information about the need for ongoing medical care, observation or examination should be included on the PER or in open attachments. That is to avoid the detainee and escorts being exposed to unnecessary risk or harm. It may frequently be appropriate to attach a copy of a Detained Persons Medical Report Form in a standard agreed format.

Medication Issued

12 Where medication has been issued, the PER must indicate whether the detainee and/or the escort have received instructions about its administration or whether specific instructions for medical personnel have been provided. Where a Detained Persons Medication Form in a standard agreed format is

available, it should be used to inform the PER and a copy should be attached for reference.

Special Needs

13 This box is to be used if the detainee has a disability or has special transport or care requirements due to medical treatment or an on-going medical condition that may affect the safety of the detainee or escorting staff during the escort. Clear details of the specific condition applicable will be particularly helpful for those escorting and/or receiving the detainee.

First Aid Given

14 Has first aid been applied to the detainee at any stage, either before arrival at the police station or while detained there? If so, details should be provided as concisely as possible. The police may tick either of the two boxes (one entry is listed in the Other section of risk categories. [The Prison Service require two separate listings.]

Security Risks

Violence

15 This should apply where, for example, the detainee has a history of violent behaviour or has recently committed an assault on a member of police staff or a fellow detainee.

Conceals Weapons

16 This should be ticked if the detainee has a history of concealing weapons or is considered likely to do so whilst in detention.

Escape Risk

17 This should be ticked where the detainee's custodial history or behaviour suggest that they present an escape risk or where intelligence is available to that effect.

Hostage Taker

18 This covers where the detainee is a known hostage taker or where information exists to suggest they may attempt to take a hostage.

Stalker/Harasser

19 Does the detainee have a restraining order or a civil injunction against them under current stalking and/or harassment legislation? Is the detainee likely to attempt to harass or intimidate witnesses?

Racial Motivation

20 Does the detainee have a history of racially motivated offences or have they been racially motivated to assault other detainees whilst in custody?

Sex Offence

21 Is the detainee a known or suspected sex offender, particularly with regard to offences against children?

Other Risks

Drug/Alcohol Issues

22 Is drug or alcohol abuse an immediate factor in the treatment/handling of the detainee? Is there an active dependency to be taken account of? Could the detainee have needles or drugs concealed upon them? Again, this is an area where input from medical staff may be important.

Suicide/Self-Harm

23 This is a very important category and should be ticked whenever the custody officer has any belief or suspicion that the detainee may try and harm themselves. That may arise from a whole range of factors, including the detainee's past or current behaviour, their stated intentions, their mood or the circumstances in which they entered custody. Liaison with medical staff will often be relevant to completing this entry.

Injuries

24 Does the detainee have any visible or known injuries prior to departure on escort?

Vulnerable

25 Is the detainee particularly vulnerable to interference or assault by other detainees or even by members of the public? That may derive from the general nature or specific circumstances of the offence in relation to which they are being held. The attitude of associates or co-defendants may also be relevant.

Force/Restraint Used

26 Has force or restraint been used, either during arrest or while the detainee has been in custody?

CS Spray Used

27 Has CS been used at any stage in the process leading up to the detainee entering custody or since they have been in custody?

First Aid Given

28 See paragraph 14. The police may tick either entry.

Other

29 This is a 'catch all' box for risks which are not covered by any of the other categories. If this box is ticked, it will be necessary to provide details in the section for 'Further information about risk'.

Attachments

Report(s)

30 The box should be ticked whenever report(s) expanding on specific risks are attached to the PER.

Pre-cons

31 Pre-convictions should be attached when readily available and this box ticked.

Handcuff Request

32 This should be ticked (and a copy of the appropriate form attached) where it is necessary to make an application to the Crown Prosecution Service for the detainee to wear handcuffs in court during their appearance.

Immigration Detention Authority

33 Detainees held on behalf of the immigration authorities will be accompanied by a form authorising their detention on that basis. The form should be attached to the PER and the relevant box ticked. Such detainees may be vulnerable because of their race.

Detainee's Property

34 Property will normally be transported in sealed bags or containers and the seal numbers should be recorded. The Prison Service uses property codes, but this column will not generally be relevant for the police.

35 Each sealed bag/container should be recorded by ticking on departure and on arrival at the final destination. Cash amounts transported outside sealed bags/containers should be specifically recorded on departure and arrival.

36 The person in charge of the escort should sign to indicate receipt of the detainee and of recorded property and cash at the point of departure. The person finally accepting the detainee at the end of the last leg of the escort should sign to indicate receipt of the detainee and of recorded property and cash from the escorting staff.

Time of last meal prior to departure

37 It is helpful for escorting staff to know when the detainee was last fed or if a meal has been offered and refused (and the reason, if known). The time of the relevant meal should be recorded here.

Photograph

38 Where a photograph of the detainee is available, it should be attached to the top copy of the PER (Part A) where indicated. Ideally, this will be small enough so as to avoid obscuring other parts of the form.

Part B—Record of Events

39 While the Record of Events should always be linked to Part A of the PER, it will not always be physically part of the same document. Therefore, to ensure any necessary cross-referencing, it is essential that the Record of Events includes the detainee's surname, forename(s), PNC and/or Prison Number(s).

40 The Record should be used to document key events such as departures, arrivals and handovers of responsibility. It should also include any notable incidents and any new information arising in relation to the detainee. Particular attention should be paid to anything bearing on the risk assessment of the detainee. Significant events should be highlighted by a tick in the final column and, if it is necessary to attach an incident report, the box referring to that should be ticked.

41 If a significant new risk becomes apparent during escort, details should be given on the Record of Events. Part A of the PER should be updated as necessary.

Other Information

Meals

42 The time of meals given or offered during escort should be recorded, as should any refusal and the reason for it.

Next Appearance and Court

43 Escorting staff should ensure these details are entered before leaving court. Where there is to be a further court appearance but the date is not yet known, the space should be marked DTBF (date to be fixed).

Home Office Circular 28/2002—Learning the Lessons from Adverse Incidents

1. There are three main purposes of this circular:

  • to give you guidance on the system currently being set up to ensure that the police service is better able to learn the lessons from adverse incidents;

  • to set out some specific lessons that have arisen from one particular case that we have been looking into; and

  • to give you some general guidance on making police cells safer.

2. **Chief officers should pass this circular on to *investigating officers within professional standards departments* and *officers responsible for custody suites*.**

Guidance on the system

Background

3. A standing committee on learning the lessons from adverse incidents was convened last year. It is chaired by the Association of Chief Police Officers (ACPO), with the Police Complaints Authority (PCA) providing the Secretariat, and with representation from the Home Office Police Leadership and Powers and Police Standards Units, Her Majesty's Inspectorate of Constabulary (HMIC), Centrex and the Crown Prosecution Service (CPS).

4. The terms of reference of the standing committee are to:

  • review adverse incidents which occur in the police service;

  • identify lessons to be learned from such incidents, with the aims of preventing similar incidents from occurring elsewhere and developing good practice; and

  • disseminate the findings and recommendations of the committee.

5. We also hope to facilitate a culture in which the police service and those working within it are willing to share information in order to help each other learn from adverse incidents. This is not about perpetuating a 'blame culture'. We simply want to make sure that, where adverse incidents have occurred, the appropriate steps are taken to ensure that the risks of such incidents occurring elsewhere are minimised, and that good practice among the police service is extended.

How the system will work

6. We want a system in which all the lessons that need to be are identified and disseminated to everyone who needs to know about them. In order to ensure that this happens, a degree of flexibility will need to be built into the system.

7. I attach a Communication Map for Learning the Lessons from Adverse Incidents, which summarises how we anticipate the system will work in practice.

8. You will see that we envisage it being possible for lessons to be identified from almost any source, both from within the police service and from outside it. From this summer, Investigating Officers (IOs) will be asked to complete a form on their investigations, giving details of any lessons that have arisen during the investigation which they consider could usefully be disseminated to either:

- the particular force concerned;
- forces in that region; or
- the police service nationally.

9. Forms should be completed and submitted to Centrex either at the end of investigations or during them if the lessons are particularly important and identifying them would not prejudice the investigation. A blank version of the form is attached to this circular. IOs need not complete the form for every investigation, but it will be important for them to ask themselves at the end of every investigation if there are any lessons that could usefully be disseminated. We would expect some lessons to arise from most investigations. Where IOs have any doubt as to whether a lesson could usefully be disseminated, they should go ahead and give details of it in the form and submit it to Centrex.

10. The PCA (and in the future the Independent Police Complaints Commission) will be asking themselves the same question at the end of all investigations in which they have been involved. And chief officers should consider if lessons can be identified from any civil actions in which their forces have been engaged, or from any other source such as complaints about direction and control or 'near misses'. In particular, 'near misses' in custody suites should be given very careful consideration to ensure that any lessons arising from them are identified.

11. Where it seems to Centrex, the PCA or chief officers that there may be a case for the lessons that they have identified being disseminated to the police service nationally, the matter should be referred to the Learning the Lessons Working Group. This is being convened under the Standing Committee (which is to become the Learning the Lessons Steering Group, with

535

responsibility for overseeing all the work on this area). The Home Office Police Leadership and Powers Unit will chair and provide the Secretariat for the Working Group. Lessons identified by Centrex or the PCA should be brought to the Group by their representatives on it. Lessons identified by chief officers should either be brought to the Group by George Hedges, Chief Constable of Durham, who will be the ACPO representative on it, or referred direct to the Home Office Police Leadership and Powers Unit. (George Hedges is soon to retire; his replacement in this role will be Ken Jones, Chief Constable of Sussex.)

12. HMIC will also be represented on the Working Group, and two experienced IOs will be invited to join it. The Group will also be free to identify lessons from other sources outside the police service, such as from the CPS, inquests or even, if appropriate, the media. The Group may in some cases decide that new or revised Home Office guidance should be issued (which will normally take the form of Home Office circulars such as this). In other cases it may be appropriate for:

- ACPO to issue new or revised guidance;
- the matter to be looked into further by HMIC;
- Centrex to revise an aspect of police training;
- the matter to be referred to one of the staff associations; or
- new Home Office research to be commissioned.

13. The most important lessons, which may suggest a need for a significant change in practice in the police service nationally or perhaps even a change in legislation, will be referred to the Steering Group.

14. Where it seems that there may be a case for the lessons identified being disseminated to forces in a particular region, the matter can be referred direct to the ACPO Standing Committee on Complaints and Discipline (currently chaired by George Hedges, but soon to be chaired by Ken Jones), or to the chief officers or police authorities in the region, or to HMIC. They should then ensure that the lessons are disseminated to those who need to know about them.

15. Where it seems that the lessons identified need only be disseminated to the individual force concerned, the matter can either be taken forward by the chief officer or police authority or referred direct to HMIC. They should then ensure that the lessons are disseminated to those who need to know about them.

16. Our work is still at a relatively early stage, and the mechanisms for identifying and disseminating lessons are still being tested. We would be grateful for any comments on these proposals for how the system will work in practice. Please send these to Simon King in the Home Office Police Leadership and Powers Unit (contact details in paragraph 49) by 31 August 2002.

17. We expect the system to be operating fully from later this summer. However, in the meantime we are keen for the process of learning the lessons from adverse incidents to start straightaway. The first specific lessons arising from one particular case that we have been looking into are given below. Other lessons that we identify will be the subject of further Home Office circulars.

First specific lessons to be learned

18. The PCA have identified four specific lessons to be learned from a case from 2001, in which a young man died in a cell in a police station.

The case

19. The young man had a substantial criminal record and had previously been imprisoned. He was also a known heroin addict, and had told the officers who arrested him that he had taken heroin that morning.

20. After he had been taken to the cell block the young man was seen by a doctor, who described him as pleasant and co-operative. She concluded that the young man was commencing drug withdrawal, and gave him some medication. She completed her notes and gave them to one of the custody officers. He then copied them incorrectly into the custody record.

21. Later in the evening the young man complained to a different custody officer that the medication had not worked and that he was in pain. This officer then telephoned a different doctor (the first doctor having now gone off duty), and described the young man's symptoms and complaint. He repeated the incorrect details of the medication given from the custody record. The second doctor said that he would not prescribe any further medication and advised the officers to 'keep an eye' on the young man and call again if he got any worse. (This doctor has stated that, had he been given correct information about the medication given, he would have made a different decision.)

22. The young man came out of his cell to make some telephone calls. The officer who returned him to his cell forgot to remove his trainers, which had long laces. He was then not checked for nearly three-quarters of an hour.

23. When he was checked he was found dead in his cell, hanging by the neck from the toilet plunger on the sink, which had provided a ligature point for his shoelaces.

The lessons

24. The first lesson is around ligature points.

25. When the cells were inspected it was found that all of them contained stainless steel toilet-and-sink units with hot and cold taps and plungers. Since this case the units have been boxed in with wood panelling, pending a final

decision as to whether they should be removed from these cells altogether. However, there may still be cells in other police stations which have similar designs. **All police stations should be checked to see if there are any cells containing taps, plungers or other easily accessible ligature points. If there are any, they should be removed.**

26. Further guidance on making police cells safer is given in paragraphs 33–47.

27. The second lesson is around the Human Rights Act 1998.

28. Although it seems that not removing the young man's trainers in this case was an oversight, one of the investigating officers did suggest that laces were not always removed due to the requirement for proportionality under the Human Rights Act. Of course it is true that people have a range of rights under the European Convention on Human Rights (ECHR), which the police must have due regard to in their dealings with members of the public and others. However, under Article 2 of the ECHR 'Everyone's right to life shall be protected by law', and the police must have the highest regard for this. Of course, it is difficult to ensure that everything that people might use to harm themselves is removed, but **items such as shoelaces and belts that can most easily be used in this way should always be removed, especially where there are grounds for believing that someone may be a suicide risk. Members of the police service can be assured that there is no legal obstacle under the Human Rights Act to doing this.**

29. The third lesson is around non-medically qualified persons 'copying' doctors' notes into custody records.

30. The consequences of notes not being copied accurately can be very serious. **Doctors should therefore be invited to make the relevant entry directly into the custody record themselves, attaching their original notes.**

31. The fourth lesson is around liaison between the Prison Service and the police service.

32. The young man in this case had previously been in prison, and was known by the Prison Service to be a suicide risk. However, there was nothing to this effect on the Police National Computer (PNC). We have discussed this issue with colleagues in the Prison Service. They are aware of it, and there is a Prison Service/ACPO Prison Intelligence Working Group initiative in Leicestershire, under which, whenever a prisoner becomes a known suicide risk or self-harms, the Leicestershire Police PNC Operator inputs the warning marker 'Suicidal' or 'Potentially Suicidal' on the PNC. It is felt that this initiative has been successful, and two further three-month pilots started at Wandsworth and Holloway Prisons on 1 July 2002. Further information on this will be made available towards the end of this year.

General guidance on making police cells safer

33. We thought that, given that one of the first lessons that we have identified is around ligature points, it would be helpful to issue some general guidance on making police cells safer. This supplements Home Office Circular 92/1968. (It should be noted that some of the recommendations in that circular have still not been implemented in all areas.)

34. This guidance is not, and cannot be, comprehensive, as people contemplating committing suicide in a police cell can be extremely resourceful. Moreover, there is no such thing as a completely safe cell. We can only aim to reduce the possible means of committing suicide by ligature to an absolute minimum.

Means of forming a ligature

35. To commit suicide by ligature a person requires both the means of forming a ligature and the means of attaching himself or herself to it. By removing one or preferably both of these, suicide by ligature becomes impossible.

36. People usually attempt to form ligatures by using personal effects such as:

- shoelaces;
- belts;
- buckles;
- pull-cords from 'training' style clothing; and
- strips of material or fibres torn or unravelled from clothing or mattresses, blankets etc. in the custody suite.

37. It is very important to appreciate that even strips of material or fibres which seem insignificant can be twisted or plaited to form a ligature. It must also be understood that even 'non-tear' materials can be torn by a sharp object, and that even blunt objects such as a 1p coin can be sharpened against cell walls, floors, or tile joints. Paper body suits can also be dangerous, with those with long zips providing a means for near-instantaneous death by ligature.

The cell environment

38. Cell doors should wherever possible be outwards-opening and have 'piano' hinges.

39. Cell hatches should always be kept locked shut. (Older-style 'flap-down', or 'pin-lock' hatches are often ill-fitting and defective. Where combined with door handles other than the standard-issue Home Office handle—the 'T- bar'-door handle—they can be extremely dangerous.)

40. As far as possible all cells should be free of:

- pipework or conduits of any form (even at ground level);
- sharp angles;
- gratings;
- holes;
- abrasive surfaces;
- broken or cracked surfaces; or
- any open joint between fittings and the cell structure.

41. No fittings should provide any means of forming a ligature. The stainless steel box units designed to be 'vandal-proof' which are still used in some police stations often have ligature points and should wherever possible be removed. All fittings should be bedded in resin-based, solid-setting, non-corrosive compounds, which will neither peel nor pick, and which are not poisonous. (The height of the openings of 'slot'-style hand wash units should not exceed 125 mm, as people have wedged their heads in larger ones and then broken their necks.)

42. Air-vents offer one of the main means of committing suicide by ligature. They should wherever possible be purpose-built, stainless steel plated and with holes no greater than 2 mm in diameter.

43. Only light fittings of designs specifically recommended by Home Office staff should be used, and they must be out of reach. (It should be noted that light fittings used by the Prison Service often have ligature points and are therefore normally unsuitable for police cells.)

44. Closed-circuit television (CCTV) cameras should where possible be installed in all cells designated for vulnerable people. All people in police cells should be monitored closely.

45. In shower areas showerheads must be as robust as possible, and with no ligature points. Shower curtains, rails etc. are inappropriate in a police custody context.

46. In exercise yards there should as far as possible be no exposed pipework, conduits etc. except at roof level. CCTV cameras and mountings must be out of reach.

47. All maintenance of police cells and custody areas should be carried out by people fully trained in issues around ligature points.

Enquiries

48. Enquiries specifically about ligature points and making police cells safer should be addressed to:

Keith Batt
Buildings and Estate Management Unit
Room 516, Clive House
Petty France
London SW1H 9AD
Tel: 020 7271 8702
Fax: 020 7271 8473
Email: Keith.Batt@homeoffice.gsi.gov.uk

49. All other enquiries about this circular should be addressed to:

Simon King
Police Leadership and Powers Unit
Room 673, 50 Queen Anne's Gate
London SW1H 9AT
Tel: 020 7273 4097
Fax: 020 7273 3482
Email: Simon.King@homeoffice.gsi.gov.uk

Index

cautions (*cont.*):
  written statements 14.4.2
CCTV 3.3.1, 4.3.2, 5.7.5, 8.2.2,
  8.3.3
cells and detention rooms
  bedding 5.4.2
  CCTV 5.7.5
  clothing, removal and replacement
    of 5.4.3
  conditions of detention 5.2.1
  handcuffs 5.3.2
  heating 5.2.3
  interviews 18.6.2, 18.7
  juvenile detainees 5.5, 5.8
  lighting 5.2.3
  mentally vulnerable
    detainees 5.3.1
  relocation 5.3.3
  restraint and conflict
    management 5.3
  risk assessments, clinical attention
    and 3.3
  secure accommodation 15.6.1,
    15.6.3
  sharing cells 5.2.2, 5.5.2
  toilets 5.2.4
  visits 5.6.3
  vulnerable detainees 5.6.3
  washing facilities 5.2.4
  welfare of detainees 5.2.1, 5.4,
    5.8
charge sheets 14.3.1–14.3.2,
  14.6
charging suspects 14.1–14.8 *see
    also* **continued detention after
    charge**
  alternative options 14.2.12, 15.2.9
  bail 14.2.1, 16.1
    conditions on 15.2.9, 16.5.2
  case study 14.6.2
  cautions 14.2.12, 14.2.13, 14.3.3
  charge sheets 14.3.1–14.3.2, 14.6
  continued detention 14.2.11
  conditional cautions 14.1, 14.2.13
  conviction, realistic prospect
    of 14.2.2
  custody records 14.6
  decision-making 14.2.1–14.2.2,
    14.8
  delay 14.2.2
  DPP's guidance 14.2.4
  early consultations, requirement
    for 14.2.7
  emergency cases 14.2.9

evidence 2.2.1, 2.8, 10.5.2, 10.8.2,
  14.2.2, 14.2.3, App 1
expiry of PACE time limits 14.2.9
extending detention 2.2.3
fitness to be charged 14.2.2
flow chart App 1
Human Rights Act 1998 14.1
information entitlements 14.1
interviews
  after charge 14.1, 14.5–14.7,
    14.8
  no comment 14.2.2
investigating officers 14.2.1–
    14.2.2
juvenile detainees 14.7, 15.6
  alternatives to charging 14.2.12
legal representatives 13.8
liberty and security, right to 14.1
mentally vulnerable detainees 14.7
more than one offence 14.2.2,
  14.2.8
notice 14.3.1–14.3.2
police
  action post referral and
    escalation procedure 14.2.10
  powers to determine
    charge 14.2.6, 14.2.8
  protection of officers 14.3.2
prepared statements 14.1, 14.6.2,
  14.8
recording the detainee's
  responses 14.6
reform 14.1
release without charge 14.2.1
reparations 14.1
reviews 10.5.2, 10.8.2, 15.4.3
silence, adverse inferences
  from 14.2.2
simple cautions 14.2.12
statements of detainees,
  prepared 14.1, 14.6.2, 14.8
terrorist suspects 14.3.2, 17.9
Threshold Test 14.2.5, 14.2.7
violent suspects 14.3.2
vulnerable persons 7.8, 14.7
written notice 14.3.1–14.3.2
written statements 14.4, 14.8
children and young persons *see*
    juvenile detainees
civilian detention officers 1.1,
    1.5.2, 1.5.3
clinical attention *see* **medical
    attention; safer detention**
clock *see* **detention clock**